PRAISE FOR
FREEZING IN THE DARK

It's no exaggeration to call *Freezing in the Dark* a masterpiece of political investigation. From hard evidence, author Ron Arnold carves a vivid, intense – and horrifying – image of today's most ruthless power mongers and political manipulators – who turn out to be left-leaning charitable donors and their armies of non-profit puppets.

"Charity" and "non-profit" lose their meaning in the world Arnold shows us, brimming with messianic billionaires who use their own capitalist profits to stop everybody else's capitalist profits, and grasping ideologues who think they're the best directors of everybody else's life.

Arnold makes the case that a real Vast Left Wing Conspiracy is rising in America, not with the usual conspiracy theorist's rhetoric of outrage and guilt by association built on sheer guesswork – which he seems to detest – but with telephone calls, emails, and face-to-face interviews with the leftists themselves.

He is so even-handed through the first half of the book, it reads more like a tribute than a critique (but he tells you what he really thinks in the second half, and in no uncertain terms).

Anyone interested in understanding American politics today will find Ron Arnold's *Freezing in the Dark* deeply revealing essential reading.

Nick Nichols
Author, Rules for Corporate Warriors

"Progressive" and "participatory democracy" have become buzzwords for liberal politicians and news media. But what exactly do the power brokers at the left end of the political spectrum mean when they use those terms? Who are they? And what happens if they and their far-flung network of well-funded activist groups get the power and control they seek?

Now, thanks to Ron Arnold's brilliant new book – *Freezing in the Dark: Money, power, politics and the vast left-wing conspiracy* – we have an inside look at the thousands of groups, hundreds of wealthy foundations and politicians, and dozens of ultra-rich revolutionaries like George Soros and Maurice Strong, who are determined to change our politics, policies and way of life – to create an "ideal society" that could be right out of *1984, Through the Looking Glass* and the Little Ice Age.

Ron doesn't just track down and chronicle where the money comes from, and who's getting it. More amazingly, he does it – not with insider spies or stolen documents – but with readily available documents that few had bothered reading, via dots that others hadn't connected, and through interviews with conspiracy leaders who were amazingly candid about what they intend to do.

If you care about freedom, hope, health and opportunity for yourself, your children or the world's least fortunate people – you need to read this book, heed its message, tell others about it, and help stop this juggernaut.

Paul Driessen
Author, Eco-Imperialism: Green power · Black death

PRAISE FOR
FREEZING IN THE DARK

Frightening! That's the only way to describe Ron Arnold's book, *Freezing in the Dark: Money, power, politics and the vast left-wing conspiracy*. Arnold's research uncovers the intricate network of special interest groups and their coordinated effort to attack capitalism and control the political landscape. Given the massive financial advantage fueling their effort, it's no wonder we are losing the battle of ideas and for our liberties. There is a cause for alarm and Arnold is sounding the alert!

Tom Borelli PhD
Free Enterprise Action Fund

To those who say that environmentalists, anti-war organizers, advocates for corporate social responsibility, and those who attack the sovereignty of nations are just a loose confederacy of deluded groups, Ron Arnold demonstrates that there really is a Vast Left Wing Conspiracy by identifying their sources of funding, revealing their plans to control everyone by centralizing power in the United Nations and supranational organizations like the European Union.

This extraordinary book describes and documents the threats to our lives, the nation, and the world that must be addressed before it is too late!

—Alan Caruba
National Anxiety Center

Publisher's Note:
It is always an event when a new book by Ron Arnold comes out. But this one is more of an event than most. We released *Freezing in the Dark* just prior to election year 2008 because it tracks today's behind-the-scenes players from their checkered yesterdays into their possible tomorrows with lessons that Americans mustn't ignore for all the election cycles to come.

Freezing in the Dark is so special because it takes us inside the electoral process and inside the minds and money of those who complain most bitterly about money in politics, The Vast Left Wing Conspiracy.

But there's much more: the feeling that you really know the people Ron writes about.

The personal profiles of left wing leaders that Ron has included give us a depth of understanding for the opposition that I've never seen in a book of political commentary. There are places—particularly in the dramatic story of how Democratic strategist Dan Carol conceived the Apollo Alliance in the wake of 9/11—that are likely to have non-progressives almost cheering for their political rivals. Which is not to say that Ron fails to smack those who need smacking, but his uncanny ability to get into the opposition's head gives us a new appreciation for their intelligence and ability—which is a more powerful warning than any rant could ever be.

—Alan Gottlieb
Merril Press

FREEZING IN THE DARK

Other books by Ron Arnold

James Watt and the Environmentalists
Regnery Gateway

The Grand Prairie Years
Dodd Mead

Ecology Wars: Environmentalism as if People Mattered

EcoTerror: The Violent Agenda to Save Nature

Undue Influence: Wealthy Foundations, Grant-Driven Environmental Groups and Zealous Bureaucrats That Control Your Future

With Alan Gottlieb

Trashing the Economy

Politically Correct Environment

Books Edited by Ron Arnold

Stealing the National Parks
by Don Hummel

Storm Over Rangelands
by Wayne Hage

People of the Tongass
by K. A. Soderberg and Jackie DuRette

It Takes A Hero
by William Perry Pendley

The Asbestos Racket
by Michael Bennett

Eight Steps towards Libertarianism
by Joseph S. Fulda

No Home on the Range
by Caren Cowan

FREEZING IN THE DARK

Money, Power, Politics,
and
The Vast Left Wing Conspiracy

Ron Arnold

Merril Press
BELLEVUE, WASHINGTON

FREEZING IN THE DARK

First Edition
Published by Merril Press

Typeset in Times New Roman and Trajan by The Free Enterprise Press,
a division of The Center for the Defense of Free Enterprise.
12500 N.E. 10th Place, Bellevue, Washington 98005.
Telephone 425-455-5038. Fax 425-451-3959.
E-mail address: books@cdfe.org.
Cover design by Northwoods Studio.

FREEZING IN THE DARK is published by Merril Press,
P.O. Box 1682, Bellevue, Washington 98009.
Additional copies of this book may be ordered from
Merril Press at $23.00 each.
Telephone 425-454-7009.

"The Embassy to Achilles" by Homer; from THE ILIAD by Homer, translated by
Robert Fagles, copyright © 1990 by Robert Fagles. Used by permission of Viking
Penguin, a division of Penguin Group (USA) Inc.

LIBRARY OF CONGRESS CATALOGING-IN-PUBLICATION DATA
Arnold, Ron.
    Freezing in the dark : money, power, politics, and the vast left wing
conspiracy / Ron Arnold. — 1st ed.
        p. cm.
    Includes bibliographical references and index.
    ISBN 978-0-936783-51-2
 1. Liberalism—United States. 2. Pressure groups—United States. 3. United
States—Politics and government—2001- I. Title.
JC574.2.U6A75 2007
320.973—dc22

                                                            2007036051

PRINTED IN THE UNITED STATES OF AMERICA

TABLE OF CONTENTS

BOOK ONE

MONEY, POWER, POLITICS

TABLE OF CONTENTS
BOOK TWO
THE VAST LEFT WING CONSPIRACY

To Janet Arnold
ad astra per aspera

ACKNOWLEDGMENTS

Freezing In The Dark is the work of many hands, like all books.

I owe a profound debt of gratitude to my first reader, Teresa Platt, the politically astute executive director of Fur Commission USA, who generously did first reading and heavy research for three of my previous books and not only gave objective and insightful critique on this book (and encouragement in the tough spots, like a big rewrite she asked for), but once more freely gave substantial research and support. Thanks for your faith in me, T.

This book would never have been finished without my long-time friend Paul Driessen, who helped in more ways than I can thank him for, especially when I had to set work aside in the dark months of my wife's long (and finally successful) battle with cancer. Paul, you are a beacon of hope.

My special thanks to George Washington University Political Science Professor Jarol B. Manheim, author of *The Death of a Thousand Cuts* and *Biz-War and the Out-of-Power Elite*, for his vital help with social network analysis and for his forbearance in my recruiting some of his best ideas.

Special thanks also to Andrew Wheeler of the Senate Environment and Public Works Committee, and ranking member, Sen. James Inhofe, for sharing their vast knowledge of pertinent but hard-to-find public documents.

David Martosko of the Center for Consumer Freedom, as well as Eric Williams of the Gallatin Group, helped with difficult research tasks.

Personal thanks to R. Russell Maylone, Curator, McCormick Library of Special Collections, Northwestern University Library, Evanston, Illinois, for diligent work finding Paula Kamen's 1992 interview with Paul and Heather Booth, which was important for the Prologue and Netwar chapters.

To Hudson Institute's John Fonte, thanks for providing key documents. Thanks to Terrence Scanlon of Capital Research Center for permission to adapt my articles that had previously appeared in *Foundation Watch*.

Henry Lamb, head of the Environmental Conservation Organization, an NGO with United Nations consultative status, vetted chapters on the UN.

To the extent possible, I have used open source materials and online resources so anyone can fact-check the text. Interviews were used only where open sources turned up empty or contained misleading gaps.

A few important people did not respond to my interview requests or refused to correct drafts, which I have noted at the proper places.

I was gratified to find that nearly all the progressive leaders I contacted *did* respond, and were forthcoming and helpful despite our political differences. Some were extraordinarily helpful.

I especially appreciate the interviews with political strategist Dan Carol covering the Apollo Alliance and many other things. He was also kind enough to forward a review chapter to his friend Rob Stein of Democracy Alliance when I could not find an address that worked.

I particularly appreciate the substantive critique (well-deserved scoldings, actually) and extremely helpful corrections by Mark Schmitt, formerly of George Soros' Open Society Institute. He took the time to review a large part of the book and saved me from some embarrassing errors.

Also, a hearty thank you to Simon Rosenberg of NDN for taking a perfectly good weekend to review a long chapter and then more time to tell me about the background of the Phoenix Group.

Robert Borosage of Campaign for America's Future asked why he should talk to me since I was going to skin him in print. Allowing that I probably was, I asked if he'd rather be skinned for fact or fiction, which must have tickled him, because he then answered my questions.

Former Clinton White House Press Secretary Mike McCurry returned my calls and helped locate some important sources.

It was not until my wife indexed the book that we realized how many *hundreds* of people in The Vast Left Wing Conspiracy I had talked to during the three years it took to write it. And then how many weren't in the index because they spoke on condition of anonymity.

To the many who helped without wanting to be named, my thanks.

To Alan Gottlieb of Merril Press for accepting *Freezing In The Dark* for publication, and to the Center for the Defense of Free Enterprise for its generous support during the long research and writing, my heartfelt thanks.

My gratitude to retired rocket scientist William H. Kay (he worked on the Saturn V moon booster) for being my *other* first reader and putting up with an old friend.

On another personal note, thanks to those readers who voted my book *EcoTerror: The Violent Agenda to Save Nature* into the Random House Reader Survey of the 100 Most Important Books of the 20th Century. I am truly honored.

And to Janet, you have always been the prize and you always will be.

As usual, any merits this book may have belong to these good people. Any errors of fact or judgment are mine alone.

Now: Buckle up. This is going to be a rough ride.

—Ron Arnold
Bellevue, Washington

BOOK ONE

MONEY, POWER, POLITICS

FREEZING IN THE DARK - X

PROLOGUE

"I<small>T IS THE REFORM THAT MAKES ALL OTHER REFORMS POSSIBLE.</small>"
That may sound like an oracle from the political beyond, but it was actually Ellen Miller, executive of a liberal Washington non-profit group, answering an interview question in 1995.[1]

I first ran across that quote while writing *Undue Influence* in 1999, researching a chapter on reformist non-profit foundations, when Ellen Miller's remarkable assertion caught my eye on a website.

What a great line, I thought—like movie dialogue.

"It is the reform that makes all other reforms possible."

The "it" was *campaign finance reform*.

Hedge fund billionaire George Soros and PBS icon Bill Moyers must have agreed with her, because their foundations subsequently donated more than $5 million to her reform group, Public Campaign.[2]

Let it bounce around your brain a moment.

It's like one of those Richard Dawkins catch-phrase-propagating memes.

"It is the reform that makes all other reforms possible."

So portentous, so emphatic, nearly mythic in power, Velcro for the mind.

I was writing a section about some foundations that had funded a particularly aggressive campaign for a ballot measure in Montana that would outlaw for-profits from contributing to ballot measure campaigns.

It would leave non-profits free to donate all they wanted. But even non-profits that accepted for-profit contributions would be excluded.[3]

The measure passed, turning Montana's initiative process into the private playground of non-profit activists and their non-profit donors.

It was a stunning and indisputable display of non-profit ambition to destroy the free enterprise system—primarily the mining industry in this case—and rule the world, even if the world in question was only the state of Montana, with its sparse population and one lone congressman.

It was an eye-opener.

1

I used Miller's oracular quote to underscore the point that foundations were giving money to stop other people from giving money—then went on to my next topic. (As things turned out, the Montana measure was struck down as unconstitutional, but the mining industry never recovered.)

When I later saw *Undue Influence* in print and read Ellen Miller's quote once more, I regretted not having pursued it further, but that's not what the book was about. Yet it raised some sharp questions:

Which other reforms?
What, exactly, did she expect of campaign finance reform?
Why did she think it was so crucial?
Was there really such a holy grail for liberals?
Where would this liberal holy grail take us?

I had other things to do—a family to care for, a non-profit organization to run, congressional testimony to give, research to direct, websites to manage, books to edit for my group's publishing house—so the questions lay dormant, stirring uneasily now and then.

A few years later, I saw headlines blaring that Congress had finally passed the Bipartisan Campaign Reform Act, or BCRA. It's better known as McCain-Feingold, named for its iconoclastic Senate sponsors, John McCain, Republican of Arizona, and Russell Feingold, Democrat of Wisconsin.[4]

McCain-Feingold went into effect the day after Election Day, 2002—in which voters increased the power of the president's party, a rare event at mid-term (only three times in the last century, 1902, 1934, and 1998).[5]

Traditionally, the party that controls the White House loses House seats in midterm elections, but Republicans increased their House majority by eight seats and narrowly regained control of the Senate. Thus, George W. Bush became only the third president in a hundred years—and the first Republican—to help his party expand its ranks in midterm elections.[6]

In practical terms, the Republican victory was helped by redistricting, the war in Iraq, and a record low voter turnout of about 30 percent—the middle class and the rich are somewhat more likely to be Republicans than the poor and far more likely to vote than the poor.[7]

So, at the end of the day on November 5, 2002, everybody who ran things in Washington was a Republican.

Democrats did not take the debacle at all well.

"Dump Bush" became a white-hot rage in Democrat hearts.

It was clear that whatever the 2004 presidential election cycle might hold in store, McCain-Feingold guaranteed that it would be like nothing in American history.

I dusted off those dormant questions and began taking notes.

Now, what about this Ellen Miller and her liberal benefactors?

Her bio was easy to find: early work with Ralph Nader groups, then important staff jobs in House and Senate committees. She was chosen for leadership by the Left's moneyed elite, first as executive director of the Washington-based political money-tracking Center for Responsive Politics, and later as leader of Public Campaign, a "clean money" advocacy group launched five years before McCain-Feingold passed.[8]

The "clean money, clean elections" reform would have "leveled the playing field" by paying for federal candidates' elections out of the United States treasury, complete with spending limits and elaborate payout formulas.

That came across as a radical pipe dream in a nation where a huge majority of voters opposed public election funding schemes as welfare for politicians, but Miller's wealthy foundation mentors seemed to think it was absolutely essential for the *survival of democracy.*

Their premise—the only thing that made any sense to me, anyway— was that, despite their large, growing network of liberal activists, despite rallying the troops with technological innovations such as emails, websites, and the cell phone, and despite their battery of devoted, wealthy foundation donors, they would never see all those "other reforms" (whatever they were), never create their "ideal society" (whatever it was), never "save democracy" (whatever that meant), without *electoral* power.

So, millions of foundation dollars went into campaign finance reform.

BUT SOMETHING WENT WRONG. Miller's key reform passed into law as the Bipartisan Campaign Reform Act, not the hoped-for Clean Money, Clean Elections Act.

McCain-Feingold wasn't pure "clean money," it was pure politics, "the art of the possible."

McCain-Feingold took the less radical step of banning "soft money" donations—large, unlimited contributions from individuals, unions, and corporations—to *political parties*, just as Congress had banned unlimited contributions directly to the *candidates* themselves back in the 1970s.[9]

It *wasn't* the reform that makes all other reforms possible.

Now, what about those mysterious "other reforms"?

Ellen Miller didn't bother to explain what it took to "save democracy."

But, while covering the environmental movement and its golden donors for more than two decades, I had scrutinized literally thousands of foundation annual reports—IRS Form 990s—that listed grants for many "other reforms": the civil rights, gun control, antiwar, and women's movements, and the move- ments for gay rights, consumer rights, abortion rights, migrant rights, animal rights, prisoner rights, plus money for liberal academics, liberal magazines, liberal Internet activists, the lot, including campaign finance reform. It was a good start on the "Vast Left Wing Conspiracy" that Joshua Micah Marshall first named in a *Slate* webzine article in 2001.[10]

Yet researching those "other reforms" was different. The environmental movement is segmented by diverse goals, diverse approaches, diverse basic assumptions, and diverse tactics, as well as by ubiquitous turf wars, fund-raising competition, ego clashes, microphone grabbing, and strategy disputes.

It takes a while, but you can assemble a roadmap to the movement's ideological terrain and its funding/activist network with diagrams, flow charts and bullet points. You can track how it tries to rule the world.

Conversely, the overall liberal movement was so scattered, shattered, and battered that it could hardly be called a movement at all. It was more like a mental hospital without doctors or nurses. Forget charts. You couldn't begin to identify Ellen Miller's "all other reforms." Liberals weren't a culture, no coherent ideology, just quarrelsome factions with loads of *issues*.

In fact, they don't even call themselves liberals anymore.

They're "progressives."

That's more important than it may sound. Linguistics Professor Geoffrey Nunberg (University of California at Berkeley) contends that "liberal" has fallen victim to a kind of negative branding at the hands of opponents: "There's no more impressive example of using language to alter substance than the right's success in turning liberal into a disparaging word."[11]

It's all Ronald Reagan's fault, suggests Nunberg.

In his farewell speech to the Republican National Convention at New Orleans in 1988, President Reagan made the name anathema:

> "The masquerade is over... It's time to talk issues; to use the dreaded L-word; to say that the policies of our opposition and the Congressional leadership of his party are liberal, liberal, liberal.[12]

It carried a sting because the upheavals of the 1960s had convinced many working-class Americans that middle-class liberals were hostile to traditional conceptions of patriotism (Vietnam War protesters), civic pride (the counterculture), personal morality (the sexual revolution), and the family (gay rights and pro-abortion activists).

Hard hats, whose unions were steadily losing members, power and prestige, became Reagan Democrats because they believed his accusations that their party had only "policies of tax and spend, economic stagnation, international weakness and accommodation, and always, always, always, blame America first."[13]

Liberal, liberal, liberal Michael Dukakis lost.

Conservative, conservative, conservative George H. W. Bush won.

The Reagan-Bush free market blitz of the '80s crushed decades of New Deal liberalism, even demoralizing far-leftists posing as liberals .

"Liberal" became such a problem that Bill Clinton had to announce his 1991 candidacy by dancing around the dreaded L-word with a jumbled semi-disavowal: "The change we must make isn't liberal or conservative. It's both, and it's different."[14]

It was a "Third Way" between left wing and right wing politics, created to win elections. It was the New Democrat wing of the Democratic Party, organized by Al From's centrist Democratic Leadership Council that Bill Clinton headed in 1990 and '91. It propelled him into the White House.[15]

During his tenure as president, Clinton's priorities included some conservative themes such as reforming welfare programs, expanding the "War on Drugs," increasing law enforcement funding, and reducing trade barriers. His agenda also included typical liberal efforts to create a universal healthcare system, restrict handgun sales, expand environmental regulations, liberalize education, defuse racial antagonisms, and lock in the jobs of workers during pregnancy or medical emergency.[16]

Clinton's Vice President, Al Gore, invented "reinventing government," a project that obtusely centralized bureaucratic power in the hands of fewer appointees. Clinton minions also re-named numerous major programs as "initiatives" to evade congressional oversight of "programs."

So he was right: "it's both and it's different."

But in all he did, he avoided the dreaded L-word as much as possible.

So DID EVERYONE ELSE. America had changed, and not many people were willing to describe themselves as liberal anymore—linguist Nunberg cited a poll figure of only 22 percent.[17]

That had already done serious damage to Democratic politicians: it left them without a philosophical reference point. They had no identifying label to symbolize their beliefs. They were having trouble winning elections.

If you can't be a liberal, what do you call yourself? A leftist? That's even more demonized. Historically, leftists take up where liberals leave off.

That was a good clue in itself.

Lots of those lurked in the Democratic closet—some of whom wanted a remake of the old radical left labor movement and the New Deal of the 1930s, others who craved a more comprehensive form of socialism. And during the Reagan-Bush years they had begun to revive Teddy Roosevelt's term, "progressive," to replace "liberal," hoping it would help revive the Left.[18]

Linguist Nunberg didn't think the label would catch on, but it did.

In 2003, he noted, "There's a lot to be said for progressive: It conveys the right message to sophisticated left-of-center voters without connoting anything negative to the majority of the electorate."[19]

That's "the pleasure of ulteriority," as Robert Frost called metaphor.[20]

In other words, it's code for anything more left wing than you could admit on television—a crafty, ambiguous mask to hide more radical ideology.

It certainly didn't connote progress in development or economic growth. To most, it still doesn't connote much of anything at all, but the progressive label shows up in the press today more than double what it did a decade ago.

It's used to describe anything at all in that scattered, shattered, and battered left-of-center mélange that rambles from the centrist Democratic Leadership Council, to the grab-bag Democratic National Committee, to the leftish Democratic Socialists of America to the way-out Revolutionary Communist Party, USA, plus the beliefs of every registered Democrat in the country, whose ideology—if they have one—is anybody's guess.

So, how do you know what all those "other [progressive] reforms" might look like?

I gave up and took a census.

LUCKY FOR ME, the left-leaning New World Foundation (Hillary Clinton was Chair of the Board 1987/88) had commissioned a 1998 Zogby International poll that asked 1,800 rank-and-file members of nine progressive groups what could galvanize them, what a progressive agenda should look like.

It gave me a baseline to compare with my census.[21]

The New World Foundation's idea for taking the Zogby poll in the first place was to stop fishing in the center, abandon the idea that the road to victory is through the middle, and get their own house in order so progressives could unite in a coherent base and win elections.

The results were reported in *The Nation* magazine by consultant David Dyssegaard Kallick (we shall meet him again in Chapter 3):

> **Racism**. Respondents ranked it as the country's single most important social problem, followed by poverty, corporate power, jobs/economy, environment, moral decline and education.
>
> **Diversity**. Beyond seeing negative consequences of racism, progressives see positive benefits in diversity. For example, 89 percent of respondents agreed that "racial and cultural diversity in our schools are very important."
>
> **Economics**. Progressives feel strongly and consistently that corporations hold too much power, and they are willing to support practical policies that reduce or balance that power.
>
> **Environment**. "Environmental concerns are as important as economic concerns," agree 94 percent of the sample group.
>
> **Healthcare**. Eighty-seven percent of this core group feel "the federal government should guarantee national health care for everyone." Seventy-seven percent feel "the profit motive should be removed from the provision of health care."
>
> **Daycare**. Progressives are eager to see solutions to the problems of daycare, with 90 percent saying government should make a major investment in daycare centers.[22]

Those 1,800 progressives supported abortion rights and favored drug prevention over incarceration, but split on gay rights, with a large number strongly in support of legalizing same-sex marriage at the federal level and 19 percent strongly opposed. School vouchers were controversial as well.

The rank and file also had trouble identifying solutions.

Racism was a problem, but they didn't like affirmative action.

Traditional liberal solutions to poverty and jobs—such as welfare payments and government jobs—didn't get much support either.

Kallick's progressive rank and file results generally didn't track well with my census of progressive leaders, which included labor unions and groups that got the big grant money from progressive foundations.

I identified progressive foundations by their membership in the National Network of Grantmakers, premier left-of-center donor axis in America, which describes itself as a "U.S. association of funders supporting progressive social change and economic justice." I included some non-members because of their involvement in campaign finance reform, particularly the Florence and John Schumann Foundation and the Pew Charitable Trusts.[23]

In their world, social change is a zero-sum game of taking power from those who have it and giving to those who don't. Economic justice is taking money from those who have too much and giving it to those who don't have enough. What kind of government does that is rarely discussed in detail.

Although a few progressive groups had thoughtful, if tentative, answers to "what does a progressive future look like," most of the big money winners were defined more by what they stood against than what they stood for.

I did not include the usual Hate America First brigades that blamed the United States for causing the 9/11 attacks.

My census found *issues groups* more than *a coherent ideology*:

Social progressives, groups that tracked most closely with Kallick's rank and file report, including such organizations as Planned Parenthood Action Fund, NARAL Pro-Choice, People for the American Way, the Foundation for National Progress (publisher of *Mother Jones*) and the Midwest Academy. They consume a substantial slice of the progressive grantmaking pie, supporting same-sex marriage, abortion rights, community organizing, assisted suicide, marijuana legalization, and anti-religious-right programs.[24]

Labor progressives, union leaders with significant left wing agendas. Andy Stern (Service Employees International Union) wants to merge many small, weak unions into a few mega-unions with real clout; Gerald McEntee (Association of Federal, State, County and Municipal Employees) wants control of the growing government employee sector; John Sweeney (AFL-CIO) wants to form a giant unions-plus-other-progressives coalition.[25]

Anti-globalization progressives, such as the International Forum on Globalization, the Funders' Network on Trade and Globalization, and Fifty Years Is Enough. They want to remove the Bretton Woods international financial institutions—the World Bank, the International Monetary Fund, and the World Trade Organization— from their government owners, and centralize them in the United Nations (of which they are technically a part, but without ownership). Kallick's rank and file had nothing to say about this.[26]

Anti-corporate progressives, such as CorpWatch, the Campaign for America's Future, and the National Lawyers Guild. They want to reduce the influence of corporations in society by imposing costly rules—with lofty names such as "Corporate Social Responsibility," "Sustainable Development," and "the Precautionary Principle"—along with corporate campaigns, shareholder protests, lawsuits, tightening regulations, and many other tactics to force companies to sue for peace and accept the demands of their antagonists. Corporate power was the rank and file's Number 3 social problem.[27]

Anti-capitalist progressives, such as Global Exchange, Rainforest Action Network, Ruckus Society, Direct Action Network, Peoples' Global Action, Black Bloc anarchists, and other "Battle of Seattle" WTO protesters. They want to restrain capitalism as being an anti-social force, or, failing that, to redirect the profit system to the public interest. Some, a minority, want to destroy it. Kallick's rank and file didn't go this deep.[28]

Environmental progressives, such as key leaders of Greenpeace, Friends of the Commons, and Environmental Defense, Inc. They want to save the global environment by rejecting modernity and stopping all development, accomplished by putting natural resources off limits, curbing consumerism, and eliminating industrial activities they consider harmful, particularly fossil fuel use, seen as causing global warming—by promoting new energy sources of seriously questionable adequacy. A few intellectuals recommend substituting "global commons" for "environment" to attract broader support. The rank and file didn't think about the environment in these terms, but only about pollution control, health problems, and cute-little-animal nature protection.[29]

Post-national progressives. They seriously consider replacing national citizenship with "denationalized forms of citizenship." Some fear a totally privatized dystopia like Neal Stephenson's *Snow Crash*, or wander in Jean Baudrillard's hyperreality, or dream of a David Korten-style localist utopia. Others merely want to cede some American sovereignty to world bodies: Council on Foreign Relations president Richard Haass warns that America's economic survival depends on global cooperation to make the international system work. This made no blip on the rank and file's radar.[30]

Campaign finance reform progressives, including Common Cause, National Voting Rights Institute, Public Citizen, the World Policy Institute and more than 80 others. They were split down several fracture lines, mainly between the "clean money now" faction and the "incrementalist" faction that supported McCain-Feingold as a politically feasible current step toward future federally funded "clean money" elections. It was the "clean money now" faction that repeatedly hammered the assertion that *America's current electoral system was a threat to democracy.* The faction was backed by many millions in foundation funding, as we'll see in Chapter 12.[31]

What did they mean by that? If present electoral arrangements weren't adequate, what other brand of democracy did they have in mind?

They weren't too forthcoming with details, beyond allegations that *corporate* contributions "bought" votes, disenfranchising minorities and the poor to the point that democracy didn't work anymore. That clearly wasn't the whole story about campaign finance reform making "all other reforms possible." To repeat: *which* other reforms? That wasn't clarified in Kallick's progressive agenda report or my progressive census. I still couldn't see what "All-Other-Reforms Democracy" might be.

So, I reluctantly began to research the hellishly contentious question: What's democracy?

Oh well, into the abyss.

I was reasonably sure they didn't mean the democracy of Pericles, the Athenian aristocrat whose great-grandfather Cleisthenes proposed the first known broad system of democratic government after the expulsion of the tyrants in 510 BC. The Golden Age over which Pericles presided, 460-430 BC—even considering the practice of slavery and voting rights only for the male elite—must have been some sort of democracy (from the Greek *demos* and *kratos*, indicating "the people rule") because his opponents were always calling Pericles a thief, accusing him of tyranny, and trying to get him thrown out. (We shall meet him again in Chapter 11.)[32]

Fast forward to 1844: the Marx and Engels partnership began asking "what's democracy?" and eventually answered that "true democracy" required "the end of class society, the nation, the state"—equal property ownership, socialized means of production, reasonably even income distribution—which meant the underdog revenge of "social revolution" was necessary, and only the proletariat had the interest and capacity to lead the revolution.[33]

David Kallick's progressives talked some of Karl and Frederick's talk— "equitable income distribution," "practical policies that reduce or balance [corporate] power," "nationalized [or at least non-profit] health care for all." Ellen Miller and her donors liked good rousing propaganda, but didn't seem at all interested in the violent overthrow of the capitalist class, or most other communist claptrap. Not much of a clue. Well, maybe just a little. (We'll talk about various Marxisms and socialisms in Chapter 17.)

Fast forward to 1960: Specific adjectives had begun to march ahead of progressive versions of democracy, such as *social* democracy, *economic* democracy, *participatory* democracy, *deliberative* democracy, and so on, each with its own special meaning, each critical of American democracy.[34]

Most became passé, but one of those democracies emerged as the lasting winner of progressive hearts and minds: *participatory democracy.*

If you Google it with quotes, you get back more than 1.5 million entries, probably more than ten thousand of them spot-on relevant to progressives.

Political scientist Jarol Manheim noted, "Like the term progressivism itself, participatory democracy is a delightfully ambiguous phrase, one that can be interpreted more or less uniquely by any number of individuals, yet one that, at the same time, binds them together with a sense of moral purpose, common cause, and deep historical roots."[35]

If participatory democracy—if *anything*—could bind cantankerous progressives together, we're onto something.

PARTICIPATORY DEMOCRACY first gained currency from the New Left, in particular from the Students for a Democratic Society and their 63-page manifesto, *The Port Huron Statement*, which was refined and adopted by sixty or so members during a 1962 conference in Port Huron, Michigan.[36]

The *Statement* was written mostly by University of Michigan graduate student Tom Hayden, with New Yorker Richard Flacks his closest associate, and others, including 19-year-old Paul Booth and Catholic Mary Varela, who made specific contributions. (We'll examine the SDS in Chapter 15.)

The actual phrase "participatory democracy," Hayden has said, came from University of Michigan professor of philosophy, Arnold Kaufman, who had taught him and other early SDSers, and who attended the Port Huron convention as a speaker.[37]

Hayden explained, "Kaufman used the term to signify that democracy, as defined in conventional liberal discourse, was far too limited when reduced to electoral choice and concepts like the free marketplace of ideas."[38]

Kaufman, in turn, took the idea from John Dewey, philosopher, psychologist and educational reformer, who defined democracy in his writings as explicitly participatory: "No man or group of men is wise enough or good enough to rule others without their consent; the positive meaning of this statement is that all those who are affected by social institutions must have a share in producing and managing them," adding that "a democracy is more than a form of government; it is primarily a mode of associated living, of conjoint community experience."[39]

Kaufman and Dewey clearly weren't very happy with representative democracy—a system with *voting* as its central institution—which America had been practicing for the past couple of centuries.

The most immediate intellectual influence on the SDS and its *Statement*, however, was the motorcycle-riding, Texas-born, Columbia University sociologist, C. Wright Mills, who encouraged the SDS with his 1960 *Letter to the New Left*. He would have done more for the SDS had he not died of heart failure at 45 in 1962, the year of their conference.

SDS members studied his *Letter*, which declared that the Old Left and its reliance on labor as the "agency of social change" were no longer truly significant. Labor had become a mere parasite on the growth of capitalism, and the new bearers of the revolution were the New Left, the student movements now breaking "out of apathy" into social activism—in the civil rights, campus reform, and peace movements.

This was heady stuff, especially since Mills asserted that apathy was what the administrators and power technicians actually desired. Mills argued in his 1956 book, *The Power Elite*, that people at the pinnacles of the economic, political, and military communities had evolved into a structure that ruled the country—the power elite—and that most people were happy to let them do it, having neither the talent nor the interest themselves.

America was becoming a society of "manipulated consent," the town meeting ideal of face-to-face democracy lost.[40]

To Mills, the clique of powerful politicians, tycoons and warlords ruled over a land of complacent drones in their nice homes and new cars.

The only proper response was moral outrage.

To Mills, representative democracy represented nobody. *The Power Elite* contains only 8 mentions of the word "vote" in its 361-page text, and only one of those touches (harshly) upon electoral democracy.[41]

The SDS in its *Port Huron Statement* talked about the *destination*—justice, fairness, social control—not the *vehicle*—elections, representation, lobbying. It laid down the principles of participatory democracy as if there were no political parties and as if electoral democracy didn't exist:

In a participatory democracy, the political life would be based in several root principles:

- that decision-making of basic social consequence be carried on by public groupings;
- that politics be seen positively, as the art of collectively creating an acceptable pattern of social relations;
- that politics has the function of bringing people out of isolation and into community, thus being a necessary, though not sufficient, means of finding meaning in personal life....[42]

Did that mean farewell to the voting booth, personal choice, and private life, and did it mean punishment for dissent from the collective?

The economic sphere would have as its basis the principles:

- that work should involve incentives worthier than money or survival. It should be educative, not stultifying; creative, not mechanical; self-directed, not manipulated, encouraging independence; a respect for others, a sense of dignity and a willingness to accept social responsibility, since it is this experience that has crucial influence on habits, perceptions and individual ethics;
- that the economic experience is so personally decisive that the individual must share in its full determination;
- that the economy itself is of such social importance that its major resources and means of production should be open to democratic participation and subject to democratic social regulation.[43]

OES THE LEFT HAVE AN IDEOLOGY that disparages the social value of wealth, where the Right respects it? Must you hate profit? And money itself? And what if you just plain didn't want to participate?

SDS historian James Miller faced the ambiguity and asked:

What, in fact, did "participatory democracy" mean? One man, one vote? Responsible leaders held accountable in regularly scheduled elections? The informed and active involvement of every citizen in local and national political affairs? Direct action as well as voting? Rule-by-consensus in a face-to-face circle of friends? Honesty and authenticity within a tight-knit community? Abolition of all traces of hierarchy and the division of labor, abolition of elections and all representative offices?[44]

I ignored that last alternative as preposterous. Big mistake.

ISTORY WAS NOT KIND to the SDS. Within a decade, the rapid growth inspired by face-to-face participatory democracy and abolition of all hierarchy had brought fatal questions: how many faces can you face at once? And who will do the grunt work without someone telling you to it's your turn to answer the mail? SDS dissolved into paralysis first and then faction fighting, violence and disrepute. It was a fading memory by the 1980s.

But the utopian ideal of participatory democracy—to give each person a voice in the direction and operation of all aspects of their lives—survived.

It was embraced by millions, enshrined in all its pious ambiguity.

Now Ellen Miller's "all other reforms" were revealed.

It wasn't just the specific reforms of Kallick's survey or the goals found in my census. The big, fuzzy, *overarching philosophy* held all that and more.

Participatory democracy was the answer to each of my questions:

Which other reforms? *Participatory democracy.*

What, exactly, did she expect of campaign finance reform? *Participatory democracy.*

Why did she think it was so crucial? *Participatory democracy.*

Was there really such a holy grail for liberals? *Participatory democracy.*

Where would this liberal holy grail take us? *Participatory democracy.*

That was why campaign finance reform was so important.

It was to get progressives into power to create participatory democracy.

That was why campaign finance reform could "save democracy."

It was the "delightfully ambiguous" *participatory* democracy they wanted to save, not representative electoral democracy.

Progressives bound together with moral purpose, common cause, and deep historical roots could harness if not eliminate electoral democracy.

But only if they could capture political power.

With political power, they could capture economic and military power.

Then *they* would be the power elite.

The epiphany, however, soon faded without answering the real question. Participatory democracy. What, exactly, does that mean?

Damn.

Whatever it was, it would take a *real* Vast Left Wing Conspiracy rooted in the culture *and* electoral politics, not just the progressive political machine of Joshua Micah Marshall's plea.

Was that possible?

Perhaps McCain-Feingold wasn't "the reform that makes all other reforms possible," but it had possibilities of its own.

The Left had never organized itself as a mass electoral movement, the efforts of Ralph Nader and the Greens notwithstanding.

McCain-Feingold suddenly gave them the opportunity.

Progressives could now form non-profit groups to do what the more centrist Democratic Party couldn't: accept and spend unlimited amounts of soft money for election campaigns.

New groups like MoveOn.org, the web-based political action committee, had come upon the scene, mobilizing millions. Their members favored the left-most contender, former Vermont Governor Howard Dean, and posted videos likening George W. Bush to Hitler (for which they later apologized).[45]

Robert Borosage, veteran organizer of the Campaign for America's Future, believed progressives were weighing in *not* from the margin. "We are the base," he told the *Washington Post*. (He will return in Chapter 15.)[46]

Billionaire George Soros pledged $10 million for a new progressive campaign committee called America Coming Together. (We'll make his acquaintance shortly, in Chapter 2.)[47]

Carl Pope, head of the 770,000-member Sierra Club and treasurer of America Coming Together, brought an ominous twist: he fought economic growth and development everywhere. (He will show up again in Chapter 4.)[48]

The 2004 presidential election cycle stormed America like nothing in history. It unleashed "the invasion of the 527s." It catapulted mega-donors like Soros into unprecedented power and rendered the Democratic Party a poor stepchild of the very rich. It sent President George W. Bush back to the White House for four more years.

None of that was supposed to happen.

Democrats licked their wounds and moved on.

Progressives—Democrat or otherwise—prepared to rise from the ashes.

Now I WAS READY to track in detail what was really happening while the headlines told us something else.

This book is what I found. I have tried to write the first part, Book I, with some of what philosophers call "the principle of charity"—roughly, seeing things through the eyes of your opponent—but don't mistake my agreeable treatment for agreement. The last part, Book II, doesn't do that.

This book has a viewpoint throughout, for which I offer no apologies.

Dan Carol, father of the Apollo Alliance, once asked me what fears and concerns led me to write this book. I answered in one word: "Choice."[49]

The *real* Vast Left Wing Conspiracy could destroy that.

A conspiracy, recall, is "planning together to break the law."

The conspiracy I mapped was planning together to *smash* the law.

What would happen to the love of liberty, the urge to invent, the desire for wealth, the drive to explore, gun ownership, individualism, property rights, the quest for personal greatness—if progressives were the power elite?

Questions.

What about personal freedoms?

Would you still be able to own a dream home? Or just a dream?

Would you still be able to own a private car? Or a private *anything*?

What about government?

Would there still be voting booths? Or consensus circles instead?

Would there still be courts and a Constitution to limit government power? Or just councils of the self-righteous that *were* government power?

What about the American spirit?

Would there still be the urge to invent that propelled so many Americans to fame and fortune? Would there still be fortune?

Would there still be adventurers driven to explore? Would they need a passport to stray beyond the city limits?

What about the economy?

Would there still be a military-industrial complex? Would there still be a military? Or industry?

Would the Secretary of Environment have veto power over all decisions, public and private? Would there still be private decisions?

What about you?

Would your religion still exist?

Would your gun?

Would you?

Asking such questions could make you dangerous. You might strip away the masks and discover that a progressive victory would leave America freezing in the dark, and in two senses:

- one, in an energy-starved, population-collapsed, pitiless primitivism;
- the other, in an autocratic, bleak, personally grim, socialist dystopia.

I wrote this book to show you why it shouldn't happen.

And how it could.

PROLOGUE NOTES

1. Peter Montague, "Big Picture Organizing - Part 6: Money in Politics," *Rachel's Environment and Health Weekly*, #426, January 26, 1995.

2. *See* Chapter 12 for details.

Richard Dawkins and memes. Dawkins is a professor of evolutionary biology at Oxford University in the United Kingdom. His 1976 book *The Selfish Gene* introduced the term "meme" to the popular lexicon. It means a unit of cultural information that propagates from one mind to another like a gene propagates from one organism to another. Memes range from tunes, catch-phrases, beliefs, clothing fashions, ways of making pots, to the technology of building arches and other skills. Campaign finance reform became a meme among liberal groups in the 1990s, inspiring belief that it was the gateway to achieving all liberal goals.

3. Ron Arnold, *Undue Influence: Wealthy Foundations, Grant-Driven Environmental Groups, and Zealous Bureaucrats That Control Your Future* (Bellevue, Washington: Free Enterprise Press, 1999), p. 143.

4. Public Law 107-155, March 27, 2002. 116 Statutes of the United States, 81. www.law.stanford.edu/library/campaignfinance/107.155.pdf., accessed May 2, 2006

5. Wikipedia entry: *United States House elections, 2002*, http://en.wikipedia.org/wiki/United_States_House_elections%2C_2002, accessed May 4, 2006.

6. Liza Porteus, "Republicans Win Control of Congress," *FoxNews.com*, November 6, 2002. www.foxnews.com/story/0,2933,69057,00.html, accessed March 23, 2006.

7. Steve Schifferes, "Analysis: The vanishing voter," *BBC News Online*, November 6, 2002. http://news.bbc.co.uk/1/hi/world/americas/2371963.stm., accessed March 23, 2006.

8. *See* Chapter 12 for details.

9. Federal Election Campaign Act of 1971, Public Law 92-225; reforms included the Revenue Act of 1971, Public Law 92-178.

10. Joshua Micah Marshall, "Wanted: A Vast Left-Wing Conspiracy," *Slate*, posted May 9, 2001, accessed at http://slate.msn.com/id/1007647/ on July 28, 2005.

11. Geoffrey Nunberg, "The Liberal Label: The substance is alive and well, but the brand is in trouble," *The American Prospect*, September 1, 2003. www.prospect.org/print/V14/8/nunberg-g.html, accessed March 23, 2006.

12. Ronald Reagan, "Remarks at the Republican National Convention in New Orleans, Louisiana, August 15, 1988," www.reagan.utexas.edu/archives/speeches/1988/081588b.htm, accessed May 5, 2006. See also, E. J. Dionne, Jr., "The Republicans in New Orleans: Reagan Promises an All-Out Drive for Bush Victory," *New York Times*, August 15, 1988, p. A1.

13. Ronald Reagan, "Remarks at the Republican National Convention," *op. cit.*

14. Bill Clinton, "Announcement Speech, Old State House, Little Rock, Arkansas, October 3, 1991." www.4president.org/speeches/billclinton1992announcement.htm, accessed September 6, 2005.

15. *See* Wikipedia entry, "Democratic Leadership Council," http://en.wikipedia.org/wiki/Democratic_Leadership_Council, accessed May 4, 2006.

16. *See* Wikipedia entry, "Bill Clinton," http://en.wikipedia.org/wiki/Bill_Clinton, accessed May 4, 2006.

17. Geoffrey Nunberg, "The Liberal Label: The substance is alive and well, but the brand is in trouble," *op. cit.*

18. Background on "progressive": "Progressive Movement," *The New Dictionary of Cultural Literacy, Third Edition*, edited by E.D. Hirsch, Jr., Joseph F. Kett, and James Trefil, (New York, Houghton Mifflin, 2002).

19. Geoffrey Nunberg, "The Liberal Label: The substance is alive and well, but the brand is in trouble," *op. cit.*

20. Robert Frost, "The Constant Symbol," in *Robert Frost: Poetry and Prose*, edited by Edward Connery Latham and Lawrence Thompson (New York: Holt, Rinehart and Winston, 1972), p. 401.

21. Poll results: David Dyssegaard Kallick, "Notes for a Progressive Agenda." Reprinted with permission from the November 23, 1998 issue of *The Nation.*

22. *Ibid.*

23. National Network of Grantmakers, www.nng.org/.

24. Funders of Planned Parenthood Action Fund include Turner Foundation ($6.1 million, 2000/2002, www.stealthpacs.org/funder.cfm?Org_ID=2835); NARAL Pro-Choice, Turner Foundation ($3.8 million, 2000/2002; www. stealthpacs.org/funder.cfm?Org_ID=29); People for the American Way Foundation, Arca Foundation ($200,000, 2004); Foundation for National Progress, Schumann Center for Media and Democracy ($110,000, 2003/2004); Midwest Academy, Charles Stewart Mott Foundation ($175,000, 2001/2004).

25. Michael McMenamin, "Labor Lost," *Reason*, November 1, 2000.

26. Randy Hayes, "Restructuring the Global Economy: Eradicating Bretton Woods and Creating New Institutions," The 2002 Johns Hopkins Symposium on Foreign Affairs series, *Paragon or Paradox? Capitalism in the Contemporary World*, March 14, 2002.

27. Jarol B. Manheim, *The Death of a Thousand Cuts: Corporate Campaigns and the Attack on the Corporation* (Mahwah, N.J.: Lawrence Erlbaum Associates, 2001).

28. Richard L. Grossman, Thomas Alan Linzey, and Daniel E. Brannen, "Ending Corporate Governance: We The People Revoking Our Plutocracy," October, 2004, www.ratical.org/corporations, accessed July 7, 2005. *See also*, Paul Hawken, Amory Lovins, L. Hunter Lovins, *Natural Capitalism: The Next Industrial Revolution* (Boston: Back Bay Books, 2000).

29. Ron Arnold, "The Politics of Environmental Defense, Inc.: Will John Kerry Listen to ED Trustee Teresa Heinz-Kerry?" *Foundation Watch* (Washington, D.C.: Capital Research Center, August, 2004). *See also*, John Zerzan, *Future Primitive*, (Brooklyn: Automedia, 1988).

30. Ruud Koopmans and Paul Statham, "Challenging the Liberal Nation-State? Postnationalism, Multiculturalism and the Collective Claims-Making of Migrants and Ethnic Minorities in Britain and Germany," *American Journal of Sociology*, 1999, 105(3):652-96. *See also*, Georgie Anne Geyer, *Americans No More: The Death of Citizenship*, (New York: The Atlantic Monthly Press, 1996). *See also*, Richard N. Haass, *The Opportunity: America's Moment to Alter History's Course*, (New York: PublicAffairs, 2005); Walter B. Wriston, *The Twilight of Sovereignty : How the Information Revolution Is Transforming Our World* (New York: Scribner Book Company, 1992). *See also* the London School of Economics (LSE) Centre for the Study of Global Governance for extensive discussions of the issue. Online at www.lse.ac.uk/Depts/global, accessed November 19, 2005.

31. See Chapter 12.

32. Jeremy McInerney, "The Age of Pericles," recorded material, (Chantilly, Virginia: The Teaching Company, Course No. 3317).

33. "Marx and Engels: The Prototypical Transnational Actors," August Nimtz, in *Restructuring World Politics: Transnational Social Movements, Networks, and Norms*, Sanjeev Khagram, James V. Riker, and Kathryn Sikkink, editors (Minneapolis: University of Minnesota Press, 2002), p.246.

34. Anthony Giddens, *The Third Way: The Renewal of Social Democracy*, (Oxford, England: Polity Press, 2000); Martin Carnoy and Derek Shearer, *Economic Democracy: the Challenge of the 1980s*, (White Plains, New York: M.E. Sharpe, Inc., 1980); Dimitrios Roussopoulos and C. George Benello (editors), *The Case for Participatory Democracy: Prospects for a New Society*, (Tonawanda, New York: Black Rose Books, 2003); Leon Stein, *Out of the Sweatshop: The Struggle for Industrial Democracy*, (New York City: Quadrangle/New York Times Book Company, 1977).

35. Jarol B. Manheim, *Biz-War and the Out-of-Power Elite: The Progressive-Left Attack on the Corporation*, (Mahwah, New Jersey, Lawrence Erlbaum Associates, 2004), *pp.* 145-146.

36. Tom Hayden (principal author), "The Port Huron Statement of the Students for a Democratic Society," Port Huron, Michigan, June 15, 1962. http://coursesa.matrix.msu.edu/~hst306/documents/huron.html, accessed June 1, 2005.

37. Tom Hayden and Dick Flacks, "The Port Huron Statement at 40," *The Nation*, August 5, 2002.

38. His major ideas are contained in his only book, Arnold S. Kaufman, *The Radical Liberal, new man in American politics* (Palo Alto, California: Atherton Press, 1968).

39. "No man…" John Dewey, *Intelligence in the Modern World: John Dewey's Philosophy*. Joseph Ratner, editor. (New York: Modern Library, 1939), p. 41. "a democracy…" John Dewey, *Democracy and education*, (New York: Macmillan Company, 1916), p. 101.

40. Charles Wright Mills, *The Power Elite*, (Oxford: The Oxford University Press, 1956), p. 309.

41. *Ibid.*, p. 356.

42. Hayden, "The Port Huron Statement," *op. cit.*

43. Ibid.

44. James Miller, *Democracy is in the Streets: From Port Huron to the Siege of Chicago* (Cambridge, Massachusetts: Harvard University Press, 1987, 1994), p. 245.

45. Timothy Karr, "MoveOn.org, The New York Post, and Media's Double Standard," *MediaChannel.org*, January 11, 2004. www.commondreams.org/views04/0110-01.htm, accessed June 25, 2006.

46. David Von Drehle, "Among Democrats, The Energy Seems To Be on the Left," *Washington Post*, July 10, 2003.

47. America Coming Together, 20004 Election Cycle, www.opensecrets.org/527s/527events.asp?orgid=10, accessed December 5, 2005.

48. Sierra Club website, "Arctic National Wildlife Refuge," www.sierraclub.org/arctic/, accessed June 25, 2006.

49. For the record, my viewpoint: In a word, I believe in choice. To paraphrase contrarian
    investor and author Doug Casey, I believe in free enterprise, small govern-
    ment, fiscal conservatism, avoiding entanglements in foreign countries, the
    maximum personal liberty commensurate with public safety, and a rule of law
    designed to enhance that freedom. This philosophy has been called "libertarian"
    and "classical liberal" in the 19th-century sense, and—Marxists love this one—
    "anarchy." It's a tradition with deep historical roots in this country. It's a
    point of view that, I hope, will eventually prevail over progressivist points of
    view worldwide.

PART I

DINNER AT BEDUCI

THE CALL
BILLIONAIRE
MISSING BRIDGES
AT DINNER

CHAPTER 1

THE CALL

Ring Ring.
Shortly after the Democrats lost the 2002 election, Harold Ickes got a message from Gina Glantz.

She was an official of the Service Employees International Union.

He was a consultant to the Democratic National Committee.

She wanted to set up a meeting to change the world.

Yes, Democrats were conducting post-mortems and blaming each other.

Yes, they regretted choosing not to attack President George W. Bush a lot more aggressively.

Mushy centrism, support for the war on terrorism, and mildly liberal programs had backfired, just as progressives had predicted.

But that's not what she wanted to talk about.

It was about beating Bush in 2004.

Needling for a Vein of Riches

Glantz specifically wanted to talk about non-profit, tax-free "527 groups," named for Section 527 of the Internal Revenue Code.

The newly enacted Bipartisan Campaign Reform Act outlawed soft money to political parties, but not to non-profit 527 groups, the workhorse political organizations that had toiled in backroom obscurity for many years.

Originally, 527s kept donors anonymous—*New York Times* editorials helped stop that by carping at them as "secret groups" and "slush funds."

Even though the "anonymous donor loophole" had been closed, 527s were still immune from the soft money ban.

Glantz envisioned 527s popping up like toadstools after a spring rain.

Money, like water, will find a way around obstacles, and 527 groups were about to become a famous way.[1]

21

With a pack of eager new 527 groups begging for some of the $4 million-plus in soft money that the SEIU had been giving Democrats every two years, Glantz thought the hodgepodge would inevitably waste money on duplicated efforts in the upcoming Dump Bush battle. They needed a way to coordinate and she needed a meeting with the proper people.

Ickes agreed to join a small group later in the month for dinner at BeDuCi, a tony Mediterranean restaurant near Washington's Dupont Circle.[2]

GINA GLANTZ

Gina Stritzler from Westfield, New Jersey was a campus radical in the Free Speech Movement at the University of California at Berkeley. She graduated in 1965 in journalism.

Home in New Jersey, she married investment manager Ronald Glantz.

1984 brought Gina Glantz her first big-time political job: national field director for the Mondale-Ferraro Committee.

In 1985, she joined with progressive grassroots organizer Angie Martin to form Martin & Glantz LLC, political consultants. Martin was credited with forming the first "citizen lobby," a model later used nationwide.

Clients included the Ford Foundation, the Gay, Lesbian, Bi-Sexual and Transgender Foundation Affinity Group, the Sierra Club, and the Planned Parenthood Federation. Martin died of breast cancer in 1997.

Glantz carried on, and in 1999 served as the national campaign manager for Bill Bradley's presidential run.

In January 2001, she sold her business and went to work for the Service Employees International Union as assistant for strategic issues and political action to president Andrew Stern.

GINA GLANTZ CONTACTED HAROLD ICKES because he was the right person in the right place: his father had been Secretary of the Interior under President Franklin D. Roosevelt, he earned his stripes as a tough labor lawyer in New York City, he was Bill Clinton's 1992 presidential campaign manager and later his deputy chief of staff, and guided Hillary Clinton's successful Senate campaign. He was now a paid consultant to the DNC, the Democratic National Committee.

Glantz also knew that Ickes had seen the McCain-Feingold menace coming far in advance, and had even issued a 12-page early warning to the executive committee of the DNC.

On March 12, 2001, when McCain-Feingold was still more than a year away from final passage, he wrote: "The ban on the use of soft money by national political parties will greatly advantage the Republicans."

While shaking his head over fellow Democrats delivering impassioned speeches for campaign reform, he calculated that if the McCain-Feingold ban on soft money had applied in the election cycle of 1999-2000, Republicans would have outspent the Democrats by a devastating $448 million to $270 million.[3]

It was simple arithmetic. McCain-Feingold would limit "hard money" contributions to no more than $2,000 for a single candidate, $5,000 to a political action committee, and $25,000 to a party.

That was the end of those multi-million-dollar checks from a select list of reliable fat cats.[4]

Under the new rules, the two parties would have to drum up a lot of small "hard money" donors to pay for a modern presidential race, and that would fatally hinder the one that most relied upon the rich.

Republicans, right?

Wrong.

Contrary to popular belief, Democrats weren't "the party of the working man" when it came to campaign contributions.

They depended on high-dollar donations from trial lawyers and tinseltown celebrities—like movie producer and real estate heir Stephen Bing, who had just poured $8.7 million into the Democratic Party's 2002 campaign coffers—and other limousine liberals. What would they do now?

HAROLD McEWAN ICKES

Harold Ickes, born in 1939, worked as a cowboy in Oregon for three years after finishing the elite Sidwell School in Washington. There he developed rugged riding skill, a stunning knack for profanity, and a legendary temper that led one writer to note, "he can explode into screaming fits, which his intense blue eyes and unkempt hair only make more maniacal."

At Stanford University, he met Professor Allard Kenneth Lowenstein, known as the "Pied Piper" for recruiting idealistic young students to New Left projects. He convinced Ickes to spend two summers registering black voters in the South, where a group of angry whites beat him so severely he had to have a shattered kidney removed.

In his third year at Columbia University School of Law, he again met Lowenstein, who was leading the national "Dump Johnson" anti-Vietnam war campaign within the Democratic Party. Ickes joined in.

In 1972 he worked for Democratic presidential candidate George McGovern. He met Bill Clinton while both were working on the Hatfield-McGovern Amendment to cut off all military aid to South Vietnam.

Ickes later worked for Democratic presidential candidates Edmund Muskie (1972), Jimmy Carter (1976), Edward M. Kennedy (1980), Walter Mondale (1984), Jesse Jackson (1988), and Bill Clinton (1992).

In 1977, Ickes joined the Long Island law firm Meyer, Suozzi, English & Klein, where he headed the labor practice. His client list included four union locals accused of links to the Columbo, Gambino, Genovese and Lucchese crime families. Attorneys began to call Meyer Suozzi "The Firm" after the 1993 Tom Cruise hit about lawyers trapped in a law firm serving the Mafia.

Ickes took over as Clinton White House Deputy Chief of Staff in 1994. Dick Morris, a Clinton advisor, said: "Whenever there was something that [Clinton] thought required ruthlessness or vengeance or sharp elbows and sharp knees or, frankly, skullduggery, he would give it to Harold."

McCain-Feingold meant those contributors couldn't be much help anymore, depriving Democrats of some $250 million every two years.[5]

The Republicans, by contrast and despite their media image as cigar-chomping Wall Street big shots, had for decades cultivated multitudes of small donors who gave "hard money" in amounts of $200 and under. They would be untouched by McCain-Feingold's limits and still keep giving.[6]

The imbalance for the Democrats was not simply significant, it was disastrous. Not only had the Democrats lost the Presidency to George W. Bush in 2000's unprecedented post-election hostilities, they had also lost their campaign financing lifeline at the hands of McCain-Feingold in 2002.

Any faint chance of taking back the White House in 2004 had vanished.

THE SHADOW CAMPAIGN

GINA GLANTZ DIDN'T CALL ICKES BECAUSE HE SAW THE PROBLEM, but because he saw the solution.

Democrats had to build a network of independent—but interlocking—non-partisan, non-profit organizations.

They had to be the kind with Washington-speak labels like 527s and 501c groups—both named for sections of the Internal Revenue Service code.

Both 527 and 501c groups would still be able to receive unlimited soft money donations under McCain-Feingold.

They weren't without drawbacks.

Even though McCain-Feingold did allow voter mobilization campaigns, money-harvesting 527 groups could only spend their soft dollars on *nonfederal* candidates.

They couldn't help members of Congress or the president with soft money, but they *could* also accept hard money—subject to campaign finance limits and reporting requirements—and spend it on federal campaigns.[7]

And they *could* use soft money for "electioneering communications," including so-called "issue advocacy" ads that tout or criticize a federal candidate's record without using forbidden "magic words," such as Vote Against Jane Doe. You *might* elect a president just with issue advocacy ads.

But there was a catch: those, too, were subject to campaign finance limits and disclosure requirements if they were aired 60 days before a general election or 30 days before a primary election, leaving those as "dead times" for all practical purposes. That was only one obstacle Ickes faced.

Most awkwardly, all 527 groups had to operate independently of the national party committees.

Presidential campaign managers are notorious for demanding total control. They would certainly fear unruly 527 campaigns that might ruin the election.

A tough problem if you were an out-of-power Democrat who wanted to defeat an incumbent Republican president with 527s.[8]

Ickes saw that the way was to start now and assemble a presidential campaign minus the candidate.

It didn't matter who that might turn out to be—Anybody But Bush.

He could count on the party faithful for that. They harbored a visceral, uncontrollable, blue-state loathing of George W. Bush. Their loyalists would hate him not just for "stealing the election" in 2000, but also for (in order of shrillness): 1) his intolerable swagger; 2) his exasperating secrecy; 3) his imperial contempt for doubters; 4) his unrefined Texas talk; 5) his "smirking chimp" face; 6) the mere fact that he existed.

It only mattered that a money machine would be ready in a parallel 527 campaign when the soft money-starved Democrats had to confront the hard money-rich Republicans. They could then mold the parallel campaign to fit whoever won the nomination.

A properly constructed 527 campaign, in effect, would be a substitute Democratic Party. It could also be the impetus for progressives who didn't want to be a Democratic substitute, but nobody quite realized that yet.[9]

Democratic National Committee Chairman Terry McAuliffe was hand-picked for the job by Bill Clinton (he guaranteed a $1.35 million loan that allowed the Clintons to buy their dream house in Chappaqua, New York, but backed out after a lawsuit by conservative Judicial Watch). McAuliffe talked to Ickes. They agreed. A parallel campaign was essential.[10]

McAuliffe immediately created a select task force to deal with the problem, a secret brain trust comprising Ickes and six others, including former White House Chief of Staff John D. Podesta.[11]

They had to figure out the details of how 527 organizations could continue the flow of soft money to supposedly non-party groups in fact run by loyal Democrats.

Ickes came up with the idea of a "presidential media fund" to pay for television issue ads to help the Democratic presidential nominee in the dangerous empty months between the end of the 2004 primaries and the Democratic national convention.

The brain trust surmised that the Democratic 2004 presidential nominee would enter the public primary financing system with its spending ceilings, leaving the candidate broke after the last primaries in June.

President Bush, of course, would opt out of the public system and be awash in private cash.

If their hunch was right, McCain-Feingold had just made it possible for very rich progressives to push the American public far to the left.

In mid-October, McAuliffe began talking up Ickes' presidential media fund idea with some of those very rich potential donors at a secret party conclave at Washington's Mayflower Hotel to change the world.[12]

CHAPTER 1 NOTES

1. 527 groups originally had no reporting requirements, meaning that donors were anonymous. However, a 527 attacked John McCain's failed presidential run in 2000, infuriating the senator and prompting him to support reporting requirements. *See* Editorial desk, "An End to Secret Campaign Funds," *New York Times*, June 29, 2000. The IRS website at www.irs.gov/charities/political/article/0,,id=96355,00.html#Period, accessed July 29, 2005, blandly states, "Unless excepted, tax-exempt political organizations are required to file periodic reports with the IRS." Only Political Action Committees filing FEC reports and non-federal state and local groups are excepted.

2. Glantz convenes the dinner meeting: Steve Weissman and Ruth Hassan, "BCRA and the 527 Groups," Campaign Finance Institute, February 9, 2005, Revised March 8, 2005, draft chapter for publication in *The Election after Reform: Money, Politics and the Bipartisan Campaign Reform Act*. Michael J. Malbin, ed., (Rowman and Littlefield, 2005); Jeanne Cummings, "A Hard Sell on 'Soft Money'," *Wall Street Journal*, December 2, 2003.

3. Ickes' advance warning: James V. Grimaldi and Thomas B. Edsall, "Super Rich Step into Political Vacuum," *Washington Post,* October 17, 2004.

4. For contribution limits and full text, see S. 27 and H.R. 2356, the McCain-Feingold Bipartisan Campaign Reform Act, which became Public Law 107-155 on March 27, 2002. Available online at http://thomas.loc.gov.

5. Bing's 2002 contributions: Opensecrets.org, Center for Responsive Politics, website accessed on July 30, 2005 www.opensecrets.org/softmoney/softindiv .asp?txtName=bing%2C+stephen&txtAmount=all&txtSort=Cycle.

6. Thomas B. Edsall, "Liberals meeting to set '04 strategy," *Washington Post*, May 25, 2003.

7. For a discussion of the federal expenditure loophole, see Colleen Kollar-Kotelly, United States District Judge: Memorandum Opinion, Motion for Injunction, *Emily's List v. Federal Election Commission*, February 25, 2005, www.fec.gov/law/litigation/mem_opinion_injunction_05CV00049.pdf, accessed July 30, 2005.

8. Peter H. Stone, "Hard Questions About Soft-Money Groups," *National Journal*, December 21, 2002.

9. Ickes and the parallel campaign concept: Dan Balz and Thomas B. Edsall, "Democrats Forming Parallel Campaign," *Washington Post*, March 10, 2004; Page A1.

10. McAuliffe loan guarantee: Associated Press, "Clintons sign contract for house in Chappaqua, N.Y." *The Telegraph* (Nashua, N.H.), September 3, 1999. McAuliffe reached the same conclusion: Edsall, "Super rich step into political vacuum."

11. The others were former White House political director Doug Sosnik, DNC Chief Operating Officer Minyon Moore, Chief of Staff Josh Wachs and counsel Joe Sandler, plus a leading Democratic consultant, Michael Whouley: Weissman and Hassan, "BCRA and the 527 Groups." See also Thomas B. Edsall, "New ways to harness soft money in works: Political groups poised to take huge donations," *Washington Post*, August 25, 2002, page A1.

12. Don Van Natta Jr. and Richard A. Oppel Jr., "Parties create ways to avoid soft money ban," *New York Times*, November 1, 2002.

CHAPTER 2

BILLIONAIRE

E IGHT MONTHS EARLIER, MORT HALPERIN got a new job.
As of February 2002, Morton H. Halperin, Ph.D. (International Relations, Yale, 1961) was out of the Council on Foreign Relations and into the Washington office of the Open Society Institute.

It was one of many non-profit organizations created by the quirky hedge fund operator, George Soros. He was known as "the man who broke the Bank of England," boasting he made a billion dollars in a single day in 1992 through currency speculation that drove down the value of the pound.

Halperin got to know Soros while both were with the Council on Foreign Relations in 1996, when Soros was a director and Halperin a senior fellow.

They worked closely on a CFR report, "The American National Interest and the United Nations," decrying U.S. unilateralism and neglect of the United Nations—President *Clinton*'s unilateralism and neglect.

Soros was then task force chairman and Halperin lent credibility as a former senior staffer of the National Security Council under Presidents Nixon and Clinton.[2]

Now Soros was Halperin's boss.

Halperin saw Soros through the lens of foreign affairs: the rich investor had built a substantial international reputation as a philanthropist supporting democratic reform through his far-flung Soros Foundations Network, with organizations in thirty-one countries, including the former Soviet Union and Central Eurasia, Haiti and Guatemala, plus two regional foundations that donated to twenty-seven countries in Africa.

Halperin understood that Soros used his foreign philanthropy as a carrot and stick for heads of state to adopt polices he favored, opening his pockets to the compliant and cutting off his personal and financial involvement if promised reforms failed to materialize.

27

Rumors circulated that he even helped engineer the overthrow of rulers he didn't like, such as Yugoslavia's Slobodan Milosevic.

Morton Abramowitz, former ambassador to South Korea and director of the Carnegie Endowment for International Peace, once said that Soros was "the only man in the United States who has his own foreign policy and can implement it."[3]

Halperin had something of a radical resumé.

His political career went back to the Johnson administration, where his position as Deputy Assistant Secretary of Defense had placed him in charge of compiling the top secret history of U.S. involvement in Vietnam that was leaked by Daniel Ellsberg to the *New York Times* and published as the "Pentagon Papers"—allegedly with Halperin's knowledge.[4]

Halperin advocated that American use of military force be subject to United Nations approval.

He was also intensely opposed to the very idea of an American intelligence community. In his contribution to the 1976 compilation, *The Lawless State: The Crimes of the U.S. Intelligence Agencies,* Halperin wrote, "Using secret intelligence agencies to defend a constitutional republic is akin to the ancient medical practice of employing leeches to take blood from feverish patients. The intent is therapeutic, but in the long run the cure is more deadly than the disease."[5]

Halperin seemed intent upon something like a Socialist America, as if he hated the nation's power and wanted to reduce the United States to a subservient global role of some sort—vague, but considerably to the left of Lyndon B. Johnson's administration.

Halperin also knew his way around the foundation world, having served as a senior associate of the Carnegie Endowment for International Peace, and as senior vice president of The Century Foundation, a progressive center based in New York that concentrates on specific policy issues, funding writing and research projects. (Soros contributed to it, and John Podesta became a trustee).[6]

Now Dr. Halperin began considering ways for OSI—the Open Society Institute—to reconstruct progressive politics in America, to foster electoral power for the Left and to counter the influence of the Right.

The problem was his boss.

George Soros had tossed the Open Society Institute into a mixed salad of insular, issue-specific programs with ingredients picked from this and that.

Soros added an issue here—where he thought there was no debate (as in assisted suicide)—and there—or a monopoly of thinking (as in drug policy)—and everywhere—or he thought fundamental to democracy (as in campaign finance reform).

Beyond a general liberal viewpoint, it had little political overlay.

GEORGE SOROS

George Soros was born in Budapest, Hungary in 1930 as György Švarc, or George Schwartz, of parents Tivadar (Theodore) and Erzebet (Elizabeth). Both were nonobservant Jews. His mother was from a wealthy family and his father a lawyer from humble origins.

Tivadar was a leading proponent of Esperanto, the invented trans-European language promoted by those who desired a world free of nationality. When George and his older brother Paul were still young, his father changed the family name to the Hungarian-sounding but actually Esperanto Soros. It means "soar" (in the future tense). Anti-nationalism is embedded in George Soros' name as well as in his character.

As a child, he felt he had extraordinary powers, of even being "God-like." It developed into an adult sense of messianic personal destiny.

The family was well-off until 1944 when Hitler sent Adolph Eichmann to oversee the extermination of Hungary's Jews. Tivadar obtained false identity papers for his family and they each fled to separate homes, hidden as Christians. All four survived the Holocaust.

With the Soviet takeover of Hungary in 1947, the impoverished Tivadar sent George, then 17, to stay with cousins in London, where he worked odd jobs and studied at the London School of Economics (LSE).

While pursuing his economics degree at the Fabian socialist LSE, Soros met the man who changed his life: Prof. Karl Popper, philosopher of science, teacher of logic and scientific method, towering intellect, and author of *The Logic of Scientific Discovery*. His technical concept of "falsification" as the test for validating scientific theories brought him wide recognition.

Popper was also a distinguished social philosopher whose passionate denunciation of all forms of totalitarianism in *The Open Society and Its Enemies* (1945) gave Soros a personal idol, a lifetime belief system, and a brand name for his future charities. Soros took the open society idea to extravagant heights: for him it transcended all other standards of civic virtue.

Soros never studied under Popper, but read his works and submitted essays to him for review and comment. In 1982, when Soros named his first foundation the Open Society Fund and informed the philosopher, Popper was not sure he recalled Soros, but was pleased by the honor.

Although a mediocre student at LSE, Soros was intensely intellectual and felt he was meant to be a philosopher, fancying himself Popper's successor. However, in midlife he realized that he had no talent for it, and, after years in psychotherapy, resigned himself to making large amounts of money for his messianic mission to promote Popper's open society concept worldwide.

Popper's two-volume *Open Society and Its Enemies* focused on closed societies that suppressed reason—ones he condemned as "magical, tribal or collectivist"—but didn't say much about the open society itself, beyond freedom of scientific inquiry and the freedom to dissent. Ironically, Soros donations go largely to collectivist dissent. The logical disconnect between Popper's concept and Soros' implementation has been noted by critics.

Zealous OSI officers often suggested to Soros some overarching project to unite American progressives, but he always said that wasn't his role.

It was more eccentricity than unconcern. True, he admitted never feeling fully American—immigrating in 1956, he said, "I did not particularly care for the United States. I had acquired some basic British prejudices; you know, the States were, well, commercial, crass, and so on."[7]

Soros may have been more than a little snobbish, but not standoffish.

To the contrary, his relatively new foundation (1992) had quickly networked with major players in the philanthropy industry.

His Open Society Institute belonged to the umbrella trade group, the Council on Foundations, as well as to the Environmental Grantmakers Association, and the progressives' own National Network of Grantmakers.

In fact, while working with Halperin in the Council on Foreign Relations in 1996, Soros joined with thirty-one other donors in a campaign finance reform consortium called the Funders' Committee for Citizen Participation.

Soros even invited Schumann Foundation President (and PBS icon) Bill Moyers to sit on his Institute's board of directors.

In sum, Soros was well connected, but he had strong preferences and idiosyncratic ideas about what to fund and what not.

It took Halperin a while to figure that out, in part because he had, in effect, walked into the Open Society Institute in the middle of a long ongoing conversation.

F IVE YEARS EARLIER, Sally Covington of the National Committee for Responsive Philanthropy (NCRP) completed an important study.

She gave it the portentous title, "Moving a Public Policy Agenda: The Strategic Philanthropy of Conservative Foundations."[8]

It was a scholarly roadmap to the conservative movement and the people who paid for it. It taunted and haunted progressives for years.

Covington presented her findings in one of the best attended sessions at the 1997 annual meeting of the philanthropy industry's powerful trade group, the Council on Foundations. Her report began:

> For more than three decades, conservative strategists have mounted an extraordinary effort to reshape politics and public policy priorities at the national, state and local level. Although this effort has often been described as a "war of ideas," it has involved far more than scholarly debate within the halls of academe. Indeed, waging the war of ideas has required the development of a vast and interconnected institutional apparatus. Since the 1960s, conservative forces have shaped public consciousness and influenced elite opinion, recruited and trained new leaders, mobilized core constituencies, and applied significant rightward pressure on mainstream institutions, such as Congress, state legislatures, colleges and universities, the federal judiciary and philanthropy itself.[9]

The rest was detail, tracking $210 million in grants from twelve conservative foundations, including the John M. Olin, Lynde and Harry Bradley and Sarah Scaife foundations, to specific think tanks such as the Heritage Foundation, advocacy groups such as the Federalist Society, public interest law firms such as Pacific Legal Foundation, and supportive media outlets such as *Commentary* and *The American Spectator*.

These foundations, Covington said, had successfully created that "vast and interconnected institutional apparatus" for overarching conservative public policy objectives, including smaller government, lower taxes and free markets.[10]

The lasting impact of her report came from its 7-point recommendation that foundations deploy their resources to project a clear alternative to the Right's political vision.[11]

Philanthropoids—unflattering jargon for foundation officers and staff—sympathized with this "Copycat Concept." But their employers didn't.

Before Halperin came on board, any number of OSI officers, eager to build a Left with the Right's stuff, importuned Soros with Covington's idea that "we need one of those."

"I do not view my role as countering the Right," became his mantra.

Most funders recoiled from creating a "vast and interconnected institutional apparatus" for the Left, protesting they were non-ideological.

Denise Gray-Felder, director of communications at the Rockefeller Foundation, said, "I really resist political labels, because I would be hard-pressed, even with a gun to my head, to say what we were, conservative or liberal."[12]

Ellen Condliffe Lageman, a New York University history and education professor, said the major foundations have indeed engaged in public policy grantmaking, but "they haven't done it to build a movement for broad change."[13]

Waldemar A. Nielsen, preeminent scholar of philanthropy and author of the classic, *The Golden Donors: A New Anatomy of the Great Foundations*, charged the leading foundations with being "chicken" when faced with the success of the conservative model. He said their reluctance "represents a lack of courage, an unwillingness to get into controversy. It's a kind of hiding out from reality."[14]

Soros wasn't hiding, he just wasn't buying the Copycat Concept.

Shortly after Covington's study appeared, he commented through his program director, Gara La Marche: "I think we are responding to a degree to the concerns raised in the NCRP report."

He wouldn't say that the Open Society Institute opposed a big left wing ideological vision, or was itself on the Left, but that it did take a very direct approach to raising the profile of its tossed salad portfolio.

"We have put a lot of emphasis on changing the debate on certain issues," La Marche said, citing drug legalization, assisted suicide, reduced prison sentences and welfare rights for immigrants regardless of legal status.

"We're obviously not trying to win any popularity contests."

La Marche ended by saying that "Soros believes foundations should use their position to take risks." By supporting grantees who take taboo positions in previously one-sided debates, he hoped to alter the climate enough to be the tipping point to get others to take the plunge.

It was the hedge fund operator in Soros, betting at the margin where the leverage is best, and getting others to come with him.

"We want company," La Marche said.[15]

Soros began funding NCRP after Sally Covington's report—$140,000 over the next few years—but for other reasons, since she soon left the group. It was misread by some as support of her Copycat Concept.[16]

B UT THE ELECTION OF PRESIDENT GEORGE W. BUSH changed things. You didn't need a report to tell you that the infrastructure to develop, test, and promote progressive ideas was inadequate, especially in comparison with the think tanks and media outlets promoting the ideas of the Right.

Liberal foundations started to think about new think tanks.

And Soros subtly changed because Bush was everything he wasn't.

By early 2001, Mark Schmitt (Yale, 1983), who handled OSI's program on Governance and Public Policy in the New York office, became sick of hearing "We need a Heritage Foundation for our side"—and Soros saying "No we don't."

"I didn't think effective organizations would be created by emulating 30-year-old organizations on 'the other side,'" Schmitt told me.[17]

He knew there was already an impressive array of progressive centers for research and analysis in virtually every major issue area.

Evidence also showed that they collectively had more funding than the handful of big centers on the Right. Analysts at Economic America, Inc., editors of *The Right Guide* and *The Left Guide*—respected directories that profiled many hundreds of right-of-center and left-of-center groups— wrote in 1998 that "financial figures are still considerably less for the Right than their counterparts on the Left." In fact, the Left led by more than 3 to 1.[18]

One faction of progressives, the environmental movement, was estimated in 1997 by the *Boston Globe* to have revenues of $4 billion *a year.*[19]

In short, despite throwing big foundation money at the issues, the Left was getting considerably less bang for the buck than the Right.

New think tanks based on the Copycat Concept might serve only to prove conclusively that the Left was an incoherent, intellectually bankrupt, self-destructive mess.

Instead, Schmitt wanted a thoughtful analysis of what the more liberal institutions were already doing, why that might be insufficient, and the role that a new organization would play in the current climate.

He also thought it might offer a more persuasive argument to Soros.

So, using a small amount of discretionary money from his program, he personally commissioned David Dyssegaard Kallick—recall, we met him in the Prologue—a former editor of the journal *Social Policy* who had also worked for foundations and several progressive think tanks including Robert Borosage's Institute for America's Future.

O N JANUARY 1, 2002—a month before Morton Halperin hired on—the Open Society Institute published the result: *Progressive Think Tanks: What Exists, What's Missing?*

Schmitt wrote cautiously in the Preface:

> Before moving forward with efforts to expand the progressive capacity to develop ideas and policy, we thought it essential to go beyond the old critique and understand just what actually exists....
>
> In short, we needed a map, one that showed all the landmarks as well as the uninhabited places, the roads connecting organizations but also the missing bridges.[20]

Covington's report was already "the old critique."

Kallick's new critique wasn't just a census map, but a dispassionate and savvy analysis of the deep potholes in progressive "roads connecting."

He took the census, all right—profiles of leading progressive think tanks such as the Progressive Policy Institute, Borosage's Institute for America's Future, the Economic Policy Institute, and the far-left Institute for Policy Studies, plus headcounts of several dozen movements, "Civil Rights, women's liberation, ecology, Black Power, Puerto Rican nationalism, gay rights, disability rights," and on and on—but Kallick caustically noted that together they made up "less than the sum of their parts."

What to do?

"Progressives are still struggling to find a coherent vision that energizes its ranks," as he well knew from the results of his 1998 poll for the New World Foundation, which we saw in the Prologue (*page 6*).

They were just a pile of kaleidoscopes: many patterns, no picture.

Organizationally, "the bewildering array of small progressive groups focusing on individual issues and the lack of bigger ones focusing on overall political perspective is a source of continual frustration to progressives."

It was the absent ideology, that damnable, elusive *ideology*.

What was it, exactly?

"Big questions are still unresolved, such as America's role as a single military superpower, centralization vs. decentralization of government power, technological change, a response to terrorism, or even globalization."

But it wasn't for lack of ideas.

Kallick told the Open Society Institute—the whole foundation world:

> What is lacking is not sharp individuals with creative ideas.
>
> What is missing is an institutional infrastructure that brings these people together with each other and with people who understand practical politics, media, and organizing.
>
> People who are adept in all these different ways at once are critically important, yet not easy to find. This is a natural outgrowth of the fact that the progressive world is very segmented, making people with broad cross-cutting experience relatively rare.

His final judgment:

> Any addition to the think tank scene today needs to work from an understanding of how social change happens and what part think tanks play in it; where we are at this historical moment and what the opportunity is for thoughtful intervention.[21]

Schmitt was pleased with Kallick's report, but warned:

> More thought needs to be given to the kind of institutions or networks that will help give philosophical coherence to progressive policies and ideas. But we hope this document lays the groundwork for that next phase of thought, and will be helpful to progressive foundations, individual donors, journalists, and policymakers themselves as we consider how to approach policy in the next phase of our nation's history.[22]

Schmitt duly sent the report up to Soros but doesn't remember actually talking to him about it. He spread it around to colleagues who had become interested in new think tanks, but says he never really pushed it.[23]

When Halperin came in fresh from the Council on Foreign Relations, the think tank conversation in OSI was five years along.

When he picked it up with Soros, dreaming about big overarching ideas to revitalize Progressive America, he ran into the same brick wall as others.

He wanted a think tank on the Left that could compete with the Heritage Foundation on the Right.

Soros didn't.

How to convince him?

Kallick's riddle:

> What about people who are "adept in all these different ways at once?"
> What about people with "broad cross-cutting experience?"
> What about people capable of "thoughtful intervention?"

Halperin knew somebody like that.

CHAPTER 2 NOTES

1. Halperin bio: Council on Foreign Relations, "Morton H. Halperin," online at www.cfr.org/bio.php?id=43, accessed August 15, 2005. Halperin and Podesta: Robert Dreyfuss, "An Idea Factory for the Democrats," *The Nation*, March 1, 2004.
2. Betsy Pisik, "Group urges U.S. to give U.N. moral, financial support," *The Washington Times,* August 20, 1996, p. A11.
3. Michael T. Kaufman, *Soros: The Life and Times of a Messianic Billionaire,* (New York: Alfred A. Knopf, 2000), p. 165.
4. Sen. Strom Thurman, "Statement on the Nomination of Dr. Morton Halperin," *Congressional Record,* July 15, 1994, p. S9106*ff.*
5. Morton H. Halperin, Jerry Berman, Robert Borosage and Christine Marwick, *The Lawless State: The Crimes of the U.S. Intelligence Agencies* (Washington: Center for National Security Studies, 1976), p. 5.
6. See www.cfr.org/publication/3887/morton_halperin_rejoins_council.html.
7. Michael T. Kaufman, *Soros: The Life and Times of a Messianic Billionaire, op. cit.,* p. 83.
8. Sally Covington, "Moving a Public Policy Agenda: The Strategic Philanthropy of Conservative Foundations," National Committee For Responsive Philanthropy, Washington, D.C., July 1997. Covington was director of NCRP's Democracy and Philanthropy Project. In 2000 she left to become founding director of the California Works Foundation, created by the California Labor Federation.
9. *Ibid.*
10. "The Plan: Do conservatives have a strategy or merely a vision?" *Philanthropy* (1:2), Spring 1997, www.philanthropyroundtable.org/magazines/1997/1.2/theplan.html, accessed July 30, 2005. The 12 foundations were: the Lynde and Harry Bradley Foundation, the Carthage Foundation, the Earhart Foundation, the Charles G. Koch, David H. Koch and Claude R. Lambe charitable foundations, the Phillip M. McKenna Foundation, the J.M. Foundation, the John M. Olin Foundation, the Henry Salvatori Foundation, the Sarah Scaife Foundation, and the Smith Richardson Foundation.
11. The recommendations were: 1) Understanding the importance of ideology and overarching frameworks.
    2) Building strong institutions by providing ample general operation support and awarding large, multi-year grants.
    3) Maintaining a national policy focus and concentrating on resources.
    4) Recognizing the importance of marketing, media, and persuasive communications.
    5) Creating and cultivating public intellectuals and policy leaders.
    6) Funding comprehensively for social transformation and policy change by awarding grants across sectors, blending research and advocacy, supporting litigation, and encouraging the public participation of core constituencies.
    7) Taking a long-haul approach.
12. Robin Epstein, "Shaking the Foundations," *City Limits Monthly*, October 1997, www.citylimits.org/content/articles/articleView.cfm?articlenumber= 526, accessed July 30, 2005.
13. *Ibid.*

14. *Ibid.* Nielsen's book is *The Golden Donors: A New Anatomy of the Great Foundations* (New York: Truman Talley Books / E. P. Dutton, 1985). For a review of the failure of progressive philanthropy to change policy, see Robert O. Bothwell, *The Decline of Progressive Policy and the New Philanthropy*, National Committee for Responsive Philanthropy, Washington, D.C., 2003, http://comm-org.wisc.edu/papers2003/bothwell/bothwellcontents.htm. I have personally discussed left-leaning philanthropy with Mr. Nielsen, who was considerably more emphatic about its shortcomings by telephone than in his writings. My personal copy of his *Golden Donors* was a gift from him.

15. Robin Epstein, "Shaking the Foundations," *op. cit.*

16. Open Society Institute, Form 990-PF, 1998-2003. These IRS filings are available at www.guidestar.org, which requires registration for access to Form 990s and offers grant information in a fee-based subscription.

17. Mark Schmitt to Ron Arnold, August 28, 2006.

18. Economics America, Inc. *The Right Guide: A Guide to Conservative and Right-of-Center Organizations* (Ann Arbor, Michigan: Economics America, Inc., 1993) and *The Left Guide: A Guide to Left-of-Center Organizations* (Ann Arbor, Michigan: Economics America, Inc., 1998).

19. Scott Allen, "Environmental Donors Set Tone - Activists Affected by Quest for Funds," *Boston Globe*, October 20, 1997, p. A1.

20. David Dyssegaard Kallick, "Progressive Think Tanks: What Exists, What's Missing," Open Society Institute, New York, January 1, 2002, p.2. Online at www.soros.org/initiatives/gov/articles_publications/publications/progressive _20020115/progressive_thinktanks.pdf, accessed August 9, 2005.

21. *Ibid.*, p. 29.

22. *Ibid.*, p. 3.

23. Mark Schmitt to Ron Arnold, August 28, 2006.

CHAPTER 3

MISSING BRIDGES

H ALPERIN BROUGHT PODESTA INTO THE THINK TANK DISCUSSION.
Podesta brought in Ickes. Their secret brain trust had a reason to want
a big think tank right now: Dump Bush and rebuild Progressive America.

Ickes and Podesta both had considerable experience with the Vast Right
Wing Conspiracy from their time in the White House, including the bizarre
331-page report titled *The Communication Stream of Conspiracy Commerce.*[1]

It had been prepared in mid-1995 by Mark Fabiani, a lawyer in the
White House Counsel's Office, and based on research by the Democratic
National Committee. It was mostly press clippings and internet messages
arranged to discredit news stories about the Clintons' Whitewater and
Travelgate scandals as malicious conspiracy theories.

The assertion was that
• false accusations against the Clintons
• originated with "fringe sources" such as conservative columnist Floyd
Brown,
• which were amplified through a complex right-wing "media feeding
chain," including newspaper mogul Richard Mellon Scaife's *Pittsburgh
Tribune-Review* and Rev. Sun Myung Moon's *Washington Times,*
• which deliberately disseminated "bad information" and
• passed it to the Internet, where it
• bounced into a convoluted series of American and British publications
• that landed in Congress,
• where it was picked up by mainstream media such as CNN.

The Internet came in for particular criticism: the report cautioned that it
"allows an extraordinary amount of unregulated data and information to be
located in one area and available to all."

That, it argued, allowed the right wing to unfairly attack Clinton because Republican congressional staffers "surf the Internet, interacting with extremists in order to exchange ideas and information."[1]

The *Conspiracy Commerce* report was quietly distributed to major news outlets in 1995, but didn't get much media attention until January, 1997, when Clinton press secretary Mike McCurry offered it to journalists at a daily briefing as documentation that they had been duped by a right wing conspiracy, and should talk to the White House instead of its detractors.

The media were incredulous.

CNN's Wolf Blitzer said, "Mike, this 300-page report that Fabiani and DNC put together—what was the purpose of it? Why would the White House waste its time putting together this 'media food chain' theory?"

When McCurry tried to defend the report, another reporter stopped him cold with: "You folks have always denied that there's a bunker mentality here, paranoia regarding Whitewater and these other issues. Isn't that exactly what this looks like—here are our enemies who are out to get us?"[2]

The report became an object of public ridicule.

The *Wall Street Journal* editorialized it as a laughable effort to squelch unfavorable stories about the Clintons with a conspiracy theory about conspiracy theories.

You could almost hear *The New Republic* chortling when it commented, "Americans are trafficking in 'unregulated' information and exchanging ideas. Imagine."[3]

The Communication Stream of Conspiracy Commerce sank into deep obscurity everywhere except the Clinton White House.

Covington, Fabiani and Kallick—the old critique, the weird critique, and the new critique.

Halperin, Podesta and Ickes—talent, brains and guts—worked over the idea of a new think tank that would help the Democrats Dump Bush and find ways to restore the Left to power.

Halperin took the idea to Soros, who repeated what he had said many times, that he did not view his goal as funding "the Left" or "the Democrats."[4]

But Soros was getting to like George Bush less and less.

Ickes and Podesta saw Soros through the lens of American politics. He was an idiosyncratic, courtly Hungarian-born hedge fund operator and currency speculator with an estimated personal fortune of $7 billion (number 28 on the *Forbes* list of richest Americans). A naturalized U.S. citizen (1965), he was known as a restless, eccentric thinker determined not to be stuck in a fixed position for long. He harbored a bizarre mixture of passions: an anti-communist streak that prompted him to establish reform programs inside the

---

JOHN DAVID PODESTA

John Podesta was born in Chicago, Illinois in 1949. His grandparents immigrated to America from Italy and Greece, and his father left high school after one year to take a factory job and support his family.

John has been a lifelong practicing Catholic.

He graduated in 1971 from Knox College in Illinois and got his law degree at Georgetown University Law School in 1976. He then worked as a trial attorney in the Department of Justice's Honors Program in the Land and Natural Resources Division (1976-1977), as a Special Assistant to the Director of ACTION, the federal volunteer agency (1978-1979), and joined the staff of Senator Patrick Leahy (D-Vermont) in 1979.

However, his political career had begun while he was still an undergraduate, working with Bill Clinton in 1970 on Democrat Joe Duffy's unsuccessful bid for a Senate seat from Connecticut.

In 1988, Podesta founded a lobbying and public affairs firm, Podesta Associates Inc., with his brother Tony. That year he conducted opposition research for Democratic presidential candidate Michael Dukakis, and compiled an arsenal of information for use against George H. W. Bush.

He also served as counsel to the Senate Agriculture Committee and the House Judiciary Committee.

Podesta is reputed to be a hard-working man of rare humor who makes both Democrats and Republicans comfortable, "a straight-shooter with a low threshold for nonsense," which is said to call forth a "mean, surly presence" his White House colleagues nicknamed "Skippy," to be avoided at all costs.

He is married to Mary S. Podesta, a Washington, D.C. attorney. They have three children. He describes himself as "an avid runner and a dedicated fan of roller coasters" and is known as a UFO buff and devotee of Fox TV's nine-season sci-fi hit, "The X Files."

Soviet Union and later an anti-capitalist streak that he tried to explain in a 1997 *Atlantic Monthly* article titled, "The Capitalist Threat:"[5]

> Although I have made a fortune in the financial markets, I now fear that the untrammeled intensification of laissez-faire capitalism and the spread of market values into all areas of life is endangering our open and democratic society. The main enemy of the open society, I believe, is no longer the communist but the capitalist threat.[6]

Cynics said he just didn't like the competition of globalizing firms. But capitalism's new enemy was also very good at getting government grants.

While Ickes and Podesta both served in the Clinton White House, millions of taxpayer dollars were paid each year from the United States Information Agency (USIA) and the U. S. Agency for International Development (USAID) to the Open Society Institute, ostensibly for education and media programs in Central Europe.[7]

The Soros mishmash of leftist causes at home ranged from financing the anti-gun lobby to abolishing capital punishment; from anti-Israel activism to promoting abortion rights; from feminism, population control, and gay liberation to anti-corporate campaigns, radical theories of education, and replacing national sovereignty with global institutions.[8]

Soros also had an eccentric track record in practical politics. He donated $175,000 for the "Shadow Conventions" of 2000, sideshows for the disaffected dreamed up by author and columnist Arianna Huffington (she also co-hosted Comedy Central's 1996 convention coverage).

They hyped the view that Democrats and Republicans alike no longer represented the American people, but only corporate profits, so a new "Third Force" was needed to "restore true democracy."[9]

Huffington's twin events were held at the same time and place as the Republican and Democratic conventions (Philadelphia and Los Angeles respectively).

Senator John McCain gave the opening speech in Philadelphia, pitching his McCain-Feingold campaign finance reform bill and then urging support for Republican presidential nominee George W. Bush.

Huffington had to rescue him from the resulting boos and catcalls.

She strode to the microphone and declared her ersatz convention a place "to hear everything with respect."[10]

Ickes and Podesta were also aware that Soros had poured $18 million into campaign finance reform.

First it was Ellen Miller's "clean money" reform that makes all other reforms possible, mostly for state-level publicly financed campaigns.

But when the 1997 Kerry-Wellstone federal "clean money" bill got lost in the congressional rinse cycle, he reluctantly supported McCain-Feingold's soft money ban—and continued donating to state public campaign finance projects, as we'll see in Chapter 12.

In a perverse way, and without much enthusiasm, he had helped pay for the present predicament.[11]

Now HALPERIN, PODESTA, AND ICKES had to think about a think tank, with or without funding from Soros, who was growing more sympathetic.

They saw that it had to be different than even Kallick foresaw, a think tank that rallied the public to progressive ideas while projecting a strong voice in the next election, something McCain-Feingold made possible.

It would be an instant response mechanism to counter anything from the Bush campaign with a quick and powerful rebuttal from the Left.

And it would be a force for rebuilding progressive politics in the long-term.

Like the conservative power machine, it would bridge the cultural and electoral arenas to create broad social change.

PODESTA AND HALPERIN QUICKLY DRAFTED A SERIES OF PAPERS describing the proposed organization and circulated them to potential funders.

The new group's purpose, Ickes told reporters, was to "more effectively communicate criticism of the conservative agenda and support for progressive alternatives."[12]

But the new vehicle wouldn't be Ickes' presidential television campaign, or a 527 at all.

It would take the other McCain-Feingold soft money route, 501c—and it would be *two* 501c organizations, a 501c3 and a 501c4.

The meaning of this IRS gobbledygook is important here:

A 501c3 is a tax exempt, nonprofit charitable organization that
- can't influence legislation except within set limits, and
- can't get involved in candidates' election campaigns at all.

A c3 *can*, however, advocate whatever public policy its leaders consider proper, as long as it doesn't degenerate into propaganda or unlawful action.

Donors can deduct contributions to c3's from their federal income tax.

A 501c4, on the other hand, is a tax exempt, nonprofit group that
- *is* allowed to engage in unlimited partisan political activity like legislative lobbying, and
- *can* also advocate the election or defeat of a candidate within certain bounds.

If you donate money to a c4, you can't deduct it from your income tax.

THE NEW c3 was named the American Majority Institute and its companion c4, the American Majority Fund—a strategic pair bridging the cultural and the electoral spheres to bring about lasting social change.

On Thursday, October 3, a bit more than a month before the mid-term elections of 2002, the two were quietly registered as District of Columbia non-profit corporations.[13]

Little more than a year later, on October 24, 2003, the think tank would be reregistered as the Center for American Progress, having been launched to great fanfare with Podesta its president and chief executive officer, Halperin its senior vice president, and Ickes not involved. It would survive the 2004 election debacle to become the new epicenter of Democratic thinking, somewhere leftward of the centrist Democratic Leadership Council.

Media reports said that Soros pledged $3 million to the Center for American Progress and convinced close friends Herb and Marion Sandler—they were founders of Golden West Financial Corporation, parent company of a savings-and-loan empire worth $80 billion—to donate the rest of its $11 million startup budget, along with an unidentified third donor.[14]

Soros and his circle—the missing bridges—were in.

CHAPTER 3 NOTES

1. Mark Fabiani, *The Communication Stream of Conspiracy Commerce,* Clinton White House Counsel's Office, summer 1995. Excerpt available online at http://parascope.com/articles/0197/media.htm. *London Telegraph* reporter Ambrose Evans-Pritchard, asserted in a September 1998 story that the report in fact had been prepared by private investigator Terry Lenzner's firm Investigative Group International, possibly at taxpayer expense (unconfirmed).

2. Excerpt of White House Press Secretary Mike McCurry's daily briefing, January 9, 1997, http://parascope.com/articles/0197/briefing.htm.

3. Micah Morrison, "The White House on Whitewater beat," *Wall Street Journal*, January 6, 1997, p. A12. William Powers, "Chain of Command," *The New Republic* (online version), February 3, 1997.

4. Mark Schmitt to Ron Arnold, August 26, 2006.

5. Quick profile of Soros: Unsigned editorial, "Who is George Soros?", *The Wall Street Journal*, November 19, 2003, online at http://www.opinionjournal.com/editorial/feature.html?id=110004282, accessed August 14, 2005.

6. George Soros, "The Capitalist Threat," *Atlantic Monthly*, February 1997.

7. Government grant amounts: 1998, $4.6 million; 1999, $4.8 million (interpolated, IRS data not available); 2000, $4.9 million; 2001, $5.8 million; 2002, $6.1 million; 2003, $8.8 million. Open Society Institute, Form 990-PF, years 1994-2003 (1999 not available), Statement 1 – Contributions, Gifts and Grants Received, available for download at www.guidestar.org.

8. Matt Bai, "Wiring the Vast Left Wing Conspiracy," *New York Times Magazine*, July 25, 2004, online at http://www.nytimes.com/2004/07/25/magazine/25DEMOCRATS.html, accessed August 14, 2005.

9. Soros donation: Open Society Institute, 2000 Form 990-PF, Grants to U.S. Public Charities, p. 264 of 348 in PDF format. The $175,000 was paid to Public Campaign on June 12, 2000. Shadow Conventions' agenda: Mike Ferullo, "Democratic 'Shadow Convention' opens Sunday," *CNN News*, August 12, 2000, online at http://archives.cnn.com/2000/ALLPOLITICS/stories/08/12/shadow.convention/, accessed August 15, 2005.

10. Cathy Newman, "McCain Heckled For Promoting Bush at 'Shadow Convention,'" *Washington Post*, July 31, 2000, page A10.

11. Unsigned editorial, "The Soros Agenda: Free speech for billionaires only," *Wall Street Journal*, Saturday, January 3, 2004, online at http://www.opinionjournal.com/editorial/feature.html?id=110004498, accessed August 13, 2005.

12. Peter H. Stone, "Hard Questions About Soft-Money Groups," *National Journal*, December 21, 2002.

13. Registration documents: Corporations Division, Business Regulation Administration, Department of Consumer and Regulatory Affairs, Government of The District of Columbia, corporate file number 223123 dated October 3, 2002. http://mblr.dc.gov/corp/lookup.

14. Soros and Sandler donations: Robert Dreyfuss, "An idea factory for the Democrats," *The Nation*, March 1, 2004. See also: Jane Mayer, "The Money Man," *New Yorker*, October 18, 2004. Other funders: see Chapter 5, "Podesta's List."

CHAPTER 4

AT DINNER

D INNER AT BEDUCI would be the first post-McCain-Feingold meeting for Ickes, and it posed some really serious problems.

Coordinating between 527s and political parties or their agents was now a felony punishable by fine and imprisonment.

Ickes, through his government relations firm, the Ickes & Enright Group, was an agent, a paid consultant to the Democratic National Committee.

So he got legal advice from Carolyn Utrecht, a well-known Washington campaign finance lawyer. As a result, he dropped the part of his connection to the DNC concerning campaign finance and communication.[1]

However, he maintained the rest of his consultant status, the part that covered matters such as the party convention, nominating rules and political advice.

He was not completely out of the DNC loop.

Just enough to avoid prosecution.[2]

In late November, Glantz got her meeting, which would spawn the money machine that became popularly known as The Vast Left Wing Conspiracy.

It got the name by happenstance:

Three days before Ickes circulated his grim warning to DNC insiders, a piece by liberal writer Joshua Micah Marshall appeared in Microsoft's webzine *Slate*, complaining that,

> Modern politics is a 24/7, multimedia game these days, and an essential part of that game is scandal-mongering—90 percent of which is about packaging. And Democrats just don't seem to have the taste or the talent for this.[3]

43

Marshall titled his article, "Wanted: A Vast Left Wing Conspiracy," playing off the tag made famous by Hillary Clinton on NBC's "Today Show" in an interview with Matt Lauer while defending her husband during the Monica Lewinski flap.[4]

Matt Lauer: You have said, I understand, to some close friends, that this is the last great battle, and that one side or the other is going down here.

Hillary Clinton: Well, I don't know if I've been that dramatic. That would sound like a good line from a movie. But I do believe that this is a battle. I mean, look at the very people who are involved in this—they have popped up in other settings. This is—the great story here for anybody willing to find it and write about it and explain it is the vast right-wing conspiracy that has been conspiring against my husband since the day he announced for president.

She had evidently been reading more Fabiani than Covington.

Marshall hadn't a clue about the impending McCain-Feingold train wreck, but in addition to coining a phrase, he also foreshadowed what the Democrats were about to get, as we shall see:

• packaging expertise in campaign groups America Coming Together, America Votes, and Moveon.org;

• hot scandal mongering in Michael Moore's movie *Fahrenheit 9/11*, Robert Greenwald's TV attack, *Outfoxed*, and Al Franken's *Air America* attempt to out-Limbaugh Limbaugh;

• and the taste and the talent in John Podesta's Center for American Progress and Robert Borosage's Campaign for America's Future.

It would be a Left Wing Conspiracy sufficiently vast to astonish even Marshall.

But nothing, compared to its underlying network, as we shall also see.

YOU HAD TO LOOK FOR BEDUCI, inconspicuous on the corner of busy P Street and 21st Street. It occupied the first floor of another one of those red brick Georgian-revival townhouses turned office building.

A casual passerby might not even notice the glassed-in porch or the little green awning over the entry.[5]

Once inside, you saw the bar on the right, felt the gray carpeting under your shoes, saw crisp linen on the tables, the chairs covered in a typically French country broad check pattern, and pleasing but unremarkable art on the white walls. The main dining room was on the left, with three smaller private dining rooms beyond.

It was the kind of place that offered appetizers such as *Escargots Etienerson* ($10.95), sauteed with rock shrimp, garlic and pinenuts, and, if you were adventurous, *Shelokbe Grilled Merguez* ($7.95) a fiery sausage faithful to the Algerian original.

Their salads had names like *Bilslayton Slata Mechwiya* ($7.95), a Tunisian roasted vegetable spread topped with tuna, capers, olives and hard-boiled egg.

Chef Jean-Claude Garrat was noted for entrées such as *Ostrich Tender-loin* ($23.95)—five generous medallions of ostrich accompanied by roast plantains, potatoes, crisp zucchini and broccoli.

For dessert you could get *Strawberry Surprise* ($21.00 for two), made on-premises by Michelle Miller, co-owner with Garrat.

The service was professional but not haughty and the wine list offered a range of good bottles at reasonable prices.

The stylish name of the restaurant meant "BElow DUpont CIrcle," even though it was west of the circle, down toward the Potomac, not south, as the "below" might indicate to a map reader.

BeDuCi. Just the place for six left wing Democrats to plot the little guy's revolution in American politics.

B ESIDES ICKES, THE WORKING DINNER INCLUDED Gina Glantz's boss, Andrew Stern, president of the SEIU; Steve Rosenthal, the AFL-CIO's political director; Ellen Malcolm, president of EMILY's List, the biggest Political Action Committee in America; Carl Pope, head of the 770,000-member Sierra Club; and Glantz.

She set the theme: in order to "get Bush," an umbrella group was needed to coordinate all left-leaning campaigners that might join the fight.

Preventing wasteful overlaps would help overcome the Republicans' large financial advantage.[6]

The harsh evidence of that financial advantage was clear to all six, not only in the 2002 vote count, and not only in the calculations Ickes had circulated, but also in the battle plan of Karl Rove's famous lost PowerPoint presentation.

The Bush administration's entire 2002 election strategy had been in-advertently leaked to the public when an intern walking to the Hay Adams Hotel, just across Lafayette Park from the White House, dropped a computer disc on June 4.

It contained two slide shows, one by Karl Rove, Bush's chief political adviser (it was titled "The Strategic Landscape") and the other by Ken Mehlman, White House political director ("The 2002 Challenge"). The disc was intended for them to show at the hotel, where an important group of visiting Republicans from California was to meet.

The plain-looking disc without White House markings was discovered in the park by a Senate aide. Once it became clear what was on the disc, the aide made copies, one of which got to Ed Henry of *Roll Call*, the twice-weekly Capitol Hill newspaper. *Roll Call* posted the PowerPoint presen-tations on its Web site for all to see.[7]

It was embarrassing for the Bush administration, but shocking to the Democrats. In 27 detailed panels, it not only plotted Democrat defeat, but showed exactly which Republicans were considered vulnerable and which were not. Among others, it said the president's own brother, Florida Governor Jeb Bush, was in danger and so was Rick Perry, the governor of Texas. But when the election was over, both statehouses had easily stayed Republican.

The whole thing could have been a deliberate scare tactic to open Republican wallets and demoralize Democrats.

It did both.[8]

THE DINERS AT BeDuCi were out of power, beleaguered by Rush Limbaugh, outmaneuvered by conservative activists and hemmed in by the new campaign finance rules.

They were ready to listen to Glantz's umbrella group ideas, which included appointing "traffic cops" who would try to find the most cost-effective methods to contact voters, run ads and build coalitions.[9]

Pope said he was in. Many colleagues would no doubt come with him. His Sierra Club was allied with the League of Conservation Voters, itself an umbrella group with board members from a number of rich environmental groups with their own "Dump Bush" agendas, including the Natural Resources Defense Council and Environmental Defense, Inc.[10]

ANDREW L. STERN

Andy Stern, president of the Service Employees International Union, was born in 1950 in West Orange, New Jersey, a lawyer's son. He graduated in 1972 from the University of Pennsylvania, where he studied business while learning activism in the civil rights and anti-Vietnam war movements.

He began as a welfare case worker in a unionized government agency, quickly became a shop steward, and fought his way to the presidency of the Local in 1978. He once mused, "Everywhere I go there's one big fight."

In 1978, he married Jane Perkins, who went on to become head of the Friends of the Earth. In 1984, John J. Sweeney, head of the SEIU, brought Stern to Washington to lead a national organizing campaign. Stern proved himself an outstanding organizer with his Janitors for Justice campaign.

As unions lost members, Stern saw that the labor movement's salvation was to recruit the only labor pool that was growing: service workers and government employees. In time, he realized even that wasn't enough.

When Sweeney left SEIU after being elected president of the AFL-CIO in 1995, Stern took his place. The Ivy League union boss soon saw a fatal weakness in the U.S. labor movement: it was fragmented, many small unions overlapped the same employers, ending up with no clout. The only solution was to merge the weak many into a few powerful mega-unions like Europe.

Most of the unions in the AFL-CIO rejected this controversial plan, so Stern pulled his SEIU out of the federation in 2005, bringing several others with him, and began working toward his consolidated mega-union dream.

Rosenthal and Stern also supported Glantz's idea, but pressed the need for ground-based Get Out The Vote operations as opposed to TV and radio "air wars." They were nursing an idea for a union-backed 527 organization that would register non-union people in the Democratic base—low-income, minority and female voters—then cultivate them with multiple contacts and get them to the polls on Election Day.

With union membership at an anemic 13 percent of the workforce, it could take the Democrats only so far. Since the AFL-CIO could spend its money solely for the benefit of dues-paying labor union members, it wouldn't be able to mobilize the large pool of non-union working Americans.

But Rosenthal and Stern's 527 *would* be, and unions *could* contribute to a 527. They could mobilize as many non-union voters as they wished.

Their idea would become **Partnership for America's Families**, Number 28 on the Top 50 list of 527 money groups, with total receipts in the 2004 election of $3,071,211.[11]

Ickes liked the idea of an umbrella group, too, and liked the idea of ground-based operations, but—not revealing McAuliffe's secret brain trust or the American Majority Institute—emphasized that media power was essential in a presidential race.

STEVEN S. ROSENTHAL

Steve Rosenthal is a close personal friend of Andy Stern; they have shared a New Jersey getaway beach house for over 25 years. Unlike Stern, Rosenthal was born into a union family (1953, New York). His father sold shoes in a union shop in Brooklyn.

Rosenthal attributes his passion for social justice to his religious mother and the Judaic tradition of *tikkun olam*, "repair the world." He graduated from State University of New York at New Paltz, where he majored in political science and became radicalized against the Vietnam war, volunteering for George McGovern's presidential campaign.

Rosenthal became New Jersey political director for the Communication Workers of America in 1985. He married a fellow CWA organizer, "a Teamster's daughter," Eileen Kirlin. They later adopted two children, Ana from Brazil, and Sam from Paraguay.

He left CWA to join Bill Clinton's presidential campaign in 1991, then served on the Democratic National Committee and in the Clinton administration as Associate Deputy Secretary of the U.S. Department of Labor for two years.

When John Sweeney was elected president of the AFL-CIO in 1995, he invited Rosenthal to come with him as political director. Rosenthal served for seven years and showed himself the leading Get Out The Vote campaign organizer in the labor movement. The door-to-door expertise he gained from the ground up played a key role in the 2004 presidential campaign.

The lag between the Democratic presidential primaries and the nominating convention would leave the surviving candidate without campaign funds for several months.

A presidential media fund could bridge that gap with issue ads and keep the candidate from vanishing in the Republican noise.

His idea would become **The Media Fund,** Number 2 on the Top 50 527 list, total election receipts $59,404,183.[12]

Malcolm, whose group had raised $22 million in the 2002 mid-term cycle, stressed fund-raising. She was also on the DNC executive committee and a veteran of many coordinated campaigns with national and state Democratic committees. Her emphasis on money was reflected in the name of the group she had founded in her basement in 1985: EMILY's List was an acronym for "Early Money Is Like Yeast"—it makes the dough rise.

The saying summed up an axiom of political fundraising, that receiving lots of donations early in a race is most helpful: they scare off challengers and help attract later donors. EMILY's List had become the biggest political action committee in America.

ELLEN REIGHLEY MALCOLM

Ellen Malcolm (born 1947) earned a psychology degree from Hollins College, a traditional private women's school in Roanoke, Virginia.

Her political interest began as a student there when she signed up in 1968 to work in Eugene McCarthy's presidential campaign.

She turned 21 early that year and inherited a fortune in IBM stock from her father, who died of cancer when she was an infant. The shares came from her paternal great-grandfather Austin Ward Ford, a partner in Bundy Manufacturing Co., one of IBM's corporate antecedents.

Like many young liberals with inherited fortunes, she tried to ignore the money because it might interfere with her political goals. After college she went to Washington and served her political apprenticeship with Common Cause, at that time a center of anti-war and anti-Watergate activism.

In 1977, she became press secretary for the National Women's Political Caucus, and began donating to feminist causes anonymously. She then served as press secretary and speech writer for Esther Peterson, Jimmy Carter's consumer affairs specialist.

Malcolm tried to preserve her anonymity by creating the Windom Foundation, named after the street where she lived, but saying it was the money of "Henrietta Windom," inventor of Tampax giving back to women, who made her rich (Tampax was actually invented by a man). When a couple showed up claiming to be Henrietta's relatives, Malcolm shed the pretense and began donating in her own name.

She decided she needed an education in finance and business and earned an MBA in marketing from George Washington University. In 1985 she reportedly invited 25 women to a meeting in her basement where they started EMILY's List to raise money for Democratic women candidates that supported abortion rights.

The great-granddaughter of an I.B.M. founder—herself a millionaire who had donated hundreds of thousands to progressive causes and spoke to donors as an equal—she knew how to make wait-and-see contributors stop sitting on their checkbooks. She was relentless at "the ask," as fund-raisers call it, not letting donors off the hook by changing the subject.[13]

Her idea would become **America Coming Together,** the Number 1 527 in the nation, total 2004 election receipts $79,795,487.[14]

Glantz had been national campaign manager for the presidential runs of Walter Mondale (1984) and Bill Bradley (2000). She was highly capable of juggling many political tasks at a time.

Her idea would become **America Votes**, the umbrella group that coordinated more than 20 Democratic interest groups trying to defeat President Bush.

Ironically, Glantz would not be its leader: Cecile Richards, daughter of former Democratic Governor of Texas, Ann Richards—and staffer with House Minority Leader Nancy Pelosi—would take over as executive director. Glantz served briefly as treasurer of America Coming Together, then went on to advise the campaign of presidential candidate Howard Dean.

America Votes would be Number 26 in the Top 50, total election receipts $3,174,936.[15]

CARL POPE WAS THE SLEEPER at BeDuCi.
His Sierra Club was a wilderness preservation group. Typical union members do not work in wilderness areas. Nor does anyone else. Wilderness, by law, is an area where "man is a visitor who does not remain."

Development of any kind is strictly forbidden. No homes. No stores. No structures of any kind. Roads are not permitted. Mechanized equipment may not enter. Even union-made pedal-powered mountain bikes can't go in.[16]

What was this man doing at BeDuCi?

Ickes, Malcolm, Rosenthal, Stern and Glantz could cast a blind eye on the Sierra Club's endless wilderness expansion policy—which systematically swallowed up huge land areas and the jobs of countless oil and gas workers, loggers, miners, and manufacturing employees—only because Pope had added to the group's original wilderness mission a broader progressive agenda.

He carved out common ground with labor on free trade, global climate change, and energy issues, and shifted the Club's activism to include anti-globalization protests, anti-corporate campaigns and social justice battles.

Then, too, he had a 770,000-member mailing list.

Pope had begun shifting the Sierra Club into a formal alliance with labor just before the Kyoto climate summit in late 1997 when stark calculations predicted massive job losses necessary to cut CO_2 emissions.

Richard Trumka's United Mine Workers viewed efforts to ban carbon-intensive fossil fuels such as coal and oil as a direct threat to their members' jobs that would leave America energy-starved and freezing in the dark.

The AFL-CIO went on record as opposing the Kyoto Protocol in 1998.[17]

In 1996, Andy Stern and his wife Jane Perkins created what they called the "Blue-Green Working Group" around their kitchen table, inviting friends from both movements (Blue collars and Green dollars) to start talking about green solutions, particularly for global warming, that keep workers in mind.

Pope and other enviro leaders kept up the dialogue with key unions including the United Steelworkers of America, Andy Stern's SEIU, Gerald McEntee's American Federation of State, County and Municipal Employees, and the Union of Needletrades, Industrial and Textile Employees (UNITE).

The Blues and Greens tried for years to converge—funded by the Nathan Cummings Foundation—but energy disputes and fate intervened. For a while they made progress toward accommodation if not agreement.

In early 2001, AFL-CIO president John Sweeney and Pope jointly called for a "package of worker-friendly domestic carbon-emission reduction measures."[18]

What those measures might be was the sticking point between the Blues and the Greens in the Working Group.

So they commissioned the foundation-funded Center for a Sustainable Economy and the labor-funded Economic Policy Institute to do a study called "Clean Energy and Jobs." In early 2002 they submitted a four-point program:

• Mandatory efficiency standards for vehicles and equipment, and regulations forcing electric utilities to buy power from renewable energy sources other than hydroelectric dams.

• Government bailout for displaced workers in a "Just Transition" program for employees such as coal miners who lose their jobs as a result of carbon-abatement policies: two years of full income replacement, health insurance, retirement contributions; four years of full-time training or educational benefits. No bailout for shareholders or management.

• A tax on the carbon content of fuels of $50 per ton of carbon, with the revenues used to 1) reduce payroll taxes on labor; 2) fund energy-efficiency incentives and 3) pay for the Just Transition programs.

• Carbon tariffs on imports of energy-intensive products such as steel, aluminum, and cement, to minimize the competitiveness impacts of the carbon tax, with tax rebates for exports.[19]

The authors saw their plan as raising general employment and Gross Domestic Product slightly.

The unions saw their plan as causing substantial unemployment in specific sectors, mainly coal mining, petroleum refining, and electric utilities.

It boiled down to trust.

When the final deals are being cut in some future Congress, can environmentalists be trusted to reject a package that meets emissions-reduction goals but doesn't have a solid "just transition" component?

Can labor be trusted to make global warming a priority, even if its legitimate concerns about protecting affected workers are fully addressed?[20]

The AFL-CIO stayed on record as opposing the Kyoto Protocol.

On a Tuesday morning, Carl Pope and Dan Becker (the Sierra Club's director of global warming and energy programs), John Adams and Robert Kennedy, Jr., of the Natural Resources Defense Council, and John Podesta met in AFL-CIO headquarters on 16th Street, a few blocks north of the White House.

They were there to discuss an agreement with Sweeney on strict energy conservation laws and a ban on petroleum production in the Arctic National Wildlife Refuge. It would unite two of the progressive movement's most important constituencies.

The date was September 11. When Sweeney entered the room he told everyone about the terrorist attacks on New York City. Within minutes they heard an explosion across the Potomac at the Pentagon. The group broke up, and the convergence failed.[21]

But now, in the dismal aftermath of the 2002 elections, cooperative action on these new 527s might be the link they were seeking.

Carl Pope was in.

Pope's group would become one of the environmental movement's "quartet" clusters, four related entities that were able to accept various kinds of political contributions:

• The Sierra Club, a 501c4 lobbying group;
• The Sierra Club Foundation, a 501c3 educational organization;
• The Sierra Club Political Committee, a Political Action Committee;
• And the **Sierra Club Voter Education Fund**, a 527 which would rank as the Number 15 fund-raiser in the top 50, total election receipts, $8,727,127—and create a maze of baffling inter-group money transfers.[22]

Their groups would be joined by **MoveOn.org** (the Number 9 527 at $12,558,215) and John Podesta's renamed American Majority Institute, the **Center for American Progress** (not a 527, a twin 501c3 / 501c4, 2003 gross receipts $11,738,685), and many others.[23]

All made possible by the new rules of McCain-Feingold.

None of the six knew any of that when they paid the bill at BeDuCi.

Nor did they have a definite plan.

They might be a Left Wing Conspiracy.

But they were not Vast yet.

As Ickes knew, that depended on the next move of The Billionaire.

CHAPTER   4   NOTES

1. Peter H. Stone, "Inside Two of the Soft Money Havens," *National Journal*, December 20, 2003.
2. Steve Weissman and Ruth Hassan, "BCRA and the 527 Groups," Campaign Finance Institute, February 9, 2005, Revised March 8, 2005, draft chapter for publication in *The Election after Reform: Money, Politics and the Bipartisan Campaign Reform Act.* Michael J. Malbin, ed., (Rowman and Littlefield, 2005)
3. Joshua Micah Marshall, "Wanted: A Vast Left-Wing Conspiracy," *Slate*, posted May 9, 2001, accessed at http://slate.msn.com/id/1007647/ on July 28, 2005.
4. "Matt Lauer Interview with Hillary Clinton," *NBC Today*, January 27, 1998, third-party transcript online at http://leany.com/Conspiracy/ hillary_clinton_transcript.htm, accessed August 3, 2005.
5. BeDuCi went out of business in 2004. Restaurant description and review material: Thomas Barnes, "BeDuCi, Washington, D.C., What a Neighborhood Restaurant Should Be," *Epinions*, September 21, 2002, accessed at www.epinions.com/content_76347903620, on July 28, 2005.
6. Jeanne Cummings, "A Hard Sell on 'Soft Money'," *The Wall Street Journal*, December 2, 2003.
7. Ed Henry, "Got Plumbers?" *Roll Call*, June 13, 2002. The PowerPoint presentations of both Rove and Mehlman were posted June 13, 2002, on the *Roll Call* website at www.rollcall.com/newspics/mehlman-rove.ppt but removed in 2005. See also Elisabeth Bumiller, "White House is red-faced as 2002 election analysis becomes public," *New York Times*, June 13, 2002; CBS News, "The Case Of The Slipped Disk," June 13, 2002, accessed at www.cbsnews.com /stories/2002/06/13/politics/main512175.shtml, July 28, 2005.
8. Peter Wallsten, "White House election gurus break the news: Jeb, you're vulnerable," *The Miami Herald*, June 15, 2002, p. 1B.
9. Thomas B. Edsall, "Liberals Meeting to Set '04 Strategy: Labor, Rights Groups Focus on Getting Out the Vote to Help Democrats," *The Washington Post*, May 25, 2003.
10. "Overview: League of Conservation Voters," *The New Stealth PACs: Tracking 501(c) Non-profit Groups Active in Elections*, Public Citizen, Washington, D.C., online at www.stealthpacs.org/profile.cfm?Org_ID=144, accessed August 1, 2005. The profile states, "The LCV is a complex organization. Aside from its flagship 501(c)(4), the group also maintains another 501(c)(4), a PAC, a 501(c)(3), and a 527 group. The existence of numerous entities makes it difficult to determine which LCV entity is responsible for which activities, a challenge that is compounded by the LCV's practice of transferring funds from one entity to another."
11. "527 Committee Activity: Top 50 Federally Focused Organizations," Center for Responsive Politics, Washington, D.C., online at www.opensecrets.org/ 527s/527cmtes.asp?level=C&cycle=2004, accessed August 1, 2005.
12. Ibid.
13. Margaret Wolf Freivogel, "Woman comes 'out of the philanthropic closet,' Heiress goes public with effort to bankroll women candidates," *St. Louis Post-Dispatch*, July 20, 1988, p.10A.

14. "527 Committee Activity: Top 50 Federally Focused Organizations," Center for Responsive Politics, Washington, D.C., online at www.opensecrets.org/527s/527cmtes.asp?level=C&cycle=2004, accessed August 1, 2005.

15. Ibid.

16. Wilderness Act of 1964, Public Law Public Law 88-577 (16 U.S. C. 1131-1136) 88th Congress, Second Session September 3, 1964, full text at www.leaveitwild.org/reports/wilderness1964PF.html, accessed August 8, 2005.

17. AFL-CIO Executive Council, "The Kyoto Protocol," resolution dated January 30, 1998, online at www.ujae.org/NewsRes/AFL-CIOClimResJan1998. pdf, accessed August 9, 2005.

18. Laura Paksus, "The Union Makes Them Strong: a blue-green alliance on climate change adopts a new agenda: jobs," *Orion*, March/April, 2005, www.greenlabor.org/pdf/Orion-Paskus.pdf, accessed August 21, 2006. In 2001, the Blue-Green Working Group received a $75,000 grant from the Nathan Cummings Foundation through the Public Health Institute, a left wing advocacy group. Cummings Foundation was behind much of the labor-enviro fusion effort, as we will see in Chapter 18.

19. James P. Barrett and J. Andrew Hoerner, with Steve Bernow and Bill Dougherty, *Clean Energy and Jobs: A comprehensive approach to climate change and energy policy*, Economic Policy Institute, February 2002, www.epinet.org/content.cfm/studies_cleanenergyandjobs, accessed August 9, 2005.

20. Questions asked by author Alden Myer, "Labor Intensive: A dialogue on global warming finds labor and environmentalists seeking ways to work together," *Nucleus, The Magazine of the Union of Concerned Scientists*, Vol. 21, Number 2, Summer 1999.

21. Keith Schneider, "Labor's Love Lost: The blue-green relationship hits the skids," *Grist Magazine*, May 2, 2002, online at www.grist.org/news/maindish/2002/05/02/love/, accessed August 9, 2005.

22. "527 Committee Activity: Top 50 Federally Focused Organizations," Center for Responsive Politics, Washington, D.C., online at www.opensecrets.org/527s/527cmtes.asp?level=C&cycle=2004, accessed August 1, 2005..

23. "527 Committee Activity: Top 50 Federally Focused Organizations," and "The Major Players: Active Advocacy Groups in the 2004 Election Cycle," Center for Responsive Politics, online at www.opensecrets.org/527s/527grps.asp, accessed August 1, 2005.

PART II

TROUBLE IN TBLISI

PODESTA'S LIST
IS IT SOUP YET?
PLAYING POKER IN A CHESS GAME
VELVET BULLDOZER

CHAPTER 5

PODESTA'S LIST

NOT LONG AFTER THE SIX HAD DINNER AT BEDUCI, Herb and Marion Sandler read one of John Podesta's think tank memos.

It had been sent by Aryeh Neier, president of George Soros' Open Society Institute.[1]

"To be frank with you," the Sandlers told reporters, "we did not know John Podesta, and we were not big admirers of Bill Clinton. But we checked John out and were astonished by what people said about him. He was strategic, he was intelligent, his values were terrific."[2]

Podesta's think tank, they explained, was "intended to be a progressive organization involved in values which are not, in my opinion, take, take, take. Cut taxes, cut government, screw poor people, which is what the conservative think tanks speak to all the time."

The Sandlers didn't really need to do much checking. If Neier wanted them to look into Podesta's unborn think tank, still named the American Majority Institute, that was enough.

Neier was Soros' trusted field commander, a leader in his own right, born to prosperous Jewish parents in Nazi Germany in 1937, a refugee in England two years later—"at the last minute," according to his memoir *Taking Liberties.*

He came to high school in America, then attended Cornell University, where he started a chapter of Students for a Democratic Society. He was national director of the American Civil Liberties Union from 1970 to 1978.

Neier co-founded the "blame America first" Human Rights Watch in 1978 (as Helsinki Watch) to investigate and expose human rights abuses. He led it until 1993, when he came aboard with Soros at age 56.[3]

57

The Sandlers crossed paths with Soros and Neier from time to time. They had been giving Human Rights Watch more than $2 million each year at the same time that Soros supported it with annual million-dollar grants.[4]

Soros had told Neier to send the memo to the Sandlers because he wasn't very interested and thought they would be. So, as *The Nation* reported:

> At the end of 2002 a California banker and backer of human rights causes named Herb Sandler came knocking on Podesta's door. He'd heard about the Halperin-Podesta venture from Aryeh Neier, former head of Human Rights Watch, who'd worked with Soros.... How much of the $30-35 million, three-year funding raised for the center comes from Sandler isn't clear, but it's probably in the range of two-thirds, since Soros committed only $3 million to the project. Podesta has a third major funder, but he won't disclose who it is, and seems overly cautious in talking about his backers.[5]

Bad guess. Actually, the Sandlers gave only $500,000 of 2003's $11.7 million. In fact, they were in a three-way tie for seventh place. And Soros gave only $2.5 million. But Marion Sandler got on the board of directors, and the next year the Sandler's foundation gave $2 million.[6]

IT WASN'T REALLY A BAD GUESS, it was unawareness of Soros' reluctance to fund a new think tank and his hedge fund approach to philanthropy: leverage everything possible with other people's money—"We want company."

Extreme leverage is a George Soros character trait. Most readers of the financial pages know about the spectacularly leveraged coup that earned him a billion dollars overnight in a giant gamble in 1992. He bet $10 billion—most of it borrowed money—that by selling enough sterling short he could force the Bank of England to devalue the British pound and make a killing.

Soros, with a keen grasp of money and politics, had calculated that bankers in the European Exchange Rate Mechanism (EERM), pegged to the German mark, would refuse to uphold the overvalued pound because at the time Germany had its own problems paying for reunification.

They did refuse, so Britain pulled out of the EERM and tried to prop up its sinking currency by itself.

Prime Minister John Major and Chancellor of the Exchequer Norman Lamont spent billions of the government's foreign reserves buying back pounds, trying desperately to shore up the value of sterling in the face of the daunting speculative tsunami that Soros started.

They ran out of foreign reserves.

The pound crashed.

On a day known thereafter as Black Wednesday, September 16, 1992, British subjects woke up to find their money worth about 20 percent less than the day before when compared to American dollars, German marks or even French francs. Soros' daring short position paid off—big.

Had he lost that bet, nobody would know his name today.[7]

Almost nobody outside the financial markets knew his name then, or how he got the clout to pull it off, but the investment world knew it very well.

In 1967, George Soros had been an arbitrage trader at a small New York City investment bank—just another drone—when he talked his employers into letting him start an offshore fund called First Eagle, long positions only, with $250,000 of his own money and $6 million of other peoples'. It went well, and two years later he launched Double Eagle, a hedge fund that would later become the Quantum Fund. He was 39.[8]

His hedge fund was registered in Curaçao in the Netherlands Antilles, a Caribbean tax haven beyond U.S. regulation. All of its investors were also beyond U.S. regulation: very rich non-U.S. citizens, mostly European.

Soros, who stayed in New York, was only its "investment advisor" collecting a management fee and a 15% incentive fee.[9]

Like most hedge funds, Quantum specialized in high risk, short term speculation on stocks, bonds, commodities, currencies, stock options and derivatives, taking long and short positions and large leveraged positions.

Soros took huge risks, spending mostly borrowed money and selling stocks the fund did not yet own. His success was astonishing: throughout the dismal bear markets of the 1970s, when most investors lost money, Quantum was profitable every year, sometimes paying double-digit returns.

In 1981, *Institutional Investor* magazine put him on the cover as "the world's greatest money manager."[10]

T HE NAME OF HIS FUND CAME FROM QUANTUM PHYSICS, especially the indeterminacy principle of Werner Heisenberg.

Soros liked "Quantum" as a symbol of the impossibility of accurately determining the future movement of markets as well as subatomic particles. He had developed his own theory that individual biases (e.g., the trend-following habits of speculators) introduce disequilibrium into an economy, so conventional "efficient market" theory doesn't work. Soros extends his theory to just about everything, giving it the clunky name "reflexivity."

In finance, he uses it to explain "boom-bust cycles." He goes further, arguing that when *any* social enterprise begins to rise, whether a market, a business, a movement, or a nation, the biases of individuals (investors, executives, movement leaders, or statesmen) create instability. They build a bandwagon effect, overvaluing or overreaching, which creates an artificial "bubble" that eventually bursts.

Soros has attributed his hedge fund success—including the Bank of England episode—to his reflexivity theory. Others call it luck.[11]

But there were thorns in the hedge: critics called him a "bandit" for his Southeast Asian currency raids. Others accused him of calculated hit-and-run tactics: quietly buying into a market—gold, for example, as he did in 1993—deliberately leaking his "secret," watching the bandwagon stampede drive the price up, then bailing out before the bubble bursts.[12]

Quantum had only one losing year in its first two decades and George Soros got very rich. Even though he failed to predict the stock market crash of '87 and took a $300 million hit, Quantum was actually up 14 percent for the calendar year—and his personal compensation of $75 million made him the second-highest-paid man on Wall Street.[13]

Leverage, extreme leverage.

In 1993, it earned him $1.1 billion. George Soros was the top earner on Wall Street, making more than the gross national product of 42 nations.

He was no longer just a drone on the cusp of fame.

The money brought access and influence through his charities. From then on, he mixed with chiefs of state as if he were one of them.

He even leveraged heads of state: in that same year he told a packed press conference in Romania that he had snubbed an invitation from the country's president, Ion Iliescu, "for lack of time."

He raced to the airport where his rented jet took him to the next country. He dined with the heads of Moldova and Bulgaria in a single day and told his travel companion, journalist Michael Lewis: "You see, I have one president for breakfast and another for dinner."

With tongue only slightly in cheek, he told Lewis of the influence his philanthropy had bought him in the former Soviet Union, "The Soviet Empire is now known as the Soros Empire."[14]

Yet this same man was known to have his chauffeur wait at the curb in Washington while he dashed in to the National Gallery of Art to admire a Vermeer, then get to the next appointment right on time.[15]

His quirks carried over into his philanthropy. By the time he decided to support the American Majority Institute, he didn't even think of funding it entirely by himself.

Leverage, extreme leverage.

P ODESTA THUS HAD NO CHOICE.
He and Halperin could only get a fraction of their budget from Soros and the Sandlers; it was just early money to make the dough rise. They had never counted on just those two, and maybe one more, despite impressions.

Podesta scrambled to line up more than thirty major donors in small private meetings. Eighteen of those quietly gave $200,000 or more.

There were no splashy galas because the money wasn't going to the Democratic Party—McCain-Feingold saw to that—instead, it was going to an ostensibly "non-partisan" 501c3 run by Democratic operatives.

But those other donors didn't come from the Soros or Sandler influence.

UPI reported that, "part of the reason for Podesta's fundraising success has been the involvement of Hillary Clinton."

Harold Ickes saw to that.

Podesta's list was chockablock with Clinton donors, a directory of the Democratic elite, even if the checks came from their private foundations.[16]

He was having better luck than the six.

CHAPTER 5 NOTES

1. Robert Dreyfuss, "An idea factory for the Democrats," *The Nation*, March 1, 2004.
2. Editorial board of the San Francisco Chronicle, "Golden West Financial Corp. - On the record: Marion and Herb Sandler," *San Francisco Chronicle*, Sunday, January 18, 2004, online at http://sfgate.com/cgi-bin/article.cgi?file=/chronicle/archive/2004/01/18/BUG1M4AC9G1.DTL, accessed August 14, 2005.
3. Neier biographical sketch at www.soros.org/about/bios/b_neier.
4. Kathleen Peratis, "Fighting for Your Rights: One Man's Story (book review of *Taking Liberties*), *Forward*, August 29, 2003, online at www.forward.com/issues/2003/03.08.29/arts4.neier.html, accessed August 16, 2005. Funding: Form 990-PF, Open Society Institute, 1999; Form 990-PF Sandler Family Supporting Foundation, 1998.
5. Robert Dreyfuss, "An idea factory for the Democrats."
6. Verifiable grantmakers documented by Form 990 grant descriptions: George Soros ($2.5 million); Marisla Foundation (Anne Getty Earhart) $1 million; Sandler Family Supporting Foundation (Herb and Marion Sandler) $500,000; LBC Foundation (Lewis B. Cullman) $500,000; Jerome Levy Foundation $500,000; New York Community Trust $300,000; three $250,000 donations (Glaser Progress Foundation, the Popplestone Foundation and the Peninsula Foundation); two $200,000 donations (M.D. Anderson Foundation; Stephen M Silberstein Foundation); Irving Harris Foundation $125,000; Coydog Foundation, $75,000; Overbrook Foundation $50,000; and two $25,000 donations, Jon S. Corzine Foundation and the Bernard and Irene Schwartz Foundation). Marion Sandler on CAP board of directors, CAP Form 990, 2004. Sandler Family Supporting Foundation $2 million grant, 2004 Form 990.
7. David Litterick, "Billionaire who broke the Bank of England," *The London Telegraph*, September 13 2002. www.telegraph.co.uk/money/main.jhtml?xml=/money/2002/09/13/cnwed113.xml, accessed August 16, 2005.
8. The investment bank was Arnhold and S. Bleichroeder, an old-world firm whose Arnhold founders had looked after the fortunes and interests of Europe's richest and most powerful individuals and families. The Bleichroeder side had come from the financial advisor to Otto von Bismark, Germany's Iron Chancellor. The bank was small but extraordinarily influential. **Quantum facts**: Stephen Taub and David Carey with Alison M. Smith, "The Wall Street 100," *Financial World*, July 21, 1992, p. 40. Full profile: Lois Pelz, *The New Investment Superstars: 13 Great Investors and Their Strategies for Superior Returns* (Hoboken, New Jersey: John Wiley & Sons, Inc., 2001), pp. 19-29.
9. Ryan Caione, "Soros Fund Management LLC - Fact Sheet," *Hoover's*, www.hoovers.com/soros-fund-management/, accessed August 15, 2005.
10. "World's greatest money manager," *Institutional Investor*, June 1981, pp 39-45.
11. Joshua Muravchik, "The Mind of George Soros," *Commentary*, March 1, 2004.
12. Paula Hawkins, "The currency bandits," *The European*; April 27, 1998. **Gold**: Sally B. Donnelly, "The man with the Midas touch," *Time*, May 31, 1993.
13. Alan Deutschman, "George Soros," *Salon*, March 27, 2001. www.salon.com/people/bc/2001/03/27/soros/index.html?sid=1020430, accessed August 16, 2005.
14. Tom Lowry, "George Soros was highest paid money manager with $1.1 billion in income," *New York Daily News*, June 15, 1994. Remark about presidents: Michael Lewis, "The speculator: a trip with George Soros," *The New Republic*, January 10, 1994.

15. Michael T. Kaufman, *Soros: The Life and Times of a Messianic Billionaire*, *op. cit.*, p. 209.

16. Grant amounts only, donors not identified: Political Money Line, "Democratic Think Tank Raises $11.7 Million," *Update: Wed Nov 17, 2004* online at https:// mail2.cni.org/Redirect/www.tray.com/fecinfo/, accessed August 17, 2205 through Google cache. Grantmaker identification: Foundation Center search through DialogWeb Database 27, August 10, 2005. Clinton help: Christian Bourge, "Liberal think tank debuts," *Capitol Hill Blue*, July 8, 2003, online www. capitolhill blue.com/cgi-bin/artman/exec/view.cgi?archive =19&num =2513&printer=1 accessed August 17, 2005.

CHAPTER 6

IS IT SOUP YET?

THREE MONTHS AFTER DINNER, THE BEDUCI BUNCH still hadn't formed their umbrella group.

The odds-on favorite seemed to be Rosenthal's 527 group, Partnership for America's Families. It was officially unveiled in late February, 2003 during the AFL-CIO winter meeting at the union–owned Westin Diplomat Resort and Spa in Hollywood, Florida.[1]

The AFL-CIO Executive Council agreed to come up with at least $20 million to launch the Partnership and help raise $10 million more.

Two federation officials and a well-regarded outsider would form the Partnership's board of directors: Chairman Gerald McEntee, who was also chair of the AFL-CIO political committee; Linda Chavez-Thompson, the federation's executive vice president; and Carl McCall, former New York comptroller and unsuccessful gubernatorial candidate in 2002.

Donna Brazile, Al Gore's presidential campaign manager, would be a consultant, with Steve Rosenthal as the executive director—two of the best Get Out The Vote experts in the nation.

The Partnership would send canvassers house to house to get Black, Latino and women voters registered and discuss issues in the battle to defeat President Bush and win pro-labor majorities in both houses of Congress in 2004.[2]

Four Democratic presidential candidates who were already vying for the party's nomination—Sen. John Edwards, Rep. Richard Gephardt, Sen. Joe Lieberman, and former Senator Carol Moseley-Braun—converged on Florida to schmooze and seek labor's coveted endorsement (frontrunner John Kerry was absent, recovering from prostate surgery).

The federation said no.[3]

63

GERALD W. McENTEE

Jerry McEntee is International President of the 1.4 million-member American Federation of State, County and Municipal Employees (AFSCME), one of the most aggressive and politically active organizing unions in the AFL-CIO. He holds a bachelor's degree in economics from LaSalle University in Philadelphia. McEntee is a co-founder and chairman of the board of the Washington-based Economic Policy Institute. He suspects rival Andy Stern of poaching new SEIU members from his union. His relationship with Steve Rosenthal has been fraught with conflict. A native of Philadelphia, McEntee and his wife Barbara live in Washington, D.C.

The hot-button issue that could tilt the election also came up: whether to go to war with Iraq.

The federation said no.[4]

But that didn't drown out the Partnership.

Federation President John J. Sweeney gave it a rousing kickoff speech: "This administration has actively sought every opportunity to pull the rug out from under working Americans, including slashing health and safety, stripping bargaining rights from federal workers and now putting over-time pay and the Federal Medical Leave Act in its sights."

Labor's top priority, he said, was to remove "our out-of-touch leaders. To do so, we are launching our largest mobilization and grass-roots effort ever."[5]

Steve Rosenthal led a seminar on politics. It turned to a discussion of Florida Governor Jeb Bush's easy re-election and the failure of the Democrats to get out the vote.

Rosenthal suggested that many of the AFL-CIO's Black, Hispanic and other minority constituency groups were not effective in mobilizing voters and should not receive large sums of money. His new Partnership would do it right in 2004, he promised.[6]

Jerry McEntee was not pleased.

Rosenthal's management style, both in the federation and in the Partnership, was too abrasive. The minority union leaders responsible for getting out the vote were mortally insulted. They defended their record and threw the blame back on poor federation funding.

When word of the seminar got out, minority constituency groups felt threatened that they weren't selected to do a minority job. They began a steady campaign against Rosenthal.

THE WAR ON FIFTH AVENUE

ON MARCH 19, 2003, GEORGE SOROS COULDN'T STAND IT ANYMORE. American and British forces attacked Iraq. His deepest beliefs had been violated and President George W. Bush had violated them.

It wasn't just that Bush struck him as a common, uncouth, Texas redneck.

Bush's declaration that "you are either with us or you are with the terrorists," shortly after the 9/11 attacks really got Soros. He said it evoked memories of Hitler from his boyhood as a Jew in hiding from the Nazis in his native Hungary.

A *U.S. News & World Report* columnist snorted, "Please. George W. Bush as Hitler? Get a grip."[7]

Bush supporters noted that the "if you're not with me you're against me" idea wasn't Hitler's. It first appeared in Luke 11:23. Jesus said it.

Soros heard Bush say he wanted Osama bin Laden "dead or alive," but not First Lady Laura Bush gently chide in a whisper, "Bushie, are you gonna get 'im?" Texas bluster and Texas humor eluded philosopher Soros.

Next, Soros became alarmed when Bush convinced Congress to pass the USA Patriot Act in October, 2001—the government's new authority to probe private lives made it look to him like American society, the world's most open, was closing.

Privacy advocates left and right found something not to like in the law.

And when Bush told the West Point graduating class in 2002 that the United States would make pre-emptive strikes against any nation it suspected of posing a terrorist threat, Soros started waking up at 3 a.m. and writing what would become *The Bubble of American Supremacy*.[8]

To Soros, his bubble theory was reflexivity applied to foreign policy.

But when America attacked Iraq, he made up his mind. Bush had to go.[9]

The Bush administration gave the Open Society Institute $8.8 million in 2003. Where it was going—and why—was not disclosed.[10]

Soros called Mort Halperin and John Podesta to dinner at his Fifth Avenue apartment in April to assess progress on the American Majority Institute and talk about his problem with Bush.

He brought in Michael Vachon, a personal assistant he had hired in 1986 as a public relations aide, now handling political projects.

The man who did not view his goal as funding "the Democrats" now asked what he could do to defeat Republican George Bush in 2004.

Could he influence the election? How? How much would it cost?

Who was competent to gauge his chances?

Podesta recommended two strategy consultants with solid credentials: Tom Novick, close to the grassroots, and Mark Steitz, inside the Beltway.[11]

Tom Novick was senior vice president of M&R Strategic Services, a firm started by toxics lawyer Arthur Malkin and former Rockefeller Family Fund executive director Donald K. Ross, who was also a founder of the Environmental Grantmakers Association.

Novick, like Ross, had begun his career as executive director of a Ralph Nader Public Interest Research Group—Ross in New York, Novick in Oregon.

Novick had gone on to the Soros-funded Western States Center as director of its Western Progressive Leadership Network. He had conducted a county-by-county analysis of the 2002 Senate races in Iowa, Missouri and other states, concluding that voter mobilization was a better investment than last-minute television ads.[12]

Mark Steitz was senior principal and founder of the Washington-based political strategy firm, TSD Communications.

Steitz began his career in the Congressional Budget Office, where he was a policy analyst from 1978 to 1986. He then served as director of communications for the Democratic National Committee under Ron Brown—while Harold Ickes and Steve Rosenthal were there—formulating the party's message for Bill Clinton's election campaigns in 1992 and again in 1996.

While in the DNC, he had assessed President George H.W. Bush's 1992 re-election chances in a report for some wealthy Democratic donors and independently came to the same conclusion as Novick about voter mobilization.[13]

Soros directed Vachon to engage both. They would work separately, each to evaluate Bush's strengths and weaknesses, submit a winning strategy, identify potential groups to fund, and come up with a budget.

He wanted a briefing on the results at the earliest possible date.

The consultants took about three months.

ROVE REDUX

N OT LONG AFTER THE DINNER WITH SOROS, another Karl Rove PowerPoint presentation mysteriously fell into Democratic hands.

Although not posted to the Web like the earlier "Lafayette Park PowerPoint," it was circulated widely enough to gain mention in the *New Yorker* magazine.

It gave Novick and Steitz access to the awesome Republican playbook, and would absorb them for weeks.[14]

This PowerPoint outlined, in ninety panels, the work of a Rove project called the 72-Hour Task Force, which conducted scientific experiments in grassroots political organizing during the three days before Election Day 2001 in five geographically scattered races.

The presentation frankly acknowledged that in the 2000 Presidential election the Democrats outperformed the final opinion-poll predictions in state after state.

Rove credited their superior on-the-ground organizing.

In 2001, the PowerPoint said, the Republicans conducted more than fifty separate tests, in New Jersey, Virginia, Pennsylvania, South Carolina, and Arkansas, some in paired districts, one for the experiment, the other as a control.

The verdict: grassroots efforts work, and grassroots efforts by local volunteers work best.

Democrats who saw the highly detailed PowerPoint thought that the Republicans' remarkable feat of picking up seats in Congress for the party in the White House during an off-year election was the 72-Hour Task Force paying off.

The meaning was obvious to Novick and Steitz: the Republicans had moved ahead of the Democrats in last-minute organizing skills.

That meant building their Soros strategy around the best Get Out The Vote talent in the party, and that meant Steitz's old DNC co-worker, Steve Rosenthal.

THINGS FALL APART

THE ROSENTHAL-MCENTEE SITUATION SIMMERED until a May 8 gathering at EMILY's List headquarters on 15th and H Streets in Washington.

It was a big meeting called to persuade all the major liberal groups—Carl Pope's environmentalist friends, Ellen Malcolm's abortion-rights friends, Heather Booth's NAACP friends, the pro-gay Human Rights Campaign, trial lawyers and others (including Harold Ickes and Gerald McEntee)—to join a proposed umbrella group named America Votes.

The purpose: to avoid duplication of effort.[15]

The centerpiece of the meeting was a presentation by Steve Rosenthal. He showed the audience examples of how not to do campaigns—designing direct mail pieces using the same images as candidate mail when it's well known that voters don't trust candidate mail; missing opportunities, like rejecting the picture of a middle-aged, cigar-chomping white man to illustrate corporate corruption because it tested as being ineffective, only to find that it had been sold to another group where it worked great.

His point was straight from Gina Glantz and dinner at BeDuCi: an umbrella group would prevent such missteps.

When Rosenthal was finished, most of the attendees supported the idea, but Jerry McEntee said he wouldn't join, openly acknowledging the strong antagonism within the Partnership for America's Families.

The implications were immediately apparent: without McEntee and the AFL-CIO's millions solidly behind its key on-the-ground expert, the Partnership would never grow into the giant voter contact machine they needed.

America Votes could succeed without McEntee, but the Democratic election campaign couldn't succeed without a giant voter contact machine.

Talk turned to creating a broader-based organization to do the job—something Ellen Malcolm called America Coming Together. And some in the room were relieved that it wasn't all union-made.[16]

Two weeks later, the McEntee-Rosenthal split grew worse. William Lucy, head of the Coalition of Black Trade Unionists, said having Rosenthal or any white operative lead minority-registration efforts amounted to "paternalism."[17]

Then Dr. Jaun Andrade, president of the U.S. Hispanic Leadership Institute, wrote a searing damnation of Rosenthal in the *Chicago Sun-Times*:

"Abandon and isolate Rosenthal before the damage he has caused becomes irreparable.... What matters is that Rosenthal have nothing to do with mobilizing Latino and African-American voters. That task belongs to established Latino and African-American leaders and their organizations."[18]

McEntee resigned from the Partnership, as did Chavez-Thompson and McCall.[19]

Andy Stern, the Ivy League union boss, had been waiting in the wings with SEIU money and a cadre of Rosenthal supporters.

He reassured unions and their allies, including women's and environmental groups, that the Partnership would survive its infighting.

Stern installed his own handpicked slate of new board members, all union leaders, including himself as chairman.[20]

Andy Stern now had his own campaign organization—without the twenty million AFL-CIO dollars.

He set a goal to raise $12 million, but could reasonably foresee the Partnership taking in only a scant $3 million.

Rosenthal and Stern recognized that it was permanently crippled.

It was time to put their efforts into another group that could later take over the Partnership—Ellen Malcolm's America Coming Together.

DA ZVIDANYA, MISTER BILLIONAIRE

ON THURSDAY, JUNE 5, GEORGE SOROS TOLD STUDENTS AND JOURNALISTS at the Higher School of Economics in Moscow—which his funding had created—that after 15 years and more than $1 billion in charity, he was saying farewell to Russia, that it was time to focus his efforts on a nation more in need of help—America.

The announcement shocked the Russians: Soros had become so much a part of their culture that they had even turned his name into a generic grant-seeking verb, "sorosovat"—as in, "I see that the university is going to *sorosovat* the Ford Foundation for a big grant," or even, "I have to *sorosovat* Sasha for two rubles until payday."

But he said his work there was done. "I was led to come to Russia because of my concern for a prospering open society, but now I have to concentrate on what goes on in America. The fight for an open society now has to be fought there," he said.

He told the *Moscow Times* that he was particularly concerned over American media and President Bush's handling of the situation in Iraq.[21]

Almost as an afterthought, Soros dismissed a reporter's suggestion that he was also intent on "regime change" in Georgia.

He said he and Georgian President Eduard Shevardnadze had smoothed over their differences during a recent telephone conversation.

He had assured the president his foundation there was only aiding "fair and free elections."[22]

His farewell unsettled the whole nation. It confirmed rumors of a pullout that had been circulating in Russian newspapers since the previous October, about the time Halperin and Podesta talked to him about a new think tank to revitalize progressive politics in America—and dump Bush.

The day after Soros said goodbye in Moscow, Podesta's American Majority Institute staff unpacked their boxes in downtown Washington offices just vacated by (and previously shared with) EMILY's List.

Podesta had already filled some key staff slots in preparation for a formal launch in September.[23]

In her new location in a waffle-iron-facade building directly across from AFL-CIO headquarters, Ellen Malcolm was working on her America Coming Together with Steve Rosenthal, Andy Stern and Carl Pope.

It was time to decide how officers would be listed on their initial Federal Election Commission and IRS filings next month.

Malcolm would take the position of president, Rosenthal was chief executive officer, Pope treasurer, and Stern on the executive committee.

They envisioned a voter contact program for five or six of 2004's battle-ground states.[24]

And America Votes was quickly getting enough commitments to file its incorporation papers.

Even so, half a year after dinner at BeDuCi, the six still hadn't formed their umbrella group.

Michael Lux, former Clinton White House aide (and former political director of People for the American Way), had been watching.

He now operated Progressive Strategies, LLC, a consulting group for wealthy left wing donors.

On July 3 he wrote a memo to his clients outlining the emerging hodge-podge and suggested they withhold support for now.

Despite signs of cooperation, he wrote, "it's definitely not soup yet."[25]

CHAPTER 6 NOTES

1. The location was controversial. The U.S. Labor Department hauled the plumbers and pipefitters union into court for "imprudent use" of members' money in buying the hotel with pension fund assets. Leigh Strope, "Union-owned hotel at center of labor department lawsuit," Associated Press, as published in the *Las Vegas Sun*, February 25, 2003.

2. Adam Clymer, "Democrats seek a stronger focus, and money," *New York Times*, May 25, 2003.

3. Joan Fleischer Tamen, "Democratic Presidential Hopefuls Make Pitches to Union Leaders in Florida," *South Florida Sun-Sentinel* (Knight-Ridder/Tribune Business News), February 25, 2003.

4. CNN, "Labor Coalition Opposes War with Iraq," *CNN News*, February 28, 2003, available online at www.commondreams.org/headlines03/0228-04.htm, accessed August 18. 2005.

5. Thomas B. Edsall, "Labor Targets Nonunion Voters - $20 Million Turnout Effort Expands Effort to Regain Influence," *Washington Post*, February 27, 2003, page A4.

6. Jeanne Cummings, "A hard sell on 'soft money' – 'Shadow Democrats' work around ban on unlimited donations," *Wall Street Journal*, December 2, 2003. See also, Harold Meyerson, "Union Do's and Don'ts for Democrats," *Washington Post*, May 28, 2003, p. 19.

7. Gloria Borger, "It's not hush money. Right? (lack of response by Democrats to comments made by George Soros, who has made large donations to the Democratic Party)," *U.S. News & World Report*; November 24, 2003.

8. Soros feelings about Bush: Edward Robinson, "George Soros Bankrolls Door-to-Door Voter Hunt in Swing States," *Bloomberg News*, September 28, 2004, http://quote.bloomberg.com/apps/news?pid=nifea&&sid=aVPlVg8vm8wg, accessed August 26, 2005. George Soros, *The Bubble of American Supremacy: Correcting the Misuse of American Power* (New York: PublicAffairs, 2004).

9. Dinner in Manhattan: Jeanne Cummings, "Soros Has a Hunch Bush Can Be Beat - Billionaire Puts His Weight, Money Behind Democratic Effort to Oust President in '04," *Wall Street Journal*, February 5, 2004. Vachon's background: Michael T. Kaufman, *Soros: The Life and Times of a Messianic Billionaire*, op. cit., p. 180.

10. Kate O'Beirne, "Agendas all their own: the perils of NGOs—non-governmental organizations," *National Review*, January 26, 2004. In 2006, Morton Halperin gave congressional testimony revealing little of what OSI did with its federal grants: Morton H. Halperin, "Non-Governmentl organizations and Development of Democracy," Statement of Morton H. Halperin, Director of U.S. Advocacy, The Open Society Institute, before the Senate Committee on Foreign Relations, June 8, 2006. (Federal Document Clearing House).

11. Podesta's recommendation: Steve Weissman and Ruth Hassan, "BCRA and the 527 Groups," Campaign Finance Institute, February 9, 2005, Revised March 8, 2005, draft chapter for publication in *The Election after Reform: Money, Politics and the Bipartisan Campaign Reform Act*. Michael J. Malbin, ed., (Rowman and Littlefield, 2005).

12. Novick bio, www.mrss.com/about_meet_bios.html#Tom_Novick, accessed August 26, 2005. Ross bio, www.mrss.com/about_ meet_bios.html# donald_ross, accessed August 26, 2005.

13. Steitz bio, www.steitz.com/bio.aspx?id=9&bio=MS, accessed August 26, 2005.

14. Nicholas Lemann, 'The Controller: Karl Rove is working to get George Bush reelected, but he has bigger plans," *The New Yorker Magazine*, May 12, 2003.

15. Umbrella group under discussion identified as America Votes: Weissman and Hassan, "BCRA and the 527 Groups."

16. Thomas B. Edsall, "Liberals Meeting to Set '04 Strategy - Labor, Rights Groups Focus on Getting Out the Vote to Help Democrats," *Washington Post*, "May 25, 2003.

17. Thomas B. Edsall, "Split Affects Drive Against Bush - Group Designed to Be Liberal Umbrella May Feel Fallout," *Washington Post*, June 5, 2003.

18. Jaun Andrade, "Unions must cut off self-anointed messiah of minority vote - Latinos and African Americans are the most pro-labor voters in America," *Chicago Sun-Times*, June 6, 2003, p. 45.

19. Thomas B. Edsall, "Labor PAC Faces Internal Spat," *Washington Post*, May 24, 2003, p. A13.

20. Incorporated April 24, 2003, District of Columbia, Corporation Division, file number 231444. Board members: Arturo Rodriguez, president of the United Farm Workers; John Wilhelm, Hotel Employees and Restaurant Employees (HERE); James Williams, painters' union; Edward Fire, International Union of Electronic Workers-Communications Workers of America; Miguel Contreras, Los Angeles County Federation of Labor; and George Gresham, 1199/SEIU, the 240,000-member health-care union in New York. *See* story: Steven Greenhouse, "Regrouping on a Labor Effort to Elect a Democrat," *New York Times*, June 6, 2003.

21. Simon Ostrovsky, "Soros Bids Adieu, Says U.S. Needs Help," *Moscow Times*, June 6, 2003, p. 1.

22. Alex Nicholson, "Soros Warns of Oligarchy," *Moscow Times*, June 10, 2003, p. 5.

23. Podesta progress: Gail Russell Chaddock, "Can the book open a new chapter for Hillary Clinton?" *Christian Science Monitor,* June 09, 2003, www. csmonitor.com/2003/0609/p01s01-uspo.html, accessed July 30, 2005. Staff: Sarah Wartell, chief operating officer (former chief of staff of Bill Clinton's National Economic Council); Neera Tanden, domestic policy (former policy director and deputy campaign manager for Hillary Clinton).

24. Malcolm's progress: Weissman and Hassan, "BCRA and the 527 Groups," *op. cit.*

25. Jeanne Cummings, "A hard sell on 'soft money'", *op. cit.*

CHAPTER 7

PLAYING POKER
IN A
CHESS GAME

W HILE STEVE ROSENTHAL GAVE HIS POLITICAL SEMINAR at the AFL-CIO
2003 winter meeting in Florida, a 31-year-old activist named Giga
Bokeria—6,000 miles away in Tbilisi, Republic of Georgia—prepared for a
flight across the Black Sea, over Romania and into Serbia's Belgrade Airport.

In Belgrade he met with members of the Otpor ("Resistance") youth
movement and learned how they used street demonstrations to topple
Yugoslavia's strongman, Slobodan Milosevic.

Bokeria wanted Georgia's student group Kmara! ("Enough!") to do the
same with President Eduard Shevardnadze.

His trip was paid for with funds from George Soros' Open Society
Institute.[1]

Zaza Gachechiladze, editor-in-chief of *The Georgian Messenger*, an
English-language daily based in Tblisi, said, "It's generally accepted public
opinion here that Mr. Soros is the person who planned Shevardnadze's overthrow."[2]

Bokeria turned to Otpor because a little over two years earlier, on
October 5, 2000, an estimated half-million protesters organized by Otpor ran
through tear gas to seize and torch the Yugoslav parliament building in a
violent but bloodless revolution.

Demanding that Balkan autocrat Slobodan Milosevic concede defeat
in the country's September 24th presidential election, Otpor and its allies
lobbed Molotov cocktails into the nearby state television building, leaving it
in flames that nobody came to fight.[3]

73

Mayhem reigned. The mob stormed the Politika newspaper and nearby government buildings. Otpor activists taking over the state TV station had to restrain others to keep them from lynching its director.

In the midst of the chaos, opposition candidate Vojislav Kostunica was ushered into the station and went on television to address the nation as the new Yugoslav president. Milosevic's Army and police chiefs saw that the game was up, and abandoned their supreme commander.[4]

Hours later Milosevic stepped down.

George Soros had paid more than $100 million to make it happen.
He knew that Bokeria could count on Otpor.[5]

SOROS AND HIS FUND FOR AN OPEN SOCIETY YUGOSLAVIA were part of a larger campaign. Milosevic had been blamed for fomenting instability in the Balkans for years, triggering wars of barbaric ethnic cleansing in Slovenia, Croatia, Bosnia and Kosovo. The U.S. and other Western governments hit the Yugoslav leader with sanctions to "make the economy scream" and with NATO bombs during the 1999 Kosovo war.

Yet he survived elections (rigged) and street protests (easily crushed).[6]

The U.S. Congress was sufficiently annoyed by "Slobo" that it approved $100 million in 1999 to assist anti-Milosevic forces—on top of the Soros money—funneled through the National Endowment for Democracy, a government-funded non-profit organization established in 1983 by the Reagan administration to "strengthen democratic institutions around the world through nongovernmental efforts."

In 1999, Soros' Open Society Institute got nearly $5 million from U.S. government agencies.[7]

Soros had operated in Belgrade since 1991, gradually building an "infrastructure of change," according to Fund president Sonja Licht.

The infrastructure consisted of cultural societies and alternative art clubs equipped with photocopiers, fax machines and computers as "islands of resistance" to the communist-renamed-socialist regime, said Licht.

The Fund, Licht said, "empowered the people themselves."

Soros bought newsprint for independent papers and kept opposition publishing houses alive.

A Soros-funded radio station called B-92 later proved a key tool in rallying opposition forces.[8]

Soros had spent seven years cultivating a civil society in Yugoslavia when students created Otpor at Belgrade University in October 1998.

Otpor was a new hope to dislodge Milosevic, and Soros began funding it immediately, according to the Fund's executive director, Ivan Vejvoda.[9]

The Clinton administration, too, was interested in regime change in Yugoslavia, but didn't resort to another war or standard CIA covert actions because key advisor Doug Schoen thought it might be possible to unite the disunited in Yugoslavia to do the job themselves.

All it would take, Schoen told President Clinton, was some American training for the fractious eighteen-party political coalition called the Democratic Opposition of Serbia (DOS)—and money, a great deal of money.[10]

Schoen knew a lot about Yugoslavia.

He had been campaign manager for Milan Panic, the Serbia-born American pharmaceutical tycoon who returned home and lost a rigged presidential election to Slobodan Milosevic in 1992.

At the time, Schoen's polling of likely voters showed that Panic, then serving as the crumbling nation's Prime Minister, was at least neck-and-neck with Milosevic and had an excellent chance of winning.

Then Milosevic's government pulled every dirty trick imaginable— keeping Panic's ads off television, bugging their phones, sending attractive young women to lure Schoen and Panic as "personal assistants," turning away qualified students and minority voters at the polls because they were known to favor Panic, ballot stuffing and miscounting votes, and on and on.[11]

Nothing was going to remove Milosevic. He couldn't be beaten.

That's what the populace knew from experience, so why vote?

Schoen had left Yugoslavia in 1992 bruised and embittered by the utter ruthless corruption of the regime. Now he wanted to come back and do it right. It may have been a simple thirst for revenge.

Bill Clinton trusted Douglas E. Schoen not because of his Harvard law degree or his Ph.D. from Oxford (where Clinton had been a Rhodes scholar), but because he had been the campaign strategist and pollster who framed the winning message for his 1996 reelection bid (working in tandem with Mark Steitz, who was framing the message from inside the Democratic National Committee).

Soon the National Democratic Institute (NDI)—using some National Endowment for Democracy money funneled through the U.S. Agency for International Development (USAID)—sent Doug Schoen, senior partner of the polling firm Penn, Schoen & Berland Associates, on a mission to the Yugoslav opposition (the Penn was Mark J. Penn, worldwide CEO of the PR firm Burson-Marsteller).

ONE OCTOBER DAY IN 1999, Schoen gave a seminar for twenty DOS political leaders in the Hungarian capital, Budapest, which straddles the Danube River, Buda on the West, Pest on the East.

They met in the luxurious Budapest Marriott Hotel on the Pest side.

Visa restrictions predictably imposed by the Milosevic government made it impossible for Schoen to travel to Serbia anymore, so he was holding the session across the northern border in Hungary.[12]

In a darkened conference room, Schoen projected the results of a recent in-depth opinion poll of 840 Serbian voters onto an overhead screen. The first chart showed Milosevic with a 70 percent unfavorable rating among Serbian voters. That was the good news.

Next chart. Most opposition leaders, including the Serbian Democratic Party's slick and dynamic co-founder, Zoran Djindjic, rated nearly as bad.

However, a moderate Serbian nationalist named Vojislav Kostunica, Djindjic's Democratic Party co-founder, had a favorable rating of 49 percent and an unfavorable rating of only 29 percent.

Nobody loved him, but nobody hated him, either.

The message was clear: if Djindjic could contain his power hunger in favor of Kostunica, they might win an election.

What did the rest of the polling suggest?

First, Serbian voters accepted simple anti-Milosevic messages about their terrible economic suffering.

Second, they wanted change to come about through the ballot box, not demonstrations.

Third, only a united opposition could depose Milosevic.

Schoen told them to take home from his seminar one word: unity.

SOROS HAD MADE SCHOEN'S SEMINAR POSSIBLE. Without his years of undermining the authority of Yugoslavia's government, the opposition leaders Schoen advised would have had no infrastructure to call upon at critical junctures: no well-funded Otpor activists able to capture Belgrade, no radio station B-92 eager to rally a scattered citizenry on cue, no web of cultural organizations prepared to get behind the protests.

It was not beginner's luck: by the time Yugoslavia was ready to revolt, Soros had plenty of experience fomenting revolution.

It began modestly. When Soros set up his Open Society Fund in New York in 1979, Karl Popper wasn't the only one it surprised: he had long cast himself as a curmudgeon, saying he didn't believe in philanthropy.

His original fund was what the law calls a "charitable lead trust," which Soros described as "a very interesting tax gimmick" allowing him to pass large sums to his heirs untaxed. But his charitable intent—and power lust—was genuine, and he soon went to work giving money away.[13]

His maiden effort was a scholarship program for Black students in Apartheid South Africa. Soros held the visionary belief that "the creation of elites among persecuted people is the most effective way to overcome prejudice." He arranged to have his bold program administered through the University of Capetown. It was a total failure.[14]

However, once he had stumbled into the usual pitfalls of philanthropy—grants being diverted by administrators, no tracking of results, sabotage by opponents—Soros gained enough savvy to begin building a string of Open Society foundations in communist countries: his native Hungary in 1984, China in 1986, the Soviet Union in 1987, and Poland in 1988.

His announced intent was to help those societies become more open by paying for such things as photocopiers, travel, theaters, filmmaking, sociological research, newspapers and magazines.

To the communist leaders of those countries it looked like a foreign capitalist was trying to erode the ruling party's monopoly over art, culture, and education.

They accused him of promoting dissent to weaken their regime.

As became evident in the Soviet collapse of 1989, they were right.

Despite KGB interference, Soros made significant gains as the Soviet economy tottered: he gave $100 million to support Soviet science when the country had no money to maintain laboratories or pay scientists' salaries.

He committed close to another $100 million to introduce non-Marxist educational materials that had previously been banned. He gave another $100 million to wire all thirty-three regional universities to the Internet.

After the Soviet collapse he spent more millions to control a drug-resistant strain of tuberculosis that was ravaging Russian prisons. He set up a program to teach former military personnel to be entrepreneurs. He gave thousands of smaller grants for favored projects.[15]

He wasn't always as successful as in Russia: Chinese Communist Party General Secretary Zhao Ziyang gave Soros permission to operate his Fund for the Reform and Opening of China (China Fund) with a $1 million annual budget. However, three years later Zhao was ousted by party hard-liners who used the Fund as evidence of his "bourgeois liberalism" and ties with "subversive foreign forces." The Fund's Chinese director was arrested and Soros accused of being a CIA agent, which he denied. He closed the Fund with little accomplished.[16]

His first solid foreign venture—in Hungary—had required delicate negotiations with Communist Party leaders, which resulted in his foundation being anchored in the Academy of Science, the highest organ of intellectual life under Communism. "Open Society" was too provocative a name, so it was simply called, "The Hungarian Academy of Science/George Soros Foundation."[17]

It was accepted as the gift of a native son returned to share his wealth with the country of his origin. It was true, but only from a certain point of view: that of an anti-communist revolutionary.

A stroke of genius was giving hundreds of copying machines to government scientific institutes, where people quickly spread ideas that had been hidden.

Before the government knew what happened they had lost control over the flow of information.

A decade later, Soros said of the endeavor:

My foundation in Hungary, which I established in 1984, contributed to this revolution. A joint venture between my New York based Open Society Fund and the Hungarian Academy of Sciences, it was an unusual undertaking exempt from many of the constraints which bedevil foundations. We were not a normal foundation; we were an institution of civil society engaged in a subversive battle against an oppressive state and party system. We played a subtle game with the authorities, in which each of us tried to take advantage of the other; but the dice were loaded in our favor because we believed in our cause and we knew what we were doing while our opponents did not.

Our aim was simple: to demonstrate the falsehood of communist dogma by fostering alternatives. We did not need to decide on priorities or the merits of particular projects; by permitting people to engage in non-party, non-governmental activities every project served an important function. With small individual grants and a budget of about $3 million a year, we supported a huge number of projects. The Ministry of Culture complained bitterly that we had more influence on cultural life in Hungary than they did. We took it as the greatest accolade.

The experience in Hungary was truly exceptional. I tried to repeat it in Poland and in China, but in both cases we failed. In China, the game was won by the authorities and the foundation became a branch of the security police so I closed it. In Poland, civil society refused to play the game with the authorities so the foundation had difficulties in functioning; it could not even get a telephone.[18]

Was Soros trying to foment revolution in America?[19]

British journalist Neil Clark, who specializes in Middle Eastern and Balkan affairs, looked at another side of the Soros drive for democracy:

> Soros deems a society "open" not if it respects human rights and basic freedoms, but if it is "open" for him and his associates to make money. And, indeed, Soros has made money in every country he has helped to prise "open." In Kosovo, for example, he has invested $50m in an attempt to gain control of the Trepca mine complex, where there are vast reserves of gold, silver, lead and other minerals estimated to be worth in the region of $5 billion. He thus copied a pattern he has deployed to great effect over the whole of eastern Europe: of advocating "shock therapy" and "economic reform," then swooping in with his associates to buy valuable state assets at knockdown prices.[20]

A more laconic assessment of the Soros drive for democracy came from Edward Luttwak, senior fellow at the Washington-based Center for Strategic and International Studies.

"He is a great believer in changing countries."[21]

CHAPTER 7 NOTES

1. Mark MacKinnon, "Georgia revolt carried mark of Soros," *Globe and Mail*, November 26, 2003.
2. *Ibid.*
3. BBC News, "Chaos grips Belgrade," Thursday, 5 October, 2000, 18:55 GMT, 19:55 UK, http://news.bbc.co.uk/1/hi/world/europe/958053.stm, accessed August 16, 2005..
4. CNN News, "World watching to see Belgrade's day after," October 6, 2000, http://archives.cnn.com/2000/WORLD/europe/10/05/yugoslavia.protest.05/index.html, accessed August 27, 2005.
5. Peter Ford, "How the Balkan strongman was toppled: Yugoslavia activists - with foreign help - offer a textbook case on dislodging a dictator without firing a shot," *Christian Science Monitor*, January 27, 2003, p. 12.
6. The background to these events is complex: in the early 1990s, Yugoslavia began to unravel along ethnic lines: Slovenia, Croatia, Macedonia, and Bosnia and Herzegovina were recognized as independent states in 1992. The remaining republics of Serbia and Montenegro declared a new "Federal Republic of Yugoslavia" (FRY) in April 1992 and, under President Slobodan Milosevic, Serbia led military interventions to unite ethnic Serbs in neighboring republics into a "Greater Serbia." These unsuccessful efforts led to Yugoslavia being ousted from the UN in 1992. In 1998-99, massive expulsions by FRY forces and Serb paramilitaries of ethnic Albanians living in Kosovo provoked the NATO bombing of Serbia and the stationing of a NATO-led force in Kosovo. For further details *see* CIA - The World Factbook, Serbia and Montenegro. http://www.cia.gov/cia/publications/factbook/geos/yi.html, accessed September 6, 2005.
7. S. 720 and H.R. 1064, Serbia Democratization Act of 1999, 106th Congress. Four major organizations received NED funding: the U.S. Information Agency (USIA), the U.S. Agency for International Development (USAID), the National Democratic Institute and its counterpart, the International Republican Institute.
8. Peter Ford, "How the Balkan strongman was toppled," *op. cit. See also*, Open Society Institute - Internet Program (OSI-IP), http://www2.soros.org/internet/foundations/FORMER_YUGOS_REPUB.html, accessed August 15, 2005. "OSI-IP was in fact the original funder of Radio B-92/Opennet activities."
9. David Holley, "The Seed Money for Democracy: George Soros Has Put Out $2.8 Billion Since 1990 To Promote a Global Open Society. His Efforts Include Funding the Student Movement That Helped Oust Milosevic in Yugoslavia," *Los Angeles Times*, 26 January 2001, p. 1.
10. Nicholas Thompson, "This Ain't Your Momma's CIA: The agency did not play the lead role in ousting Milosevic. Thank God," *Washington Monthly*, March 2001.
11. Douglas E. Schoen, "How Milosevic Stole the Election," *New York Times Magazine*, February 14, 1993, pp 32-40.
12. Michael Dobbs, "US Advice Guided Milosevic Opposition: Political Consultants Helped Yugoslav Opposition Topple Authoritarian Leader," *Washington Post*, December 11, 2000, p. A1.

13. Michael T. Kaufman, *Soros: The Life and Times of a Messianic Billionaire*, p. 163*ff.*
14. Ibid. p. 170-72.
15. Michael T. Kaufman, "Saying Goodbye to Soros," *Transitions Online*, June 16, 2003, www.tol.cz.
16. Marianne Yen, "Fund's Representatives Arrested in China; Exiles See Plot to Tie Zhao to Subversion," *Washington Post*, August 8, 1989.
17. Michael T. Kaufman, *Soros: The Life and Times of a Messianic Billionaire*, *op. cit.*, p. 193-94.
18. Avatud Eesti Fond, "Info: George Soros: Biographical Information," http://www.oef.org.ee/en/sisu/Info/Byroo/soros/
19. *See* page 28. George Soros, "The Capitalist Threat," *Atlantic Monthly*, February 1997.
20. Neil Clark, "Profile – George Soros: The billionaire trader has become eastern Europe's uncrowned king and the prophet of 'the open society.' But open to what?" *New Statesman*, June 2, 2003.
21. Edward Robinson, "George Soros Bankrolls Voter Hunt in Swing States," *Bloomberg News*, September 28, 2004.

CHAPTER 8

VELVET BULLDOZER

FIVE MONTHS AFTER THE NATIONAL DEMOCRATIC INSTITUTE began trying to convince the Serbian opposition parties to work together (reportedly with some head-knocking from the U.S. State Department to help things along), a counterpart American group, the International Republican Institute (IRI), went to work with Otpor.

IRI paid for two dozen Otpor leaders to attend a seminar from March 31 to April 3, 2000 at the Budapest Hilton Hotel in the Castle District—across the Danube from the Marriott—on the Buda side, like the Soros Foundation Hungary, two miles north on Bolyai Street.[1]

Otpor's seminar was presented by retired U.S. Army Col. Robert Helvey of the Soros-funded Albert Einstein Institution (AEI) in Boston.

Helvey was one of the world's leading trainers in nonviolent resistance methods.

He trained Otpor activists how to organize a strike, how to run a door-to-door canvass, how to develop a political strategy, how to communicate with symbols, how to overcome fear, and how to undermine the authority of a dictatorial regime.[2]

Helvey, who served two tours in Vietnam, taught not only from his own wide experience, but also from *The Politics of Nonviolent Action* (1973), written by colleague and fellow AEI director, Gene Sharp, whose book had long been hailed as the definitive work on nonviolent struggle.[3]

Helvey used parts of another Sharp book (paid for by the Open Society Institute), *From Dictatorship to Democracy: A Conceptual Framework for Liberation*, to create a simplified field guide for Otpor, a kind of "Regime Change for Dummies."[4]

The Otpor trainees took it back to Serbia, where a young member named Srdja Popovic translated it as the "Otpor User Manual."

They disseminated it to 70,000 activists across Serbia and set about energetically undermining Milosevic's authority by any means available.[5]

IN JULY, 2000, THE OPPOSITION GOT AN UNEXPECTED BREAK. Milosevic, unaware of the opposition's growing unity and hoping to rig another mandate from the people, called for elections—in September.

A little over two months. The opposition had to get into high gear fast.

Otpor members on short visits to Hungary literally had bags of cash stuffed into their hands to smuggle back into Serbia.

Otpor's revenue for the project totaled at least $25 million.[6]

With part of the money they did something totally new in Serbian experience: they used Western advertising techniques to test their political messages.

One of Serbia's best known polling firms ran a series of focus groups testing messages for DOS and Otpor, paid for by Soros and the National Endowment for Democracy.

Otpor activists took the messages door to door.[7]

But there was still the problem that the populace didn't believe that Milosevic could be beaten.

The opposition had to overcome the defeatism.

Otpor members held a brainstorming session, struggling.

Then activist Srdjan Milivojevic murmured the words "Gotov je."

Everybody froze.

Gotov je—"He's finished."

"We realized immediately that it summed up our entire campaign," said Dejan Randjic, who ran the Otpor marketing operation. "It was very simple, very powerful. It focused on Milosevic, but did not even mention him by name."[8]

They juxtaposed the slogan on a black and white sticker with Otpor's clenched-fist emblem inside a circle. It had the look of menace.

USAID paid for 80 tons of imported adhesive paper, enough to print up 2.5 million *Gotov je* stickers.

Soon *Gotov je* was plastered all over Serbia on walls, inside elevators, in bar restrooms—and across Milosevic's campaign posters.

With USAID's sticker paper came 5,000 cans of spray paint, in all colors—good for scrawling anti-Milosevic slogans, which showed up at night on walls, stairways, alleys and street pavement.[9]

Once Vojislav Kostunica was nominated as Serbia's Democratic Party presidential candidate, they had to keep the Milosevic regime from stealing the election.

With what they knew first hand and what Schoen told them about 1992, they were well prepared.

The International Republican Institute arranged training for election observers in the Hungarian town of Szeged, just ten minutes' drive from the Serbian border.

They set up mock polling stations with ballot boxes and went through the balloting process in detail with opposition party and Otpor activists.

American consultants simulated vote-counting scams and ballot-stuffing techniques, teaching monitors to spot fraud and act quickly.

They trained four-hundred election monitors who went back to Serbia and trained another fifteen thousand.[10]

The Serbian Center for Free Elections and Democracy, funded by USAID, organized a huge parallel vote count operation to check Milosevic's government tally.[11]

On Election Day, September 24, 2000, the Democratic Opposition in Serbia placed at least two trained monitors at every polling station in the country.

Otpor activists covered the country with a highly organized Get Out The Vote campaign.

When it was all over, Milosevic's State Election Commission wouldn't release the official count.

Milosevic tried to force a runoff with Kostunica.

The opposition was adamant that their vote count showed Milosevic far behind.

The opposition declared victory but Milosevic didn't budge.[11]

By October 2, widespread protests made it only a question of physically removing Milosevic, which had been the missing element in previous failures.

It had to be done with great force but without bloodshed.

Now they activated the plan.

Zoran Djindjic, Serbian Democratic Party president, gave two-hundred Otpor activists instructions as field coordinators and equipped them with field radios and secure communications.

They would help the man chosen to lead the attacks on Belgrade: Velja Ilic, mayor of the anti-Milosevic stronghold of Čačak, a town of 100,000 about 80 miles southwest of Belgrade—the place was so hostile that Milosevic could never even come there to give a speech.

Ilic was a hardened and resourceful fighter. He had recruited a task force of some four thousand men and women.

He had arranged in advance for several Federal Army officers in the local armory to supply weapons from the military arsenal.[12]

From this point on, it was only a matter of timing.

On October 2, Djindjic called the rally in Belgrade for October 5th to force Milosevic out.

Radio station B-92 broadcast announcements of the rally nonstop.
Otpor organizers began chartering buses by the dozen.

Simultaneously, Ilic distributed 2,500 Kalashniov AK-47 assault rifles and more than 600 anti-tank shoulder-launched weapons to his task force teams.

Advance patrols dug trenches on the southern approaches to Belgrade, where they deployed several hundred mortars and recoilless rifles.

On the night of October 4, the teams moved on Belgrade in a miles-long convoy that included several bulldozers on trailers, giving the operation its Serbian nickname, "The Bulldozer Revolution."[13]

On the morning of October 5, busloads of demonstrators from all over Serbia arrived and joined with Otpor leaders and Ilic's heavily armed teams. Hundreds of thousands marched on the Federal Parliament.

It was guarded by about 300 Interior Ministry Police, who had orders to "apply minimum force."

They repelled the first protestor attack with tear gas, and the opposition forces retreated to a nearby plateau. Then came the second and third attacks, which outflanked the Interior Ministry Police, who gave up and joined the crowd.

Protestors stormed the building and set it ablaze.

The Bulldozer Revolution had won.[13]

Networks for netwars.

The Western press portrayed it as a replay of the relatively bloodless 1989 anti-communist coup that thrust dissident playwright Vaclav Havel into the presidency of the Czech Republic—which Soros also helped bankroll—applying its popular nickname, "the Velvet Revolution" to Yugoslavia.

Kostunica didn't like it, telling *Time* magazine, "We are not like the Czechs. This is more than a velvet revolution."[14]

But the name stuck.

People throughout the former Soviet bloc, who had grafted *sorosavat* onto the Russian language, began to use "velvet revolution" for any Soros-sponsored downfall.

Other foreign expressions stuck.

Otpor activists, who speak mostly Serbian, call their efforts to increase turnout before the election "GOTV," for the American slogan "Get Out The Vote."

They smile because it sounds a little like *Gotov je*.[16]

And that's what Giga Bokeria wanted to take back to Georgia.

IN THE SUMMER OF 2003, Otpor activists returned Bokeria's visit and ran several three-day courses in Tbilisi.

They briefed more than a thousand Georgian students, most of them members of Kmara!, on how to dump Shevardnadze.

The Soros Foundations Network paid for it.[17]

Some of the money was probably a pass-through from all those multi-million-dollar U.S. government grants Soros was so good at getting.

Mikheil Saakashvili, the New York-educated lawyer who would replace Shevardnadze in 2004, had received the Open Society Award from Soros in 2002.

George Soros was the only man in America with his own foreign policy and the track record to prove it.

Non-profit organizations were the bearer of that revolution.

Foundations were their vanguard.

About the time Otpor went to Tblisi in the summer of 2003, Tom Novick and Mark Steitz went to Soros' mansion in Southampton on Long Island for a two-day briefing on how to dump Bush.

CHAPTER 8 NOTES

1. Roger Cohen, "Who Really Brought Down Milosevic?" *New York Times*, November 26, 2000.

2. Metta Spencer, "Gene Sharp and Serbia: Introduction: Nonviolence versus a Dictatorship," *Peace Magazine,* October-December 2001, p.14.

3. Gene Sharp, *The Politics of Nonviolent Action – Part 1: Power and Struggle; Part 2: Methods of Nonviolent Action; Part 3, Dynamics of Nonviolent Action,* (Boston: Porter Sargent Publishers, 1973).

4. Gene Sharp, *From Dictatorship to Democracy: A Conceptual Framework for Liberation,* (Cambridge: Albert Einstein Institution, 1993). Open Society Institute paid for the book: Open Society Institute Form 990-PF 1997: $29,145 "To produce From Dictatorship to Democracy."

5. Roger Cohen, "Who Really Brought Down Milosevic?" *op. cit.* Popovic as translator: John Bacher, "Video review: Bringing Down a Dictator," *Peace Magazine*, Jul-Sep 2002, p.28. www.peacemagazine.org/archive/v18n3p28. htm, accessed September 6, 2005.

6. John Bacher, "Video review: Bringing Down a Dictator." *op. cit.*

7. Nicholas Thompson, "This Ain't Your Momma's CIA: The agency did not play the lead role in ousting Milosevic. Thank God," *Washington Monthly*, March 2001.

8. Michael Dobbs, "US Advice Guided Milosevic Opposition, Political Consultants Helped Yugoslav Opposition Topple Authoritarian Leader," *Washington Post*, December 11, 2000, p. A1.

9. Christophe Chiclet, "Otpor: the youths who booted Milosevic," *Unesco Courier*, March 2001, www.unesco.org/courier/2001_03/uk/droits.htm, accessed August 29, 2005.

10. Michael Dobbs, "US Advice Guided Milosevic Opposition." *op. cit.*

11. National Democratic Institute, "Europe: Central & Eastern: Serbia," www.ndi.org/worldwide/cee/serbia/serbia.asp, accessed August 29, 2005.

12. Peter Ackerman , Jack DuVall , Steve York and Miriam Zimmerman (producers), *Bringing Down A Dictator* (film), Profile: Velimir Ilic, www.aforcemorepowerful.org/tv/bringingDownSeries/storyCast.htm.

13. Jane's Sentinel Security Assessments: The Balkans (subsection, "The Course of the Revolution"), 3 November 2000.

14. Andrew Purvis and Dejan Anastasijevic, "'This is more than a velvet revolution,' TIME talks with Yugoslavia's new President, Vojislav Kostunica," *Time Europe*, October 23, 2000, Vol. 156, No. 17.

16. Nicholas Thompson, "This Ain't Your Momma's CIA." *op. cit.* Soros paid $500,000 to Kmara!: Zenit News Agency, "George Soros' Pet Projects Include Overthrowing a Government - Financier's Radical Social Programs Aim at Changing Society," *The Globe and Mail*, December 7, 2003.

17. Mark MacKinnon, "Georgia revolt carried mark of Soros," *The Globe and Mail*, November 26, 2003.

PART III

POPULIST PLUTOCRATS

PRIVATIZING THE DEMOCRATS

THE DYE CHART

LIPSTICK ON A PIG

RAGING INCREMENTALISTS

CHAPTER 9

PRIVATIZING THE DEMOCRATS

"MEMBERS OF CONGRESS, OURS ARE NOT WESTERN VALUES, they are the universal values of the human spirit," said British Prime Minister Tony Blair to a joint session of the U.S. House and Senate.

"Anywhere, anytime ordinary people are given the chance to choose, the choice is the same: freedom, not tyranny; democracy, not dictatorship; the rule of law, not the rule of the secret police."[1]

After his speech to Congress that Thursday afternoon in July, Blair joined President George W. Bush in the Cross Hall of the White House to continue discussing the War on Terrorism at a news conference, particularly regime change in Iraq.[2]

While they fielded reporters' questions, two-hundred miles or so to the northeast on Long Island, in a very large old house near the ocean, where Duck Pond Lane joins Old Town Road in Southampton, seventeen Bush opponents gathered to bring regime change to America.

The house—with its elaborate grounds and ample guesthouse—was known as El Mirador ("The Viewpoint") and belonged to George Soros.

It was sumptuous, but sumptuous in the nearly Spartan Soros style—costly as his purse could buy, "but not expressed in fancy: rich, not gaudy." The *New Yorker* magazine remarked, "it wasn't perched on the beach, and it barely had a view of the Atlantic Ocean."[3]

But it was rich. It had been completely renovated and redecorated by his second wife Susan when they were married in 1983. Although she had not yet earned her later status as director of Bard College's decorative arts center—she was then 28 and George was 53—Susan Weber Soros was already an expert designer, and confected El Mirador into a splendid weekend salon that since has welcomed a succession of celebrities, artists, writers, statesmen and academicians invited from around the world.

This afternoon, in the salmon-pink drawing room of the main house, Soros hosted a small but well-orchestrated summit of strategists, activists, wealthy donors and lawyers to see the eagerly awaited Dump Bush briefing by Tom Novick and Mark Steitz.

It would tell Soros exactly how to Dump Bush and who to do it with. "George viewed it like someone who was looking at putting resources into an investment," Novick told *Bloomberg News*.

"He wanted detailed plans, and he wanted people running it with proven track records."[4]

He needed it for more than his own edification.

The funderati still didn't think much could be done about Bush.

Michael Lux's soup memo had effectively killed the money flow for 527s. Soros realized he was the only one among them with the gravitas to get them off their checkbooks and into the possibilities of McCain-Feingold.

The new law was the critical missing bridge in constructing a *permanent* progressive electoral network as a companion to the progressive cultural network, which together might become the social change counterpart of the Vast Right Wing Conspiracy—something the Kallick report couldn't foresee.

In ways only a few contemplated, the future of American politics hinged on the outcome of this two-day meeting.

The donors Soros invited—his insurance tycoon friend Peter Lewis; Rob Glaser, founder and CEO of RealNetworks; Rob McKay, Taco Bell heir; and Lewis and Dorothy Cullman, heirs to the Benson & Hedges tobacco fortune—came to hear how the activists planned to beat Bush.

The strategists came to back up Novick and Steitz. They included confidants Mort Halperin and John Podesta, who so far had pledges of more than $10 million for their American Majority Institute, boosted by Hillary Clinton, whose aid had become common knowledge.[5]

Two other strategists joined them, Robert O. Boorstin and Jeremy Rosner, from the Washington public opinion and consulting firm, Greenberg Quinlan Rosner Research, Inc.—and both former Clinton administration officials. Podesta had recruited Boorstin as a senior official for his think tank; he would come on board shortly.[6]

The four knew in advance what Novick and Steitz would show. They would have known even if the consultants didn't tell them: practically every Democratic strategist in Washington was working on the same problem with the same conclusions from the same raw data: recent voter preference polls, previous Get Out The Vote results, and, particularly, quietly circulated copies of Karl Rove's lost, stolen or strayed *72-Hour Task Force* PowerPoint.

The Wall Street Journal sketched their presentation:

> The electorate remains split, and Mr. Bush is vulnerable because of the troubled economy and messy aftermath of the Iraq war. They found that 17 states, most in the Midwest, are in play, but the only way Democrats could win was to upgrade their voter-mobilization machine and come up with cash to pay for TV ads during the spring when Mr. Bush is expected to use his nearly $200 million war chest to try to bury the Democratic nominee.[7]

The New Yorker:

> Steitz and Novick indicated that the 2004 election would probably be very close. The electorate was polarized, with only ten per cent of likely voters undecided. The best strategy, they said, would be to mobilize the Democratic base and persuade undecided voters with a state-of-the-art field operation. The plan was projected to cost at least seventy-five million dollars.[8]

Steitz and Novik had built their recommendations around the field operation skills of Steve Rosenthal. Since his 1995 appointment as AFL-CIO political director, he had become known as perhaps the best Get Out The Vote campaigner in the land, using a strategy based on four key principles:

- Frame the importance of elections around specific issues that matter to the voter, such as health care;
- Increase personal one-on-one, door-to-door contact with voters;
- Increase the frequency of visits with each voter; and
- Don't tell voters who to vote for, but rather educate them about the candidates' issue positions.

Steitz and Novik told Soros how Rosenthal's principles worked. They would hire hundreds of canvassers—armed with palm computers and voter databases—to walk the precincts door to door, identify registered Democrats and register new voters. Some of the palm computers would use Acxiom Corporation's sophisticated voter software to show custom video clips of the candidate's message matching the individual voter's profile. At the end of the day, each canvasser would transmit voter responses and hot button issues back to Acxiom's central computer bank in Little Rock, Arkansas.

Then, using huge databases thus updated, the canvassers would go back to see each voter as many times as possible—registering new voters as they found them—and get them to the polls on election day.

It was a nearly ideal GOTV strategy. Almost like science-fiction.

The media paid close attention to that part of the day's presentation.

The New Yorker:

As the researchers gave their presentation, Steitz recalled, "Soros was very engrossed. He leaned forward when we were talking about getting out the vote, and asked, 'You mean you actually go door to door?' All the practical aspects caught his imagination."[9]

The Wall Street Journal:

A strategy for defeating Mr. Bush by activating new voters appealed to Mr. Soros because it reflected tactics the Hungarian native—he is a naturalized U.S. citizen—began using in the early 1980s to help promote democracy in Eastern Europe.[10]

The National Review said Soros saw portions of the *72-Hour Task Force* PowerPoint:

And on that summer day in Southampton, as he viewed Rove's secret PowerPoint, Soros was clearly fascinated with the nuts and bolts of political organizing. "He was sort of leaning forward and saying, 'So they go door-to-door to the same place?'" Steitz recalled. It was not long before Soros was sold.[11]

Neither the presenters nor the reporters seemed to realize that Soros was deeply experienced in funding Get Out The Vote programs or that he was currently paying Otpor to teach GOTV to Kmara! in Tblisi.

Only the *Wall Street Journal* grasped that his interest had something to do with previous success in Eastern Europe.[12]

Then the session at El Mirador came to the details of America Coming Together, presented by Ellen Malcolm, Steve Rosenthal and Carl Pope.

Because they had been invited, there was little doubt about the outcome: Malcolm had ACT's Internal Revenue Service papers filed at 1:26 that very afternoon.

They further hoped that the donors would make ACT the centerpiece of a larger, comprehensive 527 network including the Ickes media fund and Gina Glantz's America Votes idea, but the details were not yet solid.[13]

The Chicago Tribune:

Ellen Malcolm, the founder of the EMILY's List fundraising program aimed at Democratic women, laid out a strategy for organizing a grass-roots effort to get out the vote. Though everyone agreed the election would be fought in 17 key states, Malcolm figured her group could afford organizing efforts in only about five.[14]

That wasn't good enough for Soros—"I don't want to build half a bridge!"

He told *Bloomberg News*, "If ACT could be extended to the other battleground states, it could influence the outcome of the elections. But of course, they needed money, so I got them to do all 17 states."[15]

Press reports described Soros grilling the three activists like the investor he was.

The Chicago Tribune:

"We sort of had a negotiation," Malcolm recalled. "He wanted us to raise a lot of money before he put any of his own money in."[16]

The Wall Street Journal:

But he wanted a sound corporate structure, and under his prodding the group stopped thinking about "what can we imagine getting" and started focusing on "what is necessary to win," says Mr. Steitz.[17]

The New York Times:

"He approached it like a business," said Mark Steitz, a consultant Mr. Soros hired to advise him and who had worked with Harold Ickes, a former Clinton chief of staff. "It was like funding a start-up venture."[18]

Which may have been mostly for show. The three activists would not have been invited if they hadn't been selected in advance and they wouldn't have been selected in advance if Malcolm didn't head the richest PAC in America, Rosenthal didn't hold the best field operation track record in organized labor and Pope didn't have a 770,000-name mailing list.

As for Andy Stern—present by proxy—Soros' foundation had donated $75,000 to his Service Employees International Union two years earlier for homecare worker training in Los Angeles, about the same time Stern was running a big membership recruiting campaign there. The donation was part of the Open Society Institute's "Project on Death in America" for better treatment of dying patients, one of OSI's earliest U.S.-based programs. It ran from 1994 to 2003; the grant to Stern's union was one of its last.[19]

THE LAWYERS AT THE BRIEFING WERE NEVER NAMED by the media. The lead attorney was probably Steven Ross, partner in the large Washington law firm of Akin, Gump, Strauss, Hauer & Feld LLP.

Ross' later assertion that "George Soros has conducted himself in an entirely legal fashion" during the election campaign could be read as indicating he was there when it started.[20]

Ross most likely was: he represented Soros on campaign finance matters and filed Soros' Federal Election Commission disclosures.[21]

Key legal issues about McCain-Feingold were still up in the air that day in Southampton, including its constitutionality. Eleven different lawsuits had challenged the BCRA within a month of its 2002 passage, uniting more than eighty plaintiffs, including Senator Mitch McConnell (R-Kentucky), the AFL-CIO and the Republican party. The lead defendants were the Federal Election Commission and the U.S. Department of Justice.

Two main parts of the law were under attack: the ban on soft money to political parties and the strict regulation of "electioneering communications," including "issue ads" that opponents saw as campaign ads in disguise. All the lawsuits were consolidated into one case, *McConnell v. FEC*.

A three-judge District Court gave a mixed ruling, which never went into effect. The case was immediately appealed to the U.S. Supreme Court, with an expedited hearing set for September 3.[22]

It was understood by everyone at El Mirador that, given the current uncertainties—and the uproar either way the Supreme Court went—anything ACT did would likely provoke more lawsuits, so they should be prepared.

It was also understood that the Federal Election Commission would enforce the law so lightly that just about anything goes.

The FEC had adopted new rules that made it easy for political parties to remain involved in raising large contributions. The new rules allowed lawmakers to speak at state party functions where soft money checks were collected. They defined soft-money solicitation as an overt request for dollars—thus a "suggestion" that a donor write a $100,000 check was legal.

To cap it off, in a June 22, 2002 vote, the FEC said it would treat the 527s and 501c groups as independent organizations not constrained by the soft-money ban, even though they might be thinly disguised proxies run by ex-party officials.

That made Senator McCain so furious he vowed to introduce legislation overturning the new FEC rules.

Caution was obviously in order. Malcolm had registered ACT with the IRS as a nonfederal account to accept soft money, but shortly after the Southampton meeting she also had it registered with the Federal Election Commission to accept hard money donations, which could legally be spent on federal candidates including the president.[23]

They weren't sure about the rule against coordinating with a political party or candidate. The FEC didn't seem too intent on enforcing it. They could probably mingle at big conferences, but not one-on-one. Soros owned a home in Sun Valley not far from one of the homes of candidate John Kerry, who had been a personal friend since the mid-1990s when he co-sponsored the Clean Money, Clean Elections Act that had fizzled dismally. Perhaps it would be prudent to keep shy of him, just in case he became the nominee.

WHEN THE PRESENTATIONS CLOSED, the consultants said there was no time to waste, that one horse had to be picked among the 527s to signal to donors which group would take the lead. The media reported the turning point variously.

The Washington Post:

Standing on the back deck, the evening sun angling into their eyes, Soros took aside Steve Rosenthal, CEO of the liberal activist group America Coming Together (ACT), and Ellen Malcolm, its president. They were proposing to mobilize voters in 17 battleground states. Soros told them he would give ACT $10 million.

The Wall Street Journal:

By morning, the outlines of a new organization began to emerge, and Mr. Soros pledged $10 million to get it started.

Bloomberg News:

The morning after the presentation, he pledged $10 million for ACT.

Inconsistencies aside, Soros was the early money. It made the dough rise:

Before coffee the next morning, his friend Peter Lewis, chairman of the Progressive Corp., had pledged $10 million to ACT. Rob Glaser, founder and CEO of RealNetworks, promised $2 million. Rob McKay, president of the McKay Family Foundation, gave $1 million and benefactors Lewis and Dorothy Cullman committed $500,000.

Soros also promised up to $3 million to Podesta's new think tank, the Center for American Progress.

Soros will continue to recruit wealthy donors for his campaign. Having put a lot of money into the war of ideas around the world, he has learned that "money buys talent; you can advocate more effectively."[24]

Around that pivot, American politics went a new way. McCain-Feingold had made possible an unintended privatization of political campaigns. Now the very wealthy could legally direct an election campaign as they saw fit and political parties were powerless to stop them.

The wealthy people who once simply wrote a check to the Democratic National Committee every year could now donate to 527s farther to the left than the Democratic Party's leadership.

And they did.

New power players quickly dominated the Democratic landscape, with breathtaking total contributions.

The top private pro-Democrat donors:

- **George Soros,** (investor), $23.4 million, an unprecedented amount;
- **Peter Lewis**, Progressive Corp. (auto insurance), $22.9 million;
- **Stephen Bing,** real estate heir, Shangri-La Entertainment (movie production), $13.85 million;
- **Herb & Marion Sandler**, Golden West Financial Corp. (savings and loan), $13 million;
- **Ted Waitt,** Gateway, Inc. (computers), $5 million;
- **Andrew & Deborah Rappaport,** August Capital (Silicon Valley venture capitalists), $4.26 million;
- **Alida Rockefeller Messinger**, oil heiress, $3.58 million;
- **Jeffrey & Jeanne Levy-Hinte,** (Antidote Films), $3.57 million;
- **Linda Pritzker,** Hyatt hotel heiress, $3.15 million;
- **Jonathan McHale & Christine Mattso,** TippingPoint Technologies (computer security software), $3.1 million;
- **Fred Eychaner,** Newsweb Corp., $3.07 million;
- **Susan & Terry Ragon,** InterSystems (software), $3 million;
- **Lewis B. Cullman,** tobacco heir, $2.65 million;
- **Robert Glaser,** RealNetworks (software), $2.22 million;
- **Agnes Varis,** Agvar Chemicals, (pharmaceutical ingredients), $2 million.[25]

"What is surprising is how much a relatively small group of individuals has been willing to give," said campaign finance expert Anthony Corrado, a political science professor at Colby College in Maine.[26]

The top private 527 pro-Democrat groups:

- **America Coming Together**, $79.7 million;
- Ickes' **Media Fund** (he couldn't think of a better name), $59.4 million;
- Malcolm and Ickes formed the **Joint Victory Campaign 2004** to raise funds for both America Coming Together and the Media Fund, $78.1 million (divided up between the two and factored into their separate totals);
- Andy Stern's **SEIU**, $48.4 million;
- Jerry McEntee's **AFSCME**, $25.5 million;
- **Citizens for a Strong Senate**, $21.7 million;
- **MoveOn.org**, $12.9 million;
- **New Democrat Network**, $12.7 million;
- Carl Pope's **Sierra Club**, $8.7 million;
- Ellen Malcolm's **EMILY's List**, $7.7 million;
- **Voices for Working Families**, $7.4 million;
- John Sweeney's **AFL-CIO**, $6.5 million;
- **League of Conservation Voters**, $6 million;

- **International Brotherhood of Electrical Workers**, $5.4 million;
- **Democratic Victory 2004**, $3.69 million;
- **Laborer's Union**, $3.4 million;
- **America Votes**, $3.1 million;
- Stern and Rosenthal's **Partnership for America's Families** (dissolved, absorbed by ACT in September 2003), $3.07 million;
- **Grassroots Democrats**, $2.8 million;
- **Stronger America Now**, $2.79 million;
- **Democrats 2000**, $2.54 million;
- **Coalition to Defend the American Dream**, $1.9 million;
- **Communications Workers of America**, $1.9 million;
- **Music for America**, $1.7 million;
- **Environment 2004**, $1.2 million;
- **Natural Resources Defense Council**, $1.1 million;
- **Public Campaign Action Fund**, $1.1 million;
- **Gay and Lesbian Victory Fund**, $1.1 million;
- **America's PAC**, $1 million;
- **Mainstreet USA, Inc.**, $1 million.[27]

When ACT was officially launched in early August, Soros began a series of characteristic sound-bites about unseating George W. Bush:

The Washington Post:

"The fate of the world depends on the United States and President Bush is leading us in the wrong direction."[28]

"[Beating Bush] is the central focus of my life," Soros said, his blue eyes settled on an unseen target. The 2004 presidential race, he said in an interview, is "a matter of life and death."[29]

Newsweek:

"The country is in the grips of an extremist ideology... [where] disagreement is not tolerated," he says. "Open society is always endangered. And the people in these societies must reaffirm those values for open society to survive. If Bush is re-elected, we fail the test because we [would have allowed] ourselves to be misled."[30]

Bloomberg News:

"President Bush equates freedom with American values," Soros writes. "He has a simplistic view of what is right and what is wrong: We are right, and they are wrong. This is in contradiction with the principles of an open society, which recognize that we may be wrong."[31]

The Los Angeles Times:

If Bush gets reelected, "I shall go into some kind of monastery to reflect. And frankly, I will be asking, 'What's wrong with us?'"[32]

Former allies asked, "What's wrong with Soros?"
Fred Wertheimer, CEO of Washington-based Democracy 21, told *Bloomberg News*, "He's made a decision to go from being part of the solution to being part of the problem. Our concern is that 527s are becoming a vehicle whereby large contributors can gain undue influence, and Soros has chosen to make himself the poster child for 527s."[33]

Predictably, although anti-war activists applauded him, Soros was still vilified by anti-globalization activists for his one-time advocacy of free market economies and the global capitalist system.[34]

Democratic Party officials began to worry.
When Malcolm and Ickes launched a series of fund-raising stints across the country in November, they received not only large donations, but also angry reactions, like in Seattle:

> Some of the country's top Democratic political operatives were in Seattle this week courting some rich party donors for a new campaign to help whichever Democrat faces George W. Bush next year.
> They left with donations and pledges for more for the Joint Victory Campaign, a partnership of two newly formed organizations that say they will raise more than $100 million for voter outreach and a media campaign....
> Contributors say they see the groups as the most effective way to deliver a focused message in the campaign against President Bush's re-election.
> But there is an emerging discontent among Democratic Party officials and representatives of interest groups that traditionally back the party. They worry about the loss of money, attention and effort that is shifting to the new groups, from high-profile operations backed by well-known people to little-known groups with ill-defined missions.
> "There is an absolute proliferation of these groups, and one doesn't know what the other is doing," said Washington state Democratic Party Chairman Paul Berendt.[35]

Well, what did you need the Democratic Party for, anyway?
They had The Soros Left Wing Conspiracy.
The Democratic voter base was theirs now, bought and paid for.
Privatized by progressive plutocrats.

It probably wasn't the participatory democracy most liberals had in mind.

CHAPTER 9 NOTES

1. CNN News, "Transcript of Blair's Speech to Congress," July 17, 2003, www.cnn.com/2003/US/07/17/blair.transcript/, accessed September 7, 2005.
2. The White House, Office of the Press Secretary, "President Bush, Prime Minister Blair Discuss War on Terrorism," news release, July 17, 2003, www. whitehouse.gov/news/releases/2003/07/20030717-9.html, accessed September 7, 2005.
3. William Shakespeare, *Hamlet* (1600-01), Act I, Scene III, lines 70-71. Jane Mayer, "The Money Man: Can George Soros's millions insure the defeat of President Bush?" *The New Yorker*, October 18, 2004. See also Michael T. Kaufman, *Soros: The Life and Times of a Messianic Billionaire*, (Alfred A. Knopf, New York, 2002), *op. cit.*, pp. 201*ff.*
4. Edward Robinson, "George Soros Bankrolls Voter Hunt in Swing States," *Bloomberg News*, September 28, 2004.
5. Susan Threadgill, "In March, 'Who's Who' revealed efforts by John Podesta and Harold Ickes, both former White House chiefs of staff under Bill Clinton, to found a much-anticipated 'Heritage of the left'," *Washington Monthly*, June 1, 2003.
6. Greenberg Quinlan Rosner Research: www.greenbergresearch.com.
7. Jeanne Cummings, "Soros Has a Hunch Bush Can Be Beat - Billionaire Puts His Weight, Money Behind Democratic Effort to Oust President in '04," *The Wall Street Journal*, February 5, 2004.
8. Jane Mayer, "The Money Man: Can George Soros's millions insure the defeat of President Bush?" *The New Yorker*, October 18, 2004.
9. Ibid.
10. Jeanne Cummings, "Soros Has a Hunch Bush Can Be Beat."
11. Byron York, "Dems Showed Soros Secret Rove Plan," *National Review*, April 6, 2005. Excerpt from Byron York, *The Vast Left Wing Conspiracy*, (New York: Crown Forum, 2005), pp. 53-62.
12. Otpor in Tblisi: Mark MacKinnon, "Georgia revolt carried mark of Soros," *Globe and Mail*, November 26, 2003. Federal government agency contributions to OSI: Open Society Institute Form 990-PF, 2003, Schedule B. Part 1 – Contributions.
13. IRS Form 8871, Notice of 527 Status, filed under the name ACT NOW PAC – Nonfederal Account, EIN 20–0094706, dated July 17, 2003, filed 1:26 p.m.
14. David Greising, "The new face of money in U.S. politics - Soros is spending big to oust Bush, GOP paints Soros as a radical," *Chicago Tribune*, July 25, 2004.
15. The 17 states were: Iowa, Maine, Michigan, Minnesota, New Mexico, Oregon, Pennsylvania, Washington, Wisconsin, Arizona, Arkansas, Florida, Missouri, Nevada, New Hampshire, Ohio and West Virginia. Edward Robinson, "George Soros Bankrolls Voter Hunt in Swing States," *Bloomberg News*, September 28, 2004.
16. David Greising, ""The new face of money in U.S. politics."
17. Jeanne Cummings, "Soros Has a Hunch Bush Can Be Beat."
18. Leslie Wayne, "The 2004 Campaign: The Philanthropist; And for His Next Feat, a Billionaire Sets Sights on Bush," *New York Times*, May 31, 2004.

19. Open Society Institute, Form 990-PF 2001, Expenditure Responsibility Report Required by Regulation 53.4945-5(d). Also, communication from Mark Schmitt to Ron Arnold, August 28, 2006.

20. Robert B. Bluey, "Kerry's Votes on $87 Billion 'Made Perfect Sense" Says Soros," *CNSNews.com*, October 24, 2004.

21. Ross served from 1983 to 1993 as general counsel for the U.S. House of Representatives. Profile, Steven R. Ross, www.akingump.com/attorney. cfm? attorney_id=206. Edward Robinson, "George Soros Bankrolls Voter Hunt in Swing States," *op. cit.* George Soros FEC Form 5, Committee ID C90008004.

22. *McConnell v. FEC*, No. 02-1674, December 10, 2003.

23. FEC Form 1 – Statement of Organization, America Coming Together, founded July 18, 2003. "This organization supports/opposes more than one Federal candidate, and is NOT a separate segregated fund or party committee." Filing hand delivered July 29, 2003, 10:47 a.m.

24. Edward Robinson, "George Soros Bankrolls Voter Hunt in Swing States," *Bloomberg News. op. cit.*

25. Center for Responsive Politics, "Top Individual Contributors to 527 Committees 2004 Election Cycle," www.opensecrets.org/527s/527 indivs.asp? cycle=2004.

26. Lisa Getter, "The Race for the White House; With 527s, New Power Players Take Position; Through the creation of these independent organizations, at least 45 individual donors have contributed $1 million or more in this election," *Los Angeles Times*, November 1, 2004, p. A16.

27. Center for Responsive Politics, 527 Committee Activity - Top 50 Federally Focused Organizations, www.opensecrets.org/527s/527cmtes. asp? level =C& cycle=2004

28. Thomas B. Edsall, "Liberals Form Fund To Defeat President - Aim Is to Spend $75 Million for 2004," *Washington Post*, August 8, 2003, p. A3.

29. Laura Blumenfeld, Soros's Deep Pockets vs. Bush - Financier Contributes $5 Million More in Effort to Oust President," *Washington Post*, November 11, 2003, p. A3

30. Marcus Mabry, "Rich Man's Crusade - Money wars: George Soros is spending millions to defeat George W. Bush. His critics say it's bad for democracy. Soros says Bush is worse. Inside one man's crusade to change America," *Newsweek International*, October 1, 2004.

31. Edward Robinson, "George Soros Bankrolls Voter Hunt in Swing States," *Bloomberg News, op. cit.*

32. Lisa Getter, "The Race for the White House," *Los Angeles Times.*

33. Edward Robinson, "George Soros Bankrolls Voter Hunt in Swing States," *Bloomberg News, op. cit.*

34. Thalif Deen, "'Open society' Advocate George Soros Funds Plan to Block Bush," Inter Press Service, September 12, 2003.

35. David Postman, "Democrats Worried by Emerging Liberal Force," *Seattle Times*, December 6, 2003.

CHAPTER 10

THE DYE CHART

"I LITERALLY WOKE UP the day after the 2002 elections, picked up the paper, had breakfast and we were living in a one-party country. And there it was. That was my wake-up call."

What Rob Stein woke up to was the same political anguish that led Gina Glantz and Harold Ickes to have dinner at BeDuCi.

"I said: 'O.K., there's now Republican dominance down the line. It's not only that they control the House and the Senate and the presidency. But it's growing. There's no end in sight.' It wasn't only that they had reached a milestone, but they were ascendant."[1]

It led Stein to start a mini-movement.

Robert Jay Stein was an investor and venture capitalist busy guiding his own ample wealth plus a portfolio of fledgling companies through the shocks of competitive enterprise. His wife, Ellen Perry, was a wealth management consultant likewise busy guiding a moneyed clientele away from the rags-to-riches-to-rags syndrome.

Neither needed political anguish.

But Rob Stein couldn't escape it because he was also a former Democratic operative. Back in the early 1980s he had worked on campaigns for Senator Alan Cranston of California, and from 1989 through 1992 served as strategic advisor to Ron Brown, chairman of the Democratic National Committee—while Harold Ickes, Steve Rosenthal and Mark Steitz were there.

He rose higher, tapped as chief of staff for the Clinton-Gore transition team. And higher. When the Senate confirmed President Clinton's appointment of Brown as Secretary of Commerce, Stein went with him as chief of staff of the U.S. Department of Commerce, 1993 to 1995.[2]

Now back in the private sector, Stein desperately wanted to reconstruct progressive politics in America, but his resources were limited. He had neither the money of a Soros nor the rank of an Ickes.

What he did have was an unusual combination among Clinton officials, who were mostly lawyers, lobbyists, politicians and bureaucrats with no background in business or finance: he, too, was a lawyer with intensive party and government experience, but had been in business and finance since he got out of law school as a young man in 1970.

So he asked the two most businesslike questions about the Republican ascendancy:

Question 1. How the hell did *that* happen?

Question 2. What can we do about it?

ROBERT JAY STEIN

Rob Stein, born in West Virginia in 1943, graduated from Antioch College (1966) with a Bachelor of Arts degree and earned a Juris Doctor degree (1970 - Honors) from the George Washington University Law School.

After graduation from GWU, Stein married classmate Mary Ann Efroymson, heiress to a large Indianapolis-based fortune. Both worked as lawyers during the 1970s, Rob in small Washington non-profits including the Community Nutrition Institute and Community Support Fund. The Steins had three children, Gideon (1971), Dorothy (1975) and Noah (1977).

In 1974 Rob became a board member of Real Silk Investment Company (the capital of the Efroymson family's hosiery business, Real Silk Company, which failed in 1955). Its plants were sold off and the business reregistered in 1957 as Real Silk, Inc., an investment company, later sold to Lord Abbett Affiliated Funds. Part of the Efroymson family fortune went to form the Moriah Fund, currently led by president Mary Ann Stein and son Gideon.

In the 1980s Rob Stein worked on Get Out The Vote campaigns as president of the Forum Institute, with primary fundraising by Democratic Senator Alan Cranston of California. The Institute was disbanded in 1989 when Cranston was found to have obtained large donations for the organization from Charles Keating during the scandal surrounding the failure of his Lincoln Savings and Loan. Rob Stein's marriage to Mary Ann ended in divorce.

Stein remarried, to Ellen Perry, a long-time strategic advisor for families of substantial wealth. She was the co-founder and CEO of Asset Management Advisors, a multiclient "family office" (a wealth management firm for high-net-worth families), and Teton Trust Company, its affiliated private trust. She founded Wealthbridge Partners LLC in Washington in 2002, and educates her clientele to preserve extraordinary wealth over generations. As an active private equity investor, Rob Stein has served as a member of several Washington-area "angel" investor groups, including the eMedia Club, and a venture capital group, the Private Investor Network.

His answer to Question 1 was competent if not original: over the winter and spring, staying up late at the computer night after night, Stein submerged into investigative websites such as MediaTransparency.org and RightWeb.org, slogging through left wing exposés of the right wing, digging out histories, reports, articles, book reviews, annual reports of conservative non-profits, and even confidential papers going back to the 1970s—searching, searching, searching for an explanation of the Democrats' 2002 midterm fiasco.[3]

How? How did that happen? How *the hell* did that happen?

(Why is it that the Left is unhappy until it explains the Right?)

All through that winter of Democratic discontent, while Steve Rosenthal alienated minority union leaders in Florida and Giga Bokeria studied Otpor's overthrow strategy in Serbia, Rob Stein doggedly mined the vast literature on the vast right wing to see how it became a vast conspiracy.

When he finally had it all laid out and pieced together sometime in April, he beheld a chilling narrative of unbelievably intelligent conservative power-building.

It told of
- a secret memo by a high-level judge, who advised
- a handful of resolute businessmen to give
- a constant flow of carefully targeted money to
- a growing army of made-to-order think tanks and activist groups
- to train youth, cultivate issue-framing experts, and disseminate unrelenting media messages
- about strong defense, free markets, lower taxes, smaller government, family values and challenging the left agenda everywhere.

Stein tallied up some $300 million a year; nearly $3 billion since the 1970s.[3]

He was appalled.

As he would later tell many audiences, "This is perhaps the most potent, independent institutionalized apparatus ever assembled in a democracy to promote one belief system."[4]

His answer to Question 2:

Like a shaman who descends into darkness and reemerges with promises of transformation, he finished his midnight study of the Right with visions of a new dawn for the Left.

They needed to create a Left with the Right's stuff:

But there was nothing mystical about his vision.

Stein packaged his answer to Question 1 in a no-nonsense PowerPoint slide show full of box diagrams, flow charts and bullet points, a clear-cut, easy-to-follow executive summary dissecting and displaying the entire conservative juggernaut in just 38 frames.

GOING TO THE SHOW

F ROM NOTES TAKEN BY THOSE WHO HAVE SEEN THE POWERPOINT—Stein has not
published it—we know his method was straightforward.[5]

He avoided derogatory words, never said "conspiracy." He respected the
Right's achievement as a legitimate exercise in democracy.

We know that he began with a simple anatomy of the Right that looked
something like this:[6]

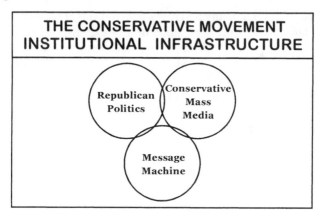

He explained what his three-ring graphic meant:

• **Republican Politics:** the Republican National Committee, state and
county Republican organizations, elected officials, and loyal partisans;

• **The Conservative Mass Media:** the message delivery system,
the television, radio and print outlets for the conservative message
machine, including talk show stars and news networks—it's the
marketplace for conservative ideas.

• **The Conservative Message Machine:** the message makers and
the message framers, a well-funded array of think tanks, legal groups,
media monitors, networking organizations, all driven by the same overarching values of free enterprise, limited government and individual
freedoms.

Stein noted that this tightly-linked infrastructure disparaged progressive
values at all levels, then he dispassionately outlined the Right's strategy:

That strategy can be traced back to one of the most prescient
documents of our time. It was a memo written in 1971 by Richmond,
Virginia corporate lawyer Lewis F. Powell, in response to a request
from his next-door neighbor, Eugene Sydnor, Jr., a board member of
the U.S. Chamber of Commerce.

Powell's eight-page memo, titled "Attack on American Free Enterprise System," is better known as "The Powell Manifesto: A
Confidential Memorandum." It contained the framework, the goals
and the ingredients for the conservative revolution that has gained
momentum and power ever since.

The Powell Manifesto addressed conservative fears directly,
beginning, "No thoughtful person can question that the American
economic system is under broad attack."
Powell laid out an obvious but daunting strategy:

"Strength lies in organization, in careful long-range planning and
implementation, in consistency of action over an indefinite period
of years, in the scale of financing available only through joint
effort, and in the political power available only through united
action and national organizations."

As history has shown, that's exactly what happened. The Powell
Manifesto charted the course for conservatives with detailed tactics to
achieve strategic strength, including:

- building a group of scholars-on-call to defend the system;
- training campus activists to be vocally pro-business;
- monitoring and critiquing the media;
- building legal organizations that could fight back in the courts;
- and building a cadre of issue-framing professionals to take a
  "more aggressive" message to the media and the public.

Powell told conservatives—and this is a direct quote:

"There should be no hesitation to attack the Naders, the Marcuses
and others who openly seek destruction of the system. There
should not be the slightest hesitation to press vigorously in all
political arenas for support of the enterprise system. Nor should
there be reluctance to penalize politically those who oppose it."

That, too, is eerily prophetic. Today we see Pacific Legal Founda-
tion attacking environmental regulations, Bill O'Reilly thumping the
"death tax" on Fox News, and Rush Limbaugh deriding any critic of the
White House.
Two months after Powell wrote the memo, President Richard M.
Nixon appointed him to the U.S. Supreme Court.
One man had mapped out the entire conservative infrastructure.[7]

Stein's PowerPoint went on like that, covering one detail after another.

- **The Money Tree:** Thirty years ago, nine conservative families provided most of the seed money that created the 60 big organiza-

tions which comprise the Message Machine. Today, the 600-member Philanthropy Roundtable provides the networking center for conservative donors (*see* The Nine Families and their Message Machine, *facing page*, which encapsulates Stein's narrative).

- **How the Message Machine works:** Flow charts show the links between money, people, messages, influence, and how conservatives set aside differences to gain power.

- **The "Investment Banking Matrix":** The key to keeping the message machine fed today is a cluster of top conservative funders and activists including Grover Norquist, president of Americans for Tax Reform; Paul Weyrich, president of the Free Congress Foundation; Irving Kristol, influential author; and Michael Grebe, president of the Bradley Foundation. They link over 200 leaders who invest an average of $250,000 a year in the conservative message machine. Some 135 of them also serve on the boards of the Big 60 groups—interlocking directorates.

- **Framing The Message:** The Machine even has experts to tell conservatives what to say if they don't quite know which words to use. Remember Frank Luntz, who was on *NOW with Bill Moyers*? He is a part of the Republican Brain Trust and has written a "bible" called *The 14 Words Never to Use* (see p. 128). It is provided to groups in the movement and explains how to frame their message.

- **Tenacity:** The Conservative Message Machine lies outside of the political life of the nation and runs day in and day out, 24/7/365, no matter which party is in office. Long term planning and permanence are its hallmarks

He ended with no grand plan, just a single slide showing where the Democrats were overmatched.[8]

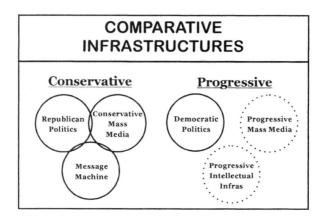

COMPARATIVE INFRASTRUCTURES

Conservative   Progressive

Republican Politics / Conservative Mass Media / Message Machine

Democratic Politics / Progressive Mass Media / Progressive Intellectual Infras

The Nine Families and their Message Machine

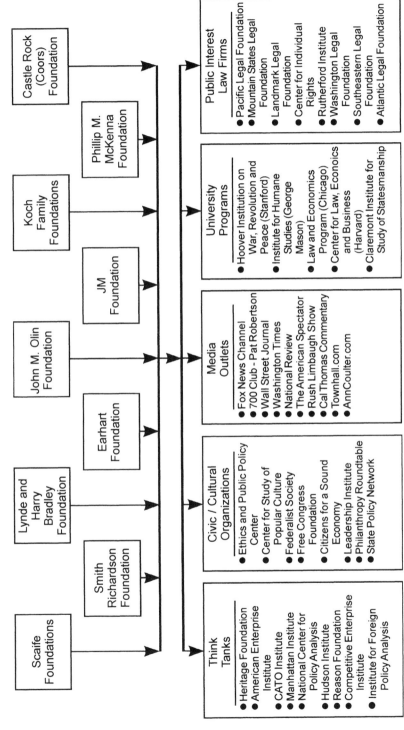

We're faced with a capacity gap between the infrastructure that conservatives have built and what progressives have.

The conservatives are tightly organized, loyal to their message, they know each other and have bonded with one another.

Progressives, on the other hand, are atomized and balkanized. Our grassroots and national groups are disconnected from our donors and our political operations. We have very few effective strategic alliances among existing organizations; very few organizations with the scale necessary to make a major impact; too few passionately progressive, politically motivated individual donors who know one another and work together; we need long-term strategic thinking; we need appropriate and necessary coordination and discipline.

He could talk it all the way through in about twenty-five minutes.

It was, in effect, a short, punchy, highly graphic update of Sally Covington's 1997 "Moving a Public Policy Agenda: The Strategic Philanthropy of Conservative Foundations," including her recommendation to project a clear alternative to the Right's political vision.[9]

It was the Powell Manifesto for the Left, addressing progressive fears directly—the Stein Manifesto.

His sole exhortation to Democrats:

Stop thinking about politics only as a succession of elections and invest in creating "long-term efficient markets" for progressive politics.[10]

He gave his show the twinkling title, "The Conservative Message Machine's Money Matrix."

It was to become the legend, the iconic narrative, the orthodoxy of the resurgent Left, and propel him to the leadership of a multi-million-dollar cell in the growing Vast Left Wing Conspiracy.

But Rob Stein didn't know that.

Now if he could only march in where Covington abdicated: convince the big left wing money that they were up against a power they could match.

By May of 2003, about the time Jerry McEntee split with Steve Rosenthal and sidetracked the Partnership for America's Families, Stein was ready to begin showing his *Matrix* piece to the big left wing money.

But how?

The big left wing money didn't know him, even though he had married into quite a bit of it right out of law school at George Washington University. His bride was classmate Mary Ann Efroymson, heiress to an Indianapolis department store fortune (the HP Wasson Co.) and the family venture into RealSilk Hosiery Company, which lost out to nylon after World War II and was restructured as an investment company. Son-in-law Rob Stein was elected to its board of directors in 1974 when he was 30.[11]

Rob and Mary Ann Stein had three children, but the marriage ended in divorce. During and after her marriage to Rob, Mary Ann Stein lawyered her way through several advocacy groups, and ended up as president of her family's foundation, the Moriah Fund, created in 1985 by Robert and Clarence Efroymson. She currently directs assets of $154 million and $8 million in annual grants, primarily to human rights, women's rights, and Jewish organizations.[12]

For all his credentials, Rob Stein still needed an escort into the halls of really high net worth. He started shopping his PowerPoint around town to friends who might know a way in. Finding the right one could be tricky in Republican Washington, where rival liberals stood on every corner peddling their magic elixir guaranteed to restore the lost glory of the Democrats.

And Rob Stein was just another guy with the key to the future.

WARRING WAL-MARTS

TWO MEN, MIKE LUX AND SIMON ROSENBERG, possessed the entrée needed to push Rob Stein through the right doors, but he wasn't close to either one. Like Stein, they were Clinton alumni, but a generation younger and about as different from one another as two Democrats could get.

Except for one thing: by early 2003 they had each assembled their own powerful political network, hoping to take control of the soft money purse that McCain-Feingold snatched from the Democratic Party—and that was $500 million in the 2000 election.[13]

Mike Lux, a far left progressive—and author of the soup memo—was first to see the opportunity. Shortly after Harold Ickes circulated his March, 2001 warning letter—a year before McCain-Feingold passed—Lux realized that if the soft money ban did pass, as seemed likely, all those outlawed contributions would go somewhere anyway.

At the time, he ran a 501c4 advocacy group called American Family Voices, immune from the proposed ban. He also ran a political consulting firm called Progressive Strategies, LLC, with a Rolodex of wealthy Democrats. He even came to sit on the board of directors of the Arca Foundation, vanguard donor to the "clean money" campaign finance reform movement.[14]

That positioned him perfectly to coordinate individual donors, issue advocacy groups, and top flight political strategists into a powerful left wing voting machine.

If he could organize a politically significant number of activist groups, he could become a one-stop account for liberal givers no longer able to write large checks to the Democratic National Committee.

So, he talked to more than 150 liberal groups, including NARAL Pro-Choice, EMILY's List, the NAACP, People for the American Way (where he had been senior vice president for political action in the late 1990s), and the League of Conservation Voters.[15]

They accepted his idea, and in August he formed the Progressive Donor Network.[16]

It took Lux eight more months to organize its public launch. He spent much of that time contacting individual donors who had contributed between $25,000 and $50,000 and organizations that spent between $50,000 and $2 million on election campaigns—and invited them to a splashy kickoff conference.[17]

MICHAEL SCOTT LUX

Mike Lux. born in Lincoln, Nebraska in 1960, is a graduate of Lincoln Northeast High School and began his organizing career as a VISTA volunteer in his home area.

From 1984 to 1987 he was executive director of Iowa Citizen Action Network, one of 32 state affiliates of Citizen Action, a three-million-member, nationwide organization that worked on consumer, environmental and social justice issues. The experience with Citizen Action made Lux one of the most radical of the Clinton White House staffers and gave him strong labor union connections. We shall see why in Chapter 15.

Lux made his way into electoral politics as a staffer for the Biden and Simon campaigns in the 1988 election cycle. He was constituency director on both the 1992 Clinton-Gore campaign and the presidential transition. From January 1993 to mid-1995 he was Special Assistant to the President for Public Liaison.

After his White House job, Lux was senior vice president for political action at People For the American Way (PFAW) and the PFAW Foundation, groups targeted against the religious Right.

In March of 1999, Lux co-founded Progressive Strategies LLC with lobbyist Thomas Sheridan, president of the Sheridan Group, to provide non-profits and PACs with comprehensive campaign management, primarily for labor unions, gun control groups and anti-tobacco groups.

In 2000, AFSCME gave $800,000 for Lux to start American Family Voices, a 501c4 issue advocacy group to attack George W. Bush. Lux formed the Progressive Donor Network as a project of AFV in 2001. PDN joined Andy and Deborah Rappaport's New Progressive Coalition in 2005.

Lux serves on the boards of the Arca Foundation, the Proteus Fund, 21st Century Democrats, Progressive Majority, the Ballot Initiative Strategy Center, and the Clinton-Gore alumni association.

Lux is married to Barbara Leigh Laur, advisor for FinnCORE, Inc., a management and development firm for non-profits. Laur has long experience in the non-profit sector. Lux and Laur live in Silver Spring, Maryland

In early April of 2002, about three weeks after McCain-Feingold passed the Senate, Lux opened the inaugural meeting of the Progressive Donor Network with a dinner featuring Senate Majority Leader Tom Daschle.[18]

The next day nearly 100 donors gathered with the presidents of major interest groups to hear presentations by House Minority Leader Richard Gephardt, Senators Barbara Boxer and John Edwards, and Democratic National Committee Chairman Terry McAuliffe.

Lux told how his American Family Voices ginned up Enron protests to disrupt White House events. CNN Crossfire hosts (and close Lux associates) James Carville and Paul Begala gave talks stressing the importance of adopting new strategies for the upcoming elections and working in tandem with independent groups in 2004 because the new campaign finance laws would take political parties out of running issue advertising.[19]

A year later, when Rob Stein needed entrée to the really big money, Lux had the muscle to oblige.

Simon Rosenberg organized the New Democrat Network, a centrist venture capital group, in 1996 at the urging of New Democrat Senators John Breaux of Louisiana and Joe Lieberman of Connecticut. At the time he was working for the Democratic Leadership Council, Al From's centrist group that laid the groundwork for Bill Clinton's '92 campaign.[20]

He took the New Democrat Network in a business-friendly, free-trade, fiscally conservative direction. His political savvy and high ambition built the NDN into one of the top dozen political action committees in the nation, doling out $5.8 million in the 2000 election cycle.[21]

Rosenberg helped organize coalitions of congressional lawmakers who embraced the NDN agenda. The New Democrat Coalition in the House had more than 70 members; 20 in the Senate. Candidates were recruited, trained and funded by the NDN, which helped elect 45 New Democrats to Congress in its first five years.[22]

He aggressively wooed business donors, particularly high-power, high-tech executives. He hosted exclusive "learning" retreats in Silicon Valley, letting donors schmooze with politicians and write large checks. Money rolled in from big names in banking, tobacco and pharmaceuticals as well as some executives of Cisco Systems and Microsoft.

Rosenberg rapidly built NDN into a vast machine, recruiting electable candidates, helping them conduct polling, holding educational seminars to make sure they knew the issues—and providing the campaign money needed to win.

NDN's advisory board reads like a *Who's Who* of Democratic politics, with Mack McLarty, former Clinton chief of staff; Mike McCurry, former White House press secretary; Joseph J. Andrew, former chairman of the Democratic National Committee; Vic Fazio, former chairman of the Democratic Congressional Campaign Committee, who did much of NDN's candidate recruiting, and many others.

The board of trustees was crammed with millionaires who cemented NDN's relations with the private sector, including Christopher Gabrieli, a Boston-based venture capitalist who had been NDN's chairman from its inception.

McCain-Feingold put NDN in the same position as Mike Lux's Progressive Donor Network—exempt from the soft money ban and well stocked with Democratic millionaires.

By the time Rob Stein began quietly showing his PowerPoint to a few friends, Rosenberg had turned NDN into a one-stop shop. Rep. Harold E. Ford, Jr. of Tennessee—who sat on NDN's executive committee—told a reporter, "It's almost like a Wal-Mart of politics."[23]

SIMON B. ROSENBERG

Simon Rosenberg was born in New York City in 1963 and grew up in New York and Connecticut. He is a graduate of Tufts University (1985). In the 1980s and early '90s, he worked as a television news writer and producer for programs that appeared on ABC News, PBS, and various cable stations.

In 1987-88 he worked in the presidential campaign of Michael Dukakis in Iowa and for Bill Clinton in the New Hampshire primary, then in the Little Rock War Room in 1991-92. From 1993-1996, he was with the Democratic National Committee and the Democratic Leadership Council.

In 1996, he was picked as director of the New Democrat Network, launched by Sens. John Breaux (D-LA) and Joe Lieberman (D-CT) as a fundraising arm of the centrist New Democrat movement, characterized by fiscal conservatism, free trade, efforts to normalize trade relations with China, bankruptcy reforms favored by business, military modernization, education reform, and investment in the high-technology economy.

Rosenberg has developed the New Democrat Network, now known by its initials, NDN, into one of the largest PACs in America. In the 2000 Gore-Bush battle, NDN doled out $5.8 million to favored candidates. The NDN 527 spent $12.7 million in the 2004 election cycle.

Rosenberg opened the way for showings of Rob Stein's "Money Matrix" PowerPoint slide show among progressive high dollar donors with his own Phoenix Group and and subsequently supported Stein's Democracy Alliance.

He was a leading candidate for the chairmanship of the Democratic National Committee in 2005, but lost out to Howard Dean.

Rosenberg is married to Caitlin Amhal Durkovich, an internet security consultant with Booz Allen Hamilton. Her father, Stephen Durkovich, is a prominent New Mexico lawyer, and her mother, Karen Durkovich, is president of the Museum of New Mexico Board of Regents. The Rosenbergs have two children and live in Washington, D.C.

MATRIX ENVY

IN THE SPRING OF 2003, Christine Varney, an NDN board member and high-ranking Democrat—a former Clinton White House aide and federal trade commissioner—hosted a breakfast at her home for Rob Stein to shop his slide show, and there he met Simon Rosenberg.

Stein told Rosenberg that he was only the third or fourth person to see the *Money Matrix* PowerPoint.

He was the first to do anything about it.

It was a most opportune meeting. Rosenberg had just emerged from a wide-ranging strategic review of NDN—it was important enough to bring in outside consultants—thinking about the next ten years and the need for an ambitious new project to build progressive infrastructure.

NDN's New York Director, Erica Payne, had even given it a name: The Phoenix Group.

Payne, a Clinton alumna herself, devised the tag after a long NDN review day, curling up with *Harry Potter and the Order of the Phoenix*.[24]

Phoenix. A fabulous bird, reborn from the ashes of its earlier life.

Progressive America.

Stein's slide show pointed directly to that rebirth.

It revealed secrets. It was charts and graphs. It was brainy. It was scary. And PowerPoints had a high bling factor.

It also didn't matter that Stein's conservative parable was nothing new in Democratic circles, borrowed in wholesale chunks from the websites he had plundered, along with ideas from liberal writings such as Sidney Blumenthal's 1986 book, *The Counter Establishment,* Michael Lind's 1997 *Up From Conservatism*, and conservative defector David Brock's new book, *Blinded by the Right.*[25]

The master-plan role of the Powell Manifesto, for example, was already an article of faith among more pious progressives.

The box diagrams and flow charts were less familiar. They showed how power works and thus gave impressive big-picture majesty to the nuts and bolts of who got how much money from where, but they, too, were not original, borrowed in concept from another source.

The genius of the thing was cramming all that into a PowerPoint with only 38 frames.

Rosenberg told me he believed Rob Stein's story would be a great tool to help fundraising for the Phoenix Group.[26]

But what would the money *really* think? He knew just the guy to ask.

Not long after George Soros hosted his Dump Bush summit in the salon at Southampton, Rosenberg made an appointment. The *New York Times Magazine* described it:

[Andy Rappaport] got a call from Simon Rosenberg, president of
the New Democrat Network, a fund-raising and advocacy group in Washington. Would Rappaport mind sitting down for a confidential meeting
with a veteran Democratic operative named Rob Stein? Sure, Rappaport
replied. What Stein showed him when they met was a PowerPoint presentation that laid out step by step, in a series of diagrams a ninth-grader
could understand, how conservatives, over a period of 30 years, had
managed to build a "message machine" that today spends more than
$300 million annually to promote its agenda.

Rappaport was blown away by the half-hour-long presentation.
"Man," he said, "that's all it took to buy the country?"[27]

It was the proper response. It led directly to the desired conclusion:
We need one of those.

Coming from Rappaport, that meant something. He was a Silicon Valley
millionaire and venture capitalist with definite ideas how he should invest his
political donations. He and his wife Deborah aimed at mobilizing younger
voters through start-up groups like Music for America and Punkvoter.com.[28]

They were intrigued with Stein's PowerPoint.

Now the pieces fell together. Rosenberg's strategic review of NDN
had found what it needed in Rob Stein's slide show.

Working with Stein to persuade the big money to make long-term political investments would become a major NDN project.

Erica Payne pestered Alan Patricof, the influential 69-year-old New
York venture capitalist—founder of Apax Partners, advisor to the World
Bank and member of elites such as the Council on Foreign Relations—to hold
a few screenings of the slide show. But only a handful of wealthy Democrats
showed up for the first Phoenix Group meeting.

RESERVATIONS SUGGESTED

ALTHOUGH HE WAS PREOCCUPIED with Steve Rosenthal, Ellen Malcolm and
the Dump Bush campaign, George Soros was attracted to Rosenberg's
Phoenix Group and Rob Stein's PowerPoint.

Its message echoed the Kallick report from a year earlier:

"What is lacking is not sharp individuals with creative ideas. What is
missing is an institutional infrastructure that brings these people together
with each other and with people who understand practical politics, media and
organizing."[29]

Soros had begun to hand off his political portfolio to his son Jonathan, a
33-year-old Harvard-trained lawyer now monitoring day-to-day the first money
going to John Podesta's Center for American Progress and Ellen Malcolm's
America Coming Together.

With Soros came Peter Lewis and his son Jonathan, a 45-year-old
restaurateur, doing the same for Daddy's money as the other Jonathan.

The two Jonathans began to travel the country asking their respective constituencies—business for Soros, the entertainment industry for Lewis—for million dollar checks to Dump Dubya.

Later in 2003, as money began flowing to America Votes and Harold Ickes' Media Fund, and then to the web-wise MoveOn.org, word got out that the Soros name was involved with the Phoenix Group. Millionaire attendance at Stein's slide show swelled to nearly 50.

Rappaport held regular meetings in Silicon Valley, drawing crowds of 80 and more. Although he didn't like the Phoenix Group name and called his West Coast crowd the Band of Progressives, he and his wife flew to New York for a session there.

As election year came, NDN chairman Chris Gabrieli held a Stein showing for the dot-com divas in Boston, with Jonathan Soros as the come-on. Rob Reiner, movie-maker and Meathead of TV's *All in the Family*, co-produced a Phoenix Group event for Hollywood glitterati. Stein was a star.

John Podesta told the *New York Times*, "I describe myself as having a master's degree in the right-wing conspiracy. Rob got the Ph.D."

THE SUNDAY JUST BEFORE THE DEMOCRATIC NATIONAL CONVENTION opened in Boston to nominate John Kerry as the Democratic candidate for president of the United States, Matt Bai's lavish 8,000-word Stein feature, "Wiring the Vast Left Wing Conspiracy," was the cover story of the *New York Times Magazine*.

Monday, *The Conservative Message Machine's Money Matrix* was publicly unveiled at "Meeting the Conservative Challenge" in the big ballroom of the Tremont Wyndham Hotel with 250 people in the audience.[30]

At every invitation-only seat was a pad, a pen, and a copy of the *New York Times Magazine*—not just a photocopy of the story, the whole thing. On a stage in the middle of the room sat Rob Stein, Simon Rosenberg, and David Brock, renegade conservative hatchet man, now CEO of his newly minted, Arca Foundation-funded progressive group, Media Matters for America.[31]

The house lights went down, Stein gave his PowerPoint, and the lights came back up. The applause was more edgy than exhilarated, at first demoralized, then infuriated, then energized.

At the end, everyone concluded: We need one of those.

Then, Bill Wasik, a senior editor at *Harper's Magazine,* asked: "How do you think a progressive message machine would differ from the conservative one? In fact, might not progressive ideas be inimical to the very idea of a message machine?"[32]

Strong question.

Stein: "The new institutions must be built with progressive values. We must build from the top down and the bottom up. In the twenty-first century, it is impossible to promote a belief system without some sort of support network that is institutionally aligned."

Weak answer.

Something's not right here, thought Wasik: there's a question left hanging somewhere.

He found it later:

What, exactly, *is* the progressive "belief system?"

The New Deal Redux? The New Left enthroned? Castro's Cuba? What?

Rob Stein's *Matrix* show unintentionally provoked that question with its charts. A whole generation of progressives had cut their teeth on certain charts that had a lot to do with progressive beliefs: the power-structure studies of left-wing sociology professor George William Domhoff—who goes by "Bill"—as laid out in his book, *Who Rules America?*[33]

The Domhoff Chart (*facing page*) presented the power structure of the U.S. not in the usual terms of the electoral system or political institutions, but rather in terms of the financial system and the influence it could buy.

Bill Domhoff, following the analysis of C. Wright Mills' *The Power Elite*, insisted that we were ruled by a small banking and corporate elite that "dominated everything in America worth dominating:" foreign policy, economic policy, population policy, environmental policy, educational policy, and legal policy—enough to be designated the "governing class."

The opening paragraph of *Who Rules America* makes the point:

> Do corporations have far too much power in the United States? Does the federal government ignore the interests of everyday people? The great majority of Americans—70 to 75 percent in some surveys—answer "yes" to both questions. This book explains why their answers are accurate even though there is freedom of speech, the possibility of full political participation, and increasing equality of opportunity due to the civil rights and women's movements. In other words, it attempts to resolve a seeming paradox that has bedeviled social scientists and political activists for a long time: How is it possible to have such extreme corporate domination in a democratic country?[34]

For Domhoff, the power elite was an outrage. It shouldn't exist.

Domhoff's work had shaped the views of virtually every activist in the ballroom of the Tremont Wyndham Hotel that convention Monday, whether they knew it or not, as we shall see in Chapter 15.

Domhoff himself was an activist as well as an academician. He was among the hundred-plus founders of the Campaign for America's Future, where he mixed with an influential network of left wing intellectuals, union leaders and activists from the Institute for Policy Studies, the Environmental Working Group, the Midwest Academy, and the Institute for Agriculture and Trade Policy, among many others (*list on pages 206-207*).

> Domhoff in a nutshell: Money is power, and social class determines who has it.
> His program, and that of his followers: undermine the ruling class and its money.

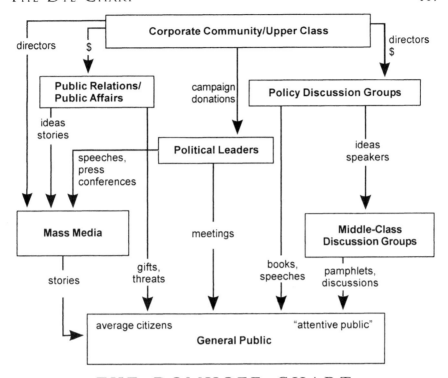

THE DOMHOFF CHART
The General Network through Which the Power Elite Tries to Shape Public Opinion
Domhoff, G. William, Who Rules America?: Power, Politics and Social Change,
5th Edition, © 2006, 2002, 1998.
Reproduced with permission of The McGraw-Hill Companies.

Domhoff got the idea of using of diagrams from political science professor Thomas R. Dye, who originated it just because he liked charts. He introduced them to political science in his book, *Who's Running America?*[35]

The Dye Chart (*page 118*) shows the same power structure as The Domhoff Chart, but more detailed and more matter-of-factly.

Dye's first paragraph in *Who's Running America?* contrasts starkly with the opening of *Who Rules America?*

> Great power in America is concentrated in a handful of people. A few thousand individuals out of 281 million Americans decide about war and peace, wages and prices, consumption and investment, employment and production, law and justice, taxes and benefits, education and learning, health and welfare, advertising and communication, life and leisure. In all societies—primitive and advanced, totalitarian and democratic, capitalist and socialist—only a few people exercise great power. This is true whether or not such power is exercised in the name of "the people."[36]

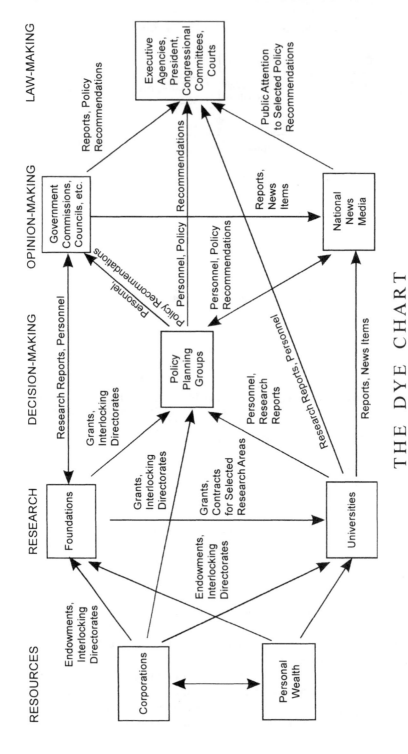

THE DYE CHART

The policy process: the view from the top. Dye, Thomas R., *Who's Running America?: The Bush Restoration*, 7th Edition, © 2002. Adapted by permission of Pearson Education Inc., Upper Saddle River, NJ.

Dye saw power in the *position*—being the executive, or editor, or dean, or senator, or president who makes the key decisions.

Domhoff saw power in the *person* holding the position—pedigree, portfolio, prospects.

The Domhoff Chart shows an outrage that must be undermined.

The Dye Chart shows an organizational system that can be captured and controlled.

Rob Stein didn't realize it, but he was trying to convince a convocation of outraged underminers to capture and control what they despised most.

Conservatives, on the other hand, didn't mind capturing and controlling the system because it never occurred to them to despise it.

And Stein's basic assumption about the Rise of the Right turned out to be considerably overstated, the role of the Powell Memo a charming fiction.

Mark Schmitt, who commissioned David Kallick's report on progressive think tanks, saw the flaw. In an *American Prospect* article, he punctured the overrated importance of the Powell Memo.

Noting—without mentioning Stein—that it was "a major feature in a PowerPoint presentation on the 'Conservative Message Machine' circulated to liberal donors," Schmitt wrote:

> Today, the Powell Memo is routinely invoked as the blueprint for virtually all of the conservative intellectual infrastructure built in the 1970s and 1980s—"a memo that changed the course of history," in the words of one analysis of the anti-environmental movement; "the attack memo that changed America," in another account.

Schmitt pointed out that most histories of the right don't attribute any significance to it at all, yet the story is practically sacred writ among those on the left.

> So why has the Powell Memo risen to this canonical status? Presumably because it helps tell the story of the institutions that support the modern right in a tidy, accessible way, and one that shows how similar institutions of the left could be designed and built. It's probably served that purpose, making the task of building an alternative intellectual infrastructure to develop progressive ideas less intimidating.
>
> But it's also a little too easy, and misleading. It implies that all liberals need to do is find our Powell, get the memo written, and implement our plan. Stand back and watch the course of history shift back our way.
>
> But the reality of the right is that there was no plan, just a lot of people writing their own memos and starting their own organizations—some succeeding, some failing, false starts, mergers, lots of money well spent, and lots of money wasted. Whether that's the model for the revival of the left, or not, it's a truth worth acknowledging.[37]

CHAPTER 10 NOTES

1. Matt Bai, "Wiring the Vast Left Wing Conspiracy," *New York Times Magazine*, July 25, 2004.
2. **Stein in Cranston campaigns:** E. J. Dionne Jr., "New Chairman Tells Democrats to Be Tough," *New York Times*, February 16, 1989. Stein and the Forum Institute: Kathleen Teltsch, "Philanthropic Groups Spur Drives for Voter Registration," *New York Times*, July 28, 1984. *See also*, "Keating Beneficiary Halts Activities," *Washington Post*, December 6, 1989, p. A10. **Stein in Commerce Department:** online bio http://www.womenangels.net/rob.html, accessed Nov. 10, 2005.
Stein Profile: **Mary Ann Efroymson background:** "317 Pass District Bar Exam," *Washington Post*, October 18, 1970, p. A29. Jim Mann, "No Consent of Spouse Required in Abortion," *Washington Post*, June 6, 1972, p. A1. RealSilk Hosiery was founded in 1922 by J.A. and L.L. Goodman and prospered for a time but fell victim to the Great Depression. It was taken over by a bank committee which gave control to patriarch Gustave Efroymson in 1932. RealSilk flourished for two decades under Efroymson family management but failed after World War II as nylon took the market. The Efroymsons laid off all the employees, sold off all their mills and facilities in 1955 and used the proceeds to reorganize as an investment company in 1957. Real Silk Company Records, 1920-1952, Indiana Historical Society – Manuscripts and Archives, Accession Number 89.0100, online http://www.indianahistory.org/library/manuscripts/ collection_guides/m0507.html, accessed Nov. 12, 2005. **Rob Stein on RealSilk board:** online bio http://www.womenangels.net/rob.html, accessed Nov. 12, 2005. **Stein in Forum Institute:** "Grants Tripled for Anti-War Studies," *San Francisco Chronicle*, May 7, 1985. "Funding Labyrinth Emerges, Cranston Group Fuinds His Son's Organization," *Daily News of Los Angeles*, July 26, 1989. "S&L Probe Hits Voter Groups," *Philadelphia Daily News*, December 6, 1989. **Ellen Perry background:** http://www.wealthbridge partners.com/website/article.asp?id=8m accessed Oct. 25, 2005.
3. Don Hazen, "The Right Wing Express," AlterNet, http://www.alternet.org/mediaculture/21192/, accessed Oct. 25, 2005. Hazen's account as well as Bai's is relied upon in the following paragraphs.
4. Bai, "Wiring the Vast Left Wing Conspiracy," *op. cit.*
5. Lewis H. Lapham, "Tentacles of Rage - The Republican propaganda mill, a brief history," *Harpers Magazine.* v.309, n.1852, September 2004.
6. Rob Stein, "The Democracy Alliance, Investing in the Future," transcription of a Seattle presentation of "The Conservative Message Machine's Money Matrix," by an anonymous attendee and forwarded to The Political Junkies website, http://www.the political junkies.net/Archived/Year%202005/Jan/Wk3/Themdems.htm, accessed Oct. 26, 2005.
7. The Powell Memo in its entirety is posted at http://reclaimdemocracy.org/corporate_accountability/powell_memo_lewis.html, accessed Nov. 14, 2005.
8. This image appears as part of a photo captioned, "NDN President Simon Rosenberg" at http://www.ndnblog.org/archives/2004_07.html, accessed Oct. 26, 2005.
The Nine Families and their Message Machine, adapted from "The Vast Right-Wing Conspiracy," by Thomas R. Dye, *Top Down Policymaking*, (New York:

Chatham House, 2001). *See also* Robert Borosage, "The Mighty Wurlitzer," *American Prospect*, V. 13, Issue 8, May 6, 2002, a review of David Brock, *Blinded by the Right: Conscience of an Ex-Conservative* (New York: Crown, 2002).

9. Sally Covington, "Moving a Public Policy Agenda: The Strategic Philanthropy of Conservative Foundations," National Committee For Responsive Philanthropy, Washington, D.C., July 1997.

10. Bai, "Wiring the Vast Left Wing Conspiracy," *op. cit.*

11. Profile at http://www.womenangels.net/rob.html, accessed Oct. 25, 2005.

12. Norm Heikens, "Family Foundations Growing in Number - and Influence," *Indianapolis Star*, July 18, 1999. Form 990, Moriah Fund, 2003. Website, The Moriah Fund, http://www.moriahfund.org, accessed Oct. 14, 2005.

13. Lorraine Woellert, "Soft Money: Is It the End—or the End Run?" *Business Week*, July 8, 2002. http://www.businessweek.com/magazine/content/02_27/ c3790074.htm, accessed Oct. 17, 2005.

14. **Mike Lux and American Family Voices:** John M. Broder, "The Labor Effort: Finding Another Loophole, a New Secretive Group Springs Up," *New York Times*, August 19, 2000. **Progressive Strategies:** profile at www.progressive strategies.net/introduction/partners, accessed Nov. 7, 2005. **Arca Foundation:** Form 990 2003, Page 5, Part VIII, Directors and Officers.

15. Thomas B. Edsall, "New Ways To Harness Soft Money In Works - Political Groups Poised To Take Huge Donations, *Washington Post*, August 25, 2002, Page A01. *See also*, Franklin Foer, "Progressive Donor Network Petty Cash - Will McCain-Feingold breed Democratic fratricide?", *The New Republic*, June 3, 2002.

16. Edward T. Pound, "Oops! The secret's out on plan to slam Bush, GOP," *U.S. News & World Report*, April 29, 2002. *See also*, Carl Cameron, "Democrats Plan Campaign Finance Alternatives," Fox News Marketwire, April 23, 2002, accessed Oct. 17, 2005.

17. Alexander Bolton, "Parties Prepared for Life After Soft Money Ban," *The Hill*, Nov. 7, 2002. *See also*, Woellert, "Soft Money: Is It the End—or the End Run?" *op. cit.*

Mike Lux Profile: Don Walton, "Activist will do his best to see GOP pays price in 2000," *Lincoln (Nebraska) Journal Star*, December 22, 1998. Profile at www.progressive strategies.net/introduction/partners, accessed Nov. 7, 2005.Progressives Strategies LLC, District of Columbia Domestic Non-Profit Corporation filing 8/17/1999 file number 992547. American Family Voices, Inc. District of Columbia Domestic Non-Profit Corporation filing 8/2/2000 file number 202862. *National Journal*: "People for Nov. 6, 1999." **Barbara Laur:** Profile at http://www.finncore.com/about_us/about_us.html, accessed Nov. 9, 2005.

18. Alexander Bolton, "Dems seek to channel soft money, *The Hill*, April 24, 2002. *See also*, Dave Boyer, "Dems to exploit finance-law loophole," *Washington Times*, April 24, 2002.

19. Pound, "Oops! The secret's out on plan to slam Bush, GOP," *op. cit.*

20. Robert Dreyfuss, "How the DLC Does It," *American Prospect*, v. 12, Issue 7, April 23, 2001.

21. Franklin Foer, "Progressive Donor Network Petty Cash - Will McCain-Feingold breed Democratic fratricide?". *op. cit.*

22. Eliza Newlin Carney, "The Money Machine Behind the Moderates," *National Journal*, Dec. 1, 2001.

23. *Ibid.*

Simon Rosenberg profile: NDN Website, http://www.ndn.org/simon_rosenberg, accessed November 15, 2005. "Rosenberg Seeks To Lead Democrats - Tufts graduate Simon Rosenberg, a political strategist with a centrist vision of the Democratic Party, is eyeing the chairmanship of the Democratic National Committee," Tufts e-news, January 29, 2005, http://enews.tufts.edu/stories/012805RosenbergSeeksToLeadDemocrats.htm, accessed November 15, 2005. **Caitlin Rosenberg:** CampaignMoney.com, NDN Political Fund "527" Contribution Details (employer statement), online at http://www.campaignmoney.com/political/527/ndn_political_fund.asp, accessed November 17, 2005. Michael Coleman, "DNC Leadership Candidate has Links to N.M.," *Albuquerque Journal*, Jan. 7, 2005.

24. Mindy Bond, "Erica Payne, Political Strategist," *The Gothamist Forum*, http://www.gothamist.com/archives/2005/01/06/erica_payne_political_strategist.php, accessed Sep. 12, 2005.

25. Sidney Blumenthal, *Rise of the Counter Establishment: From Conservative Ideology to Political Power*, (New York: Crown, 1986); Michael Lind, *Up From Conservatism: Why the Right is Wrong for America* (New York: Free Press, 1996); David Brock, *Blinded by the Right: Conscience of an Ex-Conservative* (New York: Crown, 2002).

26. Telephone conversation with Simon Rosenberg, September 25, 2006.

27. Bai, "Wiring the Vast Left Wing Conspiracy," op. cit.

28. Center for Responsive Politics, Deborah Rappaport family / August Capital / Andrew Rappaport Contributions to 527 Committees, 2004 Election Cycle: Music for America $1,600,000; New Democrat Network $1,350,000; Punk Voter Inc., $25,000. http://www.opensecrets.org/527s/527indivsdetail.asp?ID=h3003166535&Cycle=2004, accessed Dec. 12, 2005.

29. David Dyssegaard Kallick, "Progressive Think Tanks: What Exists, What's Missing," Open Society Instititute, New York, Jan. 1, 2002.

30. Rabinowitz/Dorf Communications, "Case Studies: New Democrat Network," http://www.rabinowitz-dorf.com/ndn2.html.

31. NDN Blog, "Meeting the Conservative Challenge in Boston," posted by Jason at July 28, 2004, online at http://www.ndnblog.org/archives/000443.html, accessed Oct. 3, 2005.

32. Bill Wasik, "Progressive Power," *Mother Jones*, July 27, 2004.

33. Doug Henwood, "Rotting from the head," *Left Business Observer*, Dec. 5, 2005.

34. G. William Domhoff, *Who Rules America? Power, Politics, & Social Change*, (New York: McGraw-Hill, 1998, 5th Edition 2005), p. xi.

35. **Origin of charts**: Telephone conversation with Prof. Dye, October 26, 2005.

35. Thomas R. Dye, *Who's Running America: The Bush Restoration*, (Upper Saddle River, New Jersey: Prentice Hall, 1996, 7th Edition 2002), p. 1.

36. Mark Schmitt, "The Legend of the Powell Memo," *The American Prospect* online edition, April 27, 2005, http://www.prospect.org/web/page.ww?section=root&name=ViewWeb&articleId=9606, accessed Sep. 7, 2005. Used by permission.

CHAPTER 11

LIPSTICK ON A PIG

Wᴴᴵˡᴱ Rᴏʙ Sᴛᴇɪɴ ɢᴏᴛ ᴛᴏɢᴇᴛʜᴇʀ with Simon Rosenberg in May of 2003, Democratic Senator Byron Dorgan of North Dakota read a book titled, *Moral Politics: How Liberals and Conservatives Think.*[1]

It was written in 1996 by George Lakoff, an obscure linguistics professor at the University of California at Berkeley.

It was a book about frames—not picture frames, but mental frames in our "cognitive unconscious" that shape how we see the world. Lakoff wrote that these frames are important because they influence what we strive for, the plans we make, how we act, and what we see as good and bad outcomes.

And they have a direct and profound bearing on politics—which is what fascinated Dorgan—because, as Lakoff wrote, "We discover our frames through our language; if we change our language, we change our frames."

Money may be the mother's milk of politics, as Jesse Unruh once said, but language is certainly the air it breathes. Dorgan ran the Democratic Policy Committee in the Senate. He saw the political implications, especially in Lakoff's four-word dictum:

"Reframing is social change."

Wow. You could change society by changing your language that changes the frames in voters' minds.

This was deep stuff.

Lakoff believed that experience is made possible by *preconceptual structures*, that is, paths that are hard-wired into the human brain and are roughly the same for all human beings. "We are neural beings," Lakoff wrote, "the embodied mind."[2]

123

These preconceptual structures allow us to grasp concrete things—such as hunger and pain, doing tasks and sitting still, water, stone, fire, rain, night, people, animals, artifacts, homes—as concepts, abstract ideas, not just raw perceptions. So we don't absorb information as raw material; we sift input through frames of meaning *carried in the language we use*.

Basic frames are the building blocks of thought, wrote Lakoff, which was a controversial idea in linguistics, more nearly akin to the disciplines of psychology or philosophy.

His breakaway brainchild, though, was the idea that thought is built with *metaphor*. We grasp complex and unfamiliar situations by seeing them in terms of simple and familiar concepts.[3]

For example, we build the highly abstract concept of "life" by seeing simple concrete events in a new light:

- Life is a *journey*. The person is a *traveler*, purposes are *destinations*, means are *routes*, difficulties are *obstacles*, counselors are *guides*, achievements are *landmarks*, choices are *crossroads*
- A lifetime is a *day*, death is sleep; a lifetime is a *year*, death is winter
- Life is a *struggle*, dying is losing a contest against an adversary
- Life is a *precious possession*, time is a thief, death is a loss[4]

Or another example: in debate, argument is *war*:

- He *won* the argument
- Your claims are *indefensible*
- He *shot down* all my arguments
- His criticisms were *right on target*
- If you use that *strategy*, he'll *wipe you out*[5]

And so forth.

Deep stuff indeed.

It implied that if you could frame a complicated political concept in the appropriate language, you could get people to see things in a new light and vote your way.

What intrigued Dorgan most was Lakoff's take on what conservatives know that liberals don't: American politics is about family values.

Conservative politicians favor the frame of *a strict father* (government) who sets firm rules and disciplines his family (citizens) to build strong moral backbone. The children must do what's right, work hard, and become self-reliant, responsible, adults. The father should not interfere with adult lives: the government should stay out of the business of those in society who prove their responsibility.

You can summarize their political message in eight words: "strong defense, free markets, lower taxes, smaller government and family values."[6]

G E O R G E   P.   L A K O F F

George P. Lakoff was born in Bayonne, New Jersey in May 1941 to Herman and Ida Lakoff. He earned a Ph.D. in linguistics at Indiana University in 1966, then taught at Harvard University (1965-1969) and the University of Michigan (1969-1971). He was a fellow at the Center for Advanced study in the Behavioral Sciences at Stanford (1971-1972) before taking his current position as Professor of Linguistics at the University of California at Berkeley.

As a graduate student, Lakoff rebelled against his mentor, Noam Chomsky, the most celebrated linguist of the century. Chomsky held that linguists should limit themselves to discovering the universal rules of syntax, which form the basis for language. Lakoff disagreed. He theorized that language was inherently linked to the workings of the mind, to "conceptual structures," and understanding it took more than syntax. You had to study each individual's worldview and see how ideas shaped his thought process. The dispute sparked "the linguistics wars" in the profession, and became personal and vituperative. The two have not spoken to each other since.

By contrast, progressives support a model of the "nurturant parent" who works to keep the essentially good "children" away from "corrupting influences" (such as pollution, social injustice, and poverty).

Note the contrast between the "father" in the first instance and the "parent" in the second.[7]

You can summarize their political message in ten words: "Stronger America, broad prosperity, better future, effective government and mutual responsibility."[8]

To Lakoff, it's Arnold Schwarzenegger versus Oprah Winfrey.

A year later, *U.S. News & World Report* writer Michael Barone would publish his book. *Hard America, Soft America: Competition vs. Coddling and the Battle for the Nation's Future,* commenting on this very dichotomy.

After noting that our nation seems to produce incompetent eighteen-year-olds but remarkably competent thirty-year-olds, Barone asked:

How do I explain this phenomenon? Because from ages six to eighteen Americans live mostly in what I call Soft America—the parts of our country where there is little competition and accountability. But from ages eighteen to thirty Americans live mostly in Hard America—the parts of American life subject to competition and accountability. Soft America coddles: our schools, seeking to instill self-esteem, ban tag and dodgeball, and promote just about anyone who shows up. Hard America plays for keeps: the private sector fires people when profits fall, and the military trains under live fire.[9]

Lakoff seemed to be saying coddled Americans can play for keeps too.

Dorgan, like all Democrats, had learned the hard way that there were a lot of voters out there who wanted Daddy Dubya and his strict-father Republicans to run the government. He thought Lakoff might have found a way to change that in 2004.

Senator Dorgan was so impressed he invited Lakoff to give a presentation to a Democratic Senate retreat in Cambridge, Maryland.

George Lakoff had never met a senator.

The senators had never heard of George Lakoff.

He gave it to them straight: Republicans have mastered loaded language. Democrats haven't.

Republicans frame an issue their way and pound it repeatedly until it's like a tune you can't get out of your head.

By then, their frame has become your frame.

While Democrats may have valid arguments, they are destined to lose if they accept slogans like "pro-life," "tax relief," and "family values," since anyone arguing against them looks either barbaric or stupid.

Take that phrase "tax relief." It's a message that assumes we are being oppressed by taxes and that we need to be liberated from them. The familiar frame it fits into is *persecution*. Taxpayers can relate to that.

Repeated over and over, it becomes *your* frame, and you're thinking like a conservative.

Here's the catch, Lakoff told them: if Democrats react with their own "tax relief" plan, they're unconsciously reinforcing the conservative idea that taxes are an unfair burden rather than the progressive idea that taxes are an investment in the common good.

Democrats lose from the get-go.

Lesson: if the game is fixed, don't play it.

Put the picture in your own frame.

If they call it gay marriage, you call it freedom to marry.

If they call it anti-abortion, you call it pro-choice.

If they call it free enterprise, you call it corporate greed.

You fix the game and let the Republicans stumble around in *your* universe of discourse.

THESAURUS FOR THE CHARM-IMPAIRED

LAKOFF RESERVED SPECIAL SCORN for Frank Luntz, the Republican pollster who helped Newt Gingrich frame the Contract With America in 1994.[10]

Everyone in the room knew about Frank Luntz.

He was "Republican deception personified."

He was a wildly successful market researcher. He had built his career on a simple idea: It doesn't matter what you want to tell the public, it's about what they're able to hear.

His clients were some of the most prominent Republican politicians of the last decade, including Rudolph Giuliani during his mayoral campaign in 1993, and even foreign politicians such as Silvio Berlusconi in Italy.

The Senate Democrats detested him because Luntzspeak worked in the voting booth and his watchwords won in congressional debates.[11]

Luntz said it worked because he gives his clients one consistent piece of advice: "Heed the public will."

"I've got a rule," he explained, "which is cab drivers and antique dealers know more about America than anybody else. And when the cab drivers feel a certain way, I know I need to listen."

He told a PBS interviewer, "The truth is, as much as we want to focus on politics, the American people would rather watch television. As much as we want to talk about substance, they'd rather listen to music. So I have to know what they're watching, I have to know what they're listening to, and I gotta know why."[12]

His private memos also seemed to fall into Democratic hands just as routinely as Karl Rove PowerPoints, revealing the infuriating tactics of a master framemaker who dreamed up resonant phrases and slogans.[13]

"The Healthy Forests Initiative" for the Bush timber plan.

Democrats should reframe it as "The Forest Destruction Act."[14]

"The Clear Skies Initiative" for the Bush air pollution control plan.

Democrats should reframe it as "The Dirty Air Act."

Rob Stein told PBS, "Frank Luntz doesn't do issues, he does language around issues. He figures out what words will best sell an issue, and he polls them and he tests them and he focus groups them and he comes up, issue by issue, with how to talk about it and how not to talk about it."[15]

Luntz said, "If the language works, the language works."

Most exasperating, Luntz was scholarly but not obscure.

He held a Ph.D. (Politics, Oxford University, 1987), just as Lakoff did. He taught at a prominent university (adjunct professor at the University of Pennsylvania, 1989-1996), just as Lakoff did.[16]

But Luntz's writing appeared in the *New York Times*, *Washington Post* and *Wall Street Journal*, read by millions.

Lakoff's writing appeared in unintelligible journals and esoteric books with microscopic readerships.

More to the point, Luntz was a pollster. His messages were tested and reliable Republican messages. They trounced Democratic messages.

Why? Lakoff told the senators: Democrats have been wrong to assume that voters are rational actors who make their decisions based on facts.

They aren't and they don't.

Cognitive science has proved that we are all hard-wired to respond to frames embedded deep in our unconscious minds. If the facts don't fit the frame, our brains—voter brains—simply reject them.

The Frank Luntz Memo Progressives Hate Most

The 14 Words Never to Use

Sometimes it is not what you say that matters but what you don't say. Other times a single word or phrase can undermine or destroy the credibility of a paragraph or entire presentation. This memo was originally prepared exclusively for Congressional spouses because they are your eyes and ears, a one-person reality check and truth squad combined. However, by popular demand, I have included and expanded that document because effectively communicating requires you to STOP saying words and phrases that undermine your ability to educate the American people.

So from today forward, YOU are the language police. From today forward, these are the words never to say again.

(EDITED FOR LENGTH)

NEVER SAY: Government
INSTEAD SAY: Washington
The fact is, most Americans appreciate their local government. Washington is the problem.

NEVER SAY: Privatization
INSTEAD SAY: Personalization
Many more Americans would "personalize" Social Security than "privatize" it. BANISH PRIVATIZATION FROM YOUR LEXICON.

NEVER SAY: Tax Reform
INSTEAD SAY: Tax Simplification
While a majority of Americans are generally in favor of tax reform, one-third fears that they would end up paying more in taxes.

NEVER SAY: Inheritance/Estate Tax
INSTEAD SAY: The Death Tax
While a sizeable 68% of America thinks the Inheritance/Estate Tax is unfair, fully 78% think the Death Tax is unfair.

NEVER SAY: Globalization/Capitalism
INSTEAD SAY: Free Market Economy
More Americans are afraid of the principle of globalization than even privatization. The free market economy provides opportunity to all and allows everyone to succeed.

NEVER SAY: Outsourcing
INSTEAD SAY: Taxation, Regulation, Litigation, Innovation, Education
When you use the words of your opponents you are basically accepting their definition and therefore their conclusion. We should NEVER use the word outsourcing because we will then be asked to defend or end the practice of allowing companies to ship American jobs overseas.
Rather, we should talk about the "root cause" why any company would not want to hire "the best workers in the world." And the answer: "over-taxation, over-regulation, too much litigation, and not enough innovation or quality education."

NEVER SAY: Undocumented Workers
INSTEAD SAY: Illegal Aliens
The Dems have adopted the phrase "undocumented worker" but you shouldn't. Call them exactly what they are.

NEVER SAY: Foreign Trade
INSTEAD SAY: International Trade
The word "foreign" conjures up negative images. International is a more positive concept than either foreign or global.

NEVER SAY: Drilling for oil
INSTEAD SAY: Exploring for energy
It's the picture people paint in their minds, the difference between an old-fashioned oilrig that gushes up black goop vs. 21st Century technology. Always address your concern for the environment.

NEVER SAY: Tort Reform
INSTEAD SAY: Lawsuit Abuse Reform
The term "tort" has very little meaning to the average American. "Lawsuit Abuse" is something most Americans resent.

NEVER SAY: Trial Lawyer
INSTEAD SAY: Personal Injury Lawyer
Personal injury lawyers, also known as ambulance chasers, remind people of those annoying, harassing commercials we see at 1:00 am cajoling us to sue someone.

NEVER SAY: Corporate Transparency
INSTEAD SAY: Corporate Accountability
Everyone understands and demands accountability from all sectors of the economy ... and the government.

NEVER SAY: School Choice
INSTEAD SAY: Parental Choice/ Equal Opportunity in Education
Americans are still evenly split over whether they support "school choice" in America's schools. But they are heavily in favor of "giving parents the right to choose the schools that are right for their children."

NEVER SAY: Healthcare "Choice"
INSTEAD SAY: "The Right to Choose"
This is an important nuance so often lost on political officials. Almost all Americans want "the right to choose the healthcare plan, hospital, doctor and prescription drug plan that is best for them," but far fewer Americans actually want to make that choice... too much confusion.

Luntz triggers the right frames. Democrats don't.

"If we communicate our values clearly," Lakoff said, "most people will recognize them as their own, personally more authentic and more deeply American than those put forth by conservatives."[17]

When the senators pressed Lakoff for a single turn of phrase that would capture all the values reflected in the party's many positions, he suggested, "Come home, America."[18]

The senators knew that was the theme of the McGovern campaign in 1972 and probably wouldn't work any better now. Maybe he should stick to the big ideas in *Moral Politics* and skip tactical sound bites and attack ads.

Despite a few missteps, he was a hit. Hillary Clinton invited him to dinner. Minority Leader Tom Daschle invited him to give the same presentation to a Senate caucus.[19]

He became an overnight sensation, darling of the Democrats, booked months ahead, a lecture circuit luminary who believed in free speech—he didn't charge for his talks, which was odd, even for a tenured professor at a rich state school (we'll see why in Chapter 21).

All this attention prompted Lakoff to write his most popular book, the 144-page *Don't Think of an Elephant! Know Your Values and Frame the Debate—The Essential Guide for Progressives*. It was published during the height of the 2004 presidential campaign and quickly became the bible of the Democrats, endorsed by Howard Dean, Arianna Huffington and Robert B. Reich—the great scientific salvation, handed out to campaign workers by the carton.[20]

As election results showed, he wasn't listening to the cab drivers

But then, George Lakoff didn't listen to much of anybody.

Electoral defeat didn't stop him. He carried on the framing wars with his Rockridge Institute, a progressive think tank fighting conservative think tanks with cognitive science as its sword and shield.[21]

DAD-GUM TWINKIE TALK

To no-nonsense Senator Harry Reid, Democrat of Nevada, among others, it was all just gimmickry anyway.

"I'm not a person who dwells on all these people getting together and spending hours and days coming up with the right words," Reid told the *New York Times*. To Reid, wrote the reporter, "getting the message right is just an intuitive part of politics, and he didn't need some professor to give it a name or tell him that Democrats haven't been very good at it."[22]

Common sense tells us it's good to describe things you're for in favorable-sounding terms and things you're against in unfavorable-sounding ones.

Is Lakoff's science-based euphemism and dysphemism just gimmickry?

Does it deal with issues any more than Luntz lingo?

Is his cognitive science really just political science?

Or, to reframe, is it really just partisan science?

Politicians, propagandists and peddlers alike have always sweet-talked the public, hidden important facts in fine words, and sneered at detractors. They've always directed attention where they wanted it. And—even if they're peddling science—they've always sold the sizzle, not the steak.

Is that any different from Lakoff's framing?

Take ancient Athens, for example. Everyone knows the birthplace of democracy for its Acropolis and the magnificent Parthenon that crowns it.

In 447 B.C., the ruler Pericles ordered the Parthenon built as a political maneuver calculated to win support for diverting war money in peacetime to make Athens (and himself) more impressive. By his eloquence—and money from unwilling Greek allies—Pericles built Athens into a beautiful city and a powerful empire.

How did Pericles frame his lavish expenditures? According to the Greek historian Plutarch, he told the Athenians:

> The allies have no right to consider how their money is spent, so long as Athens defends them from the Persians. It is right that, after the city provided everything necessary for war, it should devote its surplus money to the erection of buildings which would be a glory to it for all ages, while these works would create prosperity by leaving no man unemployed, and encouraging all sorts of handicraft, so that nearly the whole city would earn wages, and thus derive both its beauty and its profit from itself.[23]

How did his opponents frame it?

> They cried out in the assembly that Athens had lost her good name and disgraced herself by transferring the common treasury of the Greeks from the island of Delos to their own custody. "Greece has been outraged," they cried, "and feels itself openly tyrannized, when it sees us using the Persian War funds, which we extorted from it, for gilding and beautifying our city, as if it were a vain woman, and adorning it with precious marbles, and statues, and temples worth millions."[24]

Pericles: We did our duty, we earned the surplus, you're prospering.
      Smells like lemon-scented laundry detergent.
Opponents: We stole the money, we're an outrage, you're a tyrant.
      Smells like poopy diapers.
Or the other way around, take your pick.

It's the same with Luntz and Lakoff and their theories.
It's politics as usual, at least since the Age of Pericles.
Which smells like what is a matter of opinion.
Their results aren't.

CHAPTER 11 NOTES

1. George P. Lakoff, *Moral Politics: How Liberals and Conservatives Think*, (Chicago: University of Chicago Press, 1996, 2nd edition, May 1, 2002).
2. George P. Lakoff, *Women, Fire, and Dangerous Things*, (Chicago: University of Chicago Press, 1987). George P. Lakoff and Mark Johnson, *Philosophy in the Flesh: The Embodied Mind and Its Challenge to Western Thought*, (New York: HarperCollins Publishers, 1999).
3. George P. Lakoff and Mark Johnson, *Metaphors We Live By*, (Chicago: University of Chicago Press, 1980, 2nd edition, April 15, 2003)
4. Francis F. Steen, "George Lakoff: The Theory of Cognitive Models," Cognitive Science website http://cogweb.ucla.edu/CogSci/Lakoff.html, Communication Studies, University of California, Los Angeles, accessed Feb. 19, 2006..
5. Wikipedia entry, George Lakoff, online at http://en.wikipedia.org/wiki/George_Lakoff, accessed Feb. 20, 2006.
6. Matt Bai, "The Framing Wars," *New York Times Magazine*, July 17, 2005.
7. Wikipedia entry, George Lakoff, *op cit.*
8. Bai, "The Framing Wars," *op cit.*
9. Michael Barone, *Hard America, Soft America: Competition vs. Coddling and the Battle for the Nation's Future*, (New York: Crown Forum, 2004), pp. 13-14.
10. Rich Lowry, "Congressional Republicans Write a Contract With America," *National Review*, October 10, 1994
11. Major Garrett, "Beyond the Contract," *Mother Jones*, May 1, 1995.
12. Barak Goodman and Douglas Rushkoff, "The Persuaders," *Frontline*, PBS first aired Nov. 9, 2004. Transcript online at http://www.pbs.org/wgbh/pages/frontline/shows/persuaders/etc/script.html, accessed February 15, 2006.
13. Environmental Working Group, "Briefing: Luntz Memo on the Environment," at http://www. ewg.org/briefings/luntzmemo/, accessed February 19, 2006. *See also*, "The Luntz Memo," posted at http://www. ewg.org/briefings/luntzmemo/pdf/LuntzResearch_environment.pdf, accessed February 19, 2006.
14. David Brancaccio, "PBS Interview with George Lakoff," *NOW with Bill Moyers*, July 23, 2004, transcript posted at http://www.pbs.org/now/transcript/transcript330_full.html, accessed January 15, 2006.
15. Goodman and Rushkoff, "The Persuaders," *op. cit.*
16. The Luntz Research Companies, "Dr. Frank I. Luntz," (biography), online at http://www.luntz.com/FrankLuntz.htm.
17. George Lakoff, "Our Moral Values," *The Nation*, December 6, 2004.
18. Noam Scheiber, "Wooden Frame - Is George Lakoff misleading Democrats?" *The New Republic*, May 23, 2005.
19. Bai, "The Framing Wars," *op. cit.*

20. George P. Lakoff, *Don't Think of an Elephant! Know Your Values and Frame the Debate—The Essential Guide for Progressives*, (White River Junction, Vermont: Chelsea Green Publishing Company, 2004).

21. Lisa Vorderbrueggen, "Progressive thinkers to have forum," *Contra Costa Times*, Wed, Feb. 15, 2006.

22. Bai, "The Framing Wars," *op. cit.*

23. Plutarch (Mestrius Plutarchus, c. 46-127), "The Parallel Lives, Life of Pericles." Author's composite of English translations including "Pericles," in The Harvard Classics, Volume XII, ed. Charles W. Eliot. (New York, P.F. Collier & Sons, 1909-1914); "Plutarch's Lives," with an English Translation by Bernadotte Perrin, Loeb Edition (Cambridge, MA. Harvard University Press, 1916); "Plutarch's Lives," translated by Aubrey Stewart and George Long (London: G. Bell and Sons, 1925).

24. *Ibid.*

CHAPTER 12

RAGING
INCREMENTALISTS

IF ONLY ONE PERSON had to be blamed for the McCain-Feingold soft money ban, it would be Bill Moyers.

It certainly wasn't what the PBS icon had in mind, but he framed the campaign finance issue almost single-handedly and liberally oiled the juggernaut's wheels until the day in 2002 when the wrong law finally passed.

Back in 1979, he and producer Sherry Jones made the first documentary ever about political action committees.

They called what PACs do "the purchase of government favors."

The last scene showed yard after yard of computer printout stretching all the way across the Capitol grounds, listing campaign contributions to every member of Congress, "unfurled like toilet paper."[1]

Moyers was particularly offended by *corporate* contributions.

His visceral loathing of corporations exceeded that of Bill Domhoff, the outraged underminer. Corporate Greed. Corporate indifference.

Moyers once said, "We appear to have a government run by remote control from the U. S. Chamber of Commerce, the National Association of Manufacturers and the American Petroleum Institute. To hell with everyone else." Corporate malfeasance. Corporate corruption. Corporate scandal.[2]

He pounded that message until it was like a tune you couldn't get out of your head, as George Lakoff might say.

No one else could have pounded so effectively.

Moyers is remarkable by any measure.

He has by turns been University of Texas Class of 1956, ordained Baptist minister, press secretary to President Lyndon Johnson, newspaper publisher, author, television "deep think" journalist, and patron to the Left through his position as president of the Florence and John Schumann Foundation—now known as the Schumann Center for Media and Democracy, Inc.

It was through his philanthropy that Bill Moyers encountered Ellen Miller.

ELLEN MILLER HAD BEEN TRYING TO GET MONEY OUT OF POLITICS at the Center for Responsive Politics since 1984, filing complaints with the Federal Election Commission, tracking fundraising tactics, and later pioneering the publication of individual campaign contributions.

Miller's Center eventually made it easy for the public to follow the money on its searchable Web site, *www.opensecrets.org.*

The Center had been founded in 1983 by U.S. Senators Frank Church (D-ID) and Hugh Scott (R-PA). Its background purpose was to promote campaign finance reform by generating a continuous stream of bad publicity about money in politics.

Church had sensed that the Reagan administration was winning too well. Reaganauts had dismantled many New Deal programs and enacted tax cuts so they could never be revived.

A whole new philosophy pervaded America.

Such catchphrases as "equality of opportunity but not results" had no liberal answer.

Entrepreneurs were in.

Welfare moms were out.

Progressives felt the conservative victory was demobilizing opposition to the point that people simply disengaged from the political process.

Ironically, it wasn't just the Democrats that stayed away from the polls: Republicans too felt it was pointless to vote, only for different reasons.

Perhaps enough bad publicity about money in politics would spur campaign finance reform—and undo the Reagan legacy.

When Miller took the Center's helm, she quickly became a fixture at news conferences, preaching a razor-tongued gospel of money-pollutes-politics wherever anyone in Washington would listen.

She built a reputation for gleefully tossing out overheated zingers, like, "If the people of this country knew how bad it was, the connections, the way money pulls on legislators, they'd come to Washington and burn the Capitol down."[3]

She could have given Lakoff framing lessons: she called congressional races "auction block elections."

She scoffed at presidential primaries as "wealth primaries."

Campaign contributions were "outright bribery."[4]

In 1992, Congress fooled her and passed a comprehensive federal campaign finance bill, but President George H.W. Bush vetoed it.

That created a problem: one of her Center's golden donors gave up on campaign finance reform because it seemed to be going nowhere.[5]

Larry Hansen, vice president of Chicago's liberal Joyce Foundation and one of Ellen Miller's most loyal supporters, had to persuade his trustees to stick with it. The foundation had generously given CRP annual grants totaling $400,000 since 1988, but zeroed it out in 1993.

"I made a pitch for them to hang in there with campaign finance," Hansen told a reporter. The Joyce trustees bought it, and the money flowed again.[6]

Miller resumed her crusade mantra, "The system is rotten through and through."

She saw full public financing of election campaigns as the only adequate reform. She became an institution among quote-hungry reporters.

The trouble was, nobody in Washington listened.

THE IDEA

EIGHT BUSY BUT DISHEARTENING YEARS LATER, she reached a conclusion: Washington wasn't the place for full public financing to begin, even though she knew that was where it had to end up.

It was the right time for Janice Fine to call. Fine was an organizer for Northeast Citizen Action Resource Center (NECARC), a left wing network founded in 1984 to counteract the alarming decline in labor union power and progressive political activism.

She had a plan: she wanted to develop a model for campaign finance reform at the *state* level, and would Miller be interested in helping?

Fine explained that she got the idea from some recycled nuclear freeze activists who formed a little New England outfit called the Working Group on Electoral Democracy.[7]

They came up with the one-state-at-a-time approach and Fine presented a paper about it at a Working Group conference in the fall of 1991.

As a result, NECARC formed its Money and Politics Project with veteran Connecticut organizer Nick Nyhart as director.

Fine and Nyhart talked the Washington-based Arca Foundation into giving them a $35,000 grant for a five-state consensus-building project, using state-by-state research to criticize the role of money in New England politics.

It was natural to ask Arca because that's who paid for the Working Group's conference. Arca Foundation was Reynolds Tobacco money, about $41 million of it at the time. Arca was established in 1952 by Nancy Reynolds Bagley, led by daughter Jane (founder of Tides Foundation) from 1970 to 1980, and now run by Nancy's son, Washington socialite Smith Bagley and family. Smith is also a prominent Democratic fundraiser.[8]

Arca gave mostly to environmental causes, efforts to curb corporate influence in politics, and to fighting U.S. foreign policy towards Cuba—it would be pro-Castro Smith Bagley, another anti-capitalist capitalist, who sequestered 6-year-old refugee Elian Gonzalez in his Washington mansion during the 1999 legal battle over returning the boy to Cuba.[9]

Arca had already given more than half a million dollars to campaign reform groups such as Ralph Nader's Public Citizen and Ellen Miller's CRP.[10]

Now Fine and Nyhart wanted the research help of Miller's much bigger organization.

But it would take a million dollars to do the state-level campaigns they had in mind.

A MAJOR DONOR had been watching Ellen Miller and liked her panache. When she and Fine applied in 1992 for funding from the Florence and John Schumann Foundation, a $70 million charity based in New Jersey, they were rewarded with a substantial grant of $150,000 to NECARC and a remarkably hefty $800,000 to Miller's Center for Responsive Politics.[11]

Schumann's grant description said the money to Fine's group was "For five-state campaign finance reform project."

Nothing unusual; it was what she had asked for.

But the big money for Miller's group was to be spent "Toward reform of corrupting influence of money in electoral politics."

That was Bill Moyers talking.

The foundation's money came from Florence Ford, daughter of a founder of IBM (and relative of EMILY's List founder Ellen Malcolm), and John Schumann, president of General Motors Acceptance Corporation.

Their combined fortunes created the foundation in 1961, subsequently controlled by sons Robert and Ford Schumann.

Moyers was the hired help, with a salary of $100,043.

The position gave him a substantial voice in directing over $7 million worth of grants each year.

He made a habit of funding like-minded activists whom he later brought on his television show as guests, not disclosing the connection.

Miller, Fine and Nyhart took the Schumann money and began scouting the Northeast for a likely public campaign finance prospect.

They settled on Maine.

It was just suffering through serious political trauma.

There was an unpopular government shutdown threat, a rash of wealthy self-funded state senate candidates, and a nasty ballot-stuffing scandal involving the Speaker of the Maine House—the local press dubbed it "Ballotgate."

The system looked vulnerable.

Janice Fine went to work with a handful of activists from the Dirigo Alliance (itself a coalition of labor, environmental, and women's groups) to form the Maine Citizen Leadership Fund (MCLF), which would run the actual campaign with research help from Miller's CRP.

MCLF was funded by Arca and Schumann.

Smelling blood, the MCLF in 1993 found a sponsor who introduced public financing legislation in the Maine House of Representatives.

The bill died instantly.

Not so vulnerable.

I N JANUARY, 1994, Ellen Miller appeared on *Bill Moyers' Journal* in a segment titled, "Money Talks."

Moyers said, "Her Center for Responsive Politics is a nonpartisan group that tracks the money trail through the political jungle of Washington."

He did not say, "I gave her Center $800,000 a little over a year ago through my position in the Schumann Foundation."

Not all money talks.

During the show, Moyers fed Miller interview questions that revealed her depth of knowledge, intelligence and activist fervor.

He ended by asking her prediction: "Are we going to get a campaign reform bill out this year?"

"We are not gonna get real campaign finance reform," she stated flatly. "What I see in the House and Senate versions of reform, in fact, is freezing into place the status quo. And I think it's a kind of hoax that they're trying to pull on the American public. Which is why I think the solution ultimately will not come from Washington."

Moyers was establishing national awareness that campaign finance reform would appear first in the states.

They had to win there if they ever hoped to make Washington listen.

B IG THINGS WERE CHANGING. The happy celebration of the free market under Ronald Reagan was over.

He had wanted people to have a chance to get rich, but he didn't foresee the paper entrepreneurs and corporate raiders and leveraged buyouts.

Movies like Oliver Stone's 1987 *Wall Street,* with its "greed-is-good" villain Gordon Gekko, rubbed capitalist noses in their own triumphalism.

Prognosticator Kevin Phillips talked about it in three blistering broadsides, reflected in his book titles:

- *The Politics of Rich and Poor: Wealth and Electorate in the Reagan Aftermath* (1990)
- *Boiling Point: Democrats, Republicans and the Decline of Middle Class Prosperity* (1993)
- *Arrogant Capital: Washington, Wall Street and the Frustration of American Politics* (1994)

Phillips wrote in *The Politics of Rich and Poor*, "Many conservatives, including President George Bush himself, were becoming defensive about great wealth, wanton money-making and greed."

Moyers told him in an interview, "I was quite taken with your book."[12]

But there was more to it, mostly a loss of "social capital."

American social participation was declining all across the board—service clubs, fraternal organizations, political groups, bowling leagues—and people who belong to *any* type of group are more likely to vote.

Foundations were looking through the wrong end of the telescope: low-income voters needed something to join more than rich donors needed to be throttled. At the time, only a few obscure academicians saw that.[13]

The obsession with campaign reform never let up: in November of 1994, George Soros weighed in for the first time on electoral issues.

In a lecture at Columbia Presbyterian Medical Center on his new Project on Death in America, he briefly mentioned another "problem area I should like to do something about, but I don't yet know how:" the "distortion of our electoral process by the excessive use of TV advertising."[14]

MILLER'S MESSAGE MACHINE

ON SEPTEMBER 7, 1995, John McCain and Russ Feingold introduced S. 1219, the Senate Campaign Finance Reform Act, the unlucky incremental bill that was to suffer many defeats and reintroductions before passing seven years later to change American politics.

NECARC got a new executive director, attorney Marc Caplan, trained at the Midwest Academy, who brought new ideas and years of experience running Connecticut's Citizen Action, created in 1971 by Ralph Nader.

Caplan, Fine and Nyhart decided they could recoup NECARC's legislative losses and win in Maine through a *ballot initiative*.

They named their measure "Clean Elections" and hired activist David Donnelly to manage the petition signature gathering process.

Donnelly was an experienced campaigner who designed a layered message: condemn special interest influence while emphasizing the dazzling effects of reform and ignoring its convoluted rules.

He hustled up sixteen allied organizations, and for the footwork, he shrewdly recruited the League of Women Voters (LWV)—they wanted the bragging rights and had the largest pool of volunteers in the state.

Donnelly's campaign was spectacular.

On November 7, 1995, in a single day, more than a thousand volunteers, mostly from the LWV, collected 65,000 signatures to put the Maine Clean Elections Act on the 1996 ballot.

It would appear as Referendum Question 3: "Do you want Maine to adopt new campaign finance laws and give public funding to candidates for state office who agree to spending limits?"

Now to win the vote.

MILLER LEFT NOTHING TO CHANCE, helping to spread the ballot initiative approach nationwide, coordinating with activists in some two dozen states.

Miller decided on media saturation.

She retained the California-based Mainstream Media Project (MMP) to prepare her and a hand-picked cadre from the Working Group on Electoral Democracy and the Center for Public Integrity to use "talk radio" tactics successfully—with $120,000 from Moyers and the Schumann Foundation.[15]

With Moyers' help, Miller was invited to host a *PBS Online Newshour Forum* in late June, 1996.

In her commentary, she bemoaned the fresh failure of McCain-Feingold to pass the Senate, but giddily exulted, "Activists have seized the campaign finance reform initiative in at least 27 states."[16]

She assigned her final media blitz to New York-based Kent Communications, a professional booking company handling the 16 largest media markets.

Kent did its job well, placing Miller and her experts on more than 100 talk shows right after the parties' nominating conventions, a period of intense public and media scrutiny of the political process.

Miller also paid MMP to get reform groups to mount simultaneous call-in and op-ed campaigns to boost their talk show credibility.

On Election Day, 1996, California, Colorado and Arkansas passed modest campaign finance measures, and Maine voters answered yes to Question 3.

The measure passed by a 56 to 44 percent margin.

It would become a nationwide model.[17]

Paid for by Bill Moyers and Smith Bagley and a few rich friends.[18]

VOTER TURNOUT IN 1996 was the lowest since 1924.

Campaign spending was the highest ever.

When the news broke that Clinton, Dole, and congressional candidates had raised and spent $2.5 billion in their campaigns, people took notice.

Then the Clinton fundraising scandal surfaced, revealing that John Huang, a Democratic National Committee finance vice chair, had illegally raised more than $1 million from Korean, Thai and Indonesian influence-seekers.

People did more than take notice.

They were outraged, and let their representatives know it.

Money in politics was making front-page headlines.

Voter apathy wasn't.

Foundation administrators, the philanthropoids, had sensed the sea change in America for several years.

The Pew Charitable Trusts sensed it.

The Ford Foundation sensed it.

The Rockefeller Brothers Fund sensed it.

The Tides Foundation sensed it to the point of naming a project The SeaChange Fund for Civic Participation.

These large foundations and their peers in the philanthropy industry had previously given large sums to the environmental movement, but now felt that their work was not relevant enough to current social trends.

They did something about it.

Beginning in 1992—when Moyers gave Ellen Miller $800,000—total grants to "public affairs" projects grew much faster than philanthropic giving as a whole, nearing $1 billion annually by 1996.[19]

Campaign finance reform was about to become another "Flavor of the Moment" for fickle progressive foundations.

PRESUMPTUOUS PRETENSIONS

IN 1996, the Schumann Foundation gave more than a million dollars for campaign finance reform projects (*facing page*). $400,000 more that's not on the chart went to the Center for Responsive Politics for the usual money-in-politics projects, and for a new senior staff member.

They would need one.

On January 1, 1997, Ellen Miller stepped out of CRP and into a new job and a new world, bought for her by Bill Moyers. The Schumann Foundation's IRS Form 990-PF reported a grant to a new group called Public Campaign:

> A four-year $5,000,000 grant to support a public education campaign to awaken and galvanize broad public understanding about the issue of money in politics dedicated to the goal of building public support for fundamental reform of today's system of financing federal election campaigns.[20]

Among the seven Board of Directors members were:

Marc Caplan, NECARC;
John Moyers, Bill's son and Schumann Foundation executive director
    (and former Sierra Club public affairs staffer);
Samantha Sanchez, President of the Board and director of the Western
    States Center's Money In Politics project;
Ellen S. Miller, Executive Director, at a salary of $110,799.[21]

Moyers arranged for The Tides Center to be the group's fiscal sponsor until it received its own tax exemption, and for another donor to offer millions more—the Open Society Institute of George Soros.

Soros invited Moyers to sit on his Open Society Institute's board of directors for a four-year term, which Moyers accepted.

The Soros connection would be politically beneficial—he had given the Democratic National Committee $80,000 during the height of Bill Clinton's 1992 presidential campaign, and $100,000 during his 1996 campaign.[22]

But it wasn't just two big donors in cahoots that would make campaign finance reform the big story of the '90s.

A LITTLE BEFORE ELLEN MILLER TOOK HER NEW JOB, Moyers and Soros had joined with thirty other donors (page 143) to revitalize the Funders' Committee for Citizen Participation (FCCP), established in 1983.[23]

1996 SCHUMANN FOUNDATION GRANTS
$1,081,500 for Campaign Finance Reform

Grantee: William J. Brennan Jr. Center for Justice. $175,000. To fund a mock Supreme Court hearing and a legal scholars' conference to test the arguments for revising *Buckley v. Valeo*, the landmark Supreme Court case that blocks many campaign reforms.

Grantee: Citizens Fund. $115,000. To support public educational campaigns on money in politics in Arizona, Michigan, Georgia and Pennsylvania.

Grantee: National Voters Rights Institute. $100,000. For a groundbreaking challenge to the current system of campaign financing.

Grantee: Western States Center. $100,000. To support Western Money in Politics Project.

Grantee: League of Women Voters Education Fund. $100,000. To support publication, "Money + Politics: People Change the Equation."

Grantee: Vermont Public Interest Research Fund. $70,000. To support the Vermont Money in Politics Project.

Grantee: Public Radio International. $69,000. For "follow the money" reporting project on Marketplace, public radio's daily business and economics magazine program.

Grantee: Center for Connecticut's Future, Inc. $60,000. To fund research, public education and organizing on the issue of money in politics in Connecticut.

Grantee: Progressive Communications Systems, Inc. $57,500. To support Money in Politics Speakers Bureau pilot project.

Grantee: Environmental Working Group. $50,000. For Money in Environmental Politics Project.

Grantee: Money in Politics Radio Project. $50,000. To support on-going series of money in politics reports on Monitor Radio's national news broadcasts.

Grantee: The Public Policy and Education Fund of New York. $50,000. To support a project exploring the feasibility of organizing a campaign reform effort in New York State, culminating in a statewide conference on the issue.

Grantee: Hoosier Environmental Council. $50,000. For Restore Democracy Project.

Grantee: E-Magazine. $25,000. To support a series of two cover stories on money in environmental politics.

Grantee: Universal Health Care Action Network. $10,000. For conference of health care activists on "Integrating an Understanding of Money in Politics Into Universal Health Care Advocacy."

The FCCP had gone through its ups and downs, and 1997 happened to be one of the ups, due largely to co-chairs Larry Hansen of the Joyce Foundation and Marcia Smith of the Ford Foundation, who put some time into the basics such as planning interesting meetings—and the Clinton-Gore money scandals, of course, sparked new interest in campaign finance reform.

Quite a few of the thirty-two member foundations had realized that the action was in grassroots movements in the states—something people could join—and not in McCain-Feingold, but had no idea how to figure out which states had something interesting happening and what groups were real.

Ottinger Foundation Executive Director Meg Gage solved that with the *Funders' Handbook on Money in Politics,* a fat, detailed catalog profiling nearly 90 progressive groups working on the reform to make all other reforms possible (see protégé list, pages 144 and 145).[24]

It accelerated changes in funding that were already under way:

For example, when FCCP member donations were tallied at the end of 1996, they totaled $9 million to campaign finance reform groups.

Two years earlier, that kind of money had gone to Carl Pope's allies in the environmental movement—Ozone Action, the Wilderness Society, the National Audubon Society and others.[25]

Moyers explained the shift at a gathering of the Environmental Grantmakers Association (EGA), "We saw how environmental causes were being overwhelmed by the private funding of elections that gives big donors unequal and undeserved political influence. That's why over the past five years the Schumann brothers, Robert and Ford, and our board, have poured both income and principal into political reform through the Clean Money Initiative, the public funding of elections."[26]

Moyers didn't tell EGA his foundation's grants came from the income of:
- 2,000 shares of British Petroleum;
- 4,200 shares Conoco, Inc.;
- 10,000 shares Noble Affiliates (oil & gas);
- 10,200 shares Pioneer Natural Resource Company (oil & gas);
- 10,000 shares Royal Dutch Petroleum Company (Shell Oil); and
- 10,000 shares Shell Transportation and Trading Company (Shell Oil).

That was just a little of their big bad corporate income and principal. Schumann's Form 990s showed a lot more.

In 1997, Powell Memo debunker Mark Schmitt, Soros' Director for Governance and Public Policy at the Open Society Institute, was one of FCCP's co-chairs. He was also co-chair of the State Strategies Fund, a collaborative effort to support state-based progressive coalitions.

The FCCP was not monolithic in any sense, just a gathering of donors interested in finding out what other donors were doing. Schmitt, for example, more than once decided to not to put Open Society Institute money into something that he heard another donor say they were going to heavily fund.

FUNDERS' COMMITTEE
FOR CITIZEN PARTICIPATION

American Promise Foundation, a charity of Farmers Insurance Group of Companies: 1996 giving $2.7 million

Arca Foundation: Assets $41 million, grants paid, $1.7 million

The Aspen Institute: Assets $23.9 million, grants paid $1.2 million

Anne Bartley (daughter of Winthrop Rockefeller) no data available

Benton Foundation: Assets $17.6 million, grants paid $468,000

Carnegie Corporation of New York: Assets $1.2 billion, grants paid $55 million

Ford Foundation: Assets $1.5 billion, grants paid $439 million

James Irvine Foundation: Assets $664 million, grants paid $28.8 million

Joyce Foundation: Assets $458 million, grants paid $19.1 million

Ewing Marion Kauffman Foundation: Assets $1.6 billion, grants paid $43 million

Emma Lazarus Fund (a project of the Open Society Institute): funded in 1997 at $50 million

The John D. and Catherine T. MacArthur Foundation: Assets $2.9 billion, grants paid $130 million

McKay Foundation: Assets $5.6 million, grants paid $1.5 million

Stewart R. Mott Charitable Trust: Assets $14.8 million, grants paid $965,000

Ms. Foundation for Women, Inc.: Assets $19.9 million, grants paid $1.4 million

New World Foundation: Assets $22.7 million, grants paid $1.3 million

Norman Foundation: Assets $20.7 million, grants paid $1.1 million

Open Society Institute: Assets $297 million, grants paid $124 million

Ottinger Foundation: Assets $3.2 million, grants paid $191,000

Pew Charitable Trusts: Assets $3.2 billion, grants paid $172.8 million

Charles H. Revson Foundation: Assets $173 million, grants paid $5 million

Z. Smith Reynolds Foundation: Assets $260 million, grants paid $9.9 million

Rockefeller Brothers Fund: Assets $328 million, grants paid $11.7 million

Rockefeller Family Fund: Assets $42 million, grants paid $1.9 million

Rockefeller Foundation: Assets $3.2 billion, grants paid $94.8 million

Florence and John Schumann Foundation: Assets $70.8 million, grants paid $6.3 million

Solidago Foundation: Assets $11.2 million, grants paid $51,000

Stern Family Fund: Assets $2.5 million, grants paid $200,000

Surdna Foundation: Assets $382 million, grants paid $18.5 million

Tides Foundation: Assets $34.4 million, grants paid $6.3 million

Twentieth Century Fund: (now the Century Foundation): Assets $69 million, grants paid $1.2 million

Unitarian Universalist Veatch Program at Shelter Rock: Assets $30 million, grants paid $9.2 million

FUNDERS' COMMITTEE FOR CITIZEN PARTICIPATION PROTÉGÉS

1. 20/20 Vision for Peace and the Environment
2. Advocacy Institute
3. Alabama Arise
4. Alabama New South Foundation
5. Alaska Public Interest Research Group
6. American Friends Service Committee
    "Dollars and Democracy: The Search for the Common Good"
7. Arizona Citizens Fund
8. Arkansas Campaign Reform Project
9. Arkansas Institute for Social Justice
10. Association of Community Organizations for Reform Now (ACORN):
    "Money and Politics Project"
11. Brennan Center for Justice at New York University School of Law
    "Democracy Program"
12. Brookings Institution
13. California Public Interest Research Group Charitable Trust/CALPIRG
14. California Voter Foundation
15. Center for Connecticut's Future: "Connecticut Money and Politics Project"
16. Center for Governmental Studies
17. Center for Insurance Research
18. Center for Investigative Reporting
19. Center for Media and Democracy
20. Center for Political Reform
21. Center for Public Interest Research
22. Center for Responsive Politics
23. Center for Voting and Democracy
24. Citizen Policy and Education Fund of New Jersey "Money-in-Politics Project"
25. Citizens Fund: Campaign Finance Reform Program
26. Citizens Policy Center "Ohio Open Secrets Project"
27. Citizens Research Foundation
28. Colorado Public Interest Research Foundation
29. Common Cause
30. Commonwealth Education Project
31. Communities for a Better Environment
32. Connecticut Citizen Research Group
33. Data Center: "Money-in-Politics Project"
34. Democracy South
35. Environmental Information Center
36. Environmental Research Foundation
37. Environmental Working Group: "Money and Environmental Politics"
38. Equality State Policy Center
39. Greater Birmingham Ministries
40. Hoosier Environmental Council "Restore Democracy Coalition"
41. Illinois Issues / Illinois Campaign Finance Project
42. Institute for Washington's Future: Coalition for a Livable Washington
43. Investigative Reporters and Editors Campaign Finance Information Center

FUNDERS' COMMITTEE FOR CITIZEN PARTICIPATION PROTÉGÉS

44. League of Women Voters Education Fund / The Harwood Group:
    "Money + Politics: People Change the Equation"
45. Maine Citizen Leadership Fund Money-In-Politics Project
46. Maine Voters for Clean Elections
47. Mainstream Media Project
48. Media Access Project
49. Michigan Citizens Fund: Michigan Money-in-Politics Campaign
50. Minnesota Alliance for Progressive Action Education Fund: "Money-in-Politics Project"
51. Missouri Alliance for Campaign Reform
52. Missouri Citizen Education Fund
53. Money-in-Politics Radio Project
54. Montana Public Interest Research Group
55. Mother Jones Magazine and the Foundation for National Progress
56. National Institute on Money in State Politics
57. National Public Radio "Money, Power, and Influence Beat"
58. National Voting Rights Institute
59. Natural Resources Council of Maine
60. New Jersey Public Interest Research Group (NJPIRG) Law and Policy Center
61. New York Public Interest Research group Fund Government Reform Project
62. North Carolina Alliance for Democracy
63. Northeast Citizen Action Resource Center: "Money and Politics Project"
64. Office for Social Policy Research at Northern Illinois University
65. OMB Watch/The Unison Institute "Right-to-Know Computer Network"
66. OSPIRG Foundation
67. Pennsylvania Citizens Fund
68. Progressive Leadership Alliance of Nevada
69. Project South Money in Politics Program
70. Project Vote Smart
71. Public Campaign
72. Public Citizen
73. Public Policy and Education Fund on New York Campaign for Clean Elections
74. Radio and Television New Directors Foundation Election Project
75. Re-Visioning New Mexico: "Project Democracy"
76. Right Question Project
77. Rockefeller Institute of Government at SUNY Albany
78. Sierra Club Foundation
79. Southern Echo
80. U.S. Public Interest Research Group Education Fund
    "Americans Against Political Corruption"
81. United Vision for Idaho: "Following the Money Trail" Project
82. Vermont Public Interest Research Group: "Vermont Money and Politics Project"
83. Washington Citizen Action Education & Research Fund: "Money in Politics Project"
84. Western States Center: "Money in Western Politics Project"
85. Wisconsin Democracy Campaign
86. Working Group on Electoral Democracy
87. World Policy Institute

FCCP was like most foundation committees: a dedicated core attended meetings, while others loyally paid their dues but never once showed up.

If any one thing united them, it was their interest in funding groups only on the Left.

Meg Gage's *Handbook* showed them how to do that. It explained what each activist group did and why they should receive grants. Its profile of the Foundation for National Progress, owner of *Mother Jones* magazine, showed what public campaign financing was really for:

> *Mother Jones* writers have described public financing as a "gateway" reform, without which progressive change in areas such as health care, the environment, industrial policy, and the regulation of financial markets may be impossible.[27]

The real reason for getting money out of politics was getting leftists into politics—another "pleasure of ulteriority," as Robert Frost would say.

When total grants for campaign reform from all sources were tallied just before the election of 2004, foundation expenditures for the past decade amounted to a whopping $140 million.

However, 88 percent—$123 million—came from only eight foundations, seven of them members of FCCP: the Pew Charitable Trusts; Moyers and the Schumann Foundation; Carnegie Corporation; Joyce Foundation; George Soros' Open Society Institute; and the Ford and MacArthur foundations.[28]

The only maverick, Jerome Kohlberg Trust—which showed no need of the *Handbook*—donated $100,000 to a group that ran ads saying "Let's get the $100,000 checks out of politics," according to George Will.[29]

In May 1996, George Soros made a small investment in the future with a $2,000 campaign contribution to Senator John Kerry, Democrat of Massachusetts, and $500 to Senator Paul Wellstone, Democrat of Minnesota—and later in the year, nearly $125,000 to four Democratic committees.[30]

No Soap for Clean Money

1997 LOOKED TO BE A VERY GOOD YEAR for the campaign finance debate. In early January, newly re-elected Senator Paul Wellstone set the tone. He nearly tied the Senate in knots on the first day of the new Congress by threatening a parliamentary maneuver to block the evening adjournment— always early, so senators could attend the usual reunions—unless the leadership promised action on campaign finance reform in the first 100 days.

Rude and crude, but effective. It angered even his friends. The leaders of both parties tried for thirty minutes to cajole him out of it with general assurances but no firm date. Wellstone wouldn't budge. Finally, John McCain, the strongest Republican supporter of campaign finance reform, walked over to his desk and spoke with him privately. Wellstone withdrew his threat. Nobody knew what McCain told him, but the fracas made headlines.[31]

Two weeks later, McCain and Russ Feingold introduced S. 25, the Bipartisan Reform Act of 1997, reviving their defeated 1995 bill. Wellstone was one of the co-sponsors. So was John Kerry of Massachusetts.[32]

Kerry and Wellstone had their staffs quietly working on a federal version of the Maine clean money law. Senator Wellstone's legislative director, Brian Ahlberg, knew the clean money crowd through connections with the Citizen Action network (which we will explore in Chapter 15)—he had been one of Nader's Raiders in the Minnesota Public Interest Research Group before joining Wellstone's staff in 1991.

The staffers were busy researching the Maine law in late February when they heard that Senate Joint Resolution 18 had been introduced.

It was a proposed amendment to the Constitution of the United States giving Congress unlimited power to limit campaign finance.[33]

Senator Ernest F. Hollings, Democrat of South Carolina, and nine co-sponsors, felt the Constitution needed changing because the Supreme Court kept telling Congress it had no such power.

Congress had most recently tried in the Federal Election Campaign Act of 1971 (FECA).[34]

But the Supreme Court struck down much of that law in the landmark case of *Buckley v. Valeo* (1976).[35]

The high court ruled that, "The First Amendment denies government the power to determine that spending to promote one's political views is wasteful, excessive, or unwise. In the free society ordained by our Constitution it is not the government but the people—individually as citizens and candidates and collectively as associations and political committees—who must retain control over the quantity and range of debate on public issues in a political campaign."

That infuriated liberals, who said it equated money with free speech—the more you have, the louder you speak.

Not exactly, as the Court explained: "A restriction on the amount of money a person or group can spend on political communication during a campaign necessarily reduces the quantity of expression by restricting the number of issues discussed, the depth of their exploration, and the size of the audience reached. This is because virtually every means of communicating ideas in today's mass society requires the expenditure of money."

But what about fairness? Liberals wanted a "level playing field," as Moyers and Miller and their money loudly proclaimed.

The Court, with notable restraint, said: "The concept that government may restrict the speech of some elements of our society in order to enhance the relative voice of others is wholly foreign to the First Amendment."

Checkmate.

The only thing left for progressives was to resurface the uneven playing field with a constitutional amendment.

Two weeks later the Senate killed it by a vote of 61-38.[36]

That same day, March 18, Senators John Kerry, Paul Wellstone and John Glenn announced plans to introduce a sweeping clean money bill.[37]

In addition to public funding of candidates who could show a minimum level of public support (by collecting a set number of small donations), the bill would have provisions for limiting the duration of campaigns, said Kerry. It would also give candidates free or discounted television time, curtail interest-group advertising that targets candidates, and ban unrestricted soft money contributions.[38]

It was the best of times for the bill. The Clinton campaign scandal outraged millions. Washington pollster Richard Harwood surveyed voters and found both a yearning for reform and deep cynicism. He warned that reformers should proceed with care, "because any fix that fails to fundamentally restructure the relationship between money, politicians, and policy will lead to a greater alienation between Americans and their leaders."

The finding may have been optimistic: Harwood personally preferred public funding.[39]

It was the worst of times for the bill. The campaign reform movement being cultivated by the Funders' Committee for Citizen Participation was, like Don Quixote, riding off in all directions.

Ann McBride, president of Common Cause, the granddaddy of grass-roots political reform groups, pushed the incremental McCain-Feingold bill, saying, "Public financing is a goal we support, but it's not going to happen this year; McCain-Feingold is achievable in this Congress."

Ellen Miller said, "Incremental reform could be more dangerous than no reform at all if the public thinks we've put the money genie back in the bottle."

The reformers had circled the wagons and started shooting inside.

On June 17—the 25th anniversary of the Watergate break-in—John Kerry rose in the Senate to introduce S. 918, "A bill to reform the financing of Federal elections," titled The Clean Money, Clean Elections Act of 1997.

The reform that makes all other reforms possible.

Finally.

Senate Majority Leader Trent Lott frowned, "We're not for food stamps for politicians."

Kerry told a reporter that the real meal ticket was "paid to incumbents by large corporations and special interests."

In his introduction, he said:

Americans believe that their Government has been hijacked by special interests, that the political system responds to the needs of wealthy special interests, not the interests of ordinary, hard-working citizens. They sense, in many ways, that the Congress is not necessarily "the people's house."[40]

It had five co-sponsors: Kerry, Paul Wellstone, John Glenn, Joe Biden, and Patrick Leahy.

It was referred to the Committee on Rules and Administration.

And never seen again.

Rep. John Tierney introduced a companion bill, H.R. 2199, in the House, with 27 co-sponsors.

It was referred to the Committee on House Oversight.

And never seen again.

Such an ignominious exit could have told supporters something.

But Moyers and Soros and the Funders' Committee kept spending their foundation money on clean money.

After all, it was the gateway reform, the reform that makes all other reforms possible.

And perhaps gets leftists into office.

So they kept spending.

And spending.

And spending.

After a year at Public Campaign, Ellen Miller proved abrasive, and NECARC's Nicholas Nyhart was recruited to take her place (at $86,496).

Miller was shuffled off to TomPaine.com, a startup web-based liberal message machine run by Bill Moyers' son John as a project of the new Florence Fund, a $4.5 million chunk of the Schumann money.[41]

The spending and shuffling only gave the less radical McCain-Feingold soft money ban better odds in the next session of Congress. And the next. And the next.

And McCain-Feingold was itself sufficiently radical to raise profound concerns over suppressing free speech.[42]

One member of the Funders' Committee had never believed a federal clean money bill could pass. Its philanthropoids were scrupulously realistic. They were the kind of administrators that regarded their grants as investments and demanded tangible results for their money.

Therefore, they set realistic goals: while they gave polite lip service to the clean money movement, their heavy grants went to incremental projects that had a chance of winning.

How Do You Eat an Elephant?

"WE SIMPLY DO NOT BELIEVE the nation can legislate better campaigns," said Paul Light. "It has to come from the candidates and voters, who must both agree to a higher standard of conduct if America is to renew elections as meaningful events of democratic life."[43]

Dr. Light (Ph.D., University of Michigan, 1980) spoke as Public Policy Program director of the Pew Charitable Trusts. He was talking about a two-year, $800,000 grant to the Institute for Global Ethics in Camden, Maine.

It was for their Project on Campaign Conduct, which was to create voluntary, candidate-approved codes in two states, Ohio and Washington State, during the 1998 election cycle, then publicize the codes among voters and evaluate the results. It would finally explore the feasibility of creating a national code of ethics for the elections in 2000. It didn't pan out.

Pew President Rebecca W. Rimel had hired Light in 1995 to retarget their multi-million-dollar Public Policy Program from its earlier emphasis on bringing democracy and free markets to former Soviet bloc countries in Eastern Europe.

Rimel believed we had plenty of problems with democracy at home.

She told one reporter, "It's quite disturbing when you look at the number of people who have checked out of the civic process."[44]

She told another, "Shifting our Public Policy grantmaking to improving and restoring the American democratic process was a natural—and much needed—focus for us."[45]

As part of the money elite, she feared a legitimation crisis. Light's early Pew grants tried to head it off by finding out what was politically possible.

While Bill Moyers gave a million dollars to the National Voting Rights Institute to come up with legal strategies for clean money elections, Paul Light spent $450,000 on the League of Women Voters Education Fund for their "Money + Politics: People Change the Equation" project using "citizen assemblies" to find unbiased answers to key questions:

- Does access to wealth determine who can run for major office?
- Why are federal election campaigns so expensive?
- Do campaign contributions buy influence? and
- What are the merits of the various reform proposals?

The "assemblies" were actually focus groups sponsored by the League and run in six cities by The Harwood Group, a for-profit company owned by the same Richard Harwood who had warned against feeble reforms. The League's publicity indicated broad acceptance of public campaign finance.[46]

What they really found, according to a Harwood staffer, was:

- Elections were the place where people felt closest to democracy.
- Although public funding of elections was one possible option to restore faith in the democratic process, it was still just "welfare for politicians."
- Nobody in the public understood where campaign money came from or went to.
- They didn't care and couldn't do anything about it anyway, i.e., there was no constituency for campaign finance reform.[47]

That gave Light pause.

But he was impressed by the Harwood chief of staff who managed the project, a young lawyer and former Capitol Hill staffer named Sean Treglia. Rimel hired him in 1997 to help Light while Pew was still testing the waters.[48]

Treglia showed up for many meetings of the Funders Committee on Citizen Participation, brashly telling everyone what great work he was doing at Pew, which was one reason that George Soros funded Public Campaign with $2.5 million for hard-edged clean money advocacy, and gave nothing to a Treglia project with the American Enterprise Institute and the Citizens' Research Foundation: Pew funded it with $400,000 for an unusual seven-round summit called the Working Group on Campaign Finance Reform, with results posted on the website of the Brookings Institution.[49]

Soros misjudged that one.

The Working Group of high-powered minds probed S. 1219, the first McCain-Feingold bill, and several other reform proposals, including the clean money concept, looking for politically feasible answers.

The panel found cause for concern in the Clinton campaign finance abuses, but came away skeptical about most of the reform legislation they considered, including clean money—out of step with most FCCP funders.[50]

After the Working Group disbanded, panelists Norman Ornstein, Thomas Mann, Michael Malbin, Anthony Corrado, and Paul Taylor collaborated to identify the most urgent problems with federal campaigns:[51]

- soft money contributions to political parties;
- the abuse of "issue advocacy" advertising in political campaigns;
- the advantages of incumbency;
- the potential influence of large contributors; and
- the weakness of the FEC as a regulatory agency.

They proposed a five point, politically realistic and bipartisan reform approach: the elimination of soft money, narrowing the definition of "issue advocacy," providing free media access for qualifying candidates, establishing a tax credit for small in-state contributions, and measures to strengthen the FEC.

Corrado, Mann, and others compiled the results in *Campaign Finance Reform: A Sourcebook*. Some of it later found its way into McCain-Feingold.[52]

Most of the authors later found their way into Senator John McCain's own foundation, the Reform Institute, as advisors or paid staff.

They were stacking the incremental deck.

This early Pew research into political possibility gave the Trusts an edge in later advocacy: they knew enough to generate the missing constituency for incremental reform—or at least the perception of a constituency.

"Incremental" was the key. Pew's IRS Reports from 1997 to 2000 listed one grant after another for "incremental campaign finance reform."

- $870,000 to the Aspen Institute, 1997;
- $950,000 to the Committee for Economic Development, 1999;
- $867,000 to the University of Southern California's Annenberg School for Communication, 2000;
- $1,522,000 to George Washington University's Graduate School of Political Management, 2000;
- $1,300,000 to Anthony Corrado's Colby College, 2000.

And so on until Pew had incrementally invested over $20 million and McCain-Feingold became law.[53]

What did all those grantees spend it on?

Simple: creating a constituency where there was none.

It was no big secret. They admitted it from the start. Take that $1.3 million grant to Tony Corrado's Colby College. The official purpose says, "For project to strengthen campaign finance reform debate."[54]

What does that mean? How can a tiny college perched on Mayflower Hill above Waterville, Maine influence a huge national debate?

Colby's own news release explained:

A $1.3-million project to bring new voices into the debate over campaign finance reform was recently funded by The Pew Charitable Trusts and is being administered by Colby College. Associate Professor of Government Anthony J. Corrado, the principal investigator for the grant, is working with two influential nonprofit organizations, the Interfaith Alliance Foundation and The Greenlining Institute, and undergraduates at Colby are involved in research for the project.

Corrado, one of the leading national experts on campaign finance, sees broad public involvement in the debate as a catalyst for change. "Reform is more likely when a diverse coalition of people raise their voices in an effort to fix problems in the campaign finance system, but the notion that 'the public doesn't care' is perceived as a barrier to reform," he said. The goal of the new project is to expand the coalition of voices engaged in the discussion beyond Washington insiders and public interest groups that traditionally shaped the debate.[55]

It wasn't deceptive. It was perfectly plain.

Pew was buying a constituency—and doing it the smart way.

Pew knew about those obscure academicians (page 138) who found that people are more likely to vote if they belong to *any* type of organization, and particularly that low-income black church members have unexpectedly high rates of political participation. But it wasn't the diversity of the coalition that made people participate, it was the simple fact of *belonging*. Corrado used Pew money *to buy groups people could belong to*—any agreeable group.

By 2002 when McCain-Feingold finally passed, a lot of agreeable groups were making a lot of noise all over the country.

It was all made-to-order noise, democracy for hire.

You didn't see this backstory in the *New York Times* on McCain-Feingold Day because the *New York Times* didn't notice the news release from that little college on the hill above Waterville, Maine.

They also didn't notice that Tony Corrado worked in 1999 to recruit *businesses* for incremental reform.

Or that serious worry was emerging in corporate boardrooms about global capitalism and its legitimacy, which prompted them to be recruited.[56]

Or that Corrado had a Pew grant of $950,000 to do the recruiting through the Committee for Economic Development.

Or that he got another $1,496,000 from Pew for the big finish in 2002.

And he was only one of many.

Lesson One: manufactured constituencies make just as much noise as natural ones.

Lesson Two: do not underestimate the power of Rebecca Rimel.

After all, she's the lady who sponsored "civility" retreats for the entire U.S. House of Representatives, Democrats and Republicans, at the luxurious Greenbrier Resort—and about a third of them actually showed up in 2001, right after a nasty partisan tax-cut vote, and made nice, sort of.

Civility, one bite at a time.[57]

The core of her philanthropy at Pew was incrementalism.

She didn't call it plain "incrementalism."

She called it "raging incrementalism."

When asked about it by *Philanthropy* magazine, she responded:

> [W]e can be smart about what we do—we can be what I call "raging incrementalists," by which I mean we can be very focused and very strategic and use resources, ideas, individuals, and institutions out there to move the needle on certain key issues. It's pretty unlikely that a single foundation is going to "solve poverty" or some other huge objective. But if a foundation says that it's going to invest a lot of time, a lot of energy, and work with a lot of smart people on a very targeted specific objective, that's creative good work. That doesn't mean that they need to create new entities, although in some cases the proper organizational structures don't exist. We should really be judged by how smart and creative we can be at finding the best talent out there.[58]

Which says nothing about increments or rage. Or obscure academicians.

Although Rimel spoke in the lemon-scented evasions of foundationese—a language capable of making the deliberate destruction of rural logging communities sound like a Mother's Day beautification project—raging incrementalism was simply a strategic way to push political goalposts leftward inch by inch, year after year, rather than trying to leap tall buildings at a single bound.

It's easier, cheaper, and less visible.

Rimel's increments were little steps in a big strategy—"strategy" in its usual meaning of "a long-term plan to achieve a goal."

The goal was never explicitly stated, but it could be any large change in society that Pew might think desirable, perhaps a Socialist America on the European model of social democracy—a broadly capitalist system (that preserved foundation wealth), but with labor unions in substantial power through their own political parties, a fairly thoroughgoing welfare state with key social reforms intended to make it "more equitable and humane," including shorter work weeks, socialized medicine, long vacation and sick leave benefits, and featherbedding for surplus workers.

Public funding of elections was certainly at the heart of European social democracy, even if not very close to the heart of America.

But McCain-Feingold's ban on soft money could be a small step closer. And it looked possible. It would open the way to greater power for wealthy progressive non-profits, and imagine what they might do for democracy.

So McCain-Feingold could reasonably be construed as an incremental step toward social democracy. Get that, then come back later for more.

Rimel's raging was her steely willingness to break a little crockery (and read a few academic journals) to reach her goals.

No constituency? Buy one. None available? Create it.

Message to grantees: You'll be smart enough to find things that work, you'll get the job done together, and we'll all be happy. Or you're out.

Is it a legitimate exercise of democracy? Of course it is.

Do you have to like it? Of course you don't.

There were a lot of people who didn't like it on November 6, 2002, when McCain-Feingold went into effect.

Harold Ickes.

Andy Stern.

Gina Glantz.

Ellen Malcolm.

Steve Rosenthal.

Carl Pope.

Probably most of all, Bill Moyers.

Think of all that money.

Think of all that effort.

Think of all that outrage.

He built the Clean Money stage and gave Ellen Miller a starring role in Clean Money Act I. He wrote his friend George Soros and the Funders' Committee into the plot complications of Clean Money Act II.

Then, in a classic Third Act twist ending, Rebecca W. Rimel raged away with the incremental denouement.

If the tail credits ever roll on the unlikely docudrama, *How We Really Got McCain-Feingold,* the top name will surely be Bill Moyers.

CHAPTER 12 NOTES

1. Bill Moyers, "Journalism & Democracy: On the Importance of Being a 'Public Nuisance,'" *The Nation*, May 7, 2001. *See also*, Bill Moyers, "Why Journalism Matters," *The Record* (Bergen County, New Jersey), September 26, 2004.
2. Bill Moyers, Speech to the National Press Club, hosted by PBS to observe his thirtieth year as a broadcast journalist, Washington, March 22, 2001.
3. Bill Moyers' Journal, "Money Talks," Show #BMJ-5, *op. cit.*
4. *Ibid.*
5. S. 3, Senate Election Ethics Act, passed 56-42 May 23, 1991; H.R. 3750, House of Representatives Spending Limit and Election Reform Act, passed 273-156 November 25, 1991. The House adopted the S. 3 conference report 259-165 April 9, 1992. Bush vetoed bill May 9, 1992; Senate failed to override veto 57-42 (9 votes short of 2/3) May 13, 1992.
6. Justin Torres, "Big Money and Foundation Cash: How foundations helped spur campaign finance reform," *Philanthropy*, March / April 2001.
7. The Working Group was founded in 1988. Laura Orlando, "The Clean-Elections Movement," *Dollars and Sense* magazine, July / August 2000, www.third worldtraveler.com/Political_Reform/CleanElections_ Movement. html, accessed Nov. 16, 2005.
8. James Crotty, "Nancy Bagley: Babe of the Beltway," *Monk Magazine*, March 31, 1999, www.monk.com/display.php?p=People&id=25, accessed Sep. 15, 2005.
9. Arca Foundation website, http://www.arcafoundation.org/pages/history.htm, accessed Sep. 12, 2005. See also, Frances Robles, "Elian outing in Washington brings criticism in Miami - Motive behind party questioned," *Miami Herald*, May 9, 2000, posted www.cubanet.org/CNews/y00/may00/09e9.htm, accessed Nov 13, 2005.
10. Arca Foundation Form 990-PF, 1991, 1992.
11. Florence and John Schumann Foundation, IRS Form 990-PF, 1992, 1993.
12. "Bill Moyers Interviews Kevin Phillips,*"* *NOW with Bill Moyers*, April 9, 2004. www.pbs.org/now/transcript/transcript_phillips.html, accessed January 2, 2006.
13. Steven J. Rosenstone and John Mark Hansen, *Mobilization, Participation, and Democracy in America* (New York: Macmillan, 1993), p. 167.
14. George Soros, "Reflections on Death in America," the Alexander Ming Fisher Lecture Series at Columbia Presbyterian Medical Center, New York City, November 30, 1994, www2.soros.org/death/george_soros.htm, accessed April 14, 2006.
15. Mainstream-Media Project, "Campaign Finance Reform: Exploring the 'Clean-Money' Option, mainstream-media.net/html/campaigns/campaign_ fin_reform.html accessed Sep. 16, 2005. See also, profile of Mainstream Media Project in *Funders' Handbook on Money in Politics*, dated November 20, 1996. Funding: Schumann Foundation Form 990, 2002, Statement 14.
16. Ellen Miller, "Follow the Money," *PBS Online Newshour Forum*, October 18, 1996, www.pbs.org/newshour/forum/october96/cfr_10-18.html, accessed Sep.12, 2005.
17. David Donnelly, Janice Fine, and Ellen S. Miller, "Going Public," *Boston Review*, April / May 1997, www.bostonreview.net/BR22.2/donnelly.html. accessed Sep. 16, 2005.

18. Form 990-PF, 1996 and 1997 for Schumann and Arca Foundations.
19. Paul Van Slambrouck, "Charitable foundations turn their gazes closer to home," *Christian Science Monitor*, December 12, 1998.
20. Schumann Foundation, Form 990-PF, 1998.
21. Public Campaign, Form 990, 1998, Part V, p. 4.
22. Available for search at www.opensecrets.org. Soros donations may be tracked by year going back to the election cycle of 1992.
23. Direct evidence of the Funders' Committee has been removed from the web. It can be incompletely accessed in archived form at http://web.archive.org/web/20000413061001/http:/www.citizenparticipation.org/html/about.html.
24. "Funders' Handbook on Money in Politics – a Report by the Ottinger Foundation and the CarEth Foundation," hardcopy in author's collection, September 29, 1998. A web link to the report has been redirected and is no longer accessible.
25. "Environmental Grantmaking Foundations, 1995 Directory," (Rochester, New York: Environmental Data Research Institute, 1995).
26. Bill Moyers, Keynote speech, Environmental Grantmakers Association conference, Brainerd, Minnesota, October 16, 2001.
27. "Mother Jones Magazine and the Foundation for National Progress," profile in *Funders' Handbook on Money in Politics*, dated February 7, 1997. Hardcopy in author's collection.
28. Political Money Line, *"Campaign Finance Lobby: 1994-2000."* (subscription only). *See also*, "Who's Buying Campaign Finance 'Reform'?" American Conservative Union Foundation, 2001. *See also*, Ryan Sager, "Buying 'Reform' – Media Missed Millionaries' Scam," *New York Post*, March 17, 2005, p. 33.
29. George Will, "The Senate's Comic Opera*,"* *Jewish World Review*, March 30, 2001.
30. See www.opensecrets.org for all of George Soros' political contributions.
31. Philip Brasher, "Wellstone's tactics draw fire from his colleagues – Campaign finance move irks both parties," Associated Press as published in the *St. Paul Pioneer Press*, January 8, 1997, p. 6A.
32. S. 25, Bipartisan Campaign Reform Act of 1997, January 21, 1997, referred to the Committee on Rules and Administration. Text available online at http://thomas.loc.gov.
33. Senate Joint Resolution 18, February 27, 1997, introduced by Senators Hollings, Specter, Daschle, Bryan, Biden, Feinstein, Reed, Conrad, Dorgan, and Reid. Text available online at http://thomas.loc.gov.
34. 2 U.S.C. § 431 *et seq.* (amended 1974).
35. 424 U.S. 1 (1976), http://caselaw.lp.findlaw.com/scripts/getcase.pl?court=us&vol=424&invol=1, accessed February 22, 2006.
36. "S.J. Res. 4, the Hollings-Specter Campaign Finance Reform Constitutional Amendment," Democratic Policy Committee, http://democrats.senate.gov/~dpc/pubs/107-1-102.html, accessed February 12, 2006.
37. Reuters, "Dem Senators Want Public to Fund Campaigns*,"* *Denver Rocky Mountain News*, March 19, 1997.
38. Mary Leonard, "Citizens to the Rescue? Support for Full Public Financing of Campaigns is at its Highest Point Since Watergate," *Boston Globe*, March 16, 1997, page D1.

39. *Ibid.*

40. John Kerry, *Congressional Record, Statements on Introduced Bills and Joint Resolutions* (Senate – June 17, 1997), page S5794, online at http://thomas.loc.gov/cgi-bin/query/F?r105:2:./temp/~r105DWVho9:e17048:, accessed Nov. 4, 2005.

41. Guidestar Profile, Florence Fund, www.guidestar.org.

42. See for example, Bradley A. Smith, "John McCain's War on Political Speech - How the Arizona senator and other campaign finance reformers use the law to muffle critics and trample the First Amendment," *Reason Online*, December 2005, accessed March 16, 2006.

43. "Pew Charitable Trusts Provide Support for Ethical Elections," Institute for Global Ethics News Release, July 13, 1996, Lisa Lundgren, contact. www.globalethics.org/resources/news_releases/pew.htm, accessed November 5, 2005.

44. Paul Van Slambrouck, "Charitable foundations turn their gazes closer to home," *op. cit.*

45. Peter Key, "Pew makes a push into politics," *Philadelphia Business Journal*, March 3, 2000.

46. League of Women Voters Education Fund / The Harwood Group: "Money + Politics: People Change the Equation," *Funders' Handbook on Money in Politics, op. cit.* File was originally posted at www.funder.org/mp/groups/lwvef.html but was removed, probably earlier than 2000. Hardcopy in author's collection.

47. Sean Treglia, "Covering Philanthropy and Nonprofits Beyond 9/11," conference video, University of Southern California, Annenberg School of Communication, March 12, 2004.

48. Sean P. Treglia, Resume, www.joblink-usa.com/php/resumeaccess.phtml?rin=5363, accessed January 12, 2006. BA in Political Science, UCLA, 1985; Juris Doctor from UCLA Law School, 1989.

49. Form 990-PF, Open Society Institute, 1997. Brookings Institution, *Funders' Handbook on Money in Politics, op. cit.* File was originally posted at www.funder.org/mp/groups/BROOK.html but was removed, probably earlier than 2000. Hardcopy in author's collection.

50. The panel included experts from the Brennan Center for Justice, the Center for Responsive Politics, as well as prominent scholars and a former Chair of the Federal Election Commission.

51. Ornstein was a scholar at American Enterprise Institute, Mann at Brookings, Malbin at George Washington University Graduate School of Political Management, Corrado at Colby College in Maine, and Taylor a former *Washington Post* political reporter who quit in 1996 to form the Free TV for Straight Talk Coalition.

52. Anthony Corrado, Thomas E. Mann, Daniel R. Ortiz, Trevor Potter, and Frank J. Sorauf (Editors), *Campaign Finance Reform: A Sourcebook* (Washington, D.C., Brookings Institution Press, 1997). Reform Institute website, http://reforminstitute.org/about/advisorycommittee.shtml and http://reforminstitute.org/about/staff.shtml, accessed February 4, 2006.

53. Foundation Center grant records, Database 27, Pew Charitable Trusts, search "Abstract" attribute for string "campaign finance reform," accessed January 16, 2006.

54. *Ibid.*

55. News Release, "The Pew Charitable Trusts Fund Campaign Finance Reform Initiative," Colby College, Waterville, Maine, Release Date: Tue 13-Mar-2001, Contact: Alicia MacLeay.

56. James Heartfield, "Capitalism and Anti-capitalism." *op. cit.*

57. Kathleen Jamieson, "106th Congress Was One of The Most Civil Congresses in the Last 15 Years," Annenberg Public Policy Center of the University of Pennsylvania, Washington, D.C., March 10, 2001. www.annenberg publicpolicycenter.org/03_political_communication/civility/2001_civilityrelease030901.pdf, accessed January 5, 2007.

58. "A Matter of Trust: Rebecca Rimel tries out "raging incrementalism" at the Pew Trusts," *Philanthropy Magazine*, May/June 2000.

CHAPTER 13

CAVIAR TO THE GENERAL

JANUARY 2004

TERESA HEINZ MARRIED JOHN KERRY IN 1995. She didn't tack "Kerry" onto her name until 2003 when he began running for president.

Why not?

"Politically, it's going to be Heinz Kerry. But I don't give a shit, you know?"[1]

She didn't have to.

She was rich.

Very, very rich.

She could say what she wanted, how she wanted. And did.

She bragged about the Botox treatments that preserved her gamine good looks from decades before her 65 years.

She was just as blunt about her prenuptial agreement with Senator Kerry, a document that meant he could take out a loan only on his half of their Beacon Hill townhouse in Boston to help finance his campaign.

And Teresa admitted that she hadn't gotten around to switching her party affiliation to Democratic until 2003, same as her name.

It was going to be an interesting campaign.[2]

PRESIDENTIAL YEAR 2004 dawned with a rousing endorsement of John Kerry from the League of Conservation Voters. LCV money started rolling in by late January—$18,528 directly to the campaign—and by mid-February "six-figures" went to pay for TV ads supporting Kerry for president.[3]

That raised eyebrows for two reasons:

First, in times past, the League had received $57,300 from the Heinz Family Foundation (Teresa was chairman of its board), plus a $2,500 contribution from Teresa's personal account, which looked suspiciously like sneaky investments paying off for her husband.[4]

Second, LCV gave its endorsement at the very start of the primary season—the earliest in its 34-year history—right after Kerry won the Iowa caucuses, but before the New Hampshire primary (much less March 2, Super Tuesday), while Al Gore in 2000 had to wait until April. And Al Gore had been Mr. Environment to millions. That, too, sniffed of payoff.[5]

No, no, said LCV Political Director Mark Longabaugh when the *New York Post* asked. Senator Kerry received the League's endorsement because of his stellar 96 percent LCV voting score. (Not surprisingly, he received one of the lowest ratings from the National Association of Manufacturers.)[6]

Gore's LCV score had averaged only 63 percent over eight years in the House and 73 percent over eight years in the Senate. (Gore running mate Joe Lieberman's score was 100 percent for eight of his eleven years in the Senate.)[7]

Campaign finance laws classified Teresa as just another contributor, limiting her donations to $2,000 in the primary and $2,000 in the general election—only $4,000 tops.

That could motivate her to hide money in non-profit groups.

Longabough insisted that none of Teresa's money went to the League's 2004 contributions for her husband.

Republicans didn't believe it.

Born a Portuguese citizen in the African colony of Mozambique, Teresa Heinz Kerry was heir to the Heinz ketchup fortune and controlled three charitable organizations with combined assets of $1.2 billion, plus as many as 10 private trusts that probably held an additional half-billion dollars.[8]

Other assets such as real estate and shares in the H.J. Heinz Company brought her estimated personal fortune to the $1 billion mark.[9]

Teresa Heinz Kerry inherited all that money and control from her first husband, Senator John Heinz, Republican of Pennsylvania, just after their 25th wedding anniversary.

In 1991 he died in a horrendous midair airplane-helicopter collision that took the lives of seven people, including two first-graders in a schoolyard.[10]

John Heinz had been the love of her life. She was devastated, almost to the point of paralysis. She took Prozac to dull the grief. Friends urged her to run for her late husband's Senate seat—in part simply to revive her—but she decided against it, devoting herself to their three sons—Christopher, Andre, and H. John Heinz IV—and to managing the vast wealth her husband left her.

Philanthropy became her full-time work. She supported environmental causes, women's issues, education programs, the arts, and community development in Pittsburgh, her long-time home.

Teresa already sat on the board of directors—as vice chairman, no less— of the Environmental Defense Fund and the environmentally-oriented Winslow

Foundation. By the time John Kerry began his presidential run, she was also a trustee of the Brookings Institution, incubator of the academic crew that pushed McCain-Feingold over the top.[11]

John Kerry's friendship with George Soros rarely got press mention, and never in connection with the failed Kerry-Wellstone Clean Money Clean Elections bill that Soros had supported.

Fox News commentator Bill O'Reilly made much of Soros funding MoveOn.org and its "character assassination" ads thumping George Bush, but the Soros-Kerry personal connection never came up.

Likewise, Soros' opinion of Teresa never made news.

Whatever it was.

In 1995, to honor the memory of her late husband, Teresa set up the $20 million H. John Heinz III Center for Science, Economics and the Environment in Washington, D.C., which gave annual awards—a medallion and $250,000 cash—in the categories of Arts and Humanities, Environment, Human Condition, Public Policy, and Technology, the Economy and Employment.[12]

Teresa also gave tons of money to members of the League of Conservation Voters and many other pugnacious and politically charged green groups, including the Boston-based Clean Air Task Force, which filed a lawsuit against the federal Environmental Protection Agency alleging it had failed to identify counties that were not meeting federal smog standards.

She insisted she would continue making such grants if her husband were elected president.

Teresa's investments were so broad that, if John Kerry won, conflict of interest clashes would be inevitable, since his decisions as president would necessarily affect her assets.

There's the rub.

All of that.

To compound matters, she went stumping for her husband in her private Gulfstream II jet, *The Flying Squirrel*; she whispered to others while he gave speeches; her upper-crust charisma ("what an exotic accent" "such smart and down-to-earth remarks" "wow, killer shoes") upstaged the Senator's staid persona. If she became First Lady, the law said she could keep doing it.

All of it.

Critics noted that bankrolling lawsuits against the federal government would be a novelty for a First Lady.

Not to mention pillow talk about presidential decisions that might hurt the First Portfolio.

With George Soros implementing his own foreign policy and Teresa Heinz Kerry executing her own domestic policy, one might reasonably wonder who's running the show in a Kerry Administration.

So it was that Teresa Heinz Kerry, her mouth, and her money, became a campaign issue.[13]

THE AFRICAN QUEEN

Born Maria Teresa Thierstein Simoes-Ferreira in 1938 in Lourenço Marques, capital of Portuguese-ruled Mozambique, she was the middle child of a prominent Portuguese expatriate doctor (an oncologist) and a mother from South African / Mediterranean immigrant stock.

Teresa—pronounced "Tuh-RAY-zuh"—grew up in tea-and-tennis privilege in colonial Mozambique, and at age fourteen was sent to a Catholic boarding school in Durban, South Africa. She took her undergraduate degree in Romance languages at the elite University of Witwatersrand in Johannesburg.

Many years later, during the Kerry presidential run, she drove campaign staffers nuts by describing herself as African-American to black audiences that didn't appreciate it.

But she was dead serious about her African origins, serving listeners tidbits of nostalgia such as, "my Africa preserved the innocence of children."

She came out of Africa speaking Portuguese, French, Spanish, Italian and English.

During graduate study in Switzerland at the Interpreters' School of the University of Geneva, she went to play tennis one day and met young H. John Heinz III on the court. He was working at a Swiss bank during a year off from Harvard Business School.

It was a fairytale romance. She didn't know who he was at first—he told her only that his father "made soup" back in America. When she found out how much soup, she was stunned.

She graduated from the Interpreters' School in 1963 and moved with John to the United States, where she got a job interpreting for the Trusteeship Council of the United Nations. They were married in 1966 at the Heinz Chapel in Pittsburgh.

John entered politics and was elected a Republican Representative from Pennsylvania's 18th District in 1971 and a U.S. Senator in 1976.

The couple had been important environmental advocates for nearly a decade before John's death. Teresa had been invited onto the Environmental Defense Fund's board of trustees in 1983. The next year the Heinzes established a fund to help environmental causes—it grew into the current Heinz Family Foundation—and in 1989 Teresa worked to stop a road-building project in Brazil, then went on to the dolphin-safe tuna issue.

Teresa had persuaded old friend Wren Wirth, wife of Colorado Senator Tim Wirth, to join the board of EDF with her. Wirth later reciprocated by asking Teresa to join the board of trustees as treasurer of her Winslow Foundation, created in 1987 from the bequest of Wren's mother, Julia D. Winslow.

The Environmental Defense Fund became Teresa's pet project. She gave $447,923 in 1993 through the Heinz Family Foundation, largely to pay noted

architect William A. McDonough to design the organization's new environmentally sensitive offices in New York. McDonough in turn hired her middle
son Andre and made sure he met plenty of influentials. Andre's recollection:

> I was a project assistant for Bill for the next year, working on things
> ranging from sustainable community planning for one of the Lakota
> reservations, to working with city planning for Chattanooga, Tennessee,
> to collaborating with different ecological thinkers like Paul Hawken
> and the chemist Michael Braungart on various forms of industrial
> ecology. It was really fast exposure in one year.[14]

At the same time, Teresa also commissioned McDonough to design
her own 12,000-square-foot green-certified, nature-loving, pristine Heinz
Family Foundation Offices 32 stories above the ground in Pittsburgh's
Dominion Tower.[15]

She made sure McDonough met plenty of influentials as well. The next
year, when he was appointed Dean of the University of Virginia School of
Architecture, the rumor mill suggested that she bought him the job.[16]

Similarly, in 1996, when McDonough became the only individual to
receive the Presidential Award for Sustainable Development, the nation's
highest environmental honor, presented by President Clinton in a White
House ceremony, people wondered if Teresa was *la femme* to *cherchez*.[17]

JOHN KERRY WAS INTRODUCED TO TERESA by John Heinz at an Earth Day rally
in 1990 where both were scheduled to speak.

In 1992, he met her again at the Earth Summit in Rio de Janeiro.

President George H. W. Bush had appointed her as part of a State
Department delegation representing U.S. non-governmental organizations.

She was widowed and he was divorced. *The New Yorker* reported that
"Kerry was impressed when she took over from a Brazilian interpreter she
thought was subverting the meaning of a speech. They went to Mass at the
cathedral, and chatted in French. (When two Americans lapse into French, it
is usually for the purpose of flirting.)"[18]

They met again at a dinner party back in the capital and he offered to see
her home. They quietly became an item.

They lived together for a short time and were married on Nantucket in
the presence of her three sons and his two daughters in a civil ceremony on
Memorial Day weekend in 1995.

Step-daughters Vanessa and Alexandra Kerry did not like her at first.
They called her "step-money."[19]

Two of the Heinz sons later joined Kerry's campaign.[20]

When John Kerry began talking to a circle of confidantes in 2001 about
the feasibility of a presidential run, Teresa hated the idea, but after a long hike
alone decided it would be wrong to deny him the dream.

She had told her first husband under similar circumstances that he would run for president "over my dead body."

Time had not mellowed her.

It had toughened her.

NOBLESSE OBLIGE

AT FIRST IT WAS JUST THE RIGHT that wanted to see her tax returns. McCain-Feingold gave Teresa freedom to donate her money to a Kerry-friendly group, such as the Natural Resources Defense Council or Ellen Malcolm's America Coming Together or Harold Ickes' Media Fund or Wes Boyd and Joan Blades' MoveOn.org—and everybody knew it.

But had she done it?

John Kerry was already on the defensive over soft money ads mounted by Ickes and the Media Fund.

The Federal Election Commission received complaints over these politically active tax-exempt groups and was mulling new rules to limit them.

Even though Teresa said she wouldn't plunder the Heinz purse for her husband's campaign, she threatened that if George Bush resorted to smear tactics against her husband she would make an FEC-allowed "independent expenditure" to produce an equivalent smear against the president.

If she did make such an expenditure, it would add to the controversy, because donors can't legally "coordinate or consult" with the candidate, hard to avoid if you're husband and wife.

When Michael Moore's controversial documentary *Fahrenheit 9/11* came out, critics thought she had paid for it.

No, Miramax co-chairmen Harvey and Bob Weinstein paid Moore $6 million themselves when Disney refused to distribute it.[21]

Then came accusations that Teresa had helped to launder charitable contributions and that she gave money to a foundation with links to Hamas.[22]

She brushed it off as "noise from the Right."

One report focused on her support for the San Francisco-based Tides Foundation, noting accurately that Tides funded more than 250 radical anti-war, anti-corporate and hard line anti-development groups.[23]

The Tides linkage was particularly disturbing.

However, accusers had failed to read Teresa's Form 990 grant descriptions, which showed that the Heinz money for Tides went entirely to civic projects around Pittsburgh, some with green overtones, but nothing overly anti-business and nothing at all political.

She had essentially hired the Tides Center—a spinoff from the Tides Foundation—as a professional "back office" project manager for local things her own staff couldn't do, even requiring Tides to set up a Pittsburgh office for the purpose and file separate Form 990s. There was no evidence that any Heinz money leaked back to the weird and wooly Tides of San Francisco.

But it didn't look good for a potential First Lady to be called the "bag lady for the radical Left."

Then the September 11th Families for Peaceful Tomorrows—a nonprofit group of families of victims of the 9/11 terrorist attacks—strongly criticized President Bush's use of footage from the attacks in his television ad that began running in early March.

The Heinz Endowments were accused of funding Peaceful Tomorrows through the Tides Foundation's San Francisco back door. They weren't, but the accusation was hard to shake.[24]

Hadn't Teresa openly acknowledged that Heinz foundation money went to left wing causes that she called "progressive," and that much of it went to members of the overtly political and strongly partisan League of Conservation Voters?

Hadn't she openly acknowledged past big grants to Tides?

Wasn't it natural for people to imagine that her current Tide grants were funding Bush political opponents?

Talk shows brought the Heinz Company itself into the fray, wondering whether corporate cash was flowing to the Kerry campaign.

It prompted absurd but effective boycotts of restaurants that served their ketchup and a flood of more than 800 complaint calls from customers.

The corporation couldn't take it, and issued an exasperated news release in late March, stating, "In light of some misleading speculation, the H.J. Heinz Co. would like to make clear that neither Mrs. Teresa Heinz Kerry, Senator John Kerry, nor any member of their family is involved in the management or board of the H.J. Heinz Company."[25]

Despite a crescendo of newspaper editorial boards demanding that Teresa make her tax records public immediately, she adamantly refused.

She even filed for an extension on her 2003 income tax forms.[26]

She said it was to protect the privacy of her sons, who had complex joint trusts.

She wrote off the clamor as more "noise from the Right."

By early May the "noise from the Right" had grown into a general uproar.

She grudgingly released "financial data" and said she would provide the first two pages of her Form 1040 when it became available, expected to be in October.[27]

The summary showed she earned $5.1 million and paid $750,000 in taxes. Republicans were aghast at the low tax rate until they realized it was because of President George W. Bush's tax cut.

TERESA THE CAMPAIGN ISSUE became more familiar to Americans because of all her gallivanting about the country chatting up voters.

She went on the road seven days a week, hitting 27 states by June, sometimes making several stops in a day. She did more and more solo fundraisers, standing in for her husband and attracting supporters.

She had done a Hollywood $1,000-a-plate lunch in late February and 175 women showed up, including power players such as Paramount chairwoman and CEO Sherry Lansing—$175,000 in one stop.

To the Democratic base she was glamorous, flamboyant, fascinating.

To the Democratic campaign staff she was a Monster from the Id that filled them with primal dread every time she picked up a microphone.

She might speak adoringly about "her husband" as "the love of her life," then say it was John Heinz she meant, not John Kerry.

She might express her political views, deeply considered, well-articulated, on the disaster of global warming that meant we must abandon fossil fuels immediately—while her husband was elsewhere at the same time talking up his proposal for new clean coal-fired power plants.

She might make effective, pointed jabs at George W. Bush as "lacking curiosity," and possessing a "cynicism that is the most lethal weapon against democracy I have ever seen," then ramble into daffy medical advice she supposedly learned in Africa as a child, drifting far off message.

She might whirl into a press conference, dazzling in a custom scarf that made Hermès look cheap, with fashionable dark glasses pushed up over her hair, and then tell the reporters that when the news of the first Iowa caucus victory came through, her husband was not there to pop the champagne cork—John was on the john.

She gradually declined from "Saint Teresa," as Pittsburgh Mayor Tom Murphy dubbed her for her generosity, sidelined by her cringe factor—her naïve, bratty arrogance born of too much deference to her staggering wealth.

John Kerry's greatest character reference became his willingness to take her on.

She wasn't an embarrassment, as some said.

Her snappy and sassy ways captivated throngs.

She was just too rich for our blood.

Behind the missteps and the lurid "bag lady" headlines and the Peaceful Tomorrows allegation lurked a more insidious problem.

Environmentalist Teresa Heinz Kerry, who owned five large houses, three SUVs, a yacht and a private jet, was funding a highly political new lawsuit that could cripple or even shut down a substantial fraction of the nation's electrical generating capacity.

It was not something most Americans would look upon kindly in a First Lady.

In late April, three Heinz-funded environmental groups sued the EPA—the Environmental Protection Agency—to force it to issue perilously expensive regulations on mercury emissions from coal-fired power plants.[28]

Why three instead of just one? Her foundation's motto: "Approach challenges broadly. Encourage coalitions. Change requires collaborative responses."[29]

And thereby hangs a tale.

CHAPTER 13 NOTES

1. David Usborne, "Teresa Heinz Kerry: Too much attitude for a First Lady?" *The Independent*, London, February 7, 2004.

2. Portions of this chapter first appeared as "The Heinz Foundations and the Kerry Campaign - One Has Money, the Other Needs Money," by Ron Arnold, *Foundation Watch*, Capital Research Center, Washington, D.C., April 2004.

3. Deborah Orin and Brian Blomquist, "John's Eco-Pals got Wife's Greenbacking," *New York Post*, February 10, 2004.

4. Christopher Horner, "Playing Ketchup – Recipients of Heinz Money Making Strong Kerry Pitch," *National Review Online*, January 28, 2004, www.nationalreview.com/comment/horner200401280900.asp, accessed June 12, 2004.

5. News release, "Deb Callahan Announces LCV Endorsement of John Kerry," *League of Conservation Voters*, January 24, 2004. www.lcv.org/Features/Features.cfm?ID=2103&c=46, accessed September 15, 2004.

6. Steve Toloken, "Energy issue fueling interest," *Plastics News*, October 18, 2004.

7. Alexander Cockburn and Jeffrey St. Clair, *Al Gore: A User's Manual*, (New York: Verso, 2000).

8. Ralph Vartabedian, "Kerry's wife would keep her philanthropic role - As a first lady, Teresa Heinz Kerry's oversight of a nonprofit empire may be issue, some say," *Los Angeles Times*, April 12, 2004. The reporter reviewed Internal Revenue Service nonprofit returns, Senate financial disclosures and records at the Securities and Exchange Commission.

9. Associated Press, "Heinz Kerry Fortune Passes $1 Billion Mark," *Fox News*, June 27, 2004. www.foxnews.com/story/0,2933,123856,00.html, accessed January 22, 2006.

10. "State Mourns Heinz - Senator, 6 Others Killed by Crash of Plane, Copter over School Yard," *Harrisburg Patriot-News*, April 5, 1991. Obituary, "Sen. John Heinz," *U.S. News and World Report*, April 15, 1991.

11. Brookings Board of Trustees, as of November 2003, /web.archive.org/web/20040211164528/http://www.brookings.edu/ea/trustees.htm, accessed February 5, 2005.

12. The Heinz Awards – Shared Ideals Realized, www.heinzawards.net/about.asp?staticid=7, accessed March 20, 2006.

13. Andrew Miga, "Is she too hot for Dems?" *Boston Herald*, March 7, 2003; Dennis B. Roddy, "Right zooms in on Heinz Kerry grants - Heinz Kerry's foundation work provide grist for foes, *Pittsburgh Post-Gazette*, March 7, 2004.

14. Amanda Griscom, "My Interview With Andre - *Grist* chats with Andre Heinz, environmental activist and stepson of John Kerry," *Grist Magazine*, September 7, 2004. /www.grist.org/news/maindish/2004/09/07/griscom-heinz/ accessed January 22, 2006. Braungart was McDonough's business partner.

15. William McDonough + Partners, "Projects / Clients, Heinz Family Foundation Offices," www.mcdonoughpartners.com/projects/heinz/default.asp?projID=heinz, accessed February 21, 2006

16. News Release, "Environmental Innovator William McDonough Named Dean of University of Virginia School of Architecture," June 24, 1994, www.virginia.edu/topnews/textonlyarchive/June_1994/94-06-24_

Environmental_Innovator_William_McDonough_Named_Dean_of_University_of_Virginia_School_of_Architecture.txt, accessed February 14, 2006.

17. Resume, William McDonough, www.mcdonough.com/wam_resume.pdf, accessed March 3, 2006.

18. Judith Thurman, "The Candidate's Wife - Teresa Heinz Kerry is an uncharted element on the road to the White House," *New Yorker*, Issue of 2004-09-27, www.newyorker.com/fact/content/?040927fa_fact, accessed February 22, 2006.

19. Gayle Fee and Laura Raposa, "Heinz Kerry is still shooting from the lip," *Boston Herald*, September 21, 2004, http://thetrack.bostonherald.com/moreTrack/view.bg?articleid=45207, accessed March 4, 2006.

20. Jill Lawrence, "With Teresa, expect an unconventional campaign, *USA Today*, June 23, 2004, www.usatoday.com/news/politicselections/nation/president/2004-05-23-heinz-kerry-cover_x.htm, accessed March 4, 2006.

21. Martin Kasindorf and Judy Keen, "'Fahrenheit 9/11': Will it change any voter's mind?" *USA Today*, June 24, 2004. www.usatoday.com/news/politicselections/nation/president/2004-06-24-fahrenheit-cover_x.htm, accessed March 8, 2006.

22. FactCheck.org, "Internet 'Whispering Campaigns' Falsely Accuse Teresa Heinz," *Annenberg Political Fact Check*, August 12, 2004, www.factcheck.org/article224.html, accessed March 20, 2006.

23. Ben Johnson, "Teresa Heinz Kerry: Bag Lady for the Radical Left," *FrontPageMagazine.com*, February 13, 2004, www.frontpagemag.com/Articles/ReadArticle.asp?ID=12187 accessed September 12, 2006.

24. Eliza Newlin Carney, "In a Pickle," *National Journal*, Vol. 36, No. 17, April 24, 2004.

25. James O'Toole, "H.J. Tries to Keep Name Out of Race," *Pittsburgh Post-Gazette*, March 27, 2004; Marguerite Higgins, "Heinz denies Kerry connection," *Washington Times*, April 7, 2004.

26. Patrick Healy, "Heinz Kerry delays filing 2003 tax forms," *Boston Globe*, April 23, 2004 www.boston.com/news/nation/articles/2004/04/23/heinz_kerry_delays_filing_2003_tax_forms?mode=PF, accessed March 4, 2006.

27. CNN, "Teresa Kerry's financial data released – Wife of Democratic candidate inherited food fortune," May 12, 2004, www.cnn.com/2004/ALLPOLITICS/05/11/teresa.kerry/, accessed March 4, 2006.

28. News Release, "Conservation groups sue EPA over power plant mercury pollution," www.catf.us/press_room/20040428-Mercury.pdf, accessed January 22, 2006.

29. Heinz Family Philanthropies wesbite, www.hfp.heinz.org/aboutus/index.html, accessed March 4, 2006.

CHAPTER 14

THE INHOFE FINDING

APRIL 2004

ANDREW WHEELER thought about the question.

He tried to give a diplomatic answer, since he spoke as a panelist at a professional meeting of the American Gas Association.

But the forthright question wouldn't let him:

"Why do green groups keep filing all these lawsuits against us?"

So he just told the oil and gas people bluntly: "I've worked on the Hill a long time. I've had a lot of greens in my office. Environmental group leaders don't want development, period—they believe that *any* development harms nature, and they won't tolerate it."[1]

That was incredible, so it got an 80 percent discount.

After all, Andrew R. Wheeler was the staff director and general counsel of the Senate Environment and Public Works Committee. He had to deal with those pushy lobbyists every day. It was just Beltway burnout.

Two weeks later, four environmental groups sued the Environmental Protection Agency over mercury emissions from coal-fired power plants.

Wheeler wasn't surprised.

He had seen it coming in a number of ways.

First, a full-page *New York Times* ad—placed by the Natural Resources Defense Council and MoveOn.org—blasted President Bush for rolling back mercury regulations.[2]

171

First Arsenic Now Mercury

GEORGE BUSH'S EPA AND THE POLITICS OF POLLUTION

America learned this week that tuna, and many other fish, can contain harmful levels of toxic mercury. Forty-five states already post warnings of mercury contamination in their lakes and streams. So why is President Bush trying to weaken controls on mercury pollution?

It's déjà vu all over again. Early in his presidency, George Bush tried to allow more arsenic in drinking water. Now, he wants the EPA to let coal-fired power plants treat their mercury pollution as "non-hazardous" even though mercury threatens pregnant women and children.

The Bush administration's ploy would allow coal-fired power plants to put more mercury into the air, where it rains down on lakes and oceans, is swallowed by fish, and could wind up on your plate. Exposure to mercury can cause learning disabilities and neurological damage in kids and the developing fetus.

Guess who is praising this scheme? Coal power companies, who are big mercury polluters and big political contributors, too.

The Mercury Money Trail

The big mercury polluters and their trade associations are aggressive political players in Washington. Their executives and PACs are also generous political donors. It's no surprise that the Bush administration is following the industry's script for weakening mercury regulations.

Last time around, President Bush had to back down on arsenic in the face of a massive outcry from people across the political spectrum. Let's make history repeat itself.

Tell President Bush to get serious about reducing mercury pollution. Our kids deserve no less. Let the Bush administration and the EPA hear your voice about its proposed mercury rule. Go to www.nrdc.org

The fact that there were no mercury regulations to roll back didn't matter.

It was presidential year 2004 and environmentalists were an out-of-power elite that wanted back in power.[3]

Framing the message like Lakoff was all that mattered. Just making Bush *look* like he was rolling back regulations was good enough.

The ad came a month before the lawsuit, and neither NRDC nor MoveOn.org was a party to the suit.

The timing had been as uncanny as the ad was transparent.

It was a typical attack ad with a response coupon and a targeted "Affinity-Urgency-Action" format:

- Affinity: We think alike (we hate Bush too)
- Urgency: He's poisoning our kids (we can't dawdle)
- Action: Send money to us and nasty notes to Bush (you get bragging rights).

Within this design, the all-important message was framed to rouse strong emotions with pictures and text (*facing page*) using the time-honored direct mail trio, "Fear-Hate-Revenge:"

- Fear: That ugly power plant is belching mercury-laden coal smoke into the food chain, lakes in particular
- Hate: Our kids and pregnant women will eat that nice basket of fish, which was poisoned by President Bush and big mercury polluters
- Revenge: Hit the president with horrible messages in a massive outcry and make him stop, like you did with arsenic regulations.

But it was a sham. It wasn't really about regulating mercury, it was about true revenge: Dump Bush.

It was one of those "issue advocacy" ads that the Brookings academics had identified as a campaign finance problem: a campaign ad masquerading as an issue ad.[4]

W AS IT LEGAL?
McCain-Feingold was supposed to deal with issue advocacy, and particularly the problems caused by the 1976 Supreme Court case of *Buckley v. Valeo*.[5]

The high court had ruled that campaign finance limits applied only to "communications that in express terms advocate the election or defeat of a clearly identified candidate for federal office."

But there was that pesky footnote. At the bottom of the Court's opinion, it said that the limits apply when communications include terms "such as 'vote for,' 'elect,' 'support,' 'cast your ballot for,' 'Smith for Congress,' 'vote against,' 'defeat,' 'reject.'"

They became known as the "magic words." Without them, a communication—no matter what its real purpose—could be called issue advocacy and dodge campaign finance laws.

That wasn't a problem until the 1992 election, because pressure groups didn't think of using issue advocacy ads in electoral politics. But that year, the Christian Action Network pushed the envelope and aired what looked very much like a negative campaign ad attacking Bill Clinton for his "homosexual agenda."[6]

Since the ad never used *Buckley*'s "magic words," the Court of Appeals decided that the ad was a discussion of "Christian family values" rather than an exhortation to vote against Clinton in the upcoming presidential election.[7]

It opened the floodgates to more wink-wink nudge-nudge "issue advocacy" in 1996, when countless special interests overwhelmed the airwaves with millions of dollars in ads that looked like campaign ads, but avoided the magic words and evaded the law.

The distinction between issue ads and campaign ads had collapsed.

Senator Paul Wellstone added the amendment to McCain-Feingold that prohibited corporations (including nonprofits) and labor unions from paying for broadcasts that refer to a federal candidate (the reference could be just an image of the federal candidate, as in the NRDC / MoveOn.org ad) within 60 days of a general election or 30 days of a primary.

NRDC's March 26 ad was in the clear, coming 32 days before the next primary (Pennsylvania) and more than 180 days before the general election.

Even if it had fallen within the prohibited times, the law didn't seem to apply to print as well as broadcasts, and the U.S. Supreme Court had not addressed McCain-Feingold's applicability to 501c3 charities (such as NRDC) when it ruled that the BCRA was constitutional in December of 2003.[8]

So it was clean.

Sort of.

SENATOR JAMES M. INHOFE, Republican of Oklahoma, was livid. He was Andrew Wheeler's boss and chairman of the Senate Environment and Public Works Committee. His committee had oversight authority over the Environmental Protection Agency, and he took the job seriously. He was appalled by the NRDC / MoveOn.org ad. On the Senate floor he excoriated NRDC for false and probably illegal advertising:

> The NRDC's lobbying claim is that the President is weakening controls on mercury emissions from power plants. The facts, however, are very different.
>
> On December 15, 2003, this President proposed the first ever controls on mercury emissions from utilities.
>
> The Clinton Administration had eight years to propose such controls and did not. In nearly 3,000 days as EPA Administrator, how many

mercury regulations on power plants did former EPA Administrator Carol Browner issue? Zero. Instead, in the last month of the eighth year of the Clinton Administration, Carol Browner deftly handed a regulatory lemon to the Bush Administration that she was unwilling to impose during the Clinton Administration. What a courageous move.[9]

Senator Inhofe didn't spend much time rebutting the ad's content. He knew the Clean Air Act had mandated standards for coal- and oil-fired electric utility steam generating units ("EUSGUs" in gov-speak) that Carol Browner ducked, leaving the onus on the Bush EPA, which issued proposed standards in January of 2004.

Inhofe knew that the NRDC just didn't like President's Bush's flexible, business-friendly proposal and wanted a command-and-control, business-punishing outcome. He noted that solicitation laws in 41 states prohibited false statements and urged officials to look into it. Then he went to the real point:

> The most shocking part of all of this is not even that NRDC is running a completely false ad, or that NRDC is running a completely false ad simply to fleece people for contributions. The most shocking part is that the American taxpayer subsidizes the NRDC hundreds of thousands of dollars each year to conduct this type of activity. Public IRS records for the last several years demonstrate that NRDC regularly receives thousands of federal grant dollars every year. In 2002, the NRDC received more than half a million dollars in government grants. In 2003, NRDC was additionally awarded more than half a million dollars again in government grants. And the cycle continues year after year.[10]

Inhofe had been aware of the problem for several years as a minority member of the Senate Environment and Public Works committee. He began to do something about it when he took over as chairman of the committee in January of 2003—when Republicans formally took control of the Senate after the Democratic debacle of November 5, 2002.

The idea that the EPA and other government agencies were funding politically active nonprofit groups struck him as intolerable. One of his first acts as chairman had been to assign a Majority Staff Grants Oversight Team to research government money in nonprofit politics.

The second thing that told Andrew Wheeler to expect a lawsuit was a 17,000-word law review article by Patrick Parenteau, a former vice president of the National Wildlife Federation, now a professor at Vermont Law School.

It was titled, "Anything industry wants: environmental policy under Bush II."

It sounded oddly like a campaign ad:

In over thirty years of practicing environmental law, I have not seen anything like this. Not even the historic battles with the likes of Interior Secretary James Watt and EPA Administrator Anne Burford Gorsuch in the Reagan Administration can compare. The current administration is far more clever, disciplined, and deceptive in what it says and does than its predecessors. It has also been more effective, due to a Republican-controlled Congress, an enfeebled Democratic Party, a distracted public, and an ambivalent media. Because of this environment, there has not been an open debate on the future of environmental policy. Rather, the Bush Administration has been able to make sweeping environmental changes through a stealth campaign, masquerading under sly euphemisms like "Healthy Forests," "Clear Skies," "No Net Loss," "Stewardship Contracts," and "Sound Science." [11]

Dump Dubya. And his sly euphemist, Frank Luntz.

SLITHERING RICHES

WHEN THE COAL-FIRED POWER PLANT LAWSUIT landed in the U.S. District Court in Washington, D.C., Inhofe's oversight team was unaware that three of its plaintiffs were Heinz-funded:

- the National Wildlife Federation,
- the Izaak Walton League of America, and
- the Clean Air Task Force, which provided legal representation.

A fourth plaintiff, the Natural Resources Council of Maine (not related to NRDC), had received no Heinz grants. [12]

The majority staff was only interested in federal grants at first. They found that the National Wildlife Federation had received $600,000 from the EPA, and over $1 million from other federal agencies.

From 1996 to 2001, the Izaak Walton League had received EPA grants of $347,199. [13]

So, one of the four plaintiffs had received past EPA grants and another was using current taxpayer cash to sue the EPA, just like the Natural Resources Defense Council was using it to pay for highly political issue ads.

The oversight team already knew who else was on the taxpayer take.

They had interviewed key EPA officials and looked at years of grant records. They found dozens of environmental groups getting large amounts of government money.

The practice had exploded with the 1993 inauguration of President Bill Clinton and his installation of environmental group activists throughout the EPA bureaucracy.

It had become so political that none of those grants had been subject to competitive bidding—just gifts handed out year after year to Clinton-friendly nonprofits, without even follow-up to see what they did with the money.[14]

Nine of the grantees were intensely active in congressional lobbying or electoral campaigns:

Recipient Organization	EPA grants since 1993	Other government grants
Natural Resources Defense Council	$6.5 million	$3,528,827 (1999-2003)
Children's Environmental Health Network	$400,000	$136,729 (2001-2003)
Environmental Defense, Inc	$4.6 million	$2,447,942 (1999-2003)
The Tides Center	$2 million	$14,011,991 (1999-2003)
Consumer Federation of America	$8 million	NA
World Wildlife Fund	$1.6 million	$54 million (1998-2003)
Friends of the Earth	$200,000 (1993-1999)	NA
World Resources Institute	$8,132,060	$16.9 million (1998-2003)
National Wildlife Federation	$600,000 (1994-2003)	$1,055,600 (2000-2003)

The oversight team then made the next connection: foundations.

Who besides the government was funding these groups?

The emergence of prescriptive foundations and grant-driven environmental groups had become well-known by then, so the staff knew where to look.

The flap over Teresa Heinz Kerry's foundation grants was also fresh in the public memory, particularly reports of her donations to the League of Conservation Voters and Environmental Defense.

Had she also been funding the mercury lawsuit plaintiffs?

They quickly found the Heinz money and the Heinz Family Foundation website with its motto: "Approach challenges broadly. Encourage coalitions. Change requires collaborative responses."

How big was this coalition?

How political?

Was foundation money slithering into electoral politics?

The majority staff looked up the League of Conservations Voters' board members:

John H. Adams *Natural Resources Defense Council*	Marcia Aronoff *Environmental Defense*
Patricia Bauman *Bauman Foundation*	Brent Blackwelder (honorary) *Friends of the Earth*
Everett (Brownie) Carson *Natural Resources Council of Maine*	Wade Greene *Rockefeller Family & Associates*
John (Jay) A. Harris *Changing Horizons Fund*	Denis Hayes *Bullitt Foundation*
Rampa R. Hormel *Global Environment Project Institute*	John Hunting (honorary) *Beldon Fund*
Tom Kiernan *National Parks Conservation Association*	Fred Krupp *Environmental Defense*
Martha Marks *Republicans for Environmental Protection*	William H. Meadows III *The Wilderness Society*
Scott A. Nathan *Baupost Group*	John D. Podesta *Center for American Progress*
Lana Pollack *Michigan Environmental Council*	Samuel P. Pryor III *Appalachian Mountain Club*
Marie W. Ridder *Trust for Public Lands*	Bill Roberts *Beldon Fund*
Larry Rockefeller *American Conservation Association*	Donald K. Ross *Rockefeller Family & Associates*
Rodger O. Schlickeisen *Defenders of Wildlife*	Debbie Sease *Sierra Club*
Peggy Shepard *West Harlem Environmental Action, Inc.*	S. Bruce Smart Jr. *Former Under Secretary of Commerce (Reagan Administration)*
Ed Zuckerman *Federation of State Conservation Voter Leagues*	Theodore Roosevelt IV (honorary chair) *Lehman Brothers, Inc.*
Debra Callahan *LCV President*	Mary Jane Gallagher *League of Conservation Voters Education Fund President*

LEAGUE OF CONSERVATION VOTERS
BOARD OF DIRECTORS, 2004 / 2006

Some of the seven- and eight-figure crowd was mixed in with the activists. Aside from the obvious money and power:

Rampa R. Hormel—married into the SPAM meatpacking money;

Samuel P. Pryor III—an heir to the Fruit of the Loom underwear fortune;

Marie W. Ridder—widow of newspaper magnate Walter T. Ridder.

But that came as no surprise.

The shocks began when they found that LCV was hiding the names of contributors to their Vote For Kerry ad campaign—legally.[15]

This miraculous power came from LCV's tax status. Unlike most other 501c4 lobbying groups, LCV filed with the Federal Election Commission as a Qualified Nonprofit Corporation, a little-known category that even experts had to look up.

It's also known as an MCFL group, an acronym for the U.S. Supreme Court's 1986 decision in the case of the Federal Election Commission v. Massachusetts Citizens for Life (MCFL). The justices said that tax-exempt groups had a First Amendment right to expressly advocate the election or defeat of federal candidates as long as the groups met three criteria:

- they don't accept corporate or union money;
- they mainly have an ideological focus;
- and they are nonprofit organizations that don't make for-profit business transactions.[16]

That was no advantage until McCain-Feingold limited issue advocacy ads. But in election year 2004, groups with MCFL status and rich foundation donors like Heinz and Soros could do what others couldn't:

- run ads during McCain-Feingold's 30- and 60-day "dead times" when the airwaves are less crowded;
- pay for commercials with soft money;
- tell the public to "vote for" or "vote against" particular candidates;
- and not disclose donors.

Three other Dump Bush groups enjoyed MCFL status: NARAL Pro-Choice America, Planned Parenthood Action Fund, and Defenders of Wildlife Action Fund.

None of the pro-Bush groups did. Several considered applying: the Club for Growth, National Right to Life and the National Rifle Association.

The shocks continued.

LCV wasn't just one group.

Aside from its flagship 501c4—the League of Conservation Voters, Inc.— the group also maintained:

- another c4 (League of Conservation Voters Separate Segregated Fund);
- a PAC (League of Conservation Voters Action Fund);
- a 501c3 (League of Conservation Voters Education Fund);
- a 527 (League of Conservation Voters Environmental Voter, Inc.);
- an unincorporated project (League of Conservation Voters Accountability Project);
- and a coalition called the Environmental Victory Project, funded mostly
  by LCV, with Defenders of Wildlife Action Fund and Friends of the
  Earth Action Fund.[17]

So many LCV entities made it difficult to determine which one was
responsible for what activities. LCV also transferred funds from one entity to
another, which made a public accounting virtually impossible.

In addition, LCV was a member of Mike Lux's Progressive Donor
Network, which tied them in to more than a hundred left-leaning pressure
groups, all lusting to Dump Bush.[18]

The Sierra Club was the same way. It was the flagship c4, but also
affiliated with:

- a 501c3, the Sierra Club Foundation, which gave most of its money to
  the c4;
- a 501c3 law firm, Earthjustice Legal Defense Fund, formerly the
  Sierra Club Legal Defense Fund;
- a 527, Sierra Club Votes;
- a PAC, the Sierra Club Political Committee.

NRDC, a 501c3, had fewer tentacles. Its affiliates included:

- a 501c4, the NRDC Action Fund
- and a 527, the Environmental Accountability Fund, which was busy
  raising nearly $1 million for the 2004 election cycle

NRDC had joined with LCV and the Sierra Club to air television and
radio ads and hired campaign staffs to Dump Bush in several states including
New Mexico, Florida, Arizona, and Nevada.

The League of Conservation Voters boasted it was raising more than $6
million and fielding 25,000 volunteers to canvass voters door to door.

The Sierra Club promised to raise over $8 million and make more than
four million Dump Bush direct contacts—at least a million door-knocks, a
million and a half phone calls, two million pieces of direct mail and 350,000
emails. The Club was mobilizing its 750,000 members and recruiting more
than 12,000 new volunteers, including more young people and minorities than
ever before.[19]

And the Club's executive director, Carl Pope, served as treasurer of America Coming Together, which was raising nearly $80 million to Dump Bush. Ten million of that came from George Soros, whose friend and Open Society award winner Mikhail Saakashvili had ousted Eduard Shevardnadze in Georgia a few months earlier, in November of 2003.

It was another Soros-funded Velvet Revolution, this one called the "Rose Revolution," for symbolic "flowers of peace" that Kmara! protestors carried in their final mass blitz on the Mayor's Office, Liberty Square, Tblisi.[20]

With Georgia down, Soros was putting the finishing touches on another copy of Serbia's Bulldozer Revolution, this time for Ukraine. He was funding infrastructure to Dump Viktor Yanukovych in an "Orange Revolution" in Ukraine's upcoming November elections, just as he was funding infrastructure in America to Dump George Bush at the same time. The one in America didn't have a name yet.[21]

MoveOn.org—NRDC's *New York Times* "issue ad" partner—was busy spending $21.4 million to Dump Bush, $2.5 million of it from George Soros. MoveOn.org's website had featured two separate member-made videos portraying George W. Bush as Adolf Hitler (MoveOn.org apologized) and their online "virtual primary" found that computerized voters preferred more-left Howard Dean to more-center John Kerry.[22]

The size and clout of this network was dizzying, but it didn't get mindbinding until the mysterious Otero Mesa Report came up.

INTERLOCKING DIRECTORATES

ON MARCH 4, AN UNFAMILIAR GROUP called the Campaign to Protect America's Lands had released a 47-page report alleging that a prominent New Mexico oil and gas family had obtained permission from the Bush administration to drill on federal lands by giving money to Republicans.

On the cover, the title, "Cash, Connections and Concessions: The Yates Family, the Bush Administration and the Selling of Otero Mesa," appeared hovering above a scenic desert sunrise.[23]

The 47 pages pulsed with dramatic denunciations of the oil and gas industry, the large Yates family, their $250,000 in political contributions, terrible ethics violations by Deputy Secretary of the Interior Steve Griles—who once lobbied for the Yates clan—and general outrage at George W. Bush.

The report concentrated on the federal investigation of Griles for those alleged ethics violations in favor of the Yates companies.

There were scandalous accusations of improper access, reversal of standard policy, and shady payments.

Like Parenteau's law article, it came across as a wordy issue ad in an election year.

Like the NRDC / MoveOn.org mercury ad, there were no violations to denounce: the Interior Department's Office of the Solicitor General—which has the power to stop cabinet officers dead in their tracks—had investigated the charges and cleared Griles and the Yates family.

The report's accusations were not particularly surprising.

Every Washington insider knew the Griles investigation had been in the works for a year.

They also knew that it had been requested by Senator Joe Lieberman, who was not a Republican.[24]

Routine partisan bickering.

But nobody knew the publisher.

Who was the Campaign to Protect America's Lands?

And who paid for the Otero Mesa Report?

The group's website said it was a nonprofit, non-partisan organization "that works with former directors and employees of the Department of the Interior and other experts to publicize and stop the destruction of America's most precious assets."

But it wasn't registered with the IRS.

A note on the website explained:

CPAL is a campaign of the Environmental Integrity Project (EIP). The Environmental Integrity Project works closely with local communities to protect the public's health and resources by promoting better enforcement of federal environmental laws. EIP also seeks to protect these laws from political interference.[25]

But EIP wasn't registered with the IRS either.

A note on *its* website explained:

The Environmental Integrity Project is a nonpartisan, nonprofit organization established in March of 2002 to advocate for more effective enforcement of environmental laws. The organization was founded by Eric Schaeffer, with support from the Rockefeller Family Fund and other foundations. Mr. Schaeffer directed the U.S. Environmental Protection Agency's Office of Regulatory Enforcement until 2002, when he resigned after publicly expressing his frustration with efforts of the Bush Administration to weaken enforcement of the Clean Air Act and other laws.[26]

The name Eric Schaeffer was familiar—a Clinton leftover accustomed to eight years of big environmental groups routinely sitting around EPA Administrator Carol Browner's conference table rigging sweetheart lawsuits against corporations and looking forward to the silk stocking legal fees they would collect when they won.[27]

When EPA Administrator Christie Whitman inaugurated the Bush "market-friendly" policy of gaining industry compliance instead of just filing endless lawsuits, Schaeffer, a Democrat and a lawyer, was outraged.

His angry resignation on March 1, 2002 neatly dovetailed with his scathing testimony six days later before the Senate Governmental Affairs Committee, suggesting prior orchestration.

Chairman Joe Lieberman praised Schaeffer for his anti-Bush testimony and promised more hearings on the administration's environmental record.[28]

ROCKEFELLER FAMILY FUND

One of more than a dozen major foundations established by John D. Rockefeller and his descendants, beginning with the Rockefeller Foundation, established in New York City in 1913 by John D., Sr.

The Rockefeller Family Fund (RFF) was incorporated in New York in 1967 as a private foundation of the fourth generation—"the Cousins," as Old Money families tend to call relatives of unspecified degree.

RFF is housed in the Manhattan offices of the Rockefeller Brothers Fund, the third generation's private foundation, established in 1940 by the five sons and daughter of John D. Rockefeller, Jr. (John D. III, Winthrop, Laurance, David, Nelson and Abby).

The fourth generation's foundation was incorporated and endowed by grants from the Brothers (David, Laurance, Nelson, and John D. III's widow, Martha Baird) because the Cousins rebelled against the third generation and the vast Rockefeller machinery, refusing to be integrated into the Brothers Fund with its numerous major league programs, and began funding radical projects in a less than systematic fashion.

RFF's guidelines increasingly followed the bravado statement of Laura Rockefeller Chasin, "It's very hard to get rid of the money in a way that does more good than harm. One of the ways is to subsidize people who are trying to change the system and get rid of people like us."

They became archetypal anti-capitalist capitalists years before George Soros.

From 1985 to 1999, RFF developed into a more targeted foundation under the leadership of Nader veteran, Donald K. Ross (he invented the campus-based PIRGs), and grew into a cutting-edge network builder that wielded influence far greater than its relatively modest assets.

RFF refiled with the IRS in 1992, converting from a private foundation to a public charity, which allowed the Cousins to accept grants from larger foundations to leverage their own power, and to not only dispense the usual grants expected of a foundation, but also to operate activist projects of their own, now overseen by the fourth and fifth generations.

RFF also houses the Environmental Grantmakers Association and the anti-free trade Funders' Network on Trade and Globalization.

Schaeffer established the Environmental Integrity Project within days of his EPA resignation—with support from a foundation that would normally require weeks if not months to make funding decisions.

How did he get the Rockefeller Family Fund to work so fast?

RFF's Form 990s explained a few things: In Schedule A, topping the "highest paid employees" list for 2002, was Eric Schaeffer, salary $116,218, benefits $22,709 for nine months' work—in his first full year, 2003, he received a salary of $142,090 with $35,531 in benefits.[29]

He had been signed directly by the Rockefellers, probably in advance of his resignation, although the actual date remains secret.

The Fund had clearly been close to the EPA official for some time.

RFF had allocated $150,000 per year to operate the Environmental Integrity Project beginning in 2002, same for the Campaign to Protect America's Lands, with EIP scheduled for a $1.3 million grant in election year 2004.

This wasn't just prescriptive grantmaking like that pioneered in the '90s by the Environmental Grantmakers Association, it was outright front groups operating in-house projects with executives on the foundation's payroll.

The Fund's public charity tax status allowed it to do so.

In 2003, an RFF grant record showed:

$150,000: Funding for the Campaign to Protect America's Lands' work to stop anti-environmental public lands decisions through sustained grassroots and media efforts, expose the pro-industry agenda of top political appointees and hold public officials accountable for these decisions.

It was the Otero Mesa Report in the making.

In that light, it looked very much like RFF was paying for Lieberman's Revenge: 2002's Democratic electoral catastrophe had stripped the senator of his chairmanship in the government affairs committee. He could no longer preside in majesty over Bush-bashing hearings at will.

He had to request the Griles investigation as ranking minority member, and the investigators weren't finding anything worth prosecuting.

But reciting all the wicked allegations in a well-publicized nonprofit report would be a strong Democratic strategy for the Dump Bush campaign.

High Country News hopefully characterized the Otero Mesa Report as an "election wild card."

Its headline: "The fight to keep drillers off Otero Mesa could set the tone for the November election."[30]

Although RFF's electioneering purpose for sponsoring the report was now clear, it still seemed odd that Eric Schaeffer, primarily a clean air man, would be in charge of a lands campaign, something far from his expertise.

A little digging showed that Peter Altman, not Eric Schaeffer, was running CPAL and generating the Otero Mesa Report.

He was the former executive director of the Texas Fund for Energy and Environmental Education (TFE3), an intensely anti-corporate energy group regularly funded by RFF.

Altman had spent most of his life as an activist. He moved from New York to study at the University of Texas in Austin (B.A. sociology '94), while working part time at Ecology Action of Texas. After graduation he went to the Texas Citizen Fund, which changed its name to the Texas Fund for Energy and Environmental Education in 1998; Altman had been executive director since 1996. He had also been trained in anti-corporate direct action by Heather Booth's Midwest Academy, featured in the next chapter.

Altman also fit the RFF mold of running many projects under one tax exemption. While with TFE3, Altman cloaked his group in several unincorporated assumed names—Citizen's Clean Air Project (1997), the Sustainable Energy and Economic Development Coalition (SEED - 1998), Texas Citizen Fund (1998), and Empower Democracy (2002).

Most relevant for the anti-energy drift of the Otero Mesa Report, one of those assumed names was Campaign Exxon-Mobil (1999)—ostensibly formed to disrupt Exxon-Mobil's annual shareholder meetings in the firm's Dallas headquarters—but in fact the hub of an international network using Exxon-Mobil as an icon to incite a general attack on all fossil fuel companies as a block against global warming and a thwart against global capitalism.

Campaign ExxonMobil was part of an emerging trend in anti-capitalist activism: the convergence of environmentalist, social justice, labor, shareholder and consumerist movements in concerted and persistent attacks on single corporations.

For example, protester workshops for Exxon-Mobil's 2002 Annual Shareholders Meeting in Dallas included such variegated groups as: Women in the Zapatista Struggle; Monkeywrench Collective; Texas Green Party; P.O.C.L.A.D. (Program on Corporations, Law and Democracy); La Raza Unida; Mexika Eagle Society; Anarchist Black Cross; Texas Death Penalty Abolition Movement; American Muslim Alliance; Coalition in Solidarity with the People of Iraq; Greenpeace; Human Rights Campaign; Ruckus Society; Houston Indymedia Center; American Indian Movement Houston chapter; Texas Drug Policy Reform Movement; UPROAR; Satya; Austin Copwatch; Rhizome Collective; PODER (People Organized in Defense of Earth's Resources); and PressurePoint.

Targeting one company for attack by many groups was named "The Death of a Thousand Cuts" by political science Professor Jarol Manheim. It was intended to force corporate managements to capitulate to activist demands without concern for their products, customers, jobs or economic survival.

Exxon-Mobil Corporation was not capitulating, which roused the fury of virtually all left wing constituencies, many of which came together in 2002's particularly ferocious "Stop Exxon-Mobil" project. Peter Altman's Campaign Exxon-Mobil was one of its chief organizers.

The Stop Exxon-Mobil project's network in the U.S. included:
- CorpWatch (anti-corporate group, Tides Center project);
- PressurePoint (Seattle-based networking front, no IRS listing);
- Uproar (United People Resisting Oppression And Racism) Dallas-based radicals giving logistical support for protesters;
- Ruckus Society (activist training group);
- Greenpeace;
- United States Public Interest Research Group (U.S.PIRG);
- Global Exchange;
- Radical Encuentro (training camp and protest staging area near Dallas in Forney, Texas).

Major funders of Stop Exxon-Mobil participants were:
- Pew Charitable Trusts
- Rockefeller Foundation
- Rockefeller Brothers Fund
- Foundation for Deep Ecology
- Turner Foundation
- Surdna Foundation
- Charles Stewart Mott Foundation
- Hewlett Foundation
- Packard Foundation
- The Energy Foundation

Nodes in Europe included:
- StopEsso (single-purpose anti-corporate campaign);
- Greenpeace;
- Friends of Nature (Vienna-based, old line conservation group);
- People and Planet (United Kingdom student group);
- Seattle to Brussels Network (pan-European anti-corporate NGOs).

Nodes in Asia included:
- Friends of the Earth Japan;
- ISAR, Russian Far East Office (Institute for Social Action and Renewal in Eurasia, originally Institute for Soviet-American Relations);
- Sakhalin Environment Watch (Экологическая вахта Сахалиа).

The connection to the Russian groups was particularly intriguing.

In 1996, Exxon-Mobil and Shell entered agreements with the Russian Federation for offshore oil and gas development in the Sea of Okhotsk at the north end of remote and impoverished Sakhalin Island in the Russian Far East. It was an important part of Russia's economic growth plan.

No sooner had the ink dried on the contracts for Sakhalin-I (Exxon Neftegas Limited) and Sakhalin-II (Shell - Sakhalin Energy) than a rash of familiar anti-corporate campaigns erupted to block the development: protest demonstrations, coalition building, lawsuits, pressure on bureaucrats—networks for netwars—all suspiciously like the American model.

Most of the noise came from three groups:

- Sakhalin Environment Watch (SEW), based in Yuzhno-Sakhalinsk, capital of the Russian Federation's Sakhalin Oblast (District);
- ISAR, Washington, D.C., Moscow, Vladivostok;
- Pacific Environment and Resources Center (PERC), based in San Francisco.

SEW made itself known in Dallas at the 2002 Stop Exxon-Mobil protest when its lawyer, Diana Tarasevich, gave "testimony" in a mock "Exxon-Mobil Crimes Against Humanity Trial" at a community college.

The pro-Soviet ISAR had been founded by wealthy U.S. eccentric Harriet Crosby in 1983, changed its name after the communist collapse, opened an office in Vladivostok in 1993, and subsequently built a substantial anti-corporate environment program for the Russian Far East.

PERC worked primarily in the Russian Far East, studying species, mainly salmon and whales, that might serve as surrogates to stop forestry operations and offshore oil and gas development.

The question was, how did these groups get involved with Peter Altman's Campaign Exxon-Mobil?

IRS Form 990s revealed that the three groups had received more than $7 million from 1993 to 2003 from six American foundations:

- Rockefeller Brothers Fund ($1,176,500 grants to SEW, PERC, ISAR)
- Trust for Mutual Understanding - a Rockefeller fund ($400,000 grants to PERC and ISAR, mostly for international travel expenses)
- MacArthur Foundation ($140,000 grants to SEW and PERC)
- W. Alton Jones Foundation ($810,000 grants to SEW, PERC, ISAR)
- Charles Stewart Mott Foundation ($2,131,246 grants to PERC, ISAR)
- William and Flora Hewlett Foundation ($1,220,000 grants to PERC and ISAR)

After the Soviet Union collapsed in 1989, these American foundations and dozens of others had cultivated or created more than 90 Russian groups for anti-corporate campaigns, particularly anti-oil and gas development.

In the nonprofit world, the ruling elite keeps control through coalitions, which are their equivalent of the corporate world's interlocking directorates. *A few funders can set the agenda for hundreds of activist groups.*

Dispersed citizen action groups: Magadan Center for the Environment; Baikal Environmental Wave; Kamchatka League of Independent Experts; Ecocenter Dauria; Siberian Scientists for Global Responsibility; Union for Chemical Safety; Taiga Rangers; Altai 21st Century; Ecopatrol; Chukotka Ecological Union Kaira Club; Eco-Factor; GreenPeace Russia; others.

Moscow-based legal and political organizations lobbying and litigating against development: EcoJuris; Rodnik Public Interest Law Firm; Center for Russian Environmental Policy; Socio-Ecological Union, others.

Indigenous Peoples advocates: Sacred Earth Network (Native American - Native Siberian spiritual group); Russian Association of Indigenous Peoples of the North; EcoDal; Primorski Bureau for Public Regional Campaigning; Amur Socio-Ecological Union; many others.

Tides Center fiscal sponsorships: $140,000 passed through from the Rockefeller Brothers Fund to the Asia Pacific Environmental Exchange, training social and environmental activists, primarily in Russia; other projects.

U.S. Government grants: ISAR had received $16 million from the United States Agency for International Development (USAID) from 1993, the first year of the Clinton administration, to 2003.

The World Bank's Global Environment Facility (GEF) had allocated $144,117,000 to 20 projects in the Russian Federation, plus $86,023,000 to 15 global or regional projects involving the Russian Federation. At least $25 million of that affected the Russian Far East, slowing or stopping resource development. Most of the money in the GEF came from the United States.

The Russian network could be properly stamped: Made In The USA.
It infuriated Russian President Vladimir Putin, who would sign a law in January of 2006 with restrictive regulations on all NGOs.
They weren't just pushing resource development out of the United States, they were pushing it off the planet—the ultimate eco-imperialism.[31]
What did all this have to do with the Rockefeller Family Fund, which had not specifically funded Russian projects?
All the foundations that funded all these Russian projects were also members of the Environmental Grantmakers Association (more than 250 foundations) or the Funders Network on Trade and Globalization (over 40 funders).
Both of those donor groups are projects in the Rockefeller Family Fund.

RFF had the network to wage netwar against the Otero Mesa Report.

In all, the Rockefeller Family Fund itself spent $3.8 million on environmental grants in election year 2004.

Much of it went to overtly political c4 lobbying groups:

- $1,054,000 to People for the American Way Foundation;
- $400,000 to Defenders of Wildlife Action Fund;
- $185,000 to Federation of State Leagues of Conservation Voters;
- $110,000 to Soros and Podesta's American Majority Fund;
- $60,000 to Robert Borosage's Campaign for America's Future;
- $50,000 to U.S. Public Interest Research Group;
- $22,500 to League of Conservation Voters;
- $12,500 to the Sierra Club;
- $12,500 to MoveOn.org.

The Rockefeller Family Fund's immediate network—the Environmental Grantmakers Association and the Funders Network on Trade and Globalization—contains hundreds of foundations that support more than a thousand left wing activist groups all over the world.

That network's significance extends far beyond the election of 2004—and beyond the jurisdiction of the Environment and Public Works Committee.

On the Record

The Senate investigation had found federal grants to Tides Center of more than $16 million. The Tides Pittsburgh office that served Teresa Heinz Kerry might not be involved in radical left wing politics, but its San Francisco headquarters emphatically was.

The Tides Foundation (named after a Sausalito book store) was created as a money pass-through in 1976 by the Arca Foundation with left wing activist Drummond Pike as officer. The Tides Center was spun off in 1996 as a "back office" unit—but also run by Pike, who receives a salary from both.[32]

The Foundation and Center, as 501c3 exempt organizations, obtain grant money from foundations and individual donors and passes it through to other organizations that can't or won't obtain their own tax exemption. The Center manages and houses many of its projects in its 12-building complex, the Thoreau Center, at San Francisco's Presidio National Park, a substantial operation—it distributed nearly $66 million in grants in 2002 alone.

Tides Center serves as housemother, landlord, mentor, manager, advisor, fundraising assistant, accountant, lawyer and protector for an 8 percent override on project revenues. Its own statement:

Tides Center looks to provide a fiscal home and infrastructure support to charitable initiatives that are not incorporated as a nonprofit organization. As a nonprofit itself, Tides Center is the incorporated structure for Tides Projects.[33]

DRUMMOND MacGAVIN PIKE

Drummond Pike was born in San Rafael, California in 1948, the third of four brothers. His father, Peter Pike, was an investment banker. His mother, Catherine Cline Pike, was Marin County's first female pediatrician.

He majored in political science at the University of California at Santa Cruz and gained note as an anti-Viet Nam War protester. He was selected as campus representative to the Board of Regents during his senior year in 1969, where he was known as an aggressive student-power advocate.

In 1970, activists from the Ford Foundation-created Center for Community Change set up The Youth Project in Washington with Pike as associate director. It was a pass-through funding group (and Tides prototype) of rich old heirs who financed poor young activists in anti-business community organizing.

The Center was funded by early progressive foundations: the Stern Family Fund, Needmor Fund, DJB Foundation, J.M. Kaplan Fund, and Stewart R. Mott Charitable Trust. The Youth Project got its early money from the Carnegie and Ford foundations and the Lilly Endowment, Pike's first big-money connections.

Pike earned a master's degree in political science at Rutgers University while with the Project, then returned West to work in its San Francisco office, but was hired by Youth Project funder Alan Stephen Davis, son of insurance mogul (and AARP co-founder) Leonard Davis. Pike headed his Shalan Foundation, incorporated in New York in 1969, the year Alan married Shane Adler Davis and settled in San Francisco. Shalan was funded by Davis and two New York trusts.

In 1976, when Pike had just joined Shalan, a young couple from New Mexico approached him with a problem: they wanted to donate anonymously and needed a public foundation to handle their grants. Shalan couldn't accommodate them. To help, tobacco heiress Jane Bagley Lehman, president of Arca Foundation, stepped in and founded the Tides Foundation as a public charity with Pike as officer. Other donors came, and Pike ran Tides out of his desk drawer at Shalan for several years. His first big coup was helping Norman Lear create People for the American Way in 1980, when he also helped establish the National Network of Grantmakers, pioneer left wing donor association.

In 1981 Davis gave Pike a year to separate. At year end, Pike and Tides went independent and rented offices with Lyman Casey's Bothin Helping Fund.

Pike has since created numerous ventures: Tides Center (1996); eGrants.org (now Groundspring. org) for online giving; Tsunami Fund (a 501c4) for lobbying; Highwater, Inc. for real estate development; Working Assets for fundraising; Tides Shared Spaces, a real estate empire renting non-profit office space with addresses in New York, New Orleans, Anchorage, and Salem (Oregon); and Tides Canada for global expansion, with a prospective Tides Japan.

Wade Rathke, ACORN founder, has been a Tides director from the start.

Pike married Elizabeth "Liza" Cohen in 1982, a Berkeley grad who helped create Resource Media for environmental group outreach.

They have two children, Rachel Catherine (1984), a Gates Scholar at Cambridge in chemistry (she spent her junior year in Tanzania), and Maxwell MacGavin (1987), who graduated from Marin Academy prep school in 2005 and volunteered with ACORN Relief's Hurricane Katrina project in Houston, Texas.

Pike and his wife live in an ocean-view home in Mill Valley, an upscale suburb just across the Golden Gate from San Francisco. They also own a million-dollar chalet near Donner Summit in Truckee, California.

It's like a star nest in one of those astonishing Hubble telescope photos, cloaking some 350 bright-and-shiny up-and-coming left wing starlets in billowy smokescreens called "donor advised funds," a legal tool that shrouds donors in perfect anonymity for gifts they'd rather not acknowledge.[34]

In all, the two Tides units have distributed more than $300 million to a hodgepodge of:

- antiwar demonstrators (Peaceful Tomorrows; Iraq Peace Fund);
- gun control supporters (Americans for Gun Safety, more than a dozen state-level "gun violence" groups);
- corporate social responsibility promoters (Social Venture Network; Joshua Mailman Institute—see Chapter 16);
- anti-globalization protesters (Ruckus Society);
- anti-corporate zealots (CorpWatch);
- domestic Islamic organizations (Islamic Networks Group);
- networking technology support for the Left (Institute for Global Communications);
- abortion partisans (Pro-Choice Public Education Project);
- homosexual activists (Gay-Straight Alliance Network);
- hard-line environmentalists (Environmental Justice Institute; Transboundary Watershed Alliance);
- open borders advocates (One World Now!);
- and George Lakoff's own think tank (Rockridge Institute)[35]

Significantly, David Kallick's think tank report for Soros did not even mention Tides, although it profiled about two dozen of its projects as if they were stand-alones, not tallying the network effect.

Drummond Pike had been developing "long-term efficient markets for progressive politics" for twenty-five years before Rob Stein got the idea.[36]

Since 1993, Tides has also housed three high-profile journalism initiatives of the Pew Charitable Trusts, which caught the eye: the Pew Center for Excellence in Journalism, the Pew Center for Civic Journalism, and the Pew Center for the People and the Press. Pew was buying the management services of Tides much like Teresa Heinz Kerry, but kept control of the projects and how the money was spent.

And that brought the focus on Pew.

Rebecca Rimel and her Pew Charitable Trusts had dumped millions into left-of-center projects, with large grants to NRDC, Environmental Defense, the Sierra Club, Defenders of Wildlife, National Wildlife Federation, Izaak Walton League, Clean Air Task Force, Natural Resources Council of Maine, the Wilderness Society—most of the League of Conservation Voters' members and just about everyone else that had mounted a major attack on the EPA or George Bush.[37]

Pew had given $17.4 million to the Clear the Air Campaign, which seemed to be coordinating its Dump Bush air pollution "issue ads" with NRDC and MoveOn.org's mercury roll-back ads.

Pew also joined with the Heritage Forests Campaign, the Natural Resources Defense Council, Environmental Defense, and the Sierra Club, in a Dump Bush "Crazy George's National Forest Give-a-way" campaign.

The oversight team frequently saw the name of Ted Turner—the high-profile "Mouth from the South" CNN / Time-Warner media mogul—funding special projects for this core cluster of politically active environmental groups.

The Turner Foundation had contributed more than $20 million to the LCV since 1998, $2.6 million to the NRDC, $1 million to the Sierra Club, and nearly $2 million to Environmental Defense, Earthjustice, and Greenpeace.[38]

Of particular interest was $6.4 million that Turner's foundation gave The Partnership Project, a new entity comprised of twenty national environmental groups that pooled their heavily guarded mailing lists in a trustworthy third-party organization so the twenty could mobilize their combined constituencies all at once when circumstances required a potent network.[39]

Senator Inhofe looked at the staff's final report with its graphic money diagram (*parts illegible, below*) and concluded that there was no way to tell where taxpayer funded grants and private dollars cross, or where advocacy funding and political funding intermingle, or whether environmental groups really spent any money on actually improving the environment.

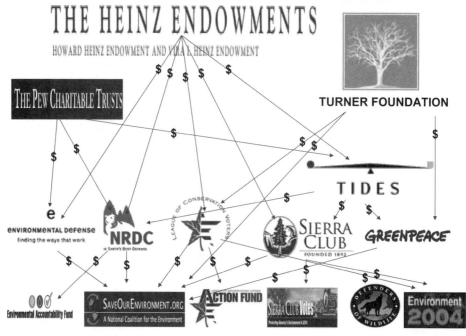

THE ENVIRO FAMILY AFFAIR

THE HEINZ ENDOWMENTS

HOWARD HEINZ ENDOWMENT AND VIRA I. HEINZ ENDOWMENT

THE PEW CHARITABLE TRUSTS

TURNER FOUNDATION

TIDES

eNVIRONMENTAL DEfENSE
finding the ways that work

NRDC
THE EARTH'S BEST DEFENSE

LEAGUE OF CONSERVATION VOTERS

SIERRA CLUB
FOUNDED 1892

GREENPEACE

Environmental Accountability Fund

SAVEOURENVIRONMENT.ORG
A National Coalition for the Environment

ACTION FUND

SIERRA CLUB Votes
Protecting America's Environment in 2004

DEFENDERS OF WILDLIFE

Environment 2004

On the Senate floor, Jim Inhofe said:

Today's environmental groups are simply Democrat political machines with millions of dollars in contributions and expenditures each year for the purpose of raising more money to pursue their agenda. Especially in this election year, the American voter should see these groups and their many affiliate organizations as they are—the newest insidious conspiracy of political action committees and perhaps the newest multi-million dollar manipulation of federal election laws.[40]

There. He said it.
Conspiracy.[41]

It was big, all right—several hundred million worth, maybe a few billion if you count the foundations' endowments—but not really so vast.

Not really, when compared to the dollars of the for-profit corporations they fought.

But then, hundreds, or even thousands of those $25,000 and $100,000 and million-dollar nonprofit grants added up to more campaigns than any industry or combination of industries could find manpower to deal with.

A few funders can set the agenda for hundreds of activist groups.

Taken together, they were indeed The Death of a Thousand Cuts, just as political science Professor Jarol Manheim called it.

A conspiracy?
A conspiracy of shared values, perhaps.
It was definitely left wing.
And if not a conspiracy, it was at least a conniving cabal.

They were just beginning to see the *real* Vast Left Wing Conspiracy.

CHAPTER 14 NOTES

1. Author's notes at the event, American Gas Association Public Affairs & Marketing Forum, Santa Fe, New Mexico, April 16, 2004.
2. Natural Resources Defense Council and MoveOn.org, "First Arsenic, Now Mercury," *New York Times*, March 26, 2004.
3. Margaret Kriz, "Out of the Loop – With Bush claiming a mandate for policies that alarm them, national environmental groups have less clout than ever before in their movement's history," *National Journal*, February 5, 2005, p. 344 *ff*. This examination of the aftermath of 2004 offers a useful history of the environmental leaders' involvement in the election campaign itself.
4. See p. 143.
5. 424 U.S. 1 (1976), http://caselaw.lp.findlaw.com/scripts/getcase.pl?court=us&vol=424&invol=1, accessed February 22, 2006.
6. Lisa Rosenberg, "A Bag of Tricks: Loopholes in the Campaign Finance System," Center for Responsive Politics, www.opensecrets.org/pubs/law_bagtricks/contents.asp, accessed February 23, 2006.
7. Federal Election Commission v. Christian Action Network, 92 F.3d 1178 (4th Cir. 1996).
8. McConnell v. FEC, 124 S. Ct.
9. Senator James Inhofe, "False Advertisement by Special Interest Groups," *Congressional Record*, April 21, 2004, *pp*. S4192-94.
10. Senate majority press release, "Inhofe Questions Legality and Veracity of MoveOn.org/NRDC Ad - Recent advertisement against President Bush may be illegal in as many as 41 states," http://epw.senate.gov/pressitem.cfm?party=rep&id=220621, April, 21, 2004, accessed March 5, 2006.
11. Patrick Parenteau, "Anything industry wants: environmental policy under Bush II. (Natural Resources Policy Under the Bush Administration)," *Duke Environmental Law & Policy Forum*, March 22, 2004.
12. The case is Izaak Walton League of America et al., v. Stephen L Johnson, Administrator, United States Environmental Protection Agency, Civil Action No. 04-694, United States District Court for the District of Columbia. Filed April 28, 2004, dismissed October 27, 2005.
13. Izaak Walton League EPA grants from 1996 to 2001 appear in the "Environmental Grants database" at the website of Landmark Legal Foundation, www.landmarklegal.org/DesktopDefault.aspx?tabid=1, accessed July 27, 2006. These grants did not appear in the EPW Committee report dated September 2004.
14. Hearing transcript, "Grants Management at the Environmental Protection Agency," U.S. Senate Committee on Environment and Public Works, Wednesday, March 3, 2004, Washington, D.C.
League of Conservation Voters board members, www.lcv.org/about-lcv/board-of-directors/ (current); in 2004, http://web.archive.org/web/20040422010026/www.lcv.org/About/AboutList.cfm?c=33, accessed February 14, 2006.
15. Liz Sidoti, "Some Groups to Run Ads Until Election Day," Associated Press, March 22, 2004.
16. 479 U.S. 238, http://caselaw.lp.findlaw.com/cgi-bin/getcase.pl?court=us&vol=479&invol=238, accessed April 7, 2006.
17. FEC filings, available for search at www.fec.gov/finance/disclosure/norcomsea.shtml; LCV website www.lcv.org.

18. See p. 101.
19. News Release, "Sierra Club 'Get Out The Vote' Campaign Mobilizes Environmental Voters, 'Direct Contact' Program Boosts Turnout in Nine Battleground States," Sierra Club, Washington, D.C., November 9, 2004.
20. For an overview, see http://en.wikipedia.org/wiki/Rose_Revolution
21. For an overview, see http://en.wikipedia.org/wiki/Orange_Revolution.
22. Fox News, "Ad Comparing Bush to Hitler Gets Heat," January 6, 2004, www.foxnews.com/story/0,2933,107426,00.html; Joy-Ann Reid, "Howard Dean Wins Virtual Primary - Dean Fails To Get 50 Percent Of Vote," *WCVB-TV*, Boston, June 27, 2003, www.thebostonchannel.com/politics/2298646/detail.html, accessed April 6, 2006.
23. Online at www.protectamericaslands.org/pdfs/yates_0304.pdf, accessed September 17, 2004.
24. Senate Committee on Homeland Security and Governmental Affairs, "Lieberman Seeks Probe of Deputy Secretary Griles' Adeherence to Ethics Agreements," April 7, 2003. Giles was later indicted in the Jack Abramoff lobbying scandal and entered a guilty plea for withholding information from Congress on Indian Affairs matters. The oil and gas leasing issue was not involved in the indictment, nor was the Yates family connected in any way.
25. www.protectamericaslands.org/about, accessed September 17, 2004.
26. www.environmentalintegrity.org/page1.cfm, accessed September 17, 2004.
27. Interview with EPA legal staff member speaking on condition of anonymity, June, 1998, confirmed with third party EPA regulatory staff, June, 1998.
28. Senate Committee on Homeland Security and Governmental Affairs, "Lieberman Challenges Bush Environmental Record," March 7, 2002. www.senate. gov/~govt-aff/index.cfm?FuseAction=PressReleases.Detail& Affiliation= C&PressRelease_id=468&Month=3&Year=2002, accessed May 4, 2006.
29. Data in this section appears in Form 990s, Rockefeller Family Fund, 2002, 2003.
30. Bobby Magill, "New Mexicans take a stand against oil and gas," *High Country News*, March 29, 2004.
31. Putin's NGO restrictions: "Law on Non-Governmental and Non-Profit Organizations," (full text) *Российская Газета (Rossiiskaya Gazeta)*, Moscow, January 17, 2006, http://www.rg.ru/2006/01/17/nko-poryadok-dok.html, accessed January 20, 2006. **Eco-imperialism**: Paul Driessen, "Roots of Eco-Imperialism," in Orrin C. Judd, *Redefining Sovereignty: Will liberal democracies continue to determine their own laws and public policies or yield these rights to transnational entities in search on universal order and justice?* (Hanover, New Hampshire: Smith and Kraus, Inc., 2005).
32. Tides website, www.tidescenter.org/aboutus.cfm; Pike's salary: Tides Center and Tides Foundation Form 990, 2004.
33. *Ibid.*
34. For an overview of donor advised funds, see Elfrena Foord, "Philanthropy 101: Donor-Advised Funds," *Journal of Financial Planning*, November 2003. Online at www.fpanet.org/journal/articles/2003_Issues/jfp1103-art8.cfm, accessed April 12, 2006.
35. Project list available for search at www.tidescenter.org/projectdirectory.cfm; See also, Tides Center Form 990, 2002.
36. See. p. 96.

37. Grant records, Pew Charitable Trusts, the Foundation Center Database, available online (fee-based) through DialogWeb, Database 27, www.dialogweb.com.

Drummond Pike profile: Beth Ashley, "Marin Profile: Pike setting his own course," *Marin Independent Journal*, December 19, 2004; Dean E. McHenry, *University of California, Santa Cruz, Early Campus History 1956-1969*, Vol. III, Interviewed by Elizabeth Spedding Calciano, Edited by E.S.C. and Randall Jarrell, Santa Cruz, 1987; Robert O. Bothwell, *The Decline of Progressive Policy and the New Philanthropy*, http://comm-org.wisc.edu/papers2003/bothwell/theorigins.htm, 2003; Tides Center, *1976-2001 - 25 Years of Working Toward Positive Social Change*, www.tidesfoundation.org/fileadmin/pdfs/tides_history.pdf; Lehman as founder: "Weddings; Susan Lehman, Trent Carmichael," *New York Times*, September 13, 1992. Corporation records of New York (March 13, 1996 - New York State does not issue organizational identification numbers), Louisiana (34571425X), Alaska (57745F), and Oregon (49844186); California property records, (home) Marin County Assessor's Parcel Number 047-151-15; (chalet) Placer County Assessor's Parcel Number 069-320-018.

38. Senate EPW Committee Majority Staff Report to the Chairman, "Political Activity of Environmental Groups and Their Supporting Foundations," U.S. Senate, Washington, D.C., September 2004.

39. For Turner's own account, see, "Interview with Ted Turner," Rotary International, www.rotaryeclubny1.com/RI%20Ted%20Turner%20Interv.htm, accessed April 12, 2006.

Graphic for committee presentation, Senate EPW Committee Majority Staff Report to the Chairman, "Political Activity of Environmental groups and Their Supporting Foundations," *op. cit.*

40. Senate Floor Statement, Senator James Inhofe, "Partisan Environmental Groups," October 4, 2004, http://inhofe.senate.gov/floorspeeches.htm accessed April 12, 2006.

41. Audrey Hudson, "Green groups accused of partisan politics; Senate report cites spending on anti-Republican agenda," *Washington Times*, October 6, 2004.

CHAPTER 15

NETWAR

JUNE 2004

"My name is Bob Borosage. I want to welcome you."
(Cheers, applause.)

"This is the Campaign for America's Future Take Back America Conference."

(Cheers, applause.)

"So I take it this crowd is ready to take back America."

(Cheers, applause.)

It was the kickoff of an intense two-day rally at the Marriott Wardman Park Hotel in Washington, featuring 115 of the most progressive leaders in America, ranging from Jesse Jackson to George Lakoff to Hillary Clinton to George Soros to Ellen Miller to Steve Rosenthal to John Podesta and beyond.

It was attended by more than 2,000 progressive activists who had come to revitalize the American Left—and to Dump Dubya, of course.[1]

The usual suspects were on hand.

Ellen Miller was now deputy director of the conference's sponsor, Campaign for America's Future, as well as its think tank companion, the Institute for America's Future (at a salary under $50,000). She wasn't very visible: her only function was to introduce a speaker and participate in a "strategic initiatives" panel discussion.

Senator Hillary Clinton showed up and told the audience about the overwhelming conservative power they were up against, à la Fabiani— "You know, I do know a little bit about the vast right wing conspiracy"—and how important it was to Beat Bush.

(Cheers, applause.)

Then she became thoughtful.

But electing leaders is only part of the equation. We, once again, have to become better citizens. You know, it is not enough for America's future that some participate and others don't. It is not enough for America's future, the future we want to see for our great country, that it seems that our highest goal in life is to be consumers. We have been given an extraordinary blessing, and at this moment in time, our country needs us, and we need people like George Soros, who is fearless, and willing to step up when it counts. So, please join me in welcoming George Soros. (Cheers, applause.)

Soros stepped to the podium and graciously praised Clinton's political acumen and particularly her foreign relations talent—but didn't mention her fundraising help with Podesta's Center for American Progress. He went to his topic:

I have a deep commitment to the principles of democracy and open society, but I felt that I best devote my energies to other parts of the world. And it is the first time that I feel that I need to stand up and do something, and become really engaged in the electoral process in this country.

Poetic license aside—as we've seen, he was no virgin—Soros set the theme:

The reason I feel that I had to get engaged is because I don't think this is a normal election. This is a referendum on the Bush administration's policies, the Bush doctrine and its application, its first application, which was the invasion of Iraq. The Bush doctrine really is quite an atrocious proposition. (Cheers, applause.)

The rest of the conference was variations on a theme—what's wrong with the Bush administration, how we're better, and how to Dump Bush.

It was significant not so much for *what* it was.

It was just another conference where you ducked out of plenary speeches that were too long, had to choose between which breakout sessions you would attend and which you would regret missing, spent most of your time in the halls talking yourself hoarse networking and plotting, and then emerged ridiculously hopeful at the end.

It was significant for *who* it was.

Each of the 115 featured leaders was a network in themselves.

Each was more than just that speaker on the podium or that panelist at the long table.

Each was their organization and its web of donors and its labyrinth of alliances.

Most importantly, each was a career that meshed early experience with maturing linkages and accomplished performance into political stature.

If you had to draw a diagram of each person-network, it would fill a big page with little dots and fine lines—groups and links, contacts and connections, friends and favors.

If you had to draw a diagram of all 115 person-networks, the mass of dots and lines would utterly blacken a big book of big pages.

ROBERT L. BOROSAGE

Robert Borosage was born in Ohio in 1945 and grew up in Michigan. He graduated from Michigan State University with a B.A. in political science in 1966. He earned a master's degree in International Affairs at George Washington University in 1968, and a Juris Doctor from Yale Law School in 1971.

In 1974 he founded the Center for National Security Studies, helped write and edit two books, "The CIA File" and "The Lawless State" (with Morton Halperin and two others). He also represented the Institute for Policy Studies (IPS)—America's premier far-left think tank and stolid opponent of U.S. policy—in a lawsuit against investigations by the Nixon administration. He won a significant settlement.

In 1979, he became director of the IPS, which was founded in 1963 and initially funded by socialist turned capitalist Samuel Rubin, from the fortune he made as founder of Faberge Perfumes, daughter Cora Weiss, and Sears heir Philip Stern, among several others.

In 1988, Borosage left IPS to serve as senior issues advisor to the presidential campaign of Jesse Jackson. He also worked with the late Senator Paul Wellstone and Senator Tom Harkin, as well as Congresswoman Carol Mosely Braun. In 1989, he founded the Campaign for New Priorities, a consortium mostly calling for reduced defense spending.

Borosage is an associate editor of *The Nation* magazine, where he worked with editor Katrina vanden Heuvel to publish "Taking Back America: And Taking Down the Radical Right" (Nation Books, 2004).

He is a member of the advisory boards of the IPS and Wellstone Action, and board chair of the Progressive Majority. He also teaches on presidential power and national security as an adjunct professor at the American University Washington School of Law.

In 1989, Borosage married Barbara Shailor, AFL-CIO director of international affairs. Shailor is known to critics as "Sweeney's brain," from her position as senior advisor to AFL-CIO President John Sweeney. Borosage and Shailor live near Washington, D.C.

A diagram of this network would be almost as dense as the one that Senator Inhofe found feeding at the American trough and extending its tentacles to Russia in Chapter 14.

And the 115 were only a little piece of The Vast Left Wing Conspiracy.

Conference host Robert L. Borosage was one of a handful of truly influential progressivists in America. He formed the Campaign / Institute for America's Future by bringing together 130 labor leaders, academics, activists and intellectuals (pages 206-207) to push America far to the left.

If you had to draw a diagram of Robert Borosage's network, it would begin with the Board of Directors of his Institute for America's Future:

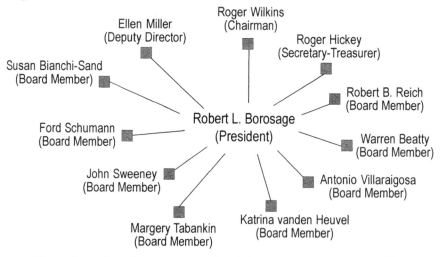

Network analysts have used up sizeable grants sorting heaps of data and writing programs to generate little star networks like this, then congratulating themselves on finding out who's running such-and-such a social network.[2]

But it's like putting together all the pieces of a puzzle and still not being able to see the picture. It doesn't show the *chain* networks, those tidbits of personal biography that help explain why the star looks the way it does:

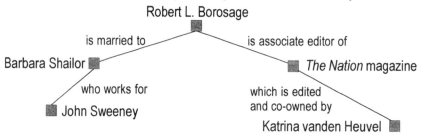

IAF's companion c4, the Campaign for America's Future, has only four board members, Borosage, Hickey, Miller and Jeff Faux, executive director of the Economic Policy Institute, a labor-based Washington think tank.[3]

Who are these people?

- Roger Wilkins, Pulitzer Prize for his *Washington Post* Watergate reporting, professor at George Mason University. Publisher, NAACP journal *Crisis*, editorial board, *The Nation* magazine.
- Roger Hickey, co-founder, Economic Policy Institute, founded CAF's New Century Alliance for Social Security and Medicare.
- Susan Bianchi-Sand, director of United American Nurses (labor arm of American Nurses Association).
- W. Ford Schumann, money behind the Schumann Center for Media and Democracy and The Florence Fund. On April 6, 2004, the Florence Fund (TomPaine.com) merged into the Institute for America's Future. Ellen Miller and $1,088,855 went to IAF.
- Ellen Miller, came to IAF/CAF in the merger with The Florence Fund.
- John Sweeney, president, AFL-CIO; member, Democratic Socialists of America.
- Margery Tabankin, executive director of both the Barbra Streisand Foundation and Steven Spielberg's Righteous Persons Foundation, board member, the Arca Foundation and Defenders of Wildlife.
- Katrina vanden Heuvel, editor and co-owner of *The Nation* magazine, trustee, The Nation Institute.
- Antonio Villaraigosa, Los Angeles City Council (elected Mayor, 2005), former Speaker of the California Assembly.
- Warren Beatty, movie actor and mogul, longtime Democratic campaign advisor (Kennedy 1968; McGovern 1972; Hart 1984, 1988); explored a presidential candidacy of his own in 1999, did not run.
- Robert Reich, professor of public policy at the University of California at Berkeley; was Clinton's Secretary of Labor; co-founded the Economic Policy Institute and *The American Prospect*.

An *all-channel* network, Borosage in the middle, simply shows that they all know each other:

A hybrid, organizational network is a little more informative.

Link lines show shared members or funding paths; lone blocks indicate remote or less-interactive connections.

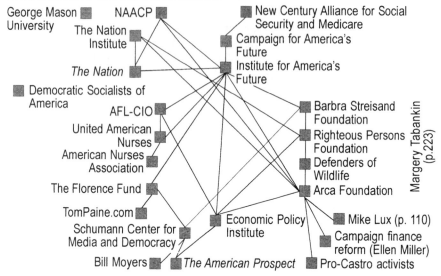

The profile becomes quite distinctive when you look at the donations to the lobbying and electoral c4, Campaign for America's Future:

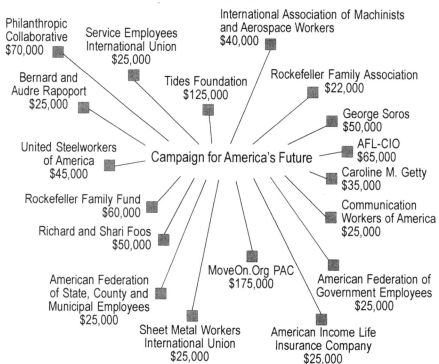

Of these eighteen donors

• eight are labor unions;
• one is a unionized insurance company catering to union members.
   • four (Soros, Getty, and the Foos and Rapoport couples) are populist plutocrats;
   • three are Rockefeller institutions (the Philanthropic Collaborative is a project of Rockefeller Philanthropy Advisors; actual donors are anonymous);
   • one, the biggest contributor, is a political action committee.
   • one, the second-largest donor, is a foundation specializing in anonymous donor advised funds; actual donors are invisible.

So we're really looking at a labor-dominated lobbying and electoral network heavily influenced by progressive plutocrats and secret donors.

It's an adversary Democratic Party network several notches to the left of the centrist Democratic Leadership Council—but not *too* many notches, just to keep it acceptable. It had taken a long time to get *that* far.

PLOWING LEFT FIELD

THE CAMPAIGN FOR AMERICA'S FUTURE was a belated outgrowth of the Corporate Democracy Act of 1980, a piece of hopeless but symbolic legislation introduced in Congress on April 2, 1980 by Democratic Representatives Benjamin S. Rosenthal (New York) and Bill Alexander (Arkansas).

It would have required corporations operating in the United States:

• to have on the board of directors a majority of non-shareholders with no connection to the company, dethroning stockholders as representatives of capital and establishing social control over the means of production;
• to establish a Public Policy Committee to judge all decisions that might significantly impact workers, suppliers, society or the environment;
• to report in advance to the U.S. Secretary of Labor any change in operations affecting more than 500 employees, which would require the company to compensate any economic or social dislocation caused by the change, and allow citizen lawsuits against the company to get payments;
• to publish an annual report showing the diversity of its employees, its compliance with environmental rules, its largest shareholders, its operations and their location in the world, and its political activities;
• to have no director who served on more than two corporate boards; violators are subject to a civil penalty of $10,000 per day (!).[4]

Corporations saw it coming. In early 1979, Mark Green, director of Ralph Nader's Congress Watch, sent a letter to 20 consumer groups whining that business was beating them. Leading activists started meeting in the "Other Roundtable," a takeoff on the powerful Business Roundtable.[5]

They discussed serious problems such as the 1977 shutdown of the Youngstown Sheet and Tube plant in Ohio that cost 5,000 jobs, and industry lobbyists asking Congress for regulatory relief during a time of economic stagnation and soaring inflation—"stagflation."[6]

From that beginning, and building on Nader's 1976 book, *Taming the Giant Corporation*, they formed a coalition called Americans Concerned About Corporate Power. They drafted the symbolic bill for Rosenthal, and began hyping a "Big Business Day" to coincide with its introduction in Congress, set for April of 1980.[7]

The core group assembled an impressive board of directors including Ralph Nader, Harvard professor emeritus John Kenneth Galbraith, food union leader William H. Wynn, auto union leader Douglas A. Fraser, Patsy J. Mink of Americans for Democratic Action, and service worker union leader James Farmer, among other notables.

The supporting coalition was equally impressive, drawing high-profile consumerists, environmentalists, academics, union leaders, religious figures, and a range of left wing activists—Robert Borosage, busy leading the Institute for Policy Studies, doesn't appear in the list.

Nader primed the pump, saying the law would "give all stakeholders in corporate decision-making a real voice in corporate governance."

A disgusted *Washington Post* columnist groused, "Ralph Nader can knock business, but can he build a carburetor?"[8]

The clause requiring corporate boards to have a disinterested majority was ridiculed as letting the passengers fly a jetliner (that was funny, pre-9/11).

Others carped that if stakeholders were as entitled to governance as stockholders, then how come there was no stake market like there is a stock market? Weren't their stakes worth anything to the holders?

The conservative Heritage Foundation published a long backgrounder debunking liberal Big Business Day and the Corporate Democracy Act.[9]

Big Business Day was supposed to become a perennial celebration, emulating the success of Earth Day ten years earlier, with teach-ins, debates, alternatives-to-big-business fairs, mock trials of corrupt companies, and nominations for a "Corporate Hall of Shame," all set against promising examples of worker-owned co-ops and rules for corporate social responsibility.

Americans Concerned About Corporate Power issued a 76-page report for the event titled, "Corporate Shadow Boards" that targeted eleven big companies for aggressive harassment. Unions in Boston staged a one-day work shutdown to dramatize the Corporate Democracy Act.[10]

Despite all they did, Big Business Day was a flop.

The Corporate Democracy Act evaporated with barely a trace.

Overt anti-capitalism simply wasn't ready for prime time in 1980 America.

The Reagan Revolution was.

The Corporate Democracy Act network dissolved.

Its nodes went their own way for the next dozen years.

Some re-networked when crises arose, then dissolved again, over and over during the Reagan and Bush years, much like a trauma patient slipping in and out of consciousness.

Then the liberals-renamed-progressives rallied with Clinton.

By the end of Clinton's first term, some nodes of the old far left network were ready to try the anti-corporate push once again, this time with a better grasp of the problem and a prettier face.

Although many veterans of the 1980 failure had sunk into permanent obscurity, others had adapted to the ascendancy of The Vast Right Wing Conspiracy (or studied G. William Domhoff's power structure charts) well enough to pattern themselves into a similar left wing elite with similar left wing structures—what political science professor Jarol Manheim calls "The Out-of-Power Elite."[11]

Robert L. Borosage's career was at the "political stature" point in 1996, with all the linkages and contacts and friends necessary to create The Campaign for America's Future, which he did on July 17.

It had softer edges than Americans Concerned About Corporate Power, a broader base to insulate it from accusations of left wing extremism, and a socially appealing name. Who could be against America's future?

Its 130 co-founders (*see overleaf*) included a dozen or so names from the failed Corporate Democracy Act battle, including Gar Alperovitz, Ira Arlook, Julian Bond, Heather Booth, Marc Caplan and Barry Commoner.[12]

The Campaign for America's Future had more help from organized labor than Americans Concerned About Corporate Power. In 1980, many unions were suspicious of the political Left, but most now followed the lead of progressive AFL-CIO president John Sweeney.

Some of the more significant of the 130 CAF co-founders were:

- Gar Alperovitz, anti-capitalist advocate of worker-owned co-ops, Political Economy professor, University of Maryland;
- Heather Booth, founder of the Midwest Academy that trained many activist members of CAF; long-time Democratic Party operative; executive director of USAction;
- John Cavanagh, executive director, Institute for Policy Studies, which was *not* insulated from accusations of left wing extremism;
- Hodding Carter III, then-president and CEO of the John A. and James L. Knight Foundation;
- Jeff Cohen, executive director of media watchdog Fairness and Accuracy in Media;

THE 130 CO-FOUNDERS OF THE CAMPAIGN FOR AMERICA'S FUTURE

1. Gar Alperovitz National Center for Economic Alternatives
2. Ira Arlook New Economy Communications
3. John Atlas National Housing Institute
4. Morton Bahr Communication Workers of America
5. Peter Barnes Redefining Progress/Working Assets
6. Ann Beaudry People for the American Way
7. George Becker United Steelworkers of America
8. Berkley Bedell Former Member of Congress
9. Lara Bergthold Act III Communications
10. Paul Berman
11. Jules Bernstein
12. Mary Frances Berry US Commission on Civil Rights
13. Susan Bianchi-Sand National Committee on Pay Equity
14. Moe Biller American Postal Workers Union
15. Norman Birnbaum Georgetown University Law Center
16. Arthur Blaustein U.C., Berkeley
17. Barry Bluestone Northeastern University, Boston
18. Julian Bond NAACP Board Chair
19. Heather Booth Founder Midwest Academy
20. Robert Borosage Campaign for America's Future
21. Jim Braude Critical Mass Media
22. Thomas Buffenbarger Machinists Union
23. Marc Caplan Northeast Action
24. David Carley
25. Hodding Carter
26. John Cavanagh Institute for Policy Studies
27. Bob Chase National Education Association
28. Richard Cloward Columbia University
29. Jeff Cohen FAIR
30. Mitchell Cohen Dissent, Co-Editor
31. Barry Commoner Queens College
32. Ken Cook Environmental Working Group
33. G. William Domhoff U.C., Santa Cruz
34. Douglas H. Dority United Food and Commercial Workers
35. Peter Dreier Occidental College
36. Dudley Dudley Women Legislator's Lobby
37. Barbara Ehrenreich Writer
38. Robert Eisner Northwestern University
39. Jeff Faux Economic Policy Institute
40. Diane Feldman The Feldman Group
41. Edward Fire International Union of Electronic Workers
42. Dick Flacks U.C., Santa Barbara
43. Nancy Folbre University of Mass. Amherst
44. Steve Fraser Houghton Mifflin
45. Betty Friedan
46. Jeannette Galanis US Student Association
47. James K. Galbraith Univ. of Texas/LBJ School
48. Herbert Gans Columbia University
49. Paul Gaston University of Virginia
50. Thomas Geoghegan Author, Which Side Are You On?
51. Todd Gitlin New York University
52. Chester Hartman PRRAC
53. Heidi Hartmann Inst. for Women's Policy Research
54. Tom Hayden California Legislature
55. Denis Hayes Earth Day founder
56. Roger Hickey Campaign for America's Future
57. Jim Hightower Hightower Radio
58. Adam Hochschild
59. Patricia Ireland National Organization for Women
60. Amy Isaacs Americans for Democratic Action
61. Jesse L. Jackson Rainbow Coalition
62. Christopher Jencks Northwestern University
63. Jaqueline Jones Brandeis University
64. Michael Kazin Author, Populist Persuasion
65. Jackie Kendall Midwest Academy
66. Charles Knight Commonwealth Institute
67. George Kourpias
68. Jonathan Kozol
69. David Kusnet Former White House speechwriter
70. Robert Kuttner American Prospect
71. Rev. Peter Laarman Judson Memorial Church

AFFILIATIONS SHOWN AT FOUNDING DATE, JULY 17, 1996

THE 130 CO-FOUNDERS OF THE CAMPAIGN FOR AMERICA'S FUTURE

72. Thea Lee AFL-CIO, Assistant Director of Public Policy
73. Nelson Lichtenstein University of Virginia
74. Judith Lichtman National Partnership for Women and Families
75. David Liederman Child Welfare League of America
76. Rev. Joseph Lowery Southern Christian Leadership Conference
77. Ray Marshall University of Texas-Austin, Former Secretary of Labor
78. Steve Max Midwest Academy
79. Jay Mazur UNITE
80. Michael McCloskey Environmentalist
81. Gerald W. McEntee AFSCME
82. Howard Metzenbaum US Senator (retired)
83. Harold Meyerson LA Weekly
84. S.M. Miller Commonwealth Institute
85. Lawrence Mishel Economic Policy Institute
86. Nan Grogan Orrock Women Legislator's Lobby, Georgia House of Representatives
87. Paul Osterman MIT/Sloan School of Management
88. Maurice S. Paprin Fund for New Priorities in America
89. Richard Parker Harvard University
90. Wallace Peterson University of Nebraska
91. Frances Fox Piven
92. Ron Pollack Families USA Foundation
93. Robert Pollin University of Massachussetts-Amherst
94. Steve Protulis National Council of Senior Citizens
95. Miles Rapoport President of Demos: A Network for Ideas & Action, Former Connecticut Secretary of State
96. Robert Reich Brandeis University, Former Secretary of Labor
97. Frank Riessman Social Policy
98. Mark Ritchie Institute for Agriculture and Trade Policy
99. Dennis Rivera Health and Human Service Employees
100. Cecil Roberts United Mine Workers of America
101. Joel Rogers University of Wisconsin
102. Richard Rorty University of Virginia
103. Sumner Rosen Jobs for All
104. Richard Rothstein
105. Lillian Rubin Institute for the Study of Social Change
106. Arlie Schardt Environmental Media Services
107. Tom Schlesinger Financial Markets Center
108. Susan Shaer Women's Action for New Direction
109. Stanley Sheinbaum
110. Jack Sheinkman ADA President
111. John Simmons Participation Associates
112. Theda Skocpol Harvard University
113. Francis Smith GreenVote
114. Paul Soglin
115. Andrew Stern Service Employees International Union
116. John J. Sweeney AFL-CIO
117. Linda Tarr-Whelan Center for Policy Alternatives
118. John E. Taylor Nat'l Community Reinvestment Coalition
119. Ellen Teninty Just Economics
120. Robert Theobald Dynamic Learning Consortium
121. Richard Trumka AFL-CIO
122. Katherine Villers Families USA Foundation
123. Philippe Villers Families USA Foundation
124. Ron Walters University of Maryland
125. Michael Walzer Dissent, Co-Editor
126. Roger Wilkins George Mason University
127. Linda Faye Williams University of Maryland
128. William Julius Wilson JFK School of Government
129. Leslie R. Wolfe Center for Women Policy Studies
130. Stephen P. Yokich United Auto Workers

AFFILIATIONS SHOWN AT FOUNDING DATE, JULY 17, 1996

- Ken Cook, Environmental Working Group;
- Jim Hightower, former Agriculture Commissioner of Texas, now a progressive media star;
- Adam Hochschild, trustee, HKH Foundation (the AMAX Mining fortune), funds many groups in CAF, also Sakhalin activists;
- Tom Hayden, former SDS president, former California state senator;
- Todd Gitlin, another SDS president, now a sociologist at Columbia University;
- Jesse L. Jackson, civil rights activist and alleged shakedown artist— Borosage worked on his 1988 presidential campaign;
- Steve Max, former SDS member, trainer at Midwest Academy;
- Mark Ritchie, president, Institute for Agriculture and Trade Policy;
- Richard Flacks, SDS alum, Vietnam-era activist, now a sociologist at the University of California at Santa Barbara, who recruited
- G. William Domhoff, whose charting of the power structure of The Vast Right Wing Conspiracy influenced all the other co-founders to build their own elite on its model—long before Rob Stein.

The real significance of Borosage's Campaign and Institute is to serve as a network node for all the other interests of the co-founders; something of a switchboard, if not clearinghouse, of The Vast Left Wing Conspiracy.

And what is such a network for?

POWER FOR THE FUTURE

IN 1996, THE YEAR BOROSAGE CREATED the Campaign for America's Future, two strategy researchers at the RAND Corporation—the noted defense and intelligence think tank (its military-style acronym stands for "Research And Development")—finished a report commissioned by the Pentagon. It was titled, "The Advent of Netwar," and began:

> In terms of conduct, netwar refers to conflicts in which a combatant is organized along networked lines or employs networks for operational control and other communications. The organizational forms that netwar actors adopt may resemble "stars" that have some centralized elements, or "chains" that are linear, but the major design will tend to be "all-channel" networks in which each principal node of an organization can communicate and interact with every other node. Further, netwar actors may develop hybrid structures that incorporate elements of some or all of the above designs in varied ways. Strong netwar actors will have not only organizational, but also doctrinal, technological, and social layers that emphasize network designs. Netwar actors may make heavy use of cyberspace, but that is not their defining characteristic—they subsist and operate in areas beyond it.[13]

The two researchers, John Arquilla and David Ronfeldt, published a follow-up RAND report in January, 2002 titled, "Networks and Netwars."
It began:

The information revolution is altering the nature of conflict across the spectrum. We call attention to two developments in particular. First, this revolution is favoring and strengthening network forms of organization, often giving them an advantage over hierarchical forms. The rise of networks means that power is migrating to nonstate actors, because they are able to organize into sprawling multiorganizational networks (especially "all-channel" networks, in which every node is connected to every other node) more readily than can traditional, hierarchical, state actors. This means that conflicts may increasingly be waged by "networks," perhaps more than by "hierarchies." It also means that whoever masters the network form stands to gain the advantage.

Second, as the information revolution deepens, the conduct and outcome of conflicts increasingly depend on information and communications. More than ever before, conflicts revolve around "knowledge" and the use of "soft power." Adversaries are learning to emphasize "information operations" and "perception management"—that is, media-oriented measures that aim to attract or disorient rather than coerce, and that affect how secure a society, a military, or other actor feels about its knowledge of itself and of its adversaries. Psychological disruption may become as important a goal as physical destruction.[14]

Like Soros' network in Eastern Europe. And in America.
Power is migrating to nonstate actors.
The Campaign for America's Future was more than a nonstate actor in the Dump Bush netwar being waged at the Take Back America Conference.
It was a permanent anti-corporate hub in a netwar against capitalism.
Each of its 130 co-founders was expert in "information operations" and "perception management." Each understood "psychological disruption."
Some were still Americans Concerned About Corporate Power, tweaked.
Heather Booth in particular. In a plenary session of the Take Back America Conference, she gave a characteristic call to action:

"The truth is that there are problems in how corporations are run. It's not just a few bad apples; it's because they are run for private profit, not the public good. We need to hold corporations accountable."[15]

SHE KNEW A WAY TO DO IT WITH "SOFT POWER." In the mid-1970s, the labor movement had developed tactics to deal with a target company by undermining its most important lifelines—bankers, customers, suppliers—with massed attacks on its reputation.

It's called the "corporate campaign," first used by labor organizer Raymond F. Rogers, Jr. in 1974. It became widely used as a substitute for strikes, which were losing their clout from declining union memberships.[16]

The "soft power" strategy of corporate campaigns was for unions to seize the moral high ground ("what we want is right and it's good for the community") in a fight showing the public that the company wasn't living up to proper codes of conduct—and finding weak points in corporate defenses.

A 1976 Rogers campaign—for the Amalgamated Clothing and Textile Workers Union in a push to unionize seven plants of the sprawling J. P. Stevens textile empire—recruited other unions, churches, political and community groups, and a "power structure analysis" group, the Corporate Data Exchange.

The Data Exchange helped Rogers to reason that Stevens should be viewed by the union not as a giant corporation with 83 plants and 44,000 employees, but as 13 men (its board of directors) with widely varying motivations.[17]

Pressuring Stevens hadn't worked. But Rogers saw that two of Stevens' directors, including chairman James D. Finley, also sat on the board of Manufacturers Hanover Corporation, a bank that needed public good will.[18]

So the allies attacked Manufacturers Hanover, demanding the Stevens directors resign, and threatening to withdraw their huge pension funds. One union, the Beltmakers, Novelty and Allied Workers Union, did remove a $6.5 million pension fund just to show that the campaign was serious and deadly.

The campaign forced Finley to resign his bank directorship—more public outcry might have led Congress to make good on its rumblings about enacting unwanted labor reforms—which isolated his company and scared off other business partners.

Stevens caved in and entered negotiations. The plants were unionized.

Recruiting support from religious, social justice, and other progressive groups had unintended consequences. They began to use labor's corporate campaign idea for their own agendas, with or without labor's cooperation.

They became very good at it—think of Greenpeace or Rainforest Action Network unfurling banners from corporate office buildings (or from a water tower near President Bush's Crawford ranch calling him the "Toxic Texan").

Nonlabor progressives ran corporate campaigns with a difference:

> [S]ome of these groups would view destruction of the corporation as a social institution as beneficial to society. Others—the clear majority— take a narrower but nonetheless antagonistic view, seeing specific corporations or industries such as mining or petroleum as net evil-doers whose elimination, or at least whose reduced success, would benefit society. These ideological and programmatic activists have no inherent stake in the viability of their targets and, as a result, are less constrained in their selection of tactics. Even though they may resemble in many ways their labor-initiated cousins, because of this alternative set of motives and objectives, we can think of the campaigns waged by these nonlabor activists as anti-corporate campaigns.[19]

Corporate campaigns have a vested interest in corporate survival.

Anti-corporate campaigns don't.

Heather Booth's whole career was tied up in both.

Her conference audience didn't need to know the details.

She was a legend.

LUMINARY IGNITION

HEATHER BOOTH WAS BORN HEATHER TOBIS in the southwest Mississippi town of Brookhaven, in the midst of World War II's pell-mell military demobilization—her father had been in the Army—on December 15, 1945.

Daughter of a liberal Jewish couple, Jerry and Hazel Tobis, she grew up in Bensonhurst in Brooklyn, New York, "in a loving family that believed in equality and taking action for what is right."[20]

Her father went into medical practice, thrived, and moved the family to Long Island in the 1950s. She felt isolated in her suburban high school. She resigned the cheerleader squad— they wouldn't let blacks on the team. Lynchings in the South led her to join CORE, the Congress of Racial Equality.

Upon graduating high school in 1963, she visited Israel. There, Yad Vashem—the Holocaust museum—transformed her: "I promised myself that in the face of injustice I would struggle for justice." It was *tikkun olam*, "repair the world," as we saw in Steve Rosenthal's profile (p. 47).[21]

That fall she enrolled at the University of Chicago—a budding struggle junkie with energy, a Brooklyn accent, and striking intelligence—where she became active in the emerging anti-war and civil rights movements.

She soon headed up a campus chapter of Friends of SNCC, the Student Nonviolent Coordinating Committee. Her father was terrified at her plan to go to Mississippi in SNCC's Freedom Summer project. She went anyway.[22]

She taught basic literacy in a freedom school so blacks could pass the literacy tests required to vote. She had been in Mississippi for one week when the bodies of three murdered civil rights workers were found. She watched cars circle her school at night while passengers threw bottles and shouted obscenities. She was frightened all the time, but stayed all summer.[23]

She was 18.

Shortly after she returned in the fall, one of her university colleagues turned up with an unwanted pregnancy that nearly drove her to suicide. Tobis found her a Chicago doctor willing to do abortions. Other women heard about it, one thing led to another, and soon she was running an illegal abortion referral service called "Jane," later handed off to a women's collective.[24]

In 1966, at a draft sit-in at the University, Tobis met Paul Booth.

He said, "Can I sit here?" She said, "It's a sit-in." He sat.

Paul was secretary of the radical Students for a Democratic Society at their national office in Chicago—he had also been a founding member.

Three days later he asked her to marry him. Five days later she said yes.[25]

INFRA THE UNDERMINERS

PAUL ROBERT BOOTH WAS BORN in Washington, D.C. in June of 1943 to Philip Booth, a New Deal Labor Department unemployment expert, and Mary Markowitz Booth, Polish immigrant who helped Jews settle in the United States after World War II and later became a psychiatric social worker.

Both parents joined the Socialist Party. They moved from Chicago to Washington in 1935 to work in the New Deal. Born into an uncommonly political family, Paul became politically active in grade school.[26]

The Booths were also active in Americans for Democratic Action, the liberal lobby established by Eleanor Roosevelt, John Kenneth Galbraith, and then-Senator Hubert Humphrey.[27]

Paul attended elite Swarthmore College in Pennsylvania (Class of '64) where he learned of Students for a Democratic Society during his sophomore year from a newsletter sent by Robert Alan Haber, its young radical president, who also came from an uncommonly political family.[28]

Al Haber and his new recruit, Thomas Emmett Hayden—who came from a totally non-political background, yet was on his way to becoming one of the most famous radicals of the Sixties—were scheduled to be in the same place as Booth in August, at the 1961 National Student Association congress in Madison, Wisconsin. They met, and by December, Paul Booth was an active member of SDS.

Al Haber created SDS in 1960 by renaming and reframing a leftist group, the Student League for Industrial Democracy (SLID, a laughable acronym), that he had joined while attending the University of Michigan in Ann Arbor.

SLID was the collegiate arm of an Old Left institution, the League for Industrial Democracy (LID), founded as the Intercollegiate Socialist Society in 1905 by celebrated novelists Upton Sinclair and Jack London. Educational reformer John Dewey had served briefly as president in 1921.[29]

Al Haber's father, William—a professor at the University of Michigan and prominent Democratic Party advisor—had been an LID supporter for years and approved his son's new affiliation. LID was well connected with liberal power players in labor unions and national politics.[30]

Al built his SLID chapter into LID's largest—with the help of friends Bob Ross and Sharon Jeffrey—by focusing on current issues and vigorous organizing. Headquarters paid for him to put on a civil rights conference under the SDS name at the university in June of 1960. They parent group sent two of their best speakers, including former socialist youth leader Michael Harrington—at 32, "the oldest young socialist in America"—who was about to gain fame from his new anti-poverty book, *The Other America.*

The gathering served as the kickoff conference for SDS, and Haber was elected its first president. He moved to LID headquarters in New York as a condition of his new position, where he worked closely with Harrington.[31]

Harrington revered Karl Marx but rejected Soviet-style communism for what he called its "perversion of socialism." He knew in detail the entire Marxist canon and could argue any point or policy with statistical prowess. Like most socialists of the era, he was a champion of militantly anticommunist trade unionism and Democratic Party welfare statism.[32]

None of that interested Al Haber or Tom Hayden or Paul Booth or the growing membership of SDS.

Students in the fledgling SDS, energized by the civil rights movement, felt that a new American radicalism needed to invent its own language and politics, not mimic old American radicalism.

They wanted to "set an agenda for a generation," to bring new life to the Left, leave Marxist cant behind, dump labor movement liberalism ("rote, not radical") and lose anticommunism ("public hysteria").[33]

They were a democracy-seeking debating society of comfortable middle-class college snots, not yet the rabid Vietnam War protesters and violent revolutionaries of later headlines. That would come.

But now, most of all, they wanted face-to-face democracy, Town Meeting dropped into modern industrial society, ways to promote controversy so they could consider all views as a community, to thrash out policy together, to take joint action against injustice, to defy power that seemed omnipotent.

That angered and even frightened the parent organization.

The League for Industrial Democracy was proud of its Marxist cant, labor movement liberalism, and militant anticommunism. They also feared student activism, which might threaten their 501c3 tax exemption.

But the times, they were a-changin'. Most radical students had come to prefer the anti-capitalism of Columbia University sociologist C. Wright Mills and his impassioned blast at American society, *The Power Elite*.[34]

Tom Hayden had even done his graduate thesis on Mills.

Like other intellectuals of the Left, Mills knew his Marx well. Unlike others, he rejected the working class as the bearer of the revolution. They had become a mere parasite on the growth of capitalism.

In his "Letter to the New Left," published in the fall of 1960 in the British journal *New Left Review*, Mills transferred that mantle to the student generation.[35]

Paul Booth said, "Mills was a model. *The Power Elite* was Bible."[36]

To the SDS, Mills was hero, oracle, ideal radical intellectual.

What attracted them to Mills was his ability to show *structure*—the interlocking directorates, the class solidarity of the political, industrial and military elites, how their combined grip worked all levers of power.

Even more significant, he showed how apathy was central to the elite's survival: average people had to be "happy robots" and *want* the elite to wield power: they themselves had neither the talent nor the interest for it.

What if they got interested?

Mills saw complacency as the worst enemy of democracy.

He called a generation out of apathy.

At a meeting in December 1961, Haber instructed Hayden to draft an SDS manifesto for a big conference set for the next June.[37]

On March 20, 1962, while Hayden was in the thick of writing the manifesto, C. Wright Mills died of a heart attack at 45.

Everyone in SDS was crushed, but Hayden felt it worst.

He had been building the manifesto around Mills and the idea of *participatory democracy,* something he learned from University of Michigan professor of philosophy, Arnold Kaufman, as we saw in the Prologue.[38]

At the time, Hayden was mired in tormenting questions, struggling with problems that never made it into the manifesto, big questions of human nature: what if the ideal of participatory democracy was based on a false estimate of human nature?[39]

Hayden's Torment: If man wasn't basically good or altruistic or "infnitely perfectible," as his first draft said, and was self-interested, lazy, and power-lusting, or even just a mixed bag, then what?

Hayden's Answer: Truly participatory democracy was not only impossible to achieve, but misguided.

Hayden realized that the framers of the American Constitution held a fairly dim view of human nature and the potential for participation.

The nation they built *allowed* participation, but didn't *insist* upon it. The machinery of the Constitution was designed to work with many or few at the ballot box. You fail to participate at your peril.

To the framers, America was a vehicle, not a destination.

The SDS wanted a destination, not a vehicle.

Hayden wrote in his unpublished notes, "This is a central fatal fact about the United States: it is a republic, not a democracy, and nearly everyone wants to keep it that way."[40]

Like his critics to come, Hayden was fully aware of the fatal fact about his participatory democracy: it is a democracy, not a republic, and almost nobody wants to change America that way.

Mills had spent his brief career raging against the republic.

But he was gone.

Now SDS had to carry on and call a generation out of apathy.

June 12, 1962: *The Port Huron Statement* was the conference centerpiece. Fifty-nine SDS members gathered near the Michigan town of Port Huron, 60 miles northeast of Detroit on the US-Canada border.

They met at a labor retreat belonging to the United Auto Workers because it was the only place cheap enough: Mildred Jeffrey, mother of SDS member Sharon Jeffrey, worked for the union and helped Al Haber negotiate a fee that SDS could afford.

Hayden's draft—47 typewritten pages covering politics, the economy, foreign policy, nuclear disarmament, civil rights, students, labor, values, and participatory democracy—prompted four days of wrangling, arguments, near-fistfights and shouting matches before the final 63-page manifesto was done.

They didn't call it a manifesto, but a *statement*, regarding it as "a work in progress" that could grow and develop as they themselves matured.

The name may also have been a New Left catch-up to the New Right's *Sharon Statement*, manifesto of the conservative Young Americans for Freedom, written by M. Stanton Evans and adopted at the group's 1960 inaugural meeting at William F. Buckley's estate in Sharon, Connecticut.[41]

Most significantly for Paul Booth, within the Port Huron document was the intellectual framework of corporate campaigns:

> We can no longer rely on competition of the many to insure that business enterprise is responsive to social needs. The many have become the few. Nor can we trust the corporate bureaucracy to be socially responsible or to develop a "corporate conscience" that is democratic. The community of interest of corporations, the anarchic actions of industrial leaders, should become structurally responsible to the people— and truly to the people rather than to an ill-defined and questionable "national interest." Labor and government as presently constituted are not sufficient to "regulate" corporations. A new re-ordering, a new calling of responsibility is necessary: more than changing "work rules" we must consider changes in the rules of society by challenging the unchallenged politics of American corporations. Before the government can really begin to control business in a "public interest," the public must gain more substantial control of government: this demands a movement for political as well as economic realignments.[42]

Mills would have cheered from his BMW motorcycle. It echoes even now in Heather Booth's Take Back America speech.

It was short on details, but it had a specific target that divided the New Left from the Old Left.

The Old Left, firmly rooted in the Marxism-Leninism of working class revolution, targeted the capitalist class, an abstract concept.

The New Left, blessed by Mills, rejected the revolutionary role of the working class in overthrowing the capitalist class and shifted focus to disempowering the actual corporation, to "control business."[43]

With a specific corporation as target, you could find the weak points, muster allies, get a bullhorn, lead a march, block the doors, hang a banner, file a lawsuit, embarrass customers, and get results—without going to the trouble of raising a Marxist army and running a Leninist government.

Paul Booth took that break with the past and turned it into a career. In 1964, his last year as vice president of the SDS, Booth and SDS president Todd Gitlin staged a demonstration against Chase Manhattan Bank in New York to protest its financing of Apartheid in South Africa.[44]

It was the first time activists had focused attention on the corporation as something *anti-social*. It became the corporate campaign cookie-cutter.

Booth developed the ability to research corporate structure—essential to the future of the corporate campaign—during the summer of 1963, when he worked in Washington D.C. at the Peace Research Center. He studied the process of taking arms out of production and shifting military workers to other corporations—and developed an extensive network of contacts among the Left and liberal policy elite in Washington.[45]

The corporate campaign became a specific subject in 1966, when SDS joined with other campus groups to create the North American Congress on Latin America (NACLA), headed by SDSer Michael Locker, who had just finished his master's degree in sociology at the University of Michigan.[46]

The impetus for NACLA's creation was the 1965 U.S. invasion of the Dominican Republic and the resulting election of a new president, Joaquin Balaguer. Fred Goff, member of the opposition Free Elections Committee, was an election monitor dismayed by the ambiguous role of the U.S.

He could find no independent source of information to help press for a transformation in U.S. foreign policy. He began looking for help to create one.

While combing U.S. campuses for recruits in the summer of 1966, he saw the work of Mike Locker, then still a graduate student researching the structure of the Dominican sugar industry.

Goff met Locker in Ann Arbor and the two immediately hit it off. Both were interested in good research, solid information that was documented and not rhetorical.

Locker said his approach was, "Knock out the rhetoric and go straight to the facts. I would call it 'scholarly propaganda,' persuading people through facts and information that what you feel is true and correct, not through rhetorical flourish and ideological citations."[47]

By the end of 1966, numerous campus groups had helped get NACLA running, housed in New York's Interchurch Center—nicknamed "the God Box"—uptown Manhattan headquarters of several Protestant denominations.

NACLA was paid for by the United Methodist Church, the Presbyterian Church, and the Division of Youth Ministries of the National Council of Churches.

NACLA historian Fred Rosen, wrote:

The times were right for that kind of research; young activists hungered for data and hard information: Who's in charge of the universities? Who owns the companies doing business in Latin America? Who controls foreign policy? Who rules the Americas? It was business as usual that NACLA's research uncovered, not scandals that could be seen as aberrations from the normal functioning of the system. Many young students, for the first time, felt as though blinders had been removed from their eyes. After the American celebration of the early postwar era, this kind of information had the power to move and to radicalize.[48]

But it would take three more years to distill their findings into a useful field manual that would shake the corporate world ever after.

In 1967, G. William Domhoff published the first edition of his landmark *Who Rules America?*, making Mills' insight into the power elite visible through charts of power flows, another step on the path to the corporate campaign.

In the same year, President Lyndon B. Johnson had 500,000 U.S. troops in Vietnam, ordered the first bombing of Haiphong, and faced massive anti-war demonstrations.

In the same year, Che Guevara led a guerilla force in Bolivia, called for "two, three, many Vietnams," and was captured and executed by U.S.-trained Bolivian soldiers.

In the same year, SDS disintegrated into anarchy, split by the rigidly ideological Progressive Labor Party and unruly Weatherman factions. Paul Booth tried to rescue the vanishing dream, but gave up and resigned.[49]

In the same year Paul Booth and Heather Tobis were married.

ALINSKY'S VARIANT

The newlyweds faced the Vietnam draft, and Paul was a highly probable target of punitive call-up for his vocal dissent in SDS—he had helped organize an anti-war march of 15,000 on the White House in 1965.[50]

To keep Paul out of the military, they had two children, Eugene (1968) and Daniel (1969), in quick succession—a deliberate decision to get a sure-fire III-A deferment.

While raising two kids, developing the Women's Radical Action Project into the Chicago Women's Liberation Union, and teaching the first course on women at Staughton Lynd's summer class for organizers, a harried Heather Booth earned a Master's degree from the University of Chicago (1970).

In the swirl of movements and causes, things changed that year :

Staughton Lynd, a former assistant professor of history at Yale, met the Booths while teaching on the University of Chicago campus—not as faculty, because they wouldn't hire him—but as part of Saul Alinsky's Industrial Areas Foundation (IAF). Lynd was a noted intellectual radical firebrand.

In December, 1965, Lynd and Tom Hayden had become the first Americans to visit Hanoi during the Vietnam war. It annoyed the U.S. government.

The State Department lifted Lynd's passport (a court temporarily gave it back) and Yale fired him. No university in the country would hire him, so he eventually accepted a job with Alinsky.[51]

Lynd took on a recent graduate of the University of Wisconsin (student body vice president) for a four-month fellowship with IAF. Her name was Marge Tabankin. She was lucky to get the spot because Alinsky firmly believed women couldn't be organizers. She was the first to prove him wrong.

Lynd assigned Tabankin to a new Alinsky project and sent her over to Paul and Heather Booth to get them and their associate, Bob Creamer, involved in the Campaign Against Pollution.[52]

It was a confrontational corporate campaign against Commonwealth Edison Company, replete with shareholder protests in annual meetings, something Alinsky invented in 1967 in a campaign against Eastman Kodak in Rochester, New York to create job openings for blacks.[53]

Saul David Alinsky was a criminologist turned community organizer.

He was a slum kid who worked his way through college and was awarded an unsolicited doctoral fellowship in criminology for reasons he never understood—he'd never even taken a class in the subject.[54]

He did his doctoral work on Chicago's Al Capone mob from inside, taken under the wing of Frank Nitti, "the Enforcer," Capone's number two man, who showed him all their gin mills, whorehouses and bookie operations.

Alinsky didn't finish his Ph.D., but took criminologist posts in Joliet State Prison and the Institute for Juvenile Research, then did union organizing with the C.I.O., getting to be good friends with labor boss John L. Lewis.

In later life, Alinsky had to turn down offers from old friends to help him out of tight spots by sending a little muscle to explain things to his opponents.

In the 1930s he ran the Back Of The Yards project, organizing the festering slums behind Chicago's stockyards that Upton Sinclair made notorious in *The Jungle* (1906). Alinsky believed the poor were smart enough to solve their own problems, given a positive program. He worked with the Chicago Catholic Diocese, the most progressive in the nation at the time. In a mostly Catholic neighborhood, he knew that without church help he would fail.

The experience made him non-ideological, non-socialist, and brutally practical. He was a pragmatist, using controversy and conflict to get results.

He despised passive and ineffectual mainstream liberalism, yet he was not rabid about it. He did not run campaigns by asking if the ends justified the means, but he did ask if *these* ends justified *these* means for *this* project.

This project was Commonwealth Edison and air pollution in Chicago.

By the time the Booths began working with him, Alinsky demanded results, not quotations from Chairman Mao or Che Guevara, which were "as germane to our highly technological, computerized society as a stagecoach on a jet runway at Kennedy airport." He said that to *Playboy* magazine.

He didn't want to turn Commonwealth Edison into a leftist hotbed, he wanted it to stop spewing sulfur dioxide into Chicago's air.

He needed real, everyday people who didn't think of themselves as "activists" or "on the left." He needed them to sign petitions supporting the state's lawsuit against Commonwealth, gather pledges and put them in a trust fund instead of paying gas bills, come to protests, keep the pressure on.

He needed "majoritarian appeals" to attract people in poor, working class, and middle class communities concerned with real, everyday issues.

Winning concessions from a big corporation was left wing enough.

And besides, local energy protests prepared you for national energy protests. And national energy policy was a path to power that could end up controlling business in the public interest, and that was *really* left wing.

Corporate campaigns, not anti-corporate campaigns.

Alinsky's lessons took.

Paul began working with the Chicago office of the American Federation of State, County and Municipal Employees (AFSCME). He helped unionize 40,000 Illinois state government workers and 7,000 white-collar city of Chicago workers, earning him the job of Illinois area director for AFSCME.[55]

Heather had become a leader in the radical feminist movement. In 1965, SDS held its winter conference in Champaign-Urbana where the role of women in society was first discussed in student circles—"The Shitwork Rebellion." It became clear that the men were denying what the women were saying to the point that the women couldn't talk, so Heather finally said, "This is ridiculous," and got a number of women to go off together and talk.

Two years later the same thing happened at a meeting of the leading University of Chicago student groups. Heather was speaking her mind on the oppression of women when one of the male student leaders told her to shut up.

She told an interviewer, "I was so stunned, I walked around and contacted every woman and we got up and left. We formed a group called the Radical Women's Action Project, or WRAP."[56]

She and two other group members, Evie Goldfield and Sue Munaker, wrote a manifesto, *Toward a Radical Movement*, in April of 1968, published by the collective New England Free Press. She was becoming an icon.[57]

At that precise moment, she was working as a teacher in a special high school for dropouts. When the assassination of Dr. Martin Luther King, Jr. provoked the April, 1968 riots, she allowed students to discuss events in the school basement and found herself facing "aiding and abetting" charges.

The job ended after she took maternity leave with her second son. She then took an editorial job and was terminated when she tried to unionize fellow workers whose pay had been cut. She sued and won.

With $10,000 from the settlement, in 1973 she and SDS Port Huron veteran Steve Max started the Midwest Academy in a church building in Chicago. It was a training school for community activists based on Alinsky's tactics, which had become widely known from his 1971 handbook, *Rules for Radicals*, published just a year before he died.[58]

Heather Booth had learned from Alinsky to mobilize the energies of ordinary people based on the power resources in their local settings, like churches and neighborhood groups. It required a shift from the purist stance that quibbled over the finer points of revolution to a willingness to deal with the practicalities of forming alliances with a mix of backgrounds, races, and views. The tensions with more ideological leftists never went away.

"The movements of the 1960s had become fragmented," Booth told an interviewer. "We wanted a center where people from diverse groups and interests could talk about a common strategy, emphasize a common vision, and build popular organizations that would last."[59]

The Academy also relied on *The NACLA Research Methodology Guide*, which finally materialized in 1970. It was the essential manual of "power structure research." It contained sections by G. William Domhoff (Personalities and Elites), Michael Locker (Corporations), and Paul Booth (Labor Organizations), each man destined for great influence.

The *NACLA Guide* was specifically intended to help identify target corporations and reveal their weak spots—the founding document of the corporate campaign.[60]

"Understanding power relationships," became the first item on the Academy's five-day course agenda. Many thousands were to take that course and spread the technique to hundreds of thousands.

Midwest Academy training followed Alinsky's principle of finding issues that could unite the "have nots" with the "have-some, want mores" to follow his thirteenth rule, *Pick the target, freeze it, personalize it and polarize it.*

The Academy's agenda sheet said:

Being right is not enough.
    An organization must also have the power to compel the person who makes the decision to give the group what it wants. In every case there are strong forces on the other side that are trying to make that decision go in the wrong way. Strategy is about getting that power. The key lies in figuring out the cost to the Decision Maker of various actions that your organization can take in the public arena, so that you can get concessions for not taking them. This is why thinking strategically matters.[61]

The principle is somewhere between a protection racket and blackmail. The difference is, it's not illegal.

"Alinsky," said Heather Booth, "is to community organizing as Freud is to psychoanalysis."[62]

By 1974, Booth had realized she could transform what began as city-level and neighborhood activism into a national-level strategy machine.

She was having trouble with the first step, developing a network of state citizen organizations.

Marc Anderson of Chicago-based Citizens for a Better Environment stepped in with the missing tactic: the canvass.[63]

It involves paid staff, usually college students on summer break, going door to door with a prepared script on an issue (such as pollution), raising money, and collecting signatures on a petition.

It proved to be a powerful tool.

Residents didn't know the canvasser was a paid solicitor, usually on commission, with a $400 per day fundraising quota and a 50 percent likelihood of job burnout during the first three days.

They signed the canvasser's petition, gave five or ten dollars, and felt like they were a progressive force battling powerful interests.

In a short time, tens of thousands of young people were canvassing.

The tactic quickly spread to Clean Water Action, Greenpeace, ACORN, the Public Interest Research Groups, Public Action, and others.

It helped pass the Clean Water Act Amendments of 1977 and the toxic waste Superfund (1980).

It had one serious drawback: the prepared script was the original 15-second sound bite. It reduced complex issues to simplistic good-or-evil skits. Everything was like that new box office hit, *Star Wars*—you were either Luke Skywalker or Darth Vader. It overdid Alinsky's thirteenth rule because it was gaining national reach: it fed the growing polarization of American society.[64]

Anti-corporate campaigns, not corporate campaigns.

In 1975 Mike Locker left NACLA to form the Corporate Data Exchange, to "discover, document, and publicize the ownership and control of American corporations." In 1977 Fred Goff left NACLA to form the Data Center, doing exactly the same. The anti-corporate campaign was on its way.[65]

THE STRUGGLE SUBSIDY

IN APRIL OF 1978, Heather Booth attended the founding conference of the Citizen Labor Energy Coalition (CLEC) at the DuPont Plaza Hotel in Washington.[66]

CLEC brought together nearly 70 labor and political organizations during America's second energy crisis to challenge the energy industry and reform energy policy.

It also had two unspoken purposes:

- first, to revive progressive politics by healing a breach between labor unions, citizen organizations, and liberal public interest groups. The Vietnam War, Black Power, and the counterculture had soured labor on both the left wing of the Democratic Party and the New Left;
- second, it was the stepping stone to Heather Booth's Citizen Action.

The Coalition was her idea, developed over the past few years in discussions with associates. In 1977, she took it to William Winpisinger, newly elected president of the International Association of Machinists (IAM).

"Wimpy," as he was known to friends, had come up through the union ranks from his start as an auto mechanic. His circle dubbed him a "seat of the pants socialist" because his radicalism came from personal outrage at injustice rather than a rationalized ideology.

In polite society, he was called a "social unionist."[67]

Winpisinger agreed to help Heather Booth—despite the urgings of AFL-CIO president George Meany to reject her proposal because of her New Left background.

Booth came to Winpinsinger not only because she knew his socialist beliefs, but more because she realized that the energy crisis had made energy issues central to economic performance and public policy making.

That had strategic as well as substantive significance. Energy would serve better than other issues to unify working- and middle-class citizens in opposition to corporate priorities and laissez-faire policies, and thus to build a progressive coalition that would naturally expand to other issues.

Energy policy was the original version of Ellen Miller's "reform that makes all other reforms possible." Nothing runs without energy.

Booth's deeper motivation was to reverse the decline of progressive political forces—labor, the New Deal coalition, the social movements of the 1960s—just as the Reagan Revolution would goad Ellen Miller in the next decade.

Like Ellen Miller, Heather Booth also attracted the attention of wealthy foundations, beginning to take on a serious role in supporting the Left. CLEC's initial funding came from the Stern Family Fund ($20,000) and the Ottinger Foundation ($15,000) through mentor David Hunter (*see* Chapter 17).[68]

The money was no surprise. The Stern Family Fund was the fortune of Sears heir Philip M. Stern, wealthy Democratic operative turned best-selling writer. He was Democratic National Committee research director (1953-1956); editor and publisher of the *Northern Virginia Sun* in Arlington (1957-1960); and John F. Kennedy's Deputy Assistant Secretary of State for Public Affairs (1961-1962) before writing a number of books on politics and campaign finance. Stern was also an angel of the Institute for Policy Studies.

The Ottinger Foundation was the money of forest products tycoon Lawrence Ottinger, founder of United States Plywood, whose widow Louise was a major New York City donor and activist for various progressive causes. Ottinger Foundation later compiled *The Funders' Handbook on Money and Politics* for the Funders' Committee on Citizen Participation.

At CLEC's founding convention, Heather Booth was chosen executive director and William Winpisinger was elected president, neatly symbolizing the alliance of social unionism and Alinsky-style New Left citizen organizing.

The Midwest Academy provided training for CLEC groups, and the Carter administration provided funding, courtesy of Alinsky colleague Marge Tabankin. She had been appointed deputy associate director of a federal program called VISTA (Volunteers In Service To America), the domestic version of the Peace Corps, part of the Johnson administration's War on Poverty.[69]

Tabankin, the youngest Carter appointee, had redirected VISTA into a New Left "institution building" program, pouring money into a network of radical groups without competitive bids or requests for proposals.

It would bring a congressional investigation a year later, and lead the Reagan administration to propose eliminating VISTA altogether. But while Tabankin remained in charge, VISTA institutionalized and empowered the Left (*see profile opposite*).[70]

MARGERY ANN TABANKIN

Margery Tabankin was born in Newark, New Jersey in 1948. While in high school there in 1963, she met Tom Hayden, who was in town recruiting organizers for the radical Students for a Democratic Society. It turned the 15-year-old into an embryonic struggle junkie, kindling nearly obsessive activism when she entered the University of Wisconsin in 1965, at the time a hotbed of anti-Vietnam war and civil rights protests.

1967: after a beating by campus police, she joined SDS and co-chaired a black student strike. In her senior year, she helped organize a nationwide anti-war boycott called "the Moratorium," was arrested five times, and elected vice president of the university's student body.

Late 1969: Tabankin left school to take a fellowship with Saul Alinsky's Industrial Areas Foundation in Chicago. There she met Paul and Heather Booth, lasting and fruitful friendships.

Early 1970: she went to Washington, campaigning (and getting arrested again) with the Youth Citizenship Fund, pushing a constitutional amendment to lower the voting age to 18, (it passed a year later).

June, 1970: Tabankin learned that her mother was dying of cancer. She returned to Newark, took care of her mother, finished her degree in political science by mail, and supported herself as a substitute English teacher at her old high school.

After her mother died, Tabankin, then 23, ran for president of the National Student Association (NSA) in 1971 and won—its first woman leader. She represented NSA at the Soviet-sponsored World Assembly for Peace in Versailles, France, February 11-13, 1972, and went to Hanoi that May on a visit arranged by Bill Zimmerman of Medical Aid for Indochina, a supplier for the Vietcong and other communist combatants. Tabankin and Zimmerman produced a documentary, *Village to Village: A Student's Journey to Vietnam,* interviewing U.S. prisoners of war to denounce American policy. Back in the U.S., Tabankin worked briefly with Tom Hayden and Jane Fonda in the Indochina Peace Campaign.

Late 1972: Tabankin returned to Washington to direct The Youth Project, the foundation-to-activist pass-through where Drummond Pike learned the non-profit ropes (*page 190*). While in this job, Tabankin married activist lawyer Tom Asher, who headed the Media Access project, but it ended in divorce, largely due to the stresses of her next job: director of VISTA (1977-1981). She was recommended for the appointment by Paul and Heather Booth, among others. She reciprocated by including them among the 120 candidate groups for VISTA funding.

In 1981 the Arca Foundation hired her as executive director, where she produced a documentary, *Heartstrings: Peter Paul and Mary in Central America*, against U.S. policy. A few years later she grew ill, diagnosed with chronic fatigue syndrome, and retired to California in 1988, but rebounded, directing the Hollywood Women's Political Committee until 1994.

She is now executive director of the Barbra Streisand Foundation and Steven Spielberg's Righteous Persons Foundation, and serves as trustee of the Arca Foundation, Defenders of Wildlife, the Institute for America's Future, People for the American Way and the Discount Foundation.

Midwest Academy got $288,490 in federal grants and contracts, plus the services of eight government-stipend VISTA volunteers for CLEC. [71]

CLEC became an effective coalition that battled industry with "Stop Big Oil" day demonstrations, the "Campaign for Fair Energy Prices" to extend price controls, lobbyists patrolling congressional offices to block natural gas price decontrol, door to door canvassing with 50,000 calls each evening, and a barrage of studies with alarming (if questionable) prophecies of deregulatory doom that garnered wide media attention. [72]

Even though CLEC had little ultimate success enacting its socialist energy policy—government price controls, a public energy company to compete with private firms, and a federal oil purchasing agency to break OPEC ties to the oil majors—it did win a number of lesser victories: a federal windfall profits tax, congressional authorization of a Conservation and Solar Bank to finance home improvements (never implemented and ignored by the Reagan administration until a court order demanded action), state utility rate reductions for residential customers, and bans on winter utility shut-offs in 23 states.

Corporate campaigns *and* anti-corporate campaigns.

Most vital to Booth, CLEC enabled her to form Citizen Action from the same citizen organizing groups she trained at the Midwest Academy—to the point that Gene Pasymowski, District Program Director of ACTION (the federal agency that administered the VISTA program) questioned whether her Academy and CLEC were really separate organizations. [73]

In 1979, five state groups met in Chicago to form Heather Booth's national federation. The founding organizations were Oregon Fair Share, Massachusetts Fair Share, Illinois Public Action Council, Connecticut Citizen Action Group (a Ralph Nader group), and Ohio Public Interest Campaign. [74]

Two of the five group leaders were former SDS activists—Michael Ansara of Massachusetts (co-founder of SDS at Harvard, Class of '68) and Ira Arlook of Ohio (PhD, Union Institute and University '77).

Marc Caplan of Connecticut would become part of Ellen Miller and Bill Moyers' campaign finance reform network, as we saw in Chapter 12.

CLEC's energy coalitions grew to encompass 25 states. The Corporate Democracy Act of 1980 came and went. Then, as the energy issue waned, Booth turned the groups into multi-issue affiliates of Citizen Action.

By 1985 CLEC itself was absorbed into Citizen Action.

Four years later Heather Booth's dream group had 32 state affiliates with nearly 3 million dues-paying members—Janice Fine's Northeast Citizen Action Resource Center (NECARC) and Mike Lux's Iowa Citizen Action Network were affiliates—and in 1989 Paul Booth got the offer of a lifetime.

AFSCME President Gerald McEntee (who had opposed U.S. involvement in the Vietnam war, to the consternation of AFL-CIO President George Meany) offered him the job of leading the nearly $20 million-a-year national organizing department at one of America's few growing unions.

It was an offer he couldn't refuse.[75]
They moved to Washington.

Heather passed Citizen Action to Ira Arlook in Ohio—whose wife Karen Nussbaum was soon to head the Clinton Labor Department's office for women's issues—and turned to organizing the Coalition for Democratic Values, a let's-update-the-New-Deal political action committee formed by Ohio Senator Howard Metzenbaum in 1990, "as a counterweight to the centrist Democratic Leadership Council," according to the *Washington Post*.[76]

THE MIDDLE-CLASS LEFT

A NEW PATTERN EMERGED.
The SDS radicals were getting rich and powerful.

Citizen Action co-founder Michael Ansara had served as assistant press secretary for Senator Eugene McCarthy's 1968 presidential campaign and went on to buy out the Share Group, a telemarketing firm in Boston he claimed to be the nation's only unionized company in the field. He became a millionaire doing business with the trade union bureaucracy, while remaining an active force in liberal Democratic circles. He was also a key fundraiser for the animal rights activist Humane Society of the United States (HSUS), but he puzzlingly retained some 95 percent of the revenues—his only client with such a high payout.[77]

Wealthy California real estate developer Charles M. Blitz became a part-time trainer for Midwest Academy and a volunteer fundraiser for Citizen Action. He solicited his fellow millionaires in the Social Venture Network, a 400-member group he co-founded in 1987 with industrial conglomerate heir Joshua Mailman to develop new ideas for socially responsible business. Members included companies like Ben & Jerry's, Domini Social Investments, and The Body Shop. The Network was a project of Drummond Pike's Tides Center.[78]

Paul Booth, organizing director of the American Federation of State, County and Municipal Employees, found himself reassigned as executive assistant to the union's president, Gerald McEntee.

Washington never looked so good. It was like being the king's counselor.

The union supplied McEntee with a car and chauffeur. Booth rode along.

When in town, McEntee had power lunches at The Palm, an expense account restaurant where his caricature hung on the wall. Booth joined in.[79]

On junkets they didn't fly first class, they flew in chartered jets and stayed in the finest hotel suites.

It was all about politics. Booth helped build AFSCME's elaborate Get Out The Vote operation, a voter registration effort, and an extensive phone bank system. The union gave generously to politicians at all levels of government.

Early in election year 1992, before the New Hampshire primaries, AFSCME's board agreed to meet with Southern dark horse presidential candidate Bill Clinton. He brought along a letter of support from 840 AFSCME members in Arkansas. He even showed them his own AFSCME membership card.

AFSCME became the first national union to back Clinton. McEntee assigned three staff members to work for him in New Hampshire.

While Paul Booth helped Bill Clinton, Heather Booth directed the field operation for Democrat Carol Moseley Braun's Illinois U.S. Senate race.

Both their candidates won.

Bill Clinton was now the POTUS, in White House-speak—the President of the United States. (Hillary was the FLOTUS.)

Jerry McEntee was the union president closest to Bill Clinton. He got to ride in Air Force One. He was invited to Friday night bull sessions at the White House mess.

Which meant that Paul Booth was executive assistant to the union president closest to Bill Clinton.

That was awkward, since his wife's Coalition for Democratic Values was supposed to be a progressive counterweight to the centrist Democratic Leadership Council, of which Bill Clinton had been the head.

It was politic for Heather Booth to become a centrist.

She quickly changed jobs, and went to work as training director of the Democratic National Committee, recruiting supporters for Clinton's political agenda.

Ira Arlook moved his office to Washington when his wife joined the Clinton Labor Department. Now he didn't live far from Citizen Action's founder.[80]

The group's Washington, D.C. director, Robert Brandon, left to form a private consulting firm, whose first client was the Democratic National Committee.

Michael Podhorzer, who had worked in the Washington office for many years, was now Paul Booth's colleague in the American Federation of State, County and Municipal Employees. Podhorzer's wife, a former associate director of Citizen Action, was Clinton's EPA chief, Carol Browner.

Cozy in the corridors of command.

Citizen Action's state affiliates began to notice changes. The organization that had championed a "single payer" health care system, based on the Canadian model, began backing much of the Clinton administration's "managed competition" health care proposal in 1993, overruling members.

At a meeting of the AFL-CIO health care committee, Jerry McEntee and AFSCME voted in favor of managed competition, abandoning its long-held single-payer position. AFSCME also poured money into television issue ads in support of the Clinton health care plan.

Then came Citizen Action's Campaign for a Responsible Congress in 1995, a hugely expensive electoral ad blitz that angered several state leaders.

Ohio spokesman Paul Ryder complained the state group never had a chance to preview television commercials Citizen Action aired attacking Ohio Republican Rep. Frank Cremeans. Massachusetts spokesman Edward Kelly charged leaders with becoming apologists for Democratic Party politics.[81]

A CORRUPTION FREE UNION

B Y ELECTION YEAR 1996, there had been much mutual back-scratching between the unions, the White House, and the Democratic Party.

Unions sent unprecedented sums to the Democratic National Committee and the Clinton-Gore campaign.

But another presidential election preoccupied union leaders: Teamsters President Ron Carey was fighting off a challenge by wealthy Detroit labor lawyer James P. Hoffa, only son of tarnished (and vanished) boss Jimmy Hoffa. Carey was not doing well.

Ron Carey was the reformer who won the union's first membership election in 1991 and gained high reputation and moral authority for building his new, corruption-free Teamsters.

Gone were the connections with wiseguys like Jimmy the Weasel, Fat Tony and Tony Pro. Carey sold the union's private jets. He stopped meetings in Hawaii. He hired a dozen staffers from groups such as People for the American Way and Planned Parenthood.[82]

But Carey's stainless independence carried over into politics: he didn't like the administration's support for NAFTA and refused to endorse Bill Clinton in 1996, but the Teamsters' treasury gave large amounts of money to the DNC anyway.

And Carey wasn't getting out to gladhand the rank-and-file like he did in 1991.

He boxed himself in and let Hoffa take the mantle of insurgent.

That worried people who wouldn't even talk to Carey back in 1991— AFL-CIO President John Sweeney, Secretary-Treasurer Richard Trumka, and AFSCME President Jerry McEntee—because he had played a crucial role in their 1995 "New Voices" election victory against incumbent Federation President Tom Donahue and his do-nothing Lane Kirkland faction, and they needed the Teamsters' continuing support.

Hoffa's campaign was outspending Carey's by at least 3 to 1, maybe 5 to 1, purportedly with mob money. The election was close, and fundraising for Carey was coming up short.

Carey campaign fundraising consultant Martin Davis, whose November Group had made a mint from Teamsters contracts under Ron Carey, was hitting brick walls trying to raise money.

All the union presidents who were willing to give generously for his re-election couldn't do it because of campaign finance laws. Their spouses could only give if they had separate funds of their own, and even those, said the campaign's lead attorney, would receive "close political scrutiny."[83]

On September 30, getting close to the election, Davis called campaign colleague Michael Ansara to his Washington home for a crisis meeting.

Ansara, whose 150-person Share Group telemarketing firm had also grown rich on Teamsters contracts, had been told to shut down its Carey re-election operation for lack of funds. He knew what Davis would tell him before he walked in the door.

They brainstormed the problem.

It boiled down to inflation levels: the Teamsters' treasury was bulging and Carey's purse was flat.

The law said they couldn't mix.

So Davis and Ansara thought creatively.

Yes, the union was barred from contributing to Mr. Carey's campaign.

No, it wasn't barred from giving money to political candidates and causes.

Yes, some of those candidates and causes seemed to have no trouble attracting wealthy donors of their own.

No, those donors weren't barred from contributing to Mr. Carey's campaign.

What if?

What if those donors gave their money to the Carey campaign instead?

What if the Teamsters would give a replacement amount—or more, maybe much more—to the donors' political causes?

Brilliant. Everybody wins.

The Carey campaign gets the funding it so desperately needs.

The political candidates and causes get more money from the Teamsters than the donors could have raised by themselves.

Ansara knew a cause that could really use some Teamsters money: the Campaign for a Responsible Congress and its sponsor, Citizen Action.

And he knew a rich donor who really liked Citizen Action.

A week later, Michael Ansara went to San Francisco for a meeting of the Social Venture Network and a talk with old friend Chuck Blitz.

Blitz, who had been a behind-the-scenes power in Clinton's 1992 election—and a major organizer of Mikhail Gorbachev's visit to the United States the same year—was interested in Ansara's proposition.

After getting a guarantee that the Teamsters money would indeed replace or double his own fundraising, Blitz agreed and went to work.

He instructed Citizen Action's deputy director Rochelle Davis to send the Teamsters two memos seeking a total of $475,000. The money, of course, would be used to fund the costly Campaign for a Responsible Congress, which at that very moment was campaigning heavily in congressional elections.

The payment was approved by Teamsters' government affairs chief William Hamilton and paid within two days.

Citizen Action wasted no time keeping its end of the bargain, and quickly arranged for three donors to give a total of $90,000 to Mr. Carey's campaign.

A week or so later, Citizen Action gave an additional $75,000 to Mike Ansara's Share Group, presumably for his services in the Carey campaign.

Blitz told Citizen Action to funnel $185,000 to a Ron Carey committee called Teamsters for a Corruption Free Union.

Citizen Action also cut a $195,000 check to the Lobby for Individual Freedom and Equality, which advocates on behalf of AIDS victims, which funneled $168,000 to Californians for Medical Rights, which advocates for the medical use of marijuana, a pet project of Blitz, but not the Teamsters.[84]

Martin Davis went to the Democratic National Committee. If Terry McAuliffe let him tap their donor list for Carey, the Teamsters would deliver hundreds of thousands of dollars to state party organizations.

Union leaders were queried and agreed to help.

Jerry McEntee solicited $20,000 for Carey from the owners of Kelley Press, an AFSCME supplier.

Paul Booth raised tens of thousands for Carey.

More than $4 million in Democratic National Committee money moved to Citizen Action and other groups, and at least $885,000 in union funds went into Carey's re-election campaign.

Carey won.

But the brilliant plan had a name: money laundering, which is a Class E felony in New York, where the plan came to the attention of federal prosecutors.

Nobody would have been the wiser but for Richard Leebove, a Detroit public-relations consultant on Hoffa's campaign who suspected the election had been stolen.

Using some highly unusual tactics, he recruited informants in the Washington Teamsters headquarters to provide sensitive documents and computer files, including the first solid evidence that money had been siphoned off the union's treasury for Carey's campaign.

He obtained private information from a donor's brokerage account.

He lied about his identity to gather information about other donors.

Leebove gave the information to the U.S. Attorney's office in New York, and they started a federal criminal probe the next day.[85]

Federal officials stripped Carey of his office and barred him from ever serving again.

In a special election Hoffa became Teamsters president.

Carey denied any knowledge of the money laundering and suspected it was a setup to install Hoffa and immunize him from any future Carey challenge.

Citizen Action shut its doors when state affiliates bolted at the scandal and funding dried up.[86]

The scandal was called "Teamstergate."

Teamsters political director William Hamilton, an alumnus of AFSCME, was convicted in federal court and sentenced to three years in prison.

Four others entered guilty pleas to funneling illegal contributions to Carey's campaign:

Davis, Nash and Ansara each got two years probation; Blitz got 6 months probation.

Ron Carey was indicted for perjury to a grand jury, but acquitted at trial.[86]

Trial testimony showed that other fundraisers in the scheme included:

- AFL-CIO president John Sweeney;
- AFSCME president Jerry McEntee;
- Paul Booth, McEntee's executive assistant;
- SEIU president Andy Stern;
- United Mine Workers president Rich Trumka; and
- 1996 Clinton-Gore reelection manager Terry McAuliffe.

Heather Booth—disconnected from Citizen Action—was not implicated.

Ira Arlook paid over $200,000 to lawyers who kept Citizen Action from prosecution.

Trumka took the Fifth Amendment against self-incrimination before a grand jury and before a congressional hearing. He was not indicted.

The Clinton administration didn't come after the rest of them.

Neither did the Bush administration.

Heather Booth helped revive the moribund Citizen Action in 1999, resurrecting it as USAction. The next year she founded the NAACP National Voter Fund.

In early 2002, she became a consultant for MoveOn.org, Campaign for America's Future, Center for Community Change, and the Proteus Fund.

BUTTING IN IN BEIJING

LATER IN 2002—in October—she and Paul traveled with SEIU President Andy Stern to the People's Republic of China. Stern was climbing out of a deep depression from the death of his beloved 13-year-old daughter Cassie, who died in his arms of complications from routine back surgery. The China trip was in part his way of putting some meaning back in his life.

There they met with Wei Jianxing, president of the All China Federation of Trade Unions (ACFTU) and member of the Communist Party politburo.

Their trip was more than an act of defiance against John Sweeney's AFL-CIO and its long-standing anticommunist policy of refusing to deal with China's government-controlled "unions."

Independent unions were banned in China. The Stern / Booth visit amounted to a breakaway assertion that China's unions were legitimate worker organizations and it was in their mutual interest to have a relationship.

What that "mutual interest" might be was unintelligible at the time. It took five years for it to become clear.

Facts: There were more than a billion people in China. The Communist rulers were allowing more and more foreign businesses to hire them at low wages. China was becoming the mother lode for American corporations.

It was simple, really. Stern went there because his employers were going there. The largest security and food service companies in the world were going to China. Wal-Mart was going to China. Boeing was going to China.

If capital globalized, labor must globalize.

China was a key to expanding the strength of American unions with global alliances of potentially global power. Only Andy Stern saw that.[87]

Historically, Chinese union leaders represented only workers in state-owned companies, because that's all there were. Their unions were really just Party-sanctioned social clubs that kept low-paid workers happy with comfortable hangouts, karaoke machines, and small cash bonuses during Chinese festivals. Their unions were totally toothless.

But now private companies from America were employing thousands of Chinese union members. Their leaders hadn't a clue how to negotiate a labor contract. They had never heard of grassroots organizing. When they approached American management, the boss just shooed them away. Unions were mere puppets of the regime, and the regime wasn't putting any muscle on American corporations to follow its own law requiring unionization.

Andy Stern went there and changed things. He went to China six times, learning, teaching, urging changes in the law. He brought a Chinese union delegation to America for seminars on how to run a real union.

By 2007, they had learned enough to unionize Wal-Mart in China, something union leaders couldn't do in the United States. They unionized others too, not getting better wages, but requiring each company they organized to contribute 2% of its local payroll to support the union's activities.[88]

It was a huge symbolic victory. Stern said, "Workers who work for the same employers, whether they are in our country or around the world, are much stronger when they work together." Globalizing the globalizers.[89]

Stern even won over the AFL-CIO's John Sweeney, who eventually went to China himself. But not in 2002. Then the fur flew.

When a *South China Morning Post* story made it appear that the first Stern delegation was officially representing the AFL-CIO, Bob Borosage's wife, Barbara Shailor—the federation's international affairs director—issued a scathing denial, denouncing the ACFTU as "not an independent trade union but rather part of Chinese government and party structure."[90]

It wasn't just three progressives pitting themselves against the federation's anticommunist policy, it was also a political jab at President George W. Bush.

It came just a few days before his meeting in Crawford, Texas with the Chinese president, Jiang Zemin.

Agreements on a new round of human rights dialogue with China were anticipated at the meeting—including worker rights issues that Jiang could now deflect because of Andy Stern and the Booths.[91]

When he returned to Washington with the Booths, Andy Stern had his aide Gina Glantz call Harold Ickes about having dinner at BeDuCi.

He had something more in mind for George W. Bush.

The Ivy League union boss very likely knew it had been named "netwar."

THE NET OUROBOROS

AT BOB BOROSAGE'S TAKE BACK AMERICA CONFERENCE, Heather Booth was more than that woman on the podium at the Marriott Wardman Park Hotel.

She was her many organizations and their many webs of many donors and their many labyrinths of many alliances.

Most importantly, she was a career that meshed early experience with maturing linkages and accomplished performance into political stature.

If you had to draw a star diagram of her social network, you'd only know that she was the dot in the middle, and all those fine lines that blackened the page went to more people than you could possibly count.

She told Bob Borosage's Take Back America conference:

> Look around in this very room. In this room are African-Americans whose grandparents were slaves. In this room are women whose mothers were denied the right to control their own bodies and some who may have faced backroom abortions. In this room are gays and lesbians who lived closeted, afraid for the loss of support of family, of their jobs, and even for loss of their lives for the love they were not allowed to speak. In this room are working women and men whose grandparents never had the time to see their children grow up, before a labor movement won the 8-hour day and its benefits. In this room are people maimed by machinery before there was OSHA. In this room are people who would not have had health care if it were not for Medicare. In this room there are people of every faith and of every class: we are the America of the Mayflower and the America of the slave ship Amistad together, the America of Ellis Island and those who crossed the Rio Grande at the mercy of the coyotes, together. We are the America of Omaha Beach and of the bridge at Selma together, the America of Cesar Chavez and the America of Justin Dart, the father of the Disability Rights movement who died last year. We are together. In this room there are people who have stood together and marched together and who together make this a better country and a better world.
>
> These are important victories. They were worth struggling for. They were worth some people dying for. They are worth living for, to retain. We have done it before and we can do it again, we need to do it again, we will do it again. And we will never go back. And to this we make our pledge. It is a solemn oath.
>
> We will be there.[92]

At the finish line on November 3, 2004, they weren't.

CHAPTER 15 NOTES

1. Robert Borosage's 2004 Take Back America Conference materials, www.ourfuture.org/projects/national_conference/2004/, accessed April 5, 2006.

Borosage biography: http://www.huffingtonpost.com/contributors/bio.php?nick=robert-l-borosage&name=Robert+L.+Borosage, accessed April 6, 2006; www.motherjones.com/radio/2005/09/borosage _bio.html, accessed April 6, 2006; telephone conversation, May 2006.

2. Valdis Krebs, "How to do Social Network Analysis," www.orgnet.com/sna.html, accessed April 7, 2006. Diagrams here are hand drawn.

3. Institute for America's Future, Form 990, 2003; Campaign for America's Future, Form 990, 2004.

4. The Corporate Democracy Act of 1980, H.R. 7010, 96th Cong., 2d Sess. (1980).

5. Merrill Brown, "Big Business Day: The Voice of the 'Stakeholder' Is Rising," *Washington Post*, April 14, 1980, WB22.

6. Gar Alperovitz, *America Beyond Capitalism: Reclaiming Our Wealth, Our Liberty, and Our Democracy* (Hoboken, New Jersey, John Wiley & Sons, 2004).

7. Merrill Brown, "Coalition Attacks Big Business," *Washington Post*, April 18, 1980, C3.

8. John Chamberlain, "Nader Can Knock Business, But Can He Build a Carburetor?" *Washington Post*, April 13, 1980; F1.

9. William Poole, "The Corporate Democracy Act and Big Business Day: Rhetoric and Reality," *Heritage Foundation Backgrounder #113*, Washington, D.C., March 11, 1980.

10. Warren Brown, "'Big Business Day' Group Is Taking Aim at 11 Firms," *Washington Post*, April 10, 1980, B3; Wilfrid C. Rodgers, "Rally may disrupt Hub construction," *Boston Globe*, April 17, 1980.

11. Jarol B. Manheim, *Biz-War and the Out-of-Power Elite: The Progressive-Left Attack on the Corporation,* (Mahwah, New Jersey, Lawrence Erlbaum Associates, 2004).

12. CAF Founders and advisors: www.ourfuture.org/aboutus/founders.cfm, accessed April 4, 2006.

13. John Arquilla and David Ronfeldt, *The Advent of Netwar* (Santa Monica, California, RAND Corporation, January 25, 1996), p. vii.

14. John Arquilla and David Ronfeldt, *Networks and Netwars: The Future of Terror, Crime, and Militancy* (Santa Monica, California, RAND Corporation, January 25, 1996), pp. 1,2.

15. Heather Booth, "Prepared Remarks," Take Back America Conference, Friday, June 6, 2003, Washington, D.C. www.ourfuture.org/docUploads/Booth.6.8.pdf, accessed May 5, 2006. These remarks were delivered at the 2003 conference.

16. Michael C. Jensen, "Union Strategist On Wall Street," *New York Times,* March 26, 1978, p. F5.

17. David Vogel, *Lobbying the Corporation: Citizen Challenges to Business Authority*, (New York, Basic Books, Inc., 1978), p. 139.

18. Michael C. Jensen, "Drive to Isolate J.P. Stevens Is Renewed," *New York Times*, March 17, 1978, p. D1.

19. Jarol B. Manheim, *Biz-War and the Out-of-Power Elite: The Progressive-Left Attack on the Corporation, op. cit.*, p. 105.

20. "Heather Booth: Living the Movement Life," essay edited by Gina Caneva from an interview conducted by Becky Kluchin, The Chicago Women's Liberation Union (CWLU) Herstory Website, *Memoirs and Biographies*, www.cwluherstory.com/CWLUMemoir/Booth.html, accessed August 5, 2005. Much of the background that follows came from two 1992 interviews in the Paula Kamen collection at McCormick Library of Special Collections, Northwestern University Library, Evanston, Illinois, interviews F. 3 and F. 4 of Series CXXV, with Paul and Heather Booth. Thanks to R. Russell Maylone, Curator, for copying them to me with permission to quote.

21. Heather Booth, "Statement," *Jewish Women and the Feminist Revolution*, www.jwa.org/feminism/_html/JWA004.htm, accessed April 28, 2006.

22. "Heather Tobis Booth," Veterans of the civil rights movement website, www.crmvet.org/vet/booth.htm, accessed August 5, 2005.

23. Carol Morello, "For Civil Rights Crusaders, Arrest Brings Relief," *Washington Post*, January 8, 2005, p. B1.

24. "Heather Booth and the roots of Jane," *Jane, an Abortion Service*, www.chicklet.com/hb.html, accessed August 5, 2005.

25. Juan Williams, *My Soul Looks Back in Wonder: Voices of the Civil Rights Experience,* (New York, N.Y., Sterling Publishing Company, Inc., 2004). p.147.

26. James Miller, *Democracy is in the Streets: From Port Huron to the Siege of Chicago*, (Cambridge, Massachusetts: Harvard University Press, 1987, paperback edition, 1994), p. 219

27. Obituary, "Mary Markowitz Booth, Psychiatric Social Worker," *Washington Post*, June 30, 2005.

28. James Miller, *Democracy is in the Streets, op. cit.*, p. 23.

29. Original sources housed in: League for Industrial Democracy, Manuscripts, Special Collections and University Archives, Stony Brook University, and the Taiment Library / Robert F. Wagner Labor Archive, Intercollegiate Socialist Society Records, 1900-1921, New York University. ISS name changed to LID in 1921, John Dewey president that year.

30. James Miller, *Democracy is in the Streets, op. cit.*, p. 30.

31. *Ibid.*, p. 38-40

32. Gary Dorrien, "Michael Harrington: Socialist to the End," *The Christian Century*, October 11, 2000, pp. 1002-1009. http://www.religion-online.org/showarticle.asp?title=1969, accessed April 29, 2006.

33. James Miller, *Democracy is in the Streets, op. cit.*, p. 106*ff*.

34. Charles Wright Mills, *The Power Elite*, (New York: Oxford University Press, 1958).

35. Charles Wright Mills, "Letter to the New Left," *New Left Review*, No. 5, September-October, 1960.

36. James Miller, *Democracy is in the Streets, op. cit.*, p. 87.

37. *Ibid,* p. 77.

38. *See* Prologue, p. 10. *See also*, Arnold S. Kaufman, *The Radical Liberal, new man in American politics* (Palo Alto, California: Atherton Press, 1968).

39. James Miller, *Democracy is in the Streets, op. cit.*, p. 96.

40. *Ibid.* p. 90.

41. Online at www.fiu.edu/~yaf/sharon.html, accessed July 9, 2006.

42. The full text is online at http://coursesa.matrix.msu.edu/~hst306/documents/huron.html, accessed August 8. 2005.

43. Barry Grey, "The middle class 'left' and the fall of Ron Carey," World Socialist Website, December 29, 1997. www.wsws.org/polemics/1997/dec1997/carey.shtml, accessed May 12, 2006.

44. James Miller, *Democracy is in the Streets*, *op. cit.*, p. 226-228.

45. *Ibid*, p. 219.

46. Fred Rosen, "'The Movement' Gives Birth to NACLA," *NACLA Report on the Americas*, Vol. 36, No. 3, November/December 2002.

47. *Ibid.*

48. *Ibid.*

49. Wikipedia entry, "Weatherman (organization)," http://en.wikipedia.org/wiki/Weatherman_(organization), accessed July 9, 2006. *See also*, Tom Wells, *The War Within: America's Battle Over Vietnam*, (Berkeley, University of California Press, 1994), p. 97.

50. James Miller, *Democracy is in the Streets*, *op. cit.*, p. 231.

51. John Chamberlain, "Passports and Equality," *Pacific Stars and Stripes*, February 23, 1966, p. 8. *See also*, Michael Miller, "'Beyond the Politics of Place': A Critical Review," Comm-Org, University of Wisconsin, October 9, 1996. Online at http://comm-org.wisc.edu/papers96/miller.html, accessed November 27, 2006.

52. Gary Delgado, *Organizing the Movement: The Roots and Growth of ACORN*, (Philadelphia: Temple University Press, 1986), p. 23.

53. Gene I. Maeroff, "Stinging the Corporations," *The Nation*, Volume: 210, Issue #24, June 22, 1970.

54. Eric Norden, Saul Alinsky Interview, *Playboy*, March, 1972.

55. James Warren, "Student Radical Turned Union Chief Faces New Challenge," *Seattle Times*, January 1, 1989, p. A8.

56. Midwest Academy, "History," www.midwestacademy.com/about_us.html, accessed May 3, 2006. Saul D. Alinsky, *Rules for Radicals: A Pragmatic Primer for Realistic Radicals* (New York, Random House, 1971; Vintage Books Edition, 1972, 1989).

57. Harry C. Boyte, "The Civic Renewal Movement in the US: On Silences and Civic Muscle, or Why Social Capital is a Useful but Insufficient Concept," Presentation to the Havens Center, University of Wisconsin-Madison, April 10, 2001.

58. North American Congress on Latin America, *NACLA Research Methodology Guide* (New York, 1970, revised edition 1971), pp 6-9 and 21-24.

59. Midwest Academy brochure, July 30, 1998, reproduced online at http://web.archive.org/web/19991109145107/www.mindspring.com/~midwestacademy/page2.html, accessed May 10, 2006.

60. As quoted in Harry C. Boyte, *The Backyard Revolution: Understanding the New Citizen Movement* (Philadelphia, Temple University, 1980), p. 39.

61. Harry C. Boyte, "A Tale of Two Playgrounds: Young People and Politics," paper presented at American Political Science Association, 2001, www.publicwork.org/pdf/speeches/TaleofTw.pdf, accessed May 10, 2006.

62. Heather Booth, Steve Max and colleague Harry Boyte wrote a defense of the canvass, acknowledging its flaws, in *Citizen Action and the New American Populism* (Philadelphia, Temple University Press, 1986), *pp.* 69-83.

63. David Vogel, *Lobbying the Corporation, op. cit.* No author, *Data Center: 25 Years of Informing Activism*, (New York: Data Center, 2002), p. 13. online at

www.datacenter.org/about/DataCenter_report.pdf, accessed July 7, 2006.

64. Andrew Battista, "Labor and Liberalism: The Citizen Labor Energy Coalition," *Labor History*, August 1999. www.findarticles.com/p/articles/mi_m0348/is_3_40/ai_55449351, accessed April 28, 2006.

65. Bob Roman, "William W. Winpisinger, 1924 – 1997," New Ground 56 – Chicago Democratic Socialists of America, January- February, 1998. www.chicagodsa.org/ngarchive/ng56.html#anchor1041945, accessed May 10, 2006.

66. The Philip M. Stern Family Fund (incorporated District of Columbia, 1959), and the Louise and Lawrence Ottinger Foundation (incorporated New York, 1945), IRS reports, 1979, 1980.

67. No author, "The New Left in Government Part II: The VISTA Program as "Institution Building," *Institutional Analysis #17*, (Washington, D.C.: Heritage Foundation, February 19, 1982). Online at www.heritage.org/Research/GovernmentReform/IA17.cfm, accessed November 26, 2006.

68. Domestic Volunteer Service Act Amendments of 1979, Hearings before the Subcommittee on Child and Human Development, Senate Committee on Labor and Human Resources, February 8, 1979 (Washington, D.C., GPO, 1979).

Tabankin biography: Nikki Finke, "A Radical Move - Margery Tabankin Has Fled the Center of Power for the Center of Status, but Without Missing an Activist Beat," *Los Angeles Times*, August 13, 1989. AP, "Anti-Bullhorn Law Challenged by Students," *Stevens Point (WI) Daily Journal*, November 21, 1969. William T. Poole, "The New Left in Government: From Protest to Policy-Making," *Institutional Analysis #9*, Heritage Foundation, Washington, D.C., November 1978. Sam Dobbins, "War Protests Mount," *Lowell Sun*, April 18, 1972. AP Wirephoto cutline: "Prisoners of War Interviewed," *Sheboygan Press*, June 12, 1972. AP, "NSA Stresses Activity, Not Demonstration," *Manitowoc Herald Times,* August 15, 1972. Doug McMillan, "A Nevada Phenomenon - Money Makes Difference for Citizen Alert," *Nevada State Journal*, March 27, 1977. Robert O. Bothwell, "The Decline of Progressive Policy and the New Philanthropy," http://comm-org.wisc.edu/papers2003/bothwell/theorigins.htm, accessed June 5, 2006. Tabankin bio, http://publicinterestpictures.org/about_us, accessed June 8, 2006.

69. "Eye On the Bureaucracy" (Vienna, Virginia, The Conservative Caucus Education and Research Foundation, January 1984), p. 2.

70. Milton R. Copulos, "CLEC: Hidden Agenda, Hidden Danger," *Heritage Foundation Institutional Analysis #26*, Washington, D.C., February 9, 1984. www.heritage.org/Research/EnergyandEnvironment/IA26.cfm, accessed May 10, 2006.

71. *Ibid.*

72. "Midwest Academy," Wikipedia entry at http://en.wikipedia.org/wiki/Midwest_Academy, accessed May 10, 2006.

73. James Warren, "Student Radical Turned Union Chief Faces New Challenge," *op. cit.*

74. Lloyd Grove, "Al From, the Life of the Party: The Head of the Democratic Leadership Council, Finding Victory in Moderation," *Washington Post*, July 24, 1992.

75. Barry Grey, "The middle class 'left' and the fall of Ron Carey," World Socialist Website, December 29, 1997. www.wsws.org/polemics/1997/dec1997/carey.shtml, accessed May 12, 2006.

76. Unnamed W.K. Kellogg Foundation interviewer, "Tides Center / Social Venture Network, Interviewee: Drummond Pike," W.K. Kellogg Foundation, October, 2003. www.wkkf.org/default.aspx?tabid=68&CID=275& Proj CID=275&ProjID=48&TID=664&NID=32&LanguageID=0, accessed May 3, 2006. Pike was also a founder of the National Network of Grantmakers, the premier organization of progressive foundations.

77. Charles Lewis and the Center for Public Integrity, "Cloud of Corruption Around Democrats' Union Patron: AFSCME and Its President, Gerald McEntee, Have Given Party More Than $3.6 million," August 9, 2000. www. publicintegrity.org/report.aspx?aid=488, accessed May 10, 2006.

78. Marianne Lavelle, "Big Money: Citizen Action Spent $7 Million On Political Ads In The 1996 Campaign – When DoGooders Get Into Bad Trouble – The Teamster Connection At Citizen Action," *U.S. News & World Report*, October 13, 1997.

79. *Ibid.*

80. Jim Larkin (pseudonym), "Labor Pains – The Teamsters: What Went Wrong? The Campaign Money Scandal of Teamster President Ron Carey," *In These Times*, December 14, 1997.

81. The following section relies on Bill Sammon, "How union treasury funded Carey: Creative plan laundered money to win Teamsters election," *Washington Times*, September 1, 1997.

82. Kevin Galvin, "Teamsters' $195,000 Goes to Pot Swap - Scheme aids Carey, Reports Say," *Denver Rocky Mountain News*, October 26, 1997.

83. Mark Maremont, "Hoffa Operative Used 'Moles,' False Identity in Teamsters Probe," *The Wall Street Journal*, December 23, 1997, p. 1. *See also*, John D. Schulz, "Who is Richard Leebove?" *Journal of Commerce*, May 4, 1998, p. 11.

84. Thomas B. Edsall, Frank Swoboda, "Mainstream politics, link to Teamsters may stunt liberal activist group," *The Washington Post*, October 26, 1997, p. A10.

85. For a detailed discussion, see Charles Lewis and the Center for Public Integrity, "Cloud of Corruption Around Democrats' Union Patron," *op. cit.*

86. "Ex-Teamsters Head Cleared: Ron Carey acquitted of perjury and corruption charges," *Newsday,* (Melville, NY), October 13, 2001. *See also* Charles Walker, "Carey Cleared of All Charges!" Socialist Action website, http:// www. geocities.com/arcticreds/carey.html accessed August 8, 2005.

87. Renuka Rayasam, "SEIU's Andy Stern: Going Global," *US News & World Report*, June 5, 2007.

88. Mei Fong and Kris Maher, "Solidarity Movement: U.S. Labor Leader Aided China's Wal-Mart Coup," *Wall Street Journal*, June 22, 2007, p. 1A.

89. Unsigned editorial, "Asialinks Daily View: U.S. Union Leader's Moves in China Could Shake Up Labor World-Wide," *Wall Street Journal*, June 22, 2007.

90. Full text: Barbara Shailor, "Letter to the Editor, South China Morning Post," online at www.newecon.org/ShailorLetter.html, accessed May 1, 2006.

91. Adam Daifallah, "Labor Unions in a Rift over Communist China: SEIU'S Stern, AFSCME'S Booth Meet with Government-controlled 'Union'; It's 'Wrong,' Says AFT'S Dorn," *New York Sun*, October 21, 2002, p. 1. (The news stories didn't mention that the federation's constitution had been amended in 1997 at its convention in Pittsburgh to drop the clause barring

any "member of the Communist party, any fascist organization, or any totalitarian movement" from serving "as an Executive Officer or member of the Executive Council."

92. Heather Booth, "Prepared Remarks," *op. cit.*

CHAPTER 16

CANDLE IN THE SUN

NOVEMBER 2004

BUSH DEFEATS KERRY

IT WAS DÉJÀ '02 ALL OVER AGAIN.
Only worse—for the Democrats.
Victorious Republicans gained seats in both House and Senate.
Dubya stood undumped.
What went wrong?

Infuriated progressives insisted that Kerry won, based on exit polls—
not unlike Otpor, minus the bulldozers, mob scenes, and AK-47s.
Other Dump Bushies just nodded when TV news reported the headline
of London's *Daily Mirror*: "How can 59,054,087 people be so DUMB?"[1]
John F. Kerry conceded at 2:14 p.m. the day after the election.
Some progressives raged over another stolen election.
Others pressed on without missing a beat.

THE RESULTS OF YOUR AUTOPSY, SIR

W HY DID KERRY LOSE?
Mischief, Message or Machine?
A corrupted election?
Who Kerry was, what he said, how he said it?
Or some unseen wildcard up the sleeve of the first McCain-Feingold election, with its massive privately financed GOTV campaigns?

T HE MISCHIEF FACTION was at work long before November 2 in a network including Rev. Jesse Jackson's Rainbow/PUSH Coalition, People for the American Way, Common Cause, the Feminist Majority Foundation, and the National Voting Rights Institute, among others.

Jackson was the cheerleader. His speeches, beginning in early 2004, routinely suggested that the fall election would be stolen just as the 2000 election had been stolen. In March, he shouted from the Florida Capitol steps, "Don't let them take that vote out of your hands," to a crowd of some 2,000 anti-Bush protesters.[2]

Conventional wisdom said the election would be decided in Florida, Pennsylvania and Ohio. He worked the Buckeye State particularly hard.

On an October visit to Cleveland, Jackson accused Republican Ohio Secretary of State J. Kenneth Blackwell (who is also black) of "trying to reverse gains made by the civil rights movement by limiting where some residents can cast their ballots."[3]

Jackson was touting a federal lawsuit filed by the Ohio and Sandusky County Democratic parties, charging that Blackwell's rule for potentially ineligible voters—that their "provisional ballots" must be cast in their own precincts—violated the federal Help America Vote Act (the rule survived two lawsuits and was enforced).[4]

Democrats cried that the court had disenfranchised minorities, but they had other problems. The Pew Research Center for the People and the Press had found that only 73 percent of African Americans supported Kerry, compared to the 90 percent that Al Gore had rallied in 2000. Kerry wasn't doing enough to court the black vote.[5]

When the polls opened on election day, the *Washington Post* reported:

Ohio, which no Republican has lost and still won the White House, appeared to be a toss-up. The University of Cincinnati's Ohio Poll yesterday put Bush at 50.1 percent and Kerry at 49.2 percent, and a Columbus Dispatch poll on Sunday called the race 50-50, the closest in the poll's history.[6]

Then came the exit polls, and things changed.

Two companies, Edison Media Research and Mitofsky International, had been hired to do exit polling for the National Election Pool, a consortium of the nation's five major broadcasters and the Associated Press.[7]

Exit polls are widely considered to be highly accurate. They are not subject to hanging chads or pregnant chads, or some of the other sources of potential polling error, because they identify actual voters leaving the polling place and ask them who they had just voted for.[8]

Early exit polls that showed Kerry leading in most battleground states were leaked to the Internet and, during the long night after the polls closed, resulted in some news outlets projecting him as the next president.

However, as of 8:45 the next morning, CNN reported that Ohio was too close to call. Bush led by more than 136,000 votes, but the Kerry campaign insisted that 250,000 provisional and absentee ballots might change the outcome.[9]

By mid-morning, as bad numbers kept developing from the ongoing vote count, Kerry campaign managers decided that Bush's lead wouldn't be erased. Ohio's 20 electoral votes—and the election—would go to Bush.

Kerry telephoned the White House before noon with his decision to concede. His concession speech was scheduled for 2:00 p.m. in front of Faneuil Hall in Boston.[10]

Bush made his victory speech at 3:00 p.m. at the Ronald Reagan Building in Washington.

Impossible! With all those lies? The lousy economy? Low ratings?

Progressives froze in stunned, shocked, horror.

Several nations, including New Zealand, Canada and Australia, politely noted their firm restrictions on immigration.

Then the convulsions began.

TomPaine.com, now a property of Robert Borosage's Campaign for America's Future, quickly ran a piece by *Harper's* contributing editor Greg Palast, asserting that:

> Most voters in Ohio thought they were voting for Kerry. CNN's exit poll showed Kerry beating Bush among Ohio women by 53 percent to 47 percent. Kerry also defeated Bush among Ohio's male voters 51 percent to 49 percent. Unless a third gender voted in Ohio, Kerry took the state.[11]

Conclusion: the exit polls were more accurate than the vote count.

The Edison/Mitofsky polls themselves raised a red flag because they showed that Kerry had won the popular vote by a margin of 3 percent, while the official tally indicated a Bush victory by 2.5 percent, a 5.5 percent discrepancy.[12]

How do you explain that?

Warren Mitofsky, one of the principals of Mitofsky International, said on the *Lehrer News Hour*, "Kerry was ahead in a number of the states in margins that looked unreasonable to us. And we suspect that the main reason was that the Kerry voters were more anxious to participate in our exit polls than the Bush voters."[13]

In such cases where the numbers don't look right, the polling companies wait for the vote returns in those same sample precincts and use that for projections.

"There were no mistakes in the projections," asserted Mitofsky.

The polling company ran a formal evaluation of its system. The final report essentially restated Mitofsky's explanation.[14]

Nothing could persuade critics.

Progressives simply believed Bush stole the election. Period.

That meant all-out netwar.

Ohio Common Cause lawyer Cliff Arnebeck drafted a lawsuit, *Moss v. Bush*, to be filed with the state Supreme Court, alleging systematic election fraud that altered the outcome of the election and claiming to have evidence. It asked the court to set aside the results, and possibly award Ohio's electoral votes to John Kerry.[15]

IT WAS WEDNESDAY AFTERNOON when John Kerry conceded the election. Two business days remained in the week, and two more weekend days.

On Monday, November 8, five days after Kerry's concession, and the same day the *Dayton Daily News* noted that "There were no reports of widespread fraud, intimidation or major glitches," Representative John Conyers, Ranking Member of the House Judiciary Committee, held a hastily arranged but expertly orchestrated hearing on "Voting Irregularities in Ohio," with nine Democratic members of Congress and fifteen networked witnesses saying exactly the opposite.[16]

Witnesses, including lawyer Arnebeck and his lead plaintiff, Rev. William Moss, alleged widespread election fraud, calling for a vote recount, an investigation of Ohio's election, and elimination of the Electoral College.[15]

Jesse Jackson's son (the congressman from Illinois' Second District) proposed, for the third time in five years, a constitutional amendment giving every U.S. citizen the right to vote anywhere, removing control from the states, centralizing the presidential electoral system in Washington, and creating a federal bureaucracy for the purpose—see page 244 for more.[17]

The Conyers hearing resulted in a 100-page report by the Democrat staff of the Judiciary Committee titled "Preserving Democracy: What Went Wrong in Ohio."[18]

It alleged: voting machine shortages; ballots counted and recounted in secret; lost, discarded, and improperly rejected registration forms and absentee ballots; touch-screen machines rigged to register "Bush" when voters pressed "Kerry"; precincts in which there were more votes recorded than registered voters; precincts in which the reported participation rate was less than 10%; high rates of "spoiled" ballots and under-votes in which no choice for president was recorded; a sworn affidavit by "a Florida computer programmer who claims he was hired to develop a voting program with a 'back door' mechanism to undetectably alter vote tallies.'"

Ohio's recount was taken and Bush won again.[19]

That wasn't good enough. The battle for another recount grew into a rage of charges and countercharges, none of which would affect the second term of President George W. Bush.

On January 6, 2005, a joint session of the House and Senate met to hear the results of the Electoral College that officially chooses the president.

Congresswoman Stephanie Tubbs Jones of Ohio and Senator Barbara Boxer of California, both Democrats, filed a rarely used objection to the results of the presidential electoral votes in Ohio "on the ground that they were not, under all of the known circumstances, regularly given."[20]

Under an 1877 law, when such an objection is made, the chambers separate and both meet for two hours of debate, then rejoin for a vote. Members may speak for only five minutes and no more than once.[21]

Senator Boxer spent her five minutes in an impassioned speech demanding debate on irregularities in Ohio: long lines of people who could not cast votes, lack of voting machines in heavily Democratic districts, rigged voting machines giving Bush extra votes, improperly disqualified provisional ballots, and more.[22]

At best, it only delayed the inevitable. The Senate rejected the challenge by a vote of 74-1 and the House by 267-31.[23]

Bush was officially re-elected.

The editors of the *Cleveland Plain Dealer* had some advice:

Memo to Rep. Stephanie Tubbs Jones and the Rev. Jesse Jackson: The election horse is dead. You can stop beating it now.

Not an ounce of political flesh remains on that carcass. Ohio has counted and recounted: President George W. Bush received 118,775 more votes than your man, Sen. John Kerry.

The senator had the good grace and sense to acknowledge the abundantly obvious, go home and resume his life.

You might consider emulating his excellent example, because what you are doing now—redoubling your effort in the face of a settled outcome—will only drive you further toward the political fringe. And that long grass already is tickling your knees.[24]

Going home was not Jesse Jackson's plan. "The 2004 election is not past tense," he maintained, pushing to dismantle the Constitution's Article II provision giving the states control of presidential voting systems—a check and balance that spreads power around instead of concentrating it.

At root, the progressive flap was about concentrating power, not about voter fairness or exit polls being more accurate than official vote tallies.

Jesse Jackson's agenda—echoing the SDS principles of participatory democracy, weakening electoral democracy—is reflected in eight constitutional amendments proposed by his son, Rep. Jesse L. Jackson, Jr. (D-IL).

JESSE JACKSON'S PROGRESSIVE AGENDA
CONSTITUTIONAL AMENDMENTS
PROPOSED BY HIS SON, REP. JESSE L. JACKSON, JR.

1. **Progressive income tax:** "The Congress of the United States shall tax all persons progressively in proportion to the income which they respectively enjoy under the protection of the United States." No co-sponsors. Introduced three times, no action.

2. **Job rights:** "Every citizen has the right to work, to free choice of employment, to just and favorable conditions of work, and to protection against unemployment. Every citizen, without any discrimination, has the right to equal pay for equal work. Every citizen who works has the right to just and favorable remuneration ensuring for themselves and their family an existence worthy of human dignity, and supplemented, if necessary, by other means of social protection. Every citizen who works has the right to form and join trade unions for the protection of their interests." No co-sponsors. Introduced three times, no action.

3. **Housing rights:** "All citizens of the United States shall have a right to decent, safe, sanitary, and affordable housing, which right shall not be denied or abridged by the United States or any State." No co-sponsors. Introduced three times, no action.

4. **Women's rights:** "Equality of rights under the law shall not be denied or abridged by the United States or by any State on account of sex. Reproductive rights for women under the law shall not be denied or abridged by the United States or any State." No co-sponsors. Introduced three times, no action.

5. **Environmental rights:** "All citizens of the United States shall have a right to a clean, safe, and sustainable environment, which right shall not be denied or abridged by the United States or any State." No co-sponsors. Introduced three times, no action.

6. **Health care rights:** "All citizens of the United States shall enjoy the right to health care of equal high quality." Co-sponsored by others. Introduced three times, no action.

7. **Public education rights:** "All citizens of the United States shall enjoy the right to a public education of equal high quality." Co-sponsored by others. Introduced three times, no action.

8. **Abolishing the Electoral College, free-range voting, popular vote for president:** "The President and Vice President shall be elected jointly by the direct vote of the citizens of the United States, without regard to whether the citizens are residents of a State. The persons having the greatest number of votes for President and Vice President shall be elected, so long as such persons have a majority of the votes cast." Co-sponsored by one other. Introduced three times, no action.

Exactly how the federal government would provide all these rights and operate the vast welfare state necessary has never been explained, but they closely resemble another agenda with which Jesse Jackson has close ties.

Barely two months before John Kerry conceded defeat, a referendum was held to remove Venezuelan President Hugo Chávez from power.

Exit polls were performed by the polling firm, Penn, Schoen & Berland Associates. Doug Schoen (we met him in Serbia in Chapter 7) issued a news release saying that final exit poll results "showed a major victory for the 'Yes' movement, defeating Chávez in the Venezuela presidential recall referendum. The poll showed 59 percent in favor of recalling Chávez, 41 percent against."[25]

However, the next morning, Chávez was declared the winner by an almost exact opposite margin. "About 58 percent said 'no' to a recall, while 42 percent said 'yes,'" wrote the *Washington Post*. The official international observer, Jimmy Carter, endorsed the official result.[26]

This discrepancy of 17 percent is three times larger than claimed for the Ohio election. Furthermore, Chávez prosecuted supporters of the recall, who gathered the millions of petitions needed—led by election monitoring activist Maria Corina Machado—for accepting foreign contributions from the National Endowment for Democracy to help pay for Schoen's exit polls, as the Endowment had done in Serbia.[27]

Chávez alleged it was foreign interference in his country. At the time, the Venezuelan Consulate had spent over $2 million funding the American Left and lobbying Washington through its new Venezuela Information Office, run by former Global Exchange operative Deborah James and paying a very clever PR man named Schellenberger we will meet in Chapter 21.[28]

Jesse Jackson didn't complain that the Venezuelan president had rigged the recall vote or prosecuted its supporters or was lobbying in the U.S.

Why should he?

Chávez was his idol. Hugo had rewritten Venezuela's Constitution just as Jesse hoped to rewrite the United States Constitution. Jackson immediately planned a trip to Venezuela, where he met with Chávez and asserted, "We must affirm this government in the family of nations."[29]

Chávez and Jackson shared a vision of participatory democracy.

Jackson told the Venezuelan Parliament—minus the Senate, which Chávez had abolished to limit the opposition—"It is not enough to have the right to vote. It is also important to have the right to education, to healthcare and all social services... Democracy cannot survive if some have too much and the majority too little; that's why people need access to land. Countries' resources should be used to empower the people."[30]

Jackson was referring to the influx of Cuban teachers and doctors sent by Fidel Castro in return for Venezuela propping up Cuba's tottering economy.

Chávez paid for free education, free health care and subsidized housing from the revenues of the national oil company, Petróleos de Venezuela.[31]

He took the firm over in a strike that ended with his firing of 20,000 skilled but dissenting oil workers, and seized personal control of its revenue.[32]

"Access to land" was supplied by paramilitary "Bolivarian Circles" that confiscated it from "some who have too much" and gave it to some who had too little—not a majority, just supporters.[33]

Jackson supports Bolivarian Circles now active in the United States.[34]

Dissent was still a problem after the recall. Chávez signed the Law on the Social Responsibility of Radio and Television, followed in 2005 by amendments to Venezuela's Criminal Code, which made it a criminal offense to insult or show disrespect ("desacato") for the president and other government authorities. Dissent could bring up to 40 months in prison.[35]

Chávez had arrogated all power into his own hands. By 2007 he would demand no term limits. His supporters would shout "Chávez Forever!"

For now, the rest wanted Chávez gone, 59 percent or 42 percent, depending on who you believe.

Jesse Jackson wanted Chávez to stay. Maybe forever.

RED STATE BLUES

HIGH RANKING DEMOCRATS did their best to take the loss in stride, putting on a game face while fuming over everything from what to look for in a candidate to ideology (go left? go right?) to on-the-ground tactics.

"You always take stock after a loss like this, and it was a big disappointment," Representative Richard A. Gephardt of Missouri (himself a failed presidential candidate) told the *New York Times*.[36]

He was of the Machine faction, believing the Democrats' organization, while impressive, paled beside the Republicans' machine for turning out votes.

"They used the infrastructure of gun organizations and religious organizations to get that done," he said, "and we've got to grapple with that."

Al From, founder of the centrist Democratic Leadership Council—Bill Clinton's launching pad—was of the Message faction: "We need to put ideas first. Over the last 40 years we've seen the turf that we compete on shrink. We've got to be a national party."

As things stood, they were a bicoastal party of tree-hugging, French-speaking, gun-banning, wind-surfing, self-righteous wine and cheese liberals.

If they chose to veer left and galvanize the base, it would mean scaring off swing voters. Swinging right would lose the Left. Catch 22.

As Nebraska's Republican Governor Mike Johanns told a reporter, each time Michael Moore spoke up for John Kerry, Mr. Kerry's support in Nebraska took a dive—Moore's scathing documentary, *Fahrenheit 9/11*, backfired, becoming a Vote For Bush campaign speech in much of America.[37]

Second guessing the voters was getting them nowhere.

They looked over the exit poll results in detail to see what went wrong.

Poll takers asked a sample of 13,660 Americans who they voted for.

They also asked a lot of other questions.

They logged demographics (age, race, gender, income, education).

They asked about party affiliation (89% of the Democrats voted for Kerry, 93% of the Republicans voted for Bush, and the Independents split three ways, 49% for Kerry, 48% for Bush and 1% for Nader).

They asked about ideology (85% of the Liberals voted for Kerry, 84% of the Conservatives voted for Bush, and the Moderates went 54% for Kerry and 45% for Bush).

Democrats weren't too surprised by the religious numbers:

VOTES BY RELIGION	BUSH	KERRY	NADER
Protestant (54%)	59%	40%	0%
Catholic (27%)	52%	47%	0%
Jewish (3%)	25%	74%	SMALL FRACTION
Other (7%)	23%	74%	1%
None (10%)	31%	67%	1%

Catholics and Jews have usually supported Democrats, while mainline Protestants have supported Republicans. The Catholic tilt for Bush didn't fit (the gay marriage issue was a Catholic "anger point"), but the Jewish vote was unexceptional.[38]

The real stunner was the ranking of issues:

MOST IMPORTANT ISSUE	BUSH	KERRY	NADER
Moral Values (22%)	80%	18%	1%
Economy/Jobs (20%)	18%	80%	0%
Terrorism (19%)	86%	14%	0%
Iraq (15%)	26%	73%	0%
Health Care (8%)	23%	77%	SMALL FRACTION
Taxes (5%)	57%	43%	0%
Education (4%)	26%	73%	SMALL FRACTION

Moral values? What about Bush and all those non-existent weapons of mass destruction in Iraq? What about the Enron scandal on his watch?

GETTING RELIGION

IT WAS STUNNING for two reasons:
- they thought they had superior moral values;
- they thought their own religious network was mobilized well enough to combat the conservatives.

It was so stunning that the *Washington Post*'s senior polling analyst Christopher Muste checked his statistics from past elections and dismissed the idea of "values voters" as nothing more than a "myth."[39]

Democrats such as Arizona Governor Janet Napolitano didn't get it: "How did a party that is filled with people with values—and I am a person with values—get tagged as the party without values?" she asked.[40]

They were blind-sided by a not-so-simple question: which values?

They had run up against conflicts simmering since the 1960s, the passionate polarization between traditional and progressive beliefs, differing systems of moral understanding.

The election of 2004 repeated the clashes—on abortion, gun rights, separation of church and state, privacy, homosexuality, families, education, laws, elections, censorship, media, and the arts—that sociologist James Davison Hunter in 1991 dubbed the "culture war."[41]

The two moralities engaged in this war can be defined by where they see moral authority coming from: in the "transcendental sphere" (God and/or religion) or in the "mundane sphere" (the self).[42]

In simple:

- Conservatives see morality as rules or a code of behavior from an authority such as a father, a government, society itself, or God. They're mostly church-goers, as exit polls showed.
- Progressives see morality as being based on proper social institutions and the development of personal virtues such as justice, wisdom, courage and humility. They're mostly secular.[43]

The values of these two moralities differ in highly specific ways, but common experience tells us they are not mutually exclusive and that people can be more (or less) conservative and more (or less) progressive, or a mix:

- Conservative values include hard work, duty and obligation, self-reliance, high levels of national pride, pro-life values (against abortion), rejection of homosexuality, belief in the importance of religion and God in one's life, and that children should learn respect and obedience. They may also include belief in life after death, and frequent attendance at religious services.

- Progressive values include the development of good character, inter-personal trust, altruism, freedom of expression, tolerance of others, personal well-being, pride in education, voluntary service, political activism, and placement of moral authority in the "mundane" sphere (non-supernatural). Some believe in "spirituality" rather than God, but others are devout church-going believers.[44]

Al From was openly worried about the God Gap: "You can't have every-body who goes to church vote Republican; you just can't," he told a forum of Democrats.[45]

But when the Democrats needed them, what happened to their "moral values" troops in the Religious Left?

The Democrats had sunk loads of effort into mobilizing them.

They put up a website to connect with religious voters.

Leah Daughtry, chief of staff of the Democratic National Committee—and pastor of the House of the Lord Church in Washington—had arranged for the Democratic National Convention to sponsor a "People of Faith" rally for John Kerry in Boston in late July.[46]

Attendees from the Jewish, Muslim and Christian faiths made the point that, despite disagreements with their partisan pals on hot button issues like gay marriage and abortion, the Democratic Party offered the best match to their social justice and anti-poverty agendas—a hopeful attitude.

In late October, Kerry realized that his one Biblical quote during the campaign had been back in the third debate—"It is not enough, my brother, to say you have faith when there are no deeds ... Faith without works is dead," from the book of James, 2:26.

So Kerry gave a speech beginning, "This campaign is about more than a set of policies; it is about a set of ideals," and then discussed the biblically based values at the root of his politics.[47]

But religious voters mentally checked off the entrenched Democratic policies of religious removal: prayer from schools and religious symbols from government buildings. Separation of church and state, mostly church.

The Kerry campaign's Mara Vanderslice frantically directed behind-the-scenes outreach to all faiths.[48]

Was it too little, too late?

Was John Kerry and the rest of the American Left not really religious, but just "something rather too solemn, mirthless, herbivorous, dull, mono-chrome, righteous, and boring," as columnist Christopher Hitchens remarked about his old days at *The Nation* magazine?[49]

Maybe so: on election day, where were the 45 million faithful in the 100,000 local congregations of the liberal National Council of Churches?

Where were the voters of the American Friends Service Committee?

Where was the National Interfaith Committee for Worker Justice?

And that old Liberation Theology bunch?

Where was that whole Religious Left network?

A Sampling of the Religious Left Network, 2004

National Council of Churches–established 1950; 36 Protestant, Anglican, Orthodox, Evangelical, historic African American and Living Peace churches; strong advocate of progressive social policy agenda; 45 million members in 100,000 churches; formed the North American Congress on Latin America (NACLA, with SDS) and the Interfaith Center on Corporate Responsibility.

Interfaith Center on Corporate Responsibility–275 faith-based institutional investors with $110 billion assets; files over 200 shareholder resolutions each year on social and environmental issues. Politically active members.

American Friends Service Committee–Quaker organization founded 1917 to provide World War I conscientious objectors with constructive alternatives to military service. AFSC's present agenda is progressivist, including social justice, peace, open borders, abolition of the death penalty, and human rights.

Pax Christi USA–Catholic peace movement, "rejects war, preparations for war, and every form of violence and domination. It advocates economic and social justice, primacy of conscience, and respect for creation."

Interfaith Alliance–founded 1994 as a liberal counterbalance to the Christian Coalition; 150,000 members in the United States, including 70 faith traditions, Jews, Christians, Muslims, Hindus, Buddhists, Sikhs, also Agnostics and Atheists. Promotes "civility, democratic values, religious liberty."

Clergy Leadership Network–a 527 committee of liberal and moderate religious leaders created for the 2004 election to counter the influence of the religious right and to Dump Bush. Funded almost entirely by America Coming Together.

Church Folks for a Better America–project of Peace Action Education Fund, education arm of the Coalition for Peace Action. Created in 2004 by a professor of theology and encouraged by numerous leftist religious leaders; it published "The Dove Ad" in August condemning Bush, the war in Iraq, and the Abu Ghraib torture scandal; called for moral recovery.

Progressive Religious Partnership–coalition of leftist religious leaders formed in 2001 by Rev. George Regas to build grassroots political action. Launch co-hosted by People for the American Way Foundation.

Pastors for Peace–founded 1988 by Interreligious Foundation for Community Organization to deliver humanitarian aid to Mexico, Central America and Cuba; blanket opposition to U.S. policy, solidarity with Fidel Castro.

Jehovah-jireh Baptist Church of Christ–Harlem ministry with programs to help inner city youth and combat gang culture. Jehovah-jireh means "God will provide," literally "God sees [to it]." The ministry supports:

National Hip Hop Political Convention–20-state political organization promoting "Hip Hop Generation" activism; first convention in 2004 attended by 6,000; agenda largely Dump Bush; deals with criminal justice, economic justice, equality, global issues; funded by Arca Foundation, others.

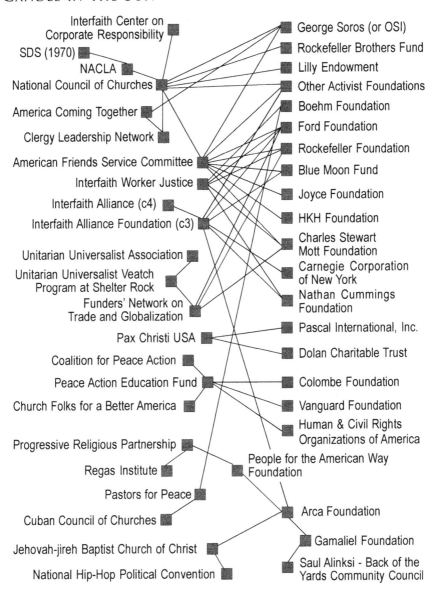

FUNDING NODES IN THE RELIGIOUS LEFT NETWORK, 2004

This diagram tracks a few of the funders and their grantees among the hundreds of other activist groups and funders in the Religious Left. As the RAND researchers found, they use "soft power"—organization, communication and doctrine—to multiply their pressure on nation states to achieve their goals. The boundary between religious groups and anti-globalization, environmental, corporate social responsibility and other progressive movements is porous; this sample is linked to many others.

The Message faction said the religious vote was split because of gay marriage initiatives on the ballot in eleven battleground states, which attracted large numbers of conservative religious voters.[50]

The Machine faction countered that they attracted large numbers of liberal religious voters, too.

Where was the Religious Left on election day.?

It was at the polls, and in larger numbers than ever.

But their GOTV machine paled beside the Republican GOTV machine.

RICH GUYS FOR KERRY

PROGRESSIVE INVESTMENT ACTIVISTS in The Vast Left Wing Conspiracy seem to consist of George Soros and a handful of his friends.

Not so. There are hundreds of them, more thoroughly networked than the Religious Left, and commanding such enormous wealth that Soros and his friends look destitute beside them: in 1999, social responsibility investment firms broke the $2 trillion mark in assets and have grown since.[51]

But Democrats in 2004 knew that high income voters went for Bush.

VOTES BY INCOME	BUSH	KERRY	NADER
Less Than $100,000 (82%)	49%	50%	0%
$100,000 or More (18%)	58%	41%	1%

They also knew that an army of very wealthy progressive investors and venture capitalists had always bailed them out before McCain-Feingold poisoned that well. Where were the progressive investment activists?

And who were they? Many of them trace their genealogy to a secret meeting held in 1981 in Estes Park, in the mountains of Colorado, convened by a bright, energetic, and idealistic 27-year-old New Yorker named Joshua Lawrence Mailman and attended by 21 friends (who were already there for the second annual conference of the National Network of Grantmakers).

Mailman and his invitees were children of privilege and inherited wealth who grew up in the LSD-drenched Zen-and-tonic '70s.

In 1976, for example, 22-year-old Mailman was arrested on psychedelic drug charges at a "therapy session" while attending Middlebury College. Five years later, shortly before the secret Estes Park meeting, Mailman told a reporter, "the earth, the air, the water, the creepy-crawlies, the ones that fly in the sky, the two-legged ones, all life is sacred." He said that while marching in a horned, wooly-headed buffalo suit during an All-Species Day Parade up Manhattan's Fifth Avenue.[52]

The 22 New Age heirs that 1981 day in Colorado wanted to do something about the Reagan Revolution then turning America far to the right.

The rich group sat in an Esalen-style circle in the mountains, "united by a core humanistic or spiritual belief in the inter-connectedness of all life," meditating on what to do, when, according to an article in *Psychology Today,* a doughnut-shaped cloud appeared overhead, which they took as an omen.[53]

They called themselves "the Dough Nuts"—"Nuts with Dough," but later "the Doughnuts," all one word—and decided to form a money-ring of like-minded inheritors of great but unearned wealth, meeting periodically and pooling their significant resources into highly leveraged progressive social change. They swore themselves to secrecy about their group; even their internal newsletters identified each other only by first names and initials.[54]

Mailman and the Doughnuts created the Threshold Foundation as a project of the secretive Tides Foundation in 1981, each giving an annual contribution of about $1 million. They set off looking for socially responsible investments and worthy activist groups to receive grants from the profits.

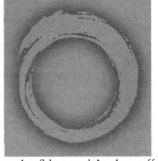

The doughnut motif survives in Threshold's artsy logo *(right)*. The fund is now a community network of 200-plus individuals and a seedbed for innumerable similar groups.

Like Soros later, Mailman was an early "wild card," a single person of huge influence acting as a catalyst for social change.

He advocates "coming up with ideas that allow relatively small amounts of money to help bring about significant positive change," which he calls "asynchronous philanthropy"—maximize the fringes, it's cheap.[55]

Since 1981, Mailman and Threshold have seeded literally *thousands* of non-profits, developed dozens of sister donor organizations, and established dozens of business networks for social responsibility around the world.[56]

Josh Mailman by himself has founded, co-founded, funded, directed, or invested in dozens of powerful nodes in the progressive investment activist network worldwide, including roles as:

- Director, the Joseph L Mailman Foundation, established by his father in 1943 from the profits of his early conglomerate, which included Air Express International and Republic Aviation.[57]
- Co-founder, trustee, Sigrid Rausing Trust, British fund donating about £15 million annually to human rights groups.[58]
- Founder, Business for Social Responsibility, 1992 network to encourage major corporations to adopt pro-social practices.[59]
- Donor, Rocky Mountain Institute, 1982 group advocating "natural capitalism," stresses efficiency and environmental restoration.
- Principal, Sirius Business Corporation, Mailman's venture capital firm, his own cute-named primary business enterprise.
- Founding shareholder, Utne Reader, progressive magazine.[60]

Threshold Foundation continues with the aid of Tides Center, the same as the Mailman Institute, a strategic planning center for activists.[61]

One of Mailman's most successful creations has been the Social Venture Network, co-founded in 1987 with Wayne Silby of the Calvert Group.

A Sampling of Social Venture Network, 2006

SVN describes itself as "a community of leaders—company founders, private investors, social entrepreneurs and key influencers—who share a commitment to building a just and sustainable world through business."

SVN develops and promotes new models of socially responsible business; maintains information clearinghouse; conducts forums with expert presenters; members are companies, foundations, activist groups, public interest law firms.

Some of the more notable of SVN's 139 current (2006) members:

Calvert Group—largest social responsibility investment management firm. Establlished 1976; first activist firm in the South African divestiture campaign in 1982; first mutual fund to sponsor a social policy shareholder resolution (1986); manages about $12 billion in assets.

Co-op America—social and environmental advocacy group founded in 1982; its subsidiary Social Investment Forum created Coalition of Environmentally Responsible Economies (CERES) and the Shareholder Action Network.

Domini Social Investments—social responsibility investment firm founded by Amy Domini, manages four funds with $1.8 billion assets; publishes the Domini 400 Social Index, rating corporations on a wide range of social and environmental criteria.

Earthjustice, formerly **Sierra Club Legal Defense Fund**—uses the courts to advance environmentalist anti-industry agenda; represents groups such as Environmental Working Group, Natural Resources Defense Council, AFL-CIO.

Human Rights Watch—founded as Helsinki Watch in 1978, investigates human rights abuses; gives Hellman/Hammett Grants to writers suffering human rights abuses; funded by Soros, Sandlers, Joshua Mailman's Rausing Trust, Ford, Rockefeller foundations. Mailman is on the board of directors.

Mother Jones Magazine—published by the Foundation for National Progress, originally the West Coast affiliate of Institute for Policy Studies.

Nathan Cummings Foundation—fortune of Sara Lee Corporation, major funder of environmental, health and social justice groups, including Sierra Club, Center for Science in the Public Interest, Government Accountability Project, National Interfaith Committee for Worker Justice.

Rainforest Action Network—anti-corporate campaign organizer, direct action environmental advocacy; operated campaigns against Citibank, Boise Cascade, Mitsubishi, Home Depot, obtained significant concessions.

Ruckus Society—founded by alumni of Greenpeace and Rainforest Action Network to train direct action activists.

TomPaine.com—currently a project of Robert Borosage's Institute for America's Future; posts progressive blogs and political essays.

W. K. Kellogg Foundation—huge breakfast cereal and food fortune now funds environmental, health and social justice projects.

SVN fills a unique niche among progressive investment activists, uniting some 250 members over time (*facing page*). Mailman's personal network is stunning:

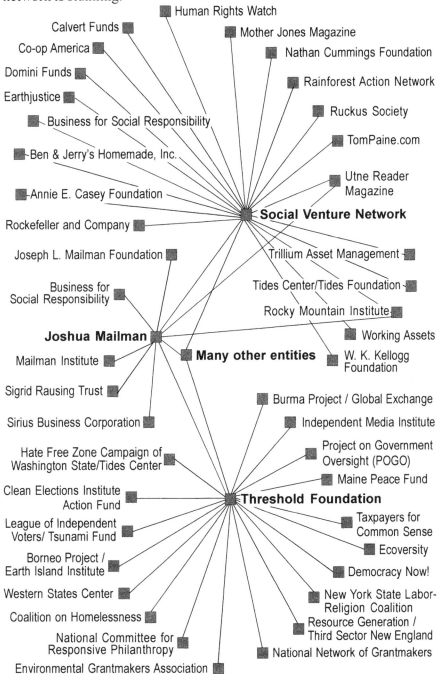

Human Rights Watch

Calvert Funds

Co-op America

Domini Funds

Earthjustice

Business for Social Responsibility

Ben & Jerry's Homemade, Inc.

Annie E. Casey Foundation

Rockefeller and Company

Joseph L. Mailman Foundation

Business for Social Responsibility

Joshua Mailman

Mailman Institute

Sigrid Rausing Trust

Sirius Business Corporation

Hate Free Zone Campaign of Washington State/Tides Center

Clean Elections Institute Action Fund

League of Independent Voters/ Tsunami Fund

Borneo Project / Earth Island Institute

Western States Center

Coalition on Homelessness

National Committee for Responsive Philanthropy

Environmental Grantmakers Association

Mother Jones Magazine

Nathan Cummings Foundation

Rainforest Action Network

Ruckus Society

TomPaine.com

Utne Reader Magazine

Social Venture Network

Trillium Asset Management

Tides Center/Tides Foundation

Rocky Mountain Institute

Working Assets

Many other entities

W. K. Kellogg Foundation

Burma Project / Global Exchange

Independent Media Institute

Project on Government Oversight (POGO)

Maine Peace Fund

Threshold Foundation

Taxpayers for Common Sense

Ecoversity

Democracy Now!

New York State Labor-Religion Coalition

Resource Generation / Third Sector New England

National Network of Grantmakers

Remember, it was in Joshua Mailman's Social Venture Network that former SDSer Michael Ansara met with Midwest Academy volunteer and multi-millionaire Charles Blitz. It was after an SVN meeting that they made the deal for the illegal Teamsters donations we saw in Chapter 15.

Blitz is also director of The Mailman Institute, which trains activists.[62]

Even elaborate network diagrams like the one on the previous page don't begin to show the wheels within wheels within wheels of the American Left.

The organizations sketched in the diagram are, of course, only part of bigger progressive investor niches, occupied by hundreds of investment groups that promote shareholder advocacy, screen out companies with unacceptable social practices, and provide social venture capital, such as:

- Social Investment Forum, non-profit trade association of progressive investment activists, created by Co-op America; has more than 500 institutional and professional members.[63] Created the
  - Advocacy & Public Policy Program, formerly the Shareholder Action Network, to provide research and organize advocacy on social investments, support anti-corporate campaigns like the Stop Exxon-Mobil project we saw in Chapter 14.
- Coalition of Environmentally Responsible Economies (CERES), also created by the Social Investment Forum (1988); promotes code of environmental conduct; members include social responsibility investment firms, major environmental groups, AFL-CIO.[64]
- Investor Responsibility Research Center, foundation-funded (Ford, Carnegie, Rockefeller) advocate for socially-aimed shareholder initiatives; publishes analyses on corporate governance issues, including Douglas Cogan's, *The Greenhouse Gambit: Business and Investment Responses to Climate Change* (1992).[65]
- Institutional Shareholder Services, founded 1985 by shareholder activists Nell Minow and Robert A.G. Monks, provides proxy voting and corporate governance services to more than 1,600 institutional and corporate clients; advice about 35,000 companies in 115 world markets; votes proxies for union-based pension funds.[66]
- Corporate Library, formed 1999 to rate governance, compensation and performance of corporations.[67]
- Corporate Campaign, Inc., Ray Rogers' consulting firm.[68]
- Progressive Asset Management, social responsibility brokerage firm formed 1987, allied with Financial West Group in 1999 to create the PAM Network of more than 60 offices and 400 representatives.[69]

Trying to draw a diagram of the whole $2 trillion progressive investor activist network would simply boggle the mind and use up a lot of ink.

Where were the Rich Guys for Kerry on election day.?

They were at the polls, and in larger numbers than ever.

But their GOTV machine paled beside the Republican GOTV machine.

LABOR MORE OR LESS FOR KERRY

On Monday, July 26, 2004, at the Democratic National Convention in Boston, while Rob Stein became the hero of progressive resurgence, Andy Stern, Ivy League president of the largest AFL-CIO union, became the skunk at the lawn party.

In the enforced harmony of John Kerry's carefully scripted nomination for President of the United States, Stern said it would be better for unions if Kerry lost.

The *Washington Post* reported:

> Andrew L. Stern, the head of the 1.6 million-member Service Employees International Union (SEIU), said in an interview with The Washington Post that both the party and its longtime ally, the labor movement, are "in deep crisis," devoid of new ideas and working with archaic structures.
>
> Stern argued that another four years of Bush administration policies might be less damaging than the stifling of needed reform within the party and the labor movement that he said would occur if Kerry becomes president.[70]

What was he thinking?

His union spent $47.7 million on behalf of Kerry's election, even though SEIU, along with the American Federation of State, County and Municipal Employees (AFSCME), delivered an early endorsement to former Vermont governor Howard H. Dean, making him an early favorite for the nomination.

And Jerry McEntee's AFSCME spent $26.1 million to elect Kerry.

Among other millions spent by other unions for Kerry.

Lack of enthusiasm for windsurfing, French-fluent, mansion owning John Forbes Kerry was in there somewhere—George Soros shared it—but hatred of Bush could compensate. That wasn't really what was eating Stern.

It was those archaic structures.

What were they? Not the Democratic Party structure, but the fragmented unions themselves.

Unions, Andy Stern saw, must think like the industries they work for in the age of mergers and acquisitions.

If capital consolidates, labor must consolidate.

If there were five unions representing garment workers, eight in heavy manufacturing, fourteen for government workers, eleven in construction and another eleven in transportation, they should be merged into one or two giant unions in each industry sector, like the mega-unions of Western Europe— where organized labor had its own political parties that shaped a socialist welfare state into the envy of unionists everywhere.

ORIGINAL NEW UNITY PARTNERSHIP UNIONS

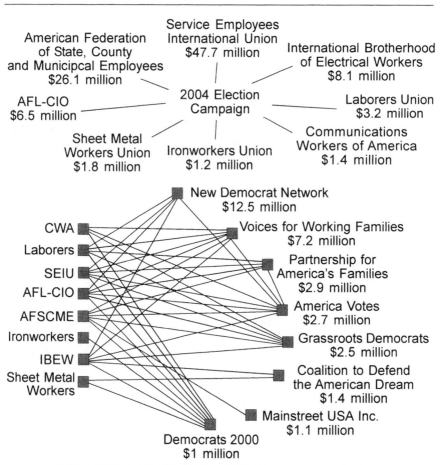

2004 TOP 8 UNION ELECTION EXPENDITURES
AND THEIR MAJOR BENEFICIARIES' EXPENDITURES

Stern wanted a fundamental revamping of the AFL-CIO from its 60 international unions down to 15 mega-unions. To hell with bosses and staffs.

Replacing America's archaic union structures with mega-unions would give labor real power, power that Kerry might want to co-opt or nullify.

Why would he want that? Stern knew from his college classes what Harvard economist John Kenneth Galbraith said in the 1950s, when labor was at its peak: the stronger unions are, the less powerful business is. The weaker they are, the more power moves to the corporate board room.

Galbraith saw the U.S. economy as a struggle of "countervailing forces," government, business, and labor. They kept each other in check, he said, assuring that ordinary Americans got a fair share of the economic pie.[71]

Would Kerry really want labor as a countervailing force *to government*?

Not likely. Stern saw that a Democrat in office could buy off labor leaders with high-level patronage jobs, trips on Air Force One, bull sessions at the White House Friday night mess, and other dazzling trinkets, while their unions faded away and power-mergers languished.

George W. Bush couldn't and wouldn't do that.

Kerry loses.

Stern and other labor leaders were ready to launch the New Unity Partnership (NUP) to jump-start the mega-merger process (*top facing page*).[72]

After Kerry lost the election, the AFL-CIO wouldn't force the needed mergers, and the NUP unions pulled out of the federation.[73]

It was another distracting mess among perpetually messy progressives. Maybe it didn't *cause* Kerry to lose, but it didn't help him win, either.

Labor unions campaigned for Kerry with a reasonable semblance of solidarity, and their cooperation with non-union groups was astonishing.

Eight unions made the 2004 Top 50 Contributor list: Andy Stern's SEIU, Jerry McEntee's AFSCME, the Electrical Workers, AFL-CIO, Laborers, Sheet Metal Workers, Communication Workers of America, and the Ironworkers. They funded eight other progressive groups in the Top 50 (*facing page*).

Recall that unions and their electoral campaign were inextricably entwined with the Soros / BeDuCi Bunch campaigns—America Coming Together, the Media Fund, the Joint Victory Campaign, America Votes, and John Podesta's Center for American Progress (its lobbying arm, the American Progress Action Fund, did most of its electoral work).

Andy Stern and his close friend Steve Rosenthal were officials of America Coming Together. The AFL-CIO, SEIU and ASFCME were part of America Votes, which charged $50,000 to join, "weeding out the unserious," and in return gave members a seat at the table, access to a highly advanced database, polling data, and strategic information.

The fifteen America Votes paying member organizations performed with uncharacteristic discipline, coordinating efforts and pooling resources. They fielded huge numbers of members covering every battleground state. Heather Booth said, "I have never seen a time when people were more focused and dedicated to working for social change." Harold Ickes' assessment: "ACT, America Votes, and the Media Fund were totally seamless."[74]

NARROWCASTING AND MICRO-TARGETING

THEY HAD HONED A SOPHISTICATED CAMPAIGN together, based on Rosenthal's one-on-one strategy, with some high-tech, high-concept, high-cost answers to the question: How do you get the attention of Americans swimming in a sea of messages?

And how do you get the right message to the right Kerry voters (for gun control, for example) while getting a different message to different Kerry voters (gun owners, for example)?

If you want to get up to 51 percent of the vote," said Law Professor Peter Swire of Ohio State University, "you probably have to assemble a coalition of 20 or 30 or 50 demographic groups. So as a modern candidate, you will want to have a strategy for how to communicate with each one of those demographic groups. You want a targeted ad on the gun control, on the pro-life, on the military, on the economic issues. You're going to want to have a message that's tailored for each one of those groups. If you don't do it, you're putting out broadcast ads in a narrowcast world."[75]

How can anyone do that? How do you identify names and addresses in 20 or 30 or 50 demographic groups and give them a highly motivating message that would infuriate other demographic groups that you need too?

Get the right campaign consultant.

Ken Strasma and his Washington-based Strategic Telemetry are the only reason that John Kerry became the Democratic nominee.

Kerry was far behind in the polls before the Iowa caucuses. Democrats there had been battered by messages from ten candidates for months on end, and getting to them was increasingly tough.

Kerry's campaign hired Strategic Telemetry because it had a secret weapon: micro-targeting.

It has a technical side and a message side. The technical part involved Strasma sifting through all the contacts that Kerry people had already made in Iowa, then running their profiles through demographic computer lists of the whole state that would tell them statistically what a Kerry voter looked like—a "Virtual ID," in Strasma-speak—a nearly magic guide to where to spend their limited resources finding more Kerry voters.[76]

But you don't actually want *every* vote. Strasma used the 1988 Iowa turnout data to estimate precinct-level turnout where Kerry needed a bit more support to pick up another delegate or two. Turning out voters where it won't translate into additional delegates is a waste. Target where the "vote goal" will win another delegate.[77]

The message side of micro-targeting has its own brand of magic: it gives politicians a chance to say things to some people they might not want others to hear.

Thus, you can take the most controversial message that wouldn't work on TV but still deliver it to the 20,000 people in a certain district who will respond to it favorably.

Strasma says, "Some of the biggest motivators in terms of issues are also the most divisive issues. On one end of the spectrum, you've got abortion rights, pro-life/pro-choice, and you've also got gun control and gun ownership rights."[78]

In politics, you have to tell people what they want to hear. Strasma's business is getting a finely targeted message to the exactly right people without getting a divisive message to the whole electorate.

It gave John Kerry the stunning comeback that caught him on the john when he won in Iowa and couldn't pop the champagne cork for Teresa.

The pleasure of ulteriority.

Meanwhile, back at the Democratic National Committee, chairman Terry McAuliffe—whose secret brain trust of 2002 had now been transmogrified into The Soros Left Wing Conspiracy—pointed to a computer on a side table in his office.

"I can get on right now and ask for single women with one child who voted in the 2000 presidential election in Missouri, and six seconds later, names and addresses will pop up on that machine," he told *USA Today*.[79]

The terminal was connected to a mammoth storehouse of computer data built from voter lists, commercially available databases and information swaps with environmental, women's and other groups allied with the party. Each communication with someone in the database was recorded.

But it's nothing like the technology Soros and friends bought for America Coming Together to use in key swing states. Every afternoon, salaried ACT canvassers were given Palm Pilots containing the names and addresses of potential voters. They were sent into the field with a lot of information about each of the voters they were visiting, profiles compiled from very advanced, very complex demographic databases. It included exactly what issues the voters were likely to respond to. Each Palm Pilot could play a short video customized to that voter's profile.[80]

If you were black, you saw the video that said, "African-American unemployment has skyrocketed to a 10-year high."

If you were a gun owner, you saw a video showing John Kerry firing a shotgun on a skeet range.

Voters were seeing different video messages tailored to their own personal demographic profiles.

Those demographic profiles were stored on microchips somewhere in Acxiom Corporation's acres of computers in Little Rock, Arkansas. And they weren't just any old profiles, not just your name, address and phone number, but also the citizen groups you belong to, catalogs you get, the cars you've bought, "and maybe even what shoes you wear and whether you like dogs or cats," said a PBS special.[81]

Acxiom client services executive Jonathan Askins said they didn't create any new products for ACT, but used a mixture of their InfoBase, with more than 176 million Americans, collected from dozens of sources of personal information such as U.S. Census data, tax records, product surveys, credit card purchases and customer records; and Personicx, which puts households in one of 70 "life stage segments" based on marital status, home ownership, presence of children, income, urbanicity, net worth, and more.[82]

All this is managed by Acxiom's AbiliTec record matching program, which verifies good names and purges bad ones (deceased, moved with no forwarding address, etc.) and prevents costly redundant contacts or mailings.

A S IN MOST HUMAN ENDEAVORS, things went wrong. For one thing, the fancy databases didn't really work all that well.

The one used by the America Votes coalition had "all kinds of glitches," causing some within the organization to feel that they had been "too hopeful," according to a report funded by the Pew Charitable Trusts.[83]

"We built the political will, now we need to build the technological will," said America Votes leader Cecile Richards.

In addition, while using the database to target voters with specially designed messages, the vaunted America Votes discipline broke down into microphone grabbing, Richards complained. Some members, she said, "try and make [their] issue the most important to voters rather than listen to what voters perceive the most important issues are."

Worse, toward the end of the campaign, the labor groups and America Votes canvassers found themselves bumping into Democratic Party and candidate campaigners because McCain-Feingold prohibited them from coordinating campaigns. The efficiency the 527s had built among themselves was wrecked in duplicated effort by the candidates and the Party.[84]

They never developed a counter to the negative ads by the Swift Boat Veterans for Truth attacking Kerry's military service in Vietnam. And they couldn't shake that windsurfing video showing Kerry gliding back and forth, back and forth, comparing it to his vacillating stance on the Iraq war.

For all that, Steve Rosenthal, leading America Coming Together, turned out the most Democratic voters of his career. ACT hit the urban core hard, still believing that was where the majority lived.

They were confident of victory. They lost. They said Bush stole it.

Matt Bai of the *New York Times Magazine* didn't think so:

> But the truth was that the Bush campaign had created an entirely new math in Ohio. It wouldn't have been possible eight years ago, or even four. But with so many white, conservative and religious voters now living in the brand-new town houses and McMansions in Ohio's growing ring counties, Republicans were able to mobilize a stunning turnout in areas where their support was more concentrated than it was in the past. Bush's operatives did precisely what they told me seven months ago they would do in these communities: they tapped into a volunteer network using local party organizations, union rolls, gun clubs and churches.[85]

Exit polls showed why John Sweeney wanted his AFL-CIO to form wide progressive alliances:

ANYONE IN HOUSEHOLD IN A UNION?	BUSH	KERRY	NADER
Yes (24%)	40%	59%	1%
No (76%)	55%	44%	0%

ARE YOU A UNION MEMBER?	BUSH	KERRY	NADER
Yes (14%)	38%	61%	1%
No (86%)	54%	45%	0%

True, America Coming Together lit up the GOTV landscape as never before. They were dazzled by their own brilliance. Their light was just a candle in the sun. As Steve Rosenthal told Matt Bai, "The rude awakening here is that I always thought there were more of us out there. And this time there were more of them." The sun had moved to the suburbs.[86]

To some extent, it wasn't only getting the Democratic base out, it was getting them to vote for Kerry. The *American Prospect*'s post-mortem:

> "I knocked on a lot of doors in 2004," says Steve Rosenthal, who headed America Coming Together, the largest liberal voter-mobilization group. "If I heard it once, I heard it a thousand times: 'You may not agree with George Bush, but you know where he stands.'" Conviction evidently trumps vacillation, even when voters are skeptical of particular convictions. One of John Kerry's pollsters says, "People looked at Bush and concluded that he'd shoot first and ask questions later. They concluded that Kerry would ask questions first. They voted for Bush."[87]

Andy Stern's SEIU picked up three days after Kerry's defeat with a new push for mega-mergers in the AFL-CIO, just as if nothing had happened.[88]

Commentators focused on the disunity it created and its undemocratic methods, ignoring the obvious question, "Where are we going with all this?"

If the AFL-CIO's 60 unions were merged into 15 mega-unions, their influence over corporations would be staggering.

Not because of their newly consolidated power to strike.

Because the newly centralized unions would have tighter control over all the money in their pension funds, which was invested where? In corporations.

Who influences all that money invested in corporations?

The Council of Institutional Investors (CII), an organization of over 140 pension fund members whose assets exceed $3 trillion:

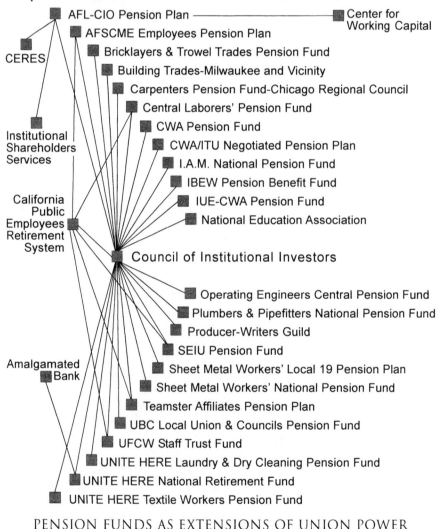

PENSION FUNDS AS EXTENSIONS OF UNION POWER

Unions and union-dominated public pension systems have substantial control of CII. Of the nine 2006 board members and seven officers, one is the executive director, two are corporate managers, four are union representatives (I.A.M., Sheet Metal Workers, Laborers, and UNITE-HERE), and nine are state pension system officials.[89]

UNITE-HERE owns Amalgamated Bank, with assets of $4 billion.[90]

The Center for Working Capital was spun off the AFL-CIO in 2001 to pressure pension trustees with research and education reports.[91]

CalPERS is the largest and most activist pension system in the nation. Its governing board is chaired and controlled by union representatives.[92]

The union pension funds in the Council of Institutional Investors (*facing page*) are also networked with numerous other activist pension funds, including CalPERS, TIAA-CREF, Hermes Pension Management, Ltd., and other progressive organizations such as CERES and Institutional Shareholders Services (*see page 256*) that bridge into the Rich Guys for Kerry crowd.[93]

Andy Stern was looking into a future of countervailing forces with power John Kenneth Galbraith never dreamed of. That Ivy education might pay off.

THE ENVIRONMENT QUESTION

When the League of Conservation Voters watched Kerry lose, they were furious, like all progressives.

Their constituents had spent many millions to Dump Dubya, but their hated nemesis stood undumped.

When their hatred worked itself out a little, they saw the exit polls.

Environmentalists everywhere were far more shocked than anyone else.

It wasn't that moral values took first place.

It was where the environment ranked in Election 2004 exit polls:

Nowhere.

CHAPTER 16 NOTES

1. Front cover, "Doh! 4 More Years of Dubya: How can 59,054,087 people be so DUMB?," *London Daily Mirror*, November 4, 2004, p. 1.

2. "Anti-Bush protesters vow to make comeback," *Tallahassee Democrat*, March 3, 2004.

3. Greg Pierce, "Jesse to the rescue?" *Washington Times*, October 6, 2004.

4. "Ohioans must go to right precinct, U.S. Court says," *Akron Beacon Journal*, October 24, 2004.

5. Pierce, "Jesse to the rescue?" *op. cit.*

6. Dan Balz and David S. Broder, "Election Day Dawns With Unpredictability - Polls Show Tie; Both Sides Have Lawyers Ready," *Washington Post*, November 2, 2004, p. A1.

7. http://www.exit-poll.net/, accessed May 29, 2006.

8. "2004 United States presidential election controversy, exit polls," Wikipedia entry, http://en.wikipedia.org/wiki/2004_U.S._presidential_election_controversy,_ exit_polls, accessed May 29, 2006.

9. "Bush camp claims certainty of victory - Kerry campaign not conceding Ohio," *CNN America Votes 2004*, November 3, 2004. www.cnn.com/2004/ALLPOLITICS/11/02/election.main/, accessed May 14, 2006.

10. "Bush wins second term as Kerry concedes - Democrat's team makes decision after looking at Ohio numbers,"*CNN America Votes 2004*, November 3, 2004. www.cnn.com/2004/ALLPOLITICS/11/03/prez.main/index.html, accessed May 14, 2006.

11. Greg Palast, "Kerry Won," TomPaine.com, November 4, 2004, www.tompaine.com/articles/kerry_won.php, accessed May 28, 2006.

12. Various authors, "Study of the 2004 Presidential Election Exit Poll Discrepancies," US Count Votes (a Utah non-profit organization), July 10, 2005. http://uscountvotes.org/ucvAnalysis/US/USCountVotes_Re_Mitofsky-Edison.pdf, accessed May 10, 2006. *See also*, Howard Kurtz, "Errors Plagued Election Night Polling Service; VNS Report Also Faults Networks in Fla. Blunder," *Washington Post*, December 22, 2000, p. A1.

13. Terence Smith, interviewer, "What went wrong?" *NewsHour with Jim Lehrer*, November 5, 2004. www.pbs.org/newshour/bb/politics/july-dec04/exitpolls_11-05.html, accessed May 29, 2006.

14. "Evaluation of Edison/Mitofsky Election System 2004," prepared by Edison Media Research and Mitofsky International for the National Election Pool (NEP), January 19, 2005, http://exit-poll.net/election-night/EvaluationJan 192005.pdf, accessed May 12, 2006.

15. *Moss v. Bush*, Verified Election Contest Petition, December 17, 2004, Supreme Court of Ohio, 2004 WL 3153018. Dismissed January 6, 2005.

16. Federal Document Clearing House, "Democrat Members of the House Judiciary Committee hold a Forum on Voting Irregularities in Ohio," November 8, 2004.

17. House Joint Resolution 36: Proposing an amendment to the Constitution of the United States to abolish the Electoral College and provide for the direct election of the President and Vice President by the popular vote of all citizens of the United States regardless of place of residence. Introduced in the House Judiciary Committee March 2, 2005, no action.

18. "Preserving Democracy: What Went Wrong in Ohio - Status Report of the House Judiciary Committee Democratic Staff," Washington, D.C., January 5, 2005.
19. "Ohio vote recount completed, Bush margin of victory shrinks about 300 votes," *Watertown Daily Times*, December 29, 2004, p. 3A.
20. Catherine Dodge, "Democratic lawmakers object to Ohio election results," *Bloomberg News*, January 6, 2005, www.bloomberg.com/apps/news?pid= 10000103&sid=aj2D7gfee2uI&refer=us, accessed May 14, 2006.
21. Electoral Count Act of February 3, 1887.
22. "Objection to counting of Ohio electoral votes," *Congressional Record, Senate*, January 6, 2005, p. S41.
23. "Congress certifies Bush's election victory," *The State* (Columbia, South Carolina), January 7, 2005, p. A15.
24. Unsigned editorial, "Please, let it go. Election was 2 months ago; inauguration is in 2 weeks; Jackson and Tubbs Jones should get on to something useful," *Cleveland Plain Dealer*, January 4, 2005, p. B8.
Jesse Jackson agenda: Online at the Library of Congress website, www.thomas.gov.
25. Michael Barone, "Exit polls in Venezuela," *USNews.com*, August 20, 2004. www.usnews.com/usnews/opinion/baroneweb/mb_040820.htm, accessed, May 22, 2006. (Barone is the author of *Hard America, Soft America*.)
26. Mary Beth Sheridan, "Chavez Defeats Recall Attempt - Monitors Endorse Venezuelan Vote - Margin is Wide," *Washington Post*, August 17, 2004, p. A1.
27. Sarah Wagner, 'Venezuelan Opposition Leader's Meeting With Bush Stirs up Controversy," June 2, 2005, *Venezuelanalysis.com*, www. venezuelanalysis.com/news.php?newsno=1643, accessed May 15, 2006.
28. Foreign Agents Registration Act filings, U.S. Department of Justice, File #5567.
29. Gregory Wilbert, "Jesse Jackson Says Venezuela No Threat, Praises Venezuelan Government Concerns," August 28, 2005, *Venezuelanalysis.com*, www.venezuelanalysis.com/news.php?newsno=1735, accessed May 15, 2006. See also, Ron Arnold, "Autocrats and Activists: How Hugo Chavez and Fidel Castro Use Venezuela's CITGO Oil to Mobilize U.S. Leftists to Subvert Free Enterprise at Home," Center for the Defense of Free Enterprise, Bellevue Washington, 2006.
30. Gregory Wilbert, "Jesse Jackson Says Venezuela No Threat, Praises Venezuelan Government Concerns," *op. cit.*
31. Juan Forero, "Free-Spending Chávez Could Swing Vote His Way," *New York Times*, August 14, 2004, p. A3.
32. Juan Forero, "Chávez Still on Top in Venezuela After Tough Year," *New York Times*, April 12, 2003, p. A3.
33. Juan Forero, "Carcas 'Circles': Vicious, or Sociable?" *New York Times*, May 23, 2002, p. A8.
34. Don Terry, "Chavez plans to offer oil to aid U.S. poor," *Chicago Tribune*, August 30, 2005, p. 6. See also, Don Terry, "Jackson steps into U.S.-Venezuela breach," *Chicago Tribune*, August 29, 2005, p. 3.
35. Carlos Lauria, "Attacks on the Press 2004: Documented cases from the Americas for 2004," Committee to Protect Journalists, www.cpj.org/attacks04/americas04/americas.html, accessed May 21, 2006. *See also* No author, "Venezuela: Curbs on Free Expression Tightened," *Human Rights Watch*, March 24, 2005, http://hrw.org/english/docs/2005/03/24/venezu10368.htm, accessed May 23, 2006.

36. Nicholas D. Kristof, "Time to get religion," *New York Times*, November 6, 2004.

37. *Ibid.*

38. Jeff Manza and Clem Brooks, "The Religious Factor in U.S. Presidential Elections," *American Journal of Sociology*, July 1997, Volume 103, Number 1.

39. Christopher Muste, "Hidden in Plain Sight: Polling Data Show Moral Values Aren't a New Factor," *Washington Post*, December 12, 2004, p. B4.

40. Adam Nagourney, "Baffled in Loss, Democrats Seek Road Forward," *New York Times*, November 7, 2004, p. A1.

41. James Davison Hunter, *Culture Wars: The Struggle to Define America*, (New York, Basic Books, 1992).

42. S. N. Eisenstadt, "The Axial Age," *European Journal of Sociology*, Volume 23, 1982.

43. Wayne E. Baker, "Voting Your Values and Moral Visions," paper submitted for the 2005 annual meetings of the American Sociological Association, January, 2005, http://webuser.bus.umich.edu/wayneb/Voting_Values_Baker.pdf.

44. Wayne E. Baker, *America's Crisis of Values: Reality and Perception*, (Princeton, New Jersey: Princeton University Press, 2005).

45. David D. Kirkpatrick, "Some Democrats Believe the Party Should Get Religion," *New York Times*, November 17, 2004, p. A20.

46. Kelley Braucar Vlahos, "Democrats Are People of Faith, Too," *Fox News*, July 29, 2004, www.foxnews.com/story/0,2933,127392,00.html, accessed June 10, 2006.

47. Jane Lampman, "In final push Kerry tries to close a perceived God gap; Democrats hope to draw swing voters from ranks of religious 'moderates,' eyeing fault lines within churches," *Christian Science Monitor*, October 26, 2004.

48. Bob Abernethy, news anchor, "Role of Faith in the Democratic Party," *PBS Religion & Ethics Newsweekly*, November 12, 2004, www.pbs.org/wnet/religionandethics/week811/news.html, accessed June 10,. 2006.

49. Christopher Hitchens, "Unfairenheit 9/11," *Slate*, June 21, 2004. www.slate.com/id/2102723/, accessed June 10, 2006.

50. Political Research Associates, "The Days After," PublicEye.org, November 17, 2004., www.publiceye.org/frontpage/election2004/statement.html, accessed July 12, 2006.

51. Social Investment Forum, "1999 Report on Socially Responsible Investing Trends in the United States," *SIF Industry Research Program*, November 4, 1999, www.socialinvest.org/areas/research/trends/1999-Trends.htm, accessed June 15, 2006.

52. UPI, "State police nab eight at Addison 'therapy session,'" *Bennington (Vermont) Banner*, September 8, 1976, p. 18. Laurie Johnston, "City is spiced by big buffet and 3 parades," *New York Times*, May 18, 1981, p. B3.

53. George Harris and Daniel Yankelovich, "What Good Are the Rich? Charitable Activities of the Affluent," *Psychology Today*, April 1989, p. 36.

54. Doughnut Newsletter, Spring 1984, Threshold Foundation. Copyright is by "Doughnuts Not Nuts With Dough." Content is mostly poems and letters.

55. Threshold Foundation website, Origins, www.thresholdfoundation.org/index.php?id=44, accessed July 8, 2006.

56. Jarol B. Manheim, *Biz-War and the Out-of-Power Elite: The Progressive-Left Attack on the Corporation*, (Mahwah, New Jersey, Lawrence Erlbaum Associates, 2004). See Chapter 2, "Dollars for Doughnuts" for a concise hstory of Joseph L. Mailman's operations.

57. Sigrid Rausing Trust website, www.sigrid-rausing-trust.org/about.htm, accessed July 14, 2006.

58. Business for Social Responsibility website, www.bsr.org/Meta/About/index.cfm, accessed July 14, 2006.

59. Numerous of Mailman's associations are given in a bio at www.clal.org/csa64.html, accessed July 14, 2006.

Network diagram adapted and updated from Jarol Manheim's *Biz-War, op. cit.*

60. Tides Center website, www.tidescenter.org/project_detail.cfm?id= 30615.0, accessed July 14, 2006.

61. *Ibid.*

62. Social Investment Forum, www.socialinvest.org/, accessed July 14, 2006.

63. CERES website, www.ceres.org/, accessed July 14, 2006.

64. IRRC website, www.irrc.org/index.html, accessed July 14, 2006.

65. Joshua Mailman, "Highly Leveraged Social Change," The Future of Social Change (seminar), May 20-21, 2002, New York City, www.clal.org/csa64. html, accessed September 20, 2006.

66. ISS website, www.issproxy.com/index.jsp, accessed July 14, 2006.

67. Corporate Library website, www.thecorporatelibrary.com/, accessed July 14, 2006.

68. Corporate Campaign, Inc. website, www.corporatecampaign.org/, accessed July 14, 2006.

69. Progressive Asset Management website, www.progressive-asset.com, accessed July 14, 2006.

70. David S. Broder, "SEIU Chief Says The Democrats Lack Fresh Ideas - Stern Asserts That a Kerry Win Could Set Back Efforts to Reform the Party," *Washington Post*, July 27, 2004, p. A2.

71. John Kenneth Galbraith, *American Capitalism: The Concept of Countervailing Power*, (Cambridge, Mass., The Riverside Press, 1952).

72. Steven Greenhouse, "Though United in Politics, Unions Face Inernal Turmoil," *New York Times*, August 1, 2004, p. A19.

73. Thomas B. Edsall, "Split of Top Unions Raises Debates on Labor Day," *Washington Post*, September 5, 2005, p. A2.

74. David B. Magleby, J. Quin Monson, and Kelly D. Patterson, "Dancing Without Partners: How Candidates, Parties and Interest Groups Interact in the New Campaign Finance Environment," Center for the Study of Elections and Democracy, Brigham Young University, 2005.

75. Barak Goodman and Douglas Rushkoff, "The Persuaders," *PBS Frontline*, 2004, transcript online at www.pbs.org/wgbh/pages/frontline/shows/persuaders/etc/script.html, accessed July 2 2006.

76. Strategic Telemetry website, "What are micro-targeting, modeling and Virtual IDs?" www.strategictelemetry.com/graphics/Micro-targeting_FAQs.pdf, accessed July 2, 2006.

77. Them Dems website, "Iowa Revisited," www.thepoliticaljunkies.net/Archived/Year2004/Jan/Wk5/Themdems5.htm, accessed July 2, 2006.

78. Barak Goodman and Douglas Rushkoff, "The Persuaders," *op. cit.*

79. Jim Drinkard, "With new law, GOP routs Democrats in fundraising," *USA Today,* August 26, 2003, www.usatoday.com/news/politicselections/2003-08-20-hard-money-usat_x.htm, accessed July 16, 2006.

80. The Associated Press, "Democrats press for every vote - Grass-roots drives under way in 14 states," MSNBC News, April 28, 2004. www.voteractivation network.com/WP/MSNBC%20-%20Democrats%20 press%20for%20 every%20vote.htm, accessed July 16, 2006.

81. Barak Goodman and Douglas Rushkoff, "The Persuaders," *op. cit.*

82. Chip Taulbee, "Acxiom Corp. returns to political roots," *Arkansas Business*, August 30, 2004.

83. David B. Magleby, J. Quin Monson, and Kelly D. Patterson, "Dancing Without Partners," *op. cit.*

84. *Ibid.*

85. Matt Bai, "Who Lost Ohio?" *New York Times Magazine*, November 21, 2004.

86. *Ibid.*

87. Robert Kuttner, "The death and life of American liberalism: the right has shown that conviction beats vacillation. Can liberals acquire some spine?" *American Prospect*, June 1, 2005.

88. Steven Greenhouse, "As Labor Leadership Gathers, Head of Largest Union Issues Call for Major Changes," *New York Times*, November 10, 2004, p. A18.

Network diagram adapted and updated from Jarol Manheim's *Biz-War, op. cit.*

89. **Generally**: Leo W. Gerard, Archon Fung, Teresa Hebb, and Joel Rogers, *Working Capital: The Power of Labor's Pensions* (Ithaca, New York: Cornell University Press, 2001). "About the Council," website of the Council of Institutional Investors, www.cii.org/about/councilboard.htm, accessed July 20, 2006.

90. "About us," website of the Amalgamated Bank, http://www.amalgamatedbank. com/site/about_history.html, accessed July 20, 2006.

91. /www.wbng.org/cwc/cwcintro.htm, accessed July 20, 2006.

92. www.calpers.ca.gov/index.jsp?bc=/about/organization/board/members/ home.xml, accessed July 20, 2006.

93. Jarol B. Manheim, *Biz-War and the Out-of-Power Elite, op. cit.*, p. 170-173.

TRANSITION

MONEY, POWER, POLITICS. WHERE IS IT TAKING US? In short, to war; netwar, to be exact.

We have now looked into the turbulent lives of many progressives and seen their ever-changing stories jumble and join and fracture and join again.

It should be clear by now that there is a truly Vast Left Wing Conspiracy in America, searching for a successor to the institutions and mass politics of social democracy and the Keynesian welfare state.

All its many parts, Bob Borosage's Campaign for America's Future, John Podesta's Center for American Progress, all the forces of the Left, could be digested into the mythic name of Simon Rosenberg's Phoenix Group.

After Kerry's loss, the Phoenix metaphor called progressives out of apathy, as C. Wright Mills and his *Letter to the New Left* called students out of apathy in the Sixties.

Phoenix. A fabulous bird, reborn from the ashes of its earlier life.

Progressive America.

What, exactly, *is* that? As SDS historian James Miller asked, "Abolition of all traces of hierarchy and the division of labor, abolition of elections and all representative offices?" Some waystation on that road?

Many of us won't put up with that.

So it's netwar. The Phoenix Group and the others recruited a new army of culture warriors to be smart, to be invincible, warriors of words and action too—capable of "thoughtful intervention," as David Kallick once wrote.

It evokes certain long-gone elders calling their greatest warrior out of the tent where he lay sulking. The wisest among them couldn't get him to fight. The cleverest among them couldn't get him to fight. So they called on his old teacher, the man who took him from his father Peleus, and instructed him in the counsels of power and trained him to be the world's greatest fighter.

The teacher reminded him:

> The old horseman Peleus had me escort you,
> that day he sent you out of Phthia to Agamemnon,
> a youngster still untrained for the great leveler, war,
> still green at debate where men can make their mark.
> So he dispatched me, to teach you all these things,
> to make you a man of words and a man of action too.

That, of course, is *The Iliad* of Homer in Robert Fagle's fine translation.[1] The warrior, of course, is that archetype of the invincible, Achilles. But only a few remember the teacher's name:

Phoenix.

271

TRANSITION   NOTE

1. "The Embassy to Achilles" by Homer; from THE ILIAD by Homer, translated
   by Robert Fagles (New York: Penguin Books, 1998), p. 266.

BOOK TWO

THE VAST LEFT WING CONSPIRACY

PART V

TUTOR OF ACHILLES

PHOENIX RISING
THE BINARY TRAP

CHAPTER 17

PHOENIX RISING

P ROGRESSIVE NON-PROFITS ARE THE BEARER OF THE REVOLUTION.
Progressive foundations are their vanguard.

What revolution?
There is no chance for a communist revolutionary upheaval in the West,
Hugo Chávez notwithstanding.
What revolution then?
The progressive social change revolution.
Those "all other reforms" that Ellen Miller never explained.
The Vast Left Wing Conspiracy.
Only progressive non-profits with funders as their vanguard have the
interest and capacity to lead the revolution.

Revolutions overthrow forms of government.
The form of government is the "house" or structure in which a people
lives, shaping their quality of life and chances to prosper.[1]
At stake in the progressive revolution is what form of government shall
prevail in the United States, indeed, in the world.

The vision is that non-profits will one day rule the world.
There are those who contemplate the end of the nation state and all
notions of sovereignty with it. Some believe it will really happen.

It may seem absurd to think that the scattered, shattered, and battered
factions we have met in this book are leading a revolution, or that the fickle
foundations we have examined are relentlessly steering their ideological course.

- We've seen Ellen Miller's Get-Money-Out-Of-Politics progressives and George Soros' Get-Money-Into-Politics progressives both fail.
- We've surveyed David Kallick's social progressives anxious about racism, poverty, diversity, corporate power, the environment, healthcare, and daycare, in that order.
- We've detected Mark Schmitt's missing bridges to Progressive America and seen a few wealthy foundations help Rob Stein and John Podesta girder some chasms.
- We've uncovered the Rockefeller Family Fund's "front-groups for front-groups" strategy smearing the oil and gas industry in an electioneering ploy that didn't work.
- Considering how long it took George Soros to opt in on funding the big overarching Phoenix Project, we should ask, like *The Nation* magazine: "In a class struggle, can the owners and dispensers of capital really be trusted to finance their own overthrow?"[2]

Good question. I think the answer is, "of course."

True, many of those owners of capital are on foundations' boards of directors. Nathan Cummings Foundation President Lance Lindblom says, "That doesn't mean foundations can't transcend them."[3]

Socialist ideology, capitalist methodology.

Marxist proletarian revolution and the overthrow of capitalism isn't the only socialism on the menu. There are other successors to the New Deal.

Social democracy is a sort of "socialism lite" that keeps capitalism but removes perceived injustices, and would leave foundations intact. It imposes steeply progressive taxation, allows private enterprise, but nationalizes some major businesses such as power companies, and runs government owned or subsidized education, healthcare, child care, and, as in Sweden, employs a huge workforce in the government bureaucracy—while leaving multi-nationals Saab and Ikea in private ownership. In Canada, social democrats, in the form of the New Democratic Party (NDP), initiated universal healthcare and free automobile insurance. The European Union, Australia, New Zealand, and others have social democratic parties and institutions.[3]

Democratic socialism (keep the words straight) eliminates markets, nationalizes the means of production, and determines production with a planned economy. It can be established either by gradually reforming capitalism from within, or by a revolutionary takeover. It is "democratic" because it is under public control, since the people vote for their representatives, who risk being "instantly" recalled if they stray. It is touted as the ideal form of government, claiming planners want to stay in power and thus obey the people. Democratic socialists disdain social democracy as not being a mild form of socialism, but a mild form of capitalism, too centrist, and not socialist enough. In an evolutionary democratic socialism, non-profits and foundations would likely transition into government agencies and thus survive in some form.[4]

Many more brands of socialism can and do allow private foundations to thrive quite nicely, for example, the United Kingdom's Fabian socialism, whichitself has evolved into the so-called Third Way, a centrism that reduces regulation of the market and even allows privatization of state-controlled industries and services so long as they keep the social safety net.[5]

There is a worldwide organization of social democratic and democratic socialist parties, despite internal disagreements: the Socialist International. Democratic socialists tend to keep the Marxist dogma of class struggle and overthrowing capitalism while social democrats mostly reject it.[6]

SI's United States affiliates include the Democratic Socialists of America—union leaders William Winpisinger and John Sweeney both joined, as we saw in Chapter 15. Cornel West did, too. We'll meet him in a moment.

In 1989, the Socialist International adopted a long 7,000-word, 100-point Declaration of Principles. It has echoed in nearly every American progressive foundation grant description since then. It emphasizes the ideals:

• *Freedom*—freedom from discrimination, plus freedom from owners of capital (private employers), and from politically powerful elites, guaranteed by government.

• *Equality and social justice*—equal treatment under the law, equal income and equal social and cultural status, plus compensation for physical, mental and social inequalities, guaranteed by government.

• *Solidarity*—mandatory unity in the fight to destroy oppressors.[7]

Socialism has a fundamental problem. Let's be clear about it.

People used to say that socialism is the politics of envy.[8]

They don't say it much anymore, but it still is. It's an embarrassing, taboo subject, severely repressed, especially in socialist Western Europe.[9]

We shouldn't have to rehash this, but we do. People forget.

The socialist version of freedom is to throttle those perceived as superior and pretend that human inequalities don't exist, while actively promoting envy as a motivational tool and self-censoring as a social control mechanism.[10]

The socialist version of equality and social justice is not the same as equality under law, it is a demand that no one be better than any other, whether the superiority be sexual, social, political, religious or material.[11]

The demand for such equality is the result of *resentment*.[12]

Social justice doesn't raise everyone to wealth and power, but seeks revenge to demote those with it, nations included.[13]

As German philosopher Max Scheler bluntly put it: "In reality envy wants nothing less than the destruction of all those who embody those higher values which arouse its anger," nations included.[14]

Socialism. Or enraged, repressed envy, depending on your politics.

Then there's the mixed economy, like the United States.

Social*istic* but not social*ism*. Ambivalent. Messy. But it's *our* mess.

JOEL GARREAU, AUTHOR AND PUBLIC INTELLECTUAL, summarized America'sadvice to those who want to come live here:

> The traditional deal America has offered immigrants is: work, pay taxes, learn English, send your kids to school and stay out of trouble with the law, and we'll pretty much leave you alone.[1]

We'll pretty much leave you alone. The American Way.
That's not how progressives want things done in America.
We've seen that American progressives can't leave anybody alone.
Why not? It's the tension between freedom and equality.
Free. American freedom is expressed as *liberty*, government's obligation to refrain from interfering with private conduct. It is the spirit behind the opening words of the Bill of Rights: *Congress shall make no law...*
Equal. Equality under law is not enough for progressives. Government *must* interfere with private conduct to achieve progressive egalitarianism. In nature, we're not equal. We have different talents, looks, brains, and luck.
Progressives don't respect that, will never leave you pretty much alone.
They will never be satisfied with equality under the law.

Conspiracy. Its essence is *planning together to break the law.*
The Vast Left Wing Conspiracy is planning together to *smash* the law.
Could they? Oh, yeah.
In netwar, power migrates to non-state actors, their networks more agile than hierarchical nation-states. Then where would progressives strike first?
Go back to David Kallick's survey, top item. Then jump feet first into the seething cauldron of that most blasting of progressive furnaces: *racism.*

NON-STATE ACTORS

IN JULY 2000, FORTY-EIGHT AMERICAN PROGRESSIVES representing thirty-eight NGOs (non-governmental organizations) signed an open letter, *A Call to Action to the United Nations.*
In early August, three of the signers presented it to the United Nations Committee on the Elimination of Racial Discrimination and also to the Sub-Commission on the Promotion and Protection of Human Rights, which were meeting in Geneva, Switzerland.[2]
It was a call to smash the law of the United States.

The NGOs included the American Civil Liberties Union, Human Rights Watch, the National Association for the Advancement of Colored People, the National Council of Churches/USA, with Jesse Jackson signing for the Rainbow/PUSH Coalition, and four prestigious university professors plus noted filmmaker Spike Lee (*complete list opposite*).[3]
Acknowledging that segregation has ended, *A Call to Action* accused America of "pervasive and persistent patterns of racial discrimination and bias that threaten their livelihood, their liberty, and even their lives."

Baye Adolfo & Desiree M. Ferguson,
National Co-Chairs,
National Conference of Black Lawyers
Anthony G. Amsterdam,
Judge Edward Weinfeld Professor of Law,
NYU Law School
Barbara R. Arnwine, Executive Director,
Lawyers' Committee for Civil Rights Under Law
($4.08 million)
Mary Frances Berry, Geraldine Segal Professor of
History, University of Pennsylvania
and Chair, U.S. Civil Rights Commission
Julian Bond, Chair,
National Association for the Advancement of
Colored People ($40.2 million)
Steve Bright, Director,
Southern Center for Human Rights ($2.23 million)
JoAnn K. Chase, Executive Director,
National Congress of American Indians ($978,779)
Kerry Kennedy Cuomo, Founder,
Robert F. Kennedy Memorial Center for Human
Rights ($4.33 million)
John E. Echohawk, Executive Director,
Native American Rights Fund ($7.57 million)

Dr. Bob Edgar, General Secretary,
National Council of Churches ($77 million, estimated)
Catherine A. Fitzpatrick, Executive Director,
International League for Human Rights ($847,863)
James F. Fitzpatrick, Chair,
International Human Rights Law Group
($4.1 million)
Dr. John Hope Franklin
James B. Duke Prof. of History, Duke University
Dr. Robert Franklin
Interdenominational Theological Center
($10.4 million)
Margaret Fung, Executive Director,
Asian American Legal Defense & Education Fund
($876,183)

Ira Glasser, Executive Director,
American Civil Liberties Union ($44.5 million)
Ronald E. Hampton, Executive Director,
National Black Police Association
Antonia Hernandez, President and
General Counsel, Mexican American Legal Defense
and Educational Fund ($4.1 million)
Wade J. Henderson, Executive Director,
Leadership Conference on Civil Rights ($745,914)
Lynn Walker Huntley, Executive V.P.,
Southern Education Foundation ($6.2 million)

Jesse Jackson, Sr., President and Founder,
Rainbow PUSH Coalition ($8.6 million)
Julie Kitka, President,
Alaska Federation of Natives ($17.8 million)
Stewart Kwoh, Executive Director,
Asian Pacific American Legal Center of Southern
California ($3.6 million)

Shelton J. "Spike" Lee
Film Producer
Judith L. Lichtman, President,
National Partnership for Women and Families
($2.2 million)
William Lucy, President,
Coalition of Black Trade Unionists
Hala Maksoud, President,
American-Arab Anti-Discrimination Committee
The Hon. Kweisi Mfume, President & CEO,
NAACP
Karen K. Narasaki, Executive Director,
National Asian Pacific American Legal Consortium
($1.2 million)

Charles Ogletree, Jesse Climenko Professor
of Law, Harvard Law School
John Payton. Co-Chair,
Lawyers' Committee for Civil Rights Under Law
($4.08 million)
Michael Posner, Executive Director,
Lawyers Committee for Human Rights ($5.3 million)
john a. powell, Executive Director,
Institute on Race & Poverty,
University of Minnesota Law School
Hugh B. Price, President,
National Urban League ($46.4 million)
Professor Speedy Rice
Gonzaga Law School
Randall Robinson, President,
TransAfrica Forum ($746,113)
Sullivan Robinson, Executive Director,
Congress of National Black Churches ($950,000)
Kenneth Roth, Executive Director,
Human Rights Watch ($46.3 million)
Len Rubenstein, Executive Director,
Physicians for Human Rights ($5.3 million)
Theodore M. Shaw, Associate Director Counsel,
NAACP Legal Defense and Education Fund, Inc.
($4.6 million)
Jane E. Smith, President and CEO,
National Council of Negro Women ($7.3 million)
John Tateishi, National Executive Director,
Japanese American Citizens League ($1.7 million)

Andrea P. Taylor, Co-Chair,
American Bar Association ($138.9 million)
Committee on Race & Racism in the
Criminal Justice System

Roger Wilkins, Institute for America's Future;
Robinson Prof. of History & American Culture,
George Mason University
Yolanda S. Wu,
NOW Legal Defense and Education Fund
($6.8 million)
Raul Yzaguirre, President,
National Council of La Raza ($16 million)
James Zogby, President,
Arab American Institute ($646,092)

It asserted that, "on-going racial discrimination in the United States is particularly pernicious because its new forms are often obscured under guises such as the 'war on drugs' and crime prevention."

MOST IN AMERICA'S WHITE MAJORITY do not regard themselves as racist or see racism as a personal problem.[4]

America's foremost Black public intellectual, Cornel West (professor of religion at Princeton, more than 20 honorary degrees, a National Book Award, honorary chair of the Democratic Socialists of America, and a role in *The Matrix* movie sequels as "Councilor West") wants them to know, "The accumulated effect of the black wounds and scars suffered in a white-dominated society is a deep-seated anger, a boiling sense of rage, and a passionate pessimism regarding America's will to justice."[5]

We'll pretty much leave you alone does not compute in that universe.

> As I begin to recognize that the Negro is symbol of sin, I catch myself hating the Negro. But then I recognize that I am a Negro. There are two ways out of this conflict. Either I ask others to pay no attention to my skin, or else I want them to be aware of it. I try then to find value for what is bad—since I have unthinkingly conceded that the black man is the color of evil. In order to terminate this neurotic situation, in which I am compelled to choose an unhealthy, conflictual solution, fed on fantasies, hostile, inhuman in short, I have only one solution: to rise above this absurd drama that others have staged around me, to reject the two terms that are equally unacceptable, and, through one human being, to reach out for the universal.[6]

That's Frantz Fanon from more than fifty years ago. This is, too:

> What? While I was forgetting, forgiving, and wanting only to love, my message was flung back in my face like a slap. The white world, the only honorable one, barred me from all participation. A man was expected to behave like a man. I was expected to behave like a black man—or at least like a nigger. I shouted a greeting to the world and the world slashed away my joy. I was told to stay within bounds, to go back where I belonged.[7]

But today, African Americans belong wherever they wish.

Nontheless, social acceptance and self-acceptance remain elusive—particularly the exorcism of individual and collective self-hatreds from the profound trauma of slavery and its aftermath—even for the majority that happens to be middle-class.

We'll pretty much leave you alone doesn't work if your ancestors were involuntary immigrants. Nobody pretty much left slaves alone.

For that, most whites offer sanction for the struggle to be free, not pity for past or present pain, which is not a mortgage on anybody else's soul.[8]

Especially not for self-inflicted wounds of predatory violence in gangsta rap, or promiscuous hypersexuality in booty rap, or cruel misogyny in hip-hop, says Johnnetta B. Cole, Ph.D. (Northwestern University, 1969; past president of Spelman College, 1987-1997).

She wrote in *Ebony*, "Angry young men hurling epithets at their homeboys and female counterparts, and hypnotic songs and videos depicting mindless violence, conspicuous material excess and hostile sexism may be closer to representing new stereotypes of Black buffoonery than paving the way to Black progress."[9]

Anyone can grasp the struggle for racial equality, but why did the signers direct their *Call to Action* to the United Nations in Geneva?

Spokesman Wade Henderson, executive director of the Washington-based Leadership Conference on Civil Rights, told reporters that the groups had brought the issue before the United Nations because they were "frustrated by the lack of response at the state or federal level to endemic racial discrimination," and wanted UN help in "holding the United States accountable for the intractable and persistent problems of discrimination faced by men and women at the hands of the criminal justice system."[10]

Julian Bond, signing as chair of NAACP, said it "represents our sincere conviction that we have exhausted our domestic remedies in the United States." Maybe the American electorate doesn't agree with his agenda.[11]

NAACP trusted the United Nations: it had long enjoyed consultative status as an NGO with the UN, and was instrumental in shaping the United Nations Charter in 1945, as we shall see in Chapter 20.

A Call to Action was more than Cornel West's passionate pessimism and will to justice (he was not a signer).

It was a foundation-funded, progressive flanking attack on the fundamental structure of America, an end-run around the very system that allowed radical critics like West (and Bond) to gain respect, renown, and reward.

Hudson Institute scholar John Fonte concluded that since the NGOs couldn't win through normal American constitutional democracy, they went "outside of American democracy and beyond its Constitution."[12]

A CALL TO ACTION WAS WRITTEN LIKE A RESOLUTION, with eleven *Whereases* and three *Therefores*.

Five of its *Whereases* charged America with specific violations:

- racial profiling—using race as a presumption of guilt, subjecting people of color to arrest, police brutality and even death;
- disparities in sentencing and incarceration—African-American men comprise 50 percent of the prison population, but only 6 percent of the general population;
- the death penalty is tainted by race and class bias—42 percent of death row inmates are African-American;

- women of color face race *and* gender discrimination in the criminal justice system;
- the U.S. is failing to uphold its obligations under the International Convention on the Elimination of Racial Discrimination (ICERD).

The three *Therefores* urged that:

- the United States must "remove its reservations" from the ICERD Convention;
- the United Nations should send investigators to "examine the human rights violations of racial discrimination and race bias in the U.S. criminal justice system;"
- the United Nations should roundly thrash America at the upcoming World Conference Against Racism, Racial Discrimination, Xenophobia and Related Intolerance (WCAR), to be held in Durban, South Africa, the next August.

The United Nations had held two such world conferences on racism, one in 1978, and another in 1983. These two conferences focused on national obligations to victims of racial discrimination and the importance of legislative, judicial, and administrative action to address the problem.

In recognition of the fact that global racism hadn't gone away, a third was scheduled for August 31 to September 7, 2001.

A Call to Action was intended to enhance the buzz of the two-year run-up to the conference.

The *Call*'s most serious demand was removing America's "reservations" to the ICERD Convention.

What were those reservations? Why did the United States put them there? And why did the signers want them gone?

The Convention, passed by the United Nations in 1965, required that:

All ratifying nations:

Shall declare an offense punishable by law all dissemination of ideas based on racial superiority or hatred, incitement to racial discrimination, as well as all acts of violence or incitement to such acts against any race or group of persons of another color or ethnic origin, and also the provision of any assistance to racist activities, including the financing thereof;[13]

Shall declare illegal and prohibit organizations, and also organized and all other propaganda activities, which promote and incite racial discrimination, and shall recognize participation in such organizations or activities as an offense punishable by law.[14]

The Convention also required that all ratifying nations:

> Adopt immediate and effective measures, particularly in the fields of teaching, education, culture and information, with a view to combating prejudices.[15]

After 29 years in premeditated limbo, ICERD was ratified by the U.S. Senate in 1994.[16]

Even a Democrat-controlled Senate during the Clinton presidency couldn't swallow that infusion of intrusion without gagging:

> The Senate's advice and consent is subject to the following reservations:
>
> 1. That the Constitution and laws of the United States contain extensive protections of individual freedom of speech, expression and association. Accordingly, the United States does not accept any obligation under this Convention to restrict those rights, through the adoption of legislation or any other measures, to the extent that they are protected by the Constitution and laws of the United States.
>
> 2. That the Constitution and laws of the United States establish extensive protections against discrimination, reaching significant areas of non-governmental activity. Individual privacy and freedom from governmental interference in private conduct, however, are also recognized as among the fundamental values which shape our free and democratic society. To the extent that the Convention calls for a broader regulation of private conduct, the United States does not accept any obligation under this Convention to enact legislation or take other measures, to the extent that they are protected by the Constitution and laws of the United States.[17]

That's what the signers of *A Call to Action* wanted removed.
Reservations intended to protect the United States Constitution.
The Bill of Rights that's supposed to protect citizens from government.

I won't leave you alone.

Overthrowing the form of government.
Planning together to smash the law.

Why?

TYPES AND STEREOTYPES

THE SIGNERS WERE NOT AN OPPRESSED RABBLE. Liberators never are.
They were professionals all, leaders well paid to talk about oppressed rabbles.

The 38 groups that signed *A Call to Action* had combined revenues in 2000 of at least $428 million. That didn't count an estimated $77 million belonging to the National Council of Churches and its humanitarian partner Church World Service (churches are not required to reveal their incomes or file IRS Form 990s).[18]

Sample African American / Latina executive compensation in 2000:

- Kweisi Mfune – NAACP – salary $220,000, benefits $5,395, expense account $7,510;
- Barbara R. Arnwine – Lawyers' Committee for Civil Rights Under Law – salary $194,000, benefits $5,820;
- Mary Lynn Walker Huntley – Southern Education Foundation – salary $187,866, benefits $27,430;
- Antonia Hernandez – Mexican American Legal Defense and Educational Fund – salary $135,000, benefits $5,400;
- Robert Franklin – Interdenominational Theological Center – salary $100,000, benefits $20,936, expense account $38,000.
- Wade Henderson – Leadership Conference on Civil Rights – salary $62,822, benefits $5,911.

They had come a little ways from Mississippi Summer.

The others, academics and individual signers, were comfortably off, some rich, all advantaged and honored.

Behind them stood many, many foundations.

Human Rights Watch alone was funded by more than 200 foundations—and had been created by the Ford Foundation in 1978 as Helsinki Watch, a Cold War human rights watchdog, reorganized as Human Rights Watch in 1988. It's a favorite of George Soros and the Sandlers (Chapter 5).

In 2000, Human Rights Watch Executive Director Kenneth Roth was paid a salary of $182,500 with benefits of $18,250.

Twenty-eight of the groups received coordinated grants in 2000 from four high-profile foundations (*chart opposite*):

- The Ford Foundation gave $44.1 million to 21 groups.
- The Open Society Institute of George Soros gave $5.8 million to 11 groups.
- The Carnegie Corporation of New York gave $2 million to 10 groups.
- The Rockefeller Foundation gave $1.1 million to 11 groups.

Not-so-equal all-white foundation executive compensation in 2000:

- Susan B. Berresford – Ford Foundation – salary $582,382, benefits $152,715, expense account $8,629;
- Aryeh Neier – Open Society Institute – salary $220,045, benefits $28,148;

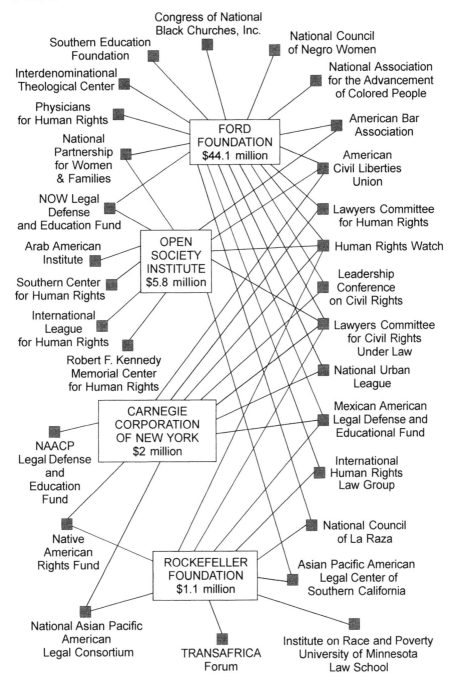

FOUR HIGH-PROFILE FUNDERS AND GRANTEES
A CALL TO ACTION

- Vartan Gregorian – Carnegie Corporation of New York – salary $500,000, benefits $61,968; deferred compensation (housing allowance) $50,000; value of options $60,500;
- Gordon Conway – Rockefeller Foundation – salary $550,951, benefits $84,113.

That was only *some* of the money behind *A Call to Action*.
Overthrowing the form of government.
Planning together to smash the law.
Why?

A CALL TO ACTION GOT LITTLE MEDIA PLAY in Geneva or anywhere else. Contrary to the original intent, its complaints sounded like a perverse call to quotas: no more arrests, prosecutions, or incarcerations than the suspect's proportionality—"Sorry, officer, but you can't arrest my client today because your department has exceeded its racial, ethnic, or gender percentile."

It came across as a Get Out Of Jail Free Card for minorities.

Then, on a Thursday late in October of 2000, just before the Bush/Gore presidential election, representatives of the 38 American NGOs met at United Nations headquarters in New York with UN High Commissioner for Human Rights Mary Robinson, the first woman president of Ireland (1990-1997), who would be serving as Secretary General of the 2001 world racism conference in South Africa.[19]

The meeting looked very much like a news conference. Julian Bond and Wade Henderson led the NGO delegation and gave the open letter to High Commissioner Robinson with no mention of its debut in Geneva.

Robinson then joined the NGOs in pressuring the United States to comply with *A Call to Action*—not surprising, because a few months earlier she had accommodated other NGO protests by issuing a blast against the First Amendment for thwarting censorship of U.S.-based websites they deemed racist (the Web services of many neo-Nazi organizations, Holocaust deniers, and "scientific racism" groups banned by international hate speech laws are hosted in the United States).[20]

The dramatic climax was special guest Saikou Diallo, father of 22-year-old Amadou Diallo, a street peddler and African immigrant who had been shot to death by four white New York City police officers. They took him for a suspected serial rapist, mistakenly thought he was armed, and fired 41 shots. Nineteen police bullets hit Diallo, who held only a wallet.

The four NYPD officers were acquitted of felony charges by a jury of four Blacks and eight Whites. The father told reporters his son's death was an international matter and a clear example of a human rights violation. "I just want some justice for my son's death," he said. "Even if the policemen are not given the death penalty, they must get some punishment."[21]

The NGOs couldn't have made a better case.

Betty King sat in on the meeting. She was United States ambassador to the UN's Economic and Social Council (ECOSOC, in UN-speak).

She was furious.

Ambassador King—Black, born in the Caribbean (St. Vincent), educated in Canada, graduate studies in the U.S., fellowship at Harvard—told a reporter, "There was no advance notice."

It was a carefully staged set-up.

King said, "I'm not insensitive to the issues. I have a son who walks the streets of New York every day. And I saw representatives of countries with far more severe human rights violations vigorously taking notes to use against us later."

Her parting shot: High Commissioner Robinson called this meeting only to single out the United States.[22]

Betty King didn't know the half of it.

AMERICA THE HIDEOUS

WHILE MARY ROBINSON PUBLICLY REBUKED THE UNITED STATES in New York City on Thursday, Wade Henderson's coalition prepared to privately rebuke the United States in San Francisco on Friday.

It was the second of three "Leadership Meetings" called by the International Human Rights Law Group—the first was in Atlanta, the third would be in Phoenix.

The three meetings were convened by United Nations Commission on Human Rights member Gay J. McDougall (Yale Law School, 1972; London School of Economics and Political Science, '78; MacArthur Foundation "genius grant" fellowship '99)—she was also executive director of the Washington-based International Human Rights Law Group.

The "Leadership" consisted of fifty-nine individuals who hadn't signed *A Call to Action,* facilitated by thirteen activists from groups that had.

The invitees represented forty-six NGOs with combined annual revenues of more than $200 million. They were asked to discuss and recommend specific positions the U.S. government should take at the racism conference, then submit a report to the U.S. Inter-Agency Task Force on the World Conference—a high-level lineup of federal executives in charge of government-wide preparations.

Such task forces had been assigned for previous UN conferences—gun control, environment, women's rights, population, drug problem, and so on.

They were part of Al Gore's "reinventing government" initiative, but continued into the Bush administration.

Expenses for the meetings and the report were paid by the Ford Foundation ($700,000) and the Charles Stewart Mott Foundation ($100,000).

The meetings brought out the real agenda—behind closed doors.[23]

A Call to Action turned out to be the polite version, a sanitized sop for the public.

The *Report of the US Leadership Meetings on the World Conference Against Racism* unfolded recommendations to demolish the social and economic systems of the United States along with their underlying principles.[24]

The 28-page *Report* broke into five "Themes," reflecting the planned agenda of the August conference in South Africa: 1) Causes; 2) Victims; 3) Prevention; 4) Reparations; and 5) Strategies.

The high spots:

First Theme: Causes of Racism

THIS THEME HAD BY FAR THE LARGEST NUMBER OF SUBSECTIONS—eleven— each a statement of blame.

Some blames contained a "fixit," a rage-filled demand, really, but couched in disinfected lawyer-speak—the mother-tongue of foundationese, endemic to UN documents.

First blame out of the gate: free market capitalism—primary cause of racism.

First fixit: a totally new Socialist America based on state control of both economy and society:

[Page 3] Free-market capitalism, as the basis of an increasingly globalized economy, was repeatedly criticized by some participants as a fundamentally flawed system. It was roundly agreed that there are inherent iniquities [*sic*] involved when people have to live in a capitalistic society without equal access to capital. Participants expressed the conviction that it is possible to organize a more just, equitable and socially responsible system; one that does not focus on the accumulation of enormous wealth by some, and the exploitation of the labor, land and resources of others. It was emphasized that in order to create opportunities and promote development for a greater number of people and communities, the profit-seeking interests that currently drive globalization must be tempered by state and corporate responsibility.[25]

Second blame: not enough government payments or recognition for minorities.

Second fixit: the U. S. government must give minorities more money and status, as implied in United Nations declarations and treaties.

[Page 4] Participants were deeply troubled by the consistent failure of the US government to recognize that an adequate standard of living is a right, not a privilege. It was strongly urged that the United States respect, protect and promote the full range of human rights, in particular economic and social rights, as enshrined in the Universal Declaration of Human Rights and in the International Convention on the Elimination of All Forms of Racial Discrimination.

Third blame: U.S. immigration policy restricts entry and deports illegal aliens based on race and country of origin.

Third fixit: the United States government must remove its borders, let everybody in who wants in, treat them as honored guests, and stop saying "illegal aliens."

[Page 4] Participants expressed concern that many migrant workers, in particular unskilled laborers and undocumented migrants, are at the mercy of their employers and are easily expelled when their labor is no longer required. They are frequently characterized as "illegal aliens" (although only activities, not people, can ever be "illegal"), which is then used as a justification for denying them their fundamental human rights and freedoms.

Participants fully supported the recommendation that the US government and state authorities guarantee minimum labor protections to all workers, including documented and undocumented migrant workers.

Ninth blame: There is a resurgence of hate groups in America and around the world.

Ninth fixit: Crack down on free speech and snoop on racists.

[Page 6] In particular, the participants were troubled by the fact that the Internet is being manipulated by hate mongers to recruit new members and market a message of intolerance and fear. It was noted that other media have also played a role in the dissemination of hate propaganda and the perpetuation of negative racial and ethnic stereotypes, including certain radio and television programs.

There was also round criticism of opportunistic politicians in the United States, Australia, Austria, France and elsewhere, who are spreading racist rhetoric and ideologies under the guise of "conservatism" or "nationalism". It was recommended that federal and state authorities enhance their efforts to monitor hate groups and hate propaganda.

Eleventh blame: Denial.

No fixit.

[Page 7] Denial is a global phenomenon, one form of which is the tendency to attribute the problems of non-whites to their own deficiencies. Denial of institutional racism is especially easy and effective in the absence of a readily identifiable perpetrator. Denial can at times be overcome with statistical and other evidence of racial discrimination and disparities. However, even in the face of blatant violations or inequities, alternative reasons and justifications will often be proffered. Denial is even a factor among some people who are or have been themselves victims of racism and racial discrimination.

It was pointed out that the rhetoric emphasizing the "progress" we have made in overcoming this country's racial problems actually ignores how deeply imbedded racism and racial discrimination is, and obfuscates the point that a great deal more should have been done by now.

Second Theme: Victims

A BRIEF SECTION trying to identify and catalog who is a bigger victim than whom, biggest victim wins.

[Page 7] On the question of who is hurt by racism, the participants in the Leadership Meetings responded that racism, racial discrimination, xenophobia and related intolerance diminish the humanity in all of us, contribute to the disintegration of society as a whole, and result in conflict, poverty and the wasting of human potential. Participants emphasized the need to examine the full range of harm that is done to society and to victims of racism, including socio-economic, physical and psychological damage.

Third Theme: Prevention

W ARDING OFF RACISM WAS HARDER. The participants identified four key priority areas: Education, inter-group relations, the Internet and economic rights.

Education: This section contains the only use of "multi-cultural" in the *Report*:

[Page 8] Participants uniformly supported the view that education is essential to preventing racism, racial discrimination, xenophobia and related intolerance. Anti-racism education must begin at the earliest possible age and continue throughout a person's lifetime. Also noted as a key element was the development and use of multi-cultural curricula that celebrate the contributions made to society and to history by different racial, ethnic and cultural groups.

Inter-group relations: Remarkable only for a revealing minority priority:

[Page 8] The language of "victims" may be perceived as disempowering. Therefore, the term may not resonate with or be embraced by all people and groups that are affected by racism.
[Page 9] Diminish "competitive victimhood."

Economic Rights: Wordy assertion reminiscent of a 1934 Walt Disney song.[26]

[Page 9] A recurring theme in the Leadership Meetings was the need to address the denial of economic rights in this country, especially as people of color are disproportionately among the economically disadvantaged. One expert proposed that a "living wage" should not merely be an idealistic notion, but a reality to be strived for in both public and private sectors. The consensus among the participants was that health care and social safety nets should be universally available and accessible, and that every person should be guaranteed their equal right to an equal, high-quality education.

Fourth Theme: Reparations

THE UNITED STATES WAS ADAMANT that reparations for slavery would not be a Conference agenda item, nor would the related charge of crimes against humanity be countenanced.

Debt forgiveness as a form of reparation to Third World nations for slavery and colonialism, particularly nations in Africa, including notorious kleptocracies, was high on the U.S. no-negotiation list—agencies had too much experience watching American food aid withheld from its intended recipients by corrupt governments as a form of political punishment.

A Call to Action signer Randall Robinson, president of the TransAfrica Forum, was equally adamant that reparations *would* be on the agenda. He was author of the book *The Debt: What America Owes to Blacks,* promoting the idea of cash payments for back wages owed to slave descendants.

It caused a split: Juan Williams, author of *Eyes on the Prize: America's Civil Rights Years* and a host on National Public Radio, argued that cash would "sell out future generations for a one-time payment that would end all white guilt, all sense of a common American family dealing with the tragedy of racial inequality. Reparations would make all black people beggars at the American banquet."[27]

The NGOs knew they were up against a brick wall.

They also knew how to get around it.

[Page 9] The participants in the Leadership Meetings noted at the outset that the agenda item on remedies and redress will require the United States to examine some of the most controversial and sensitive issues relating to racism and racial discrimination, in particular affirmative action and reparations.

[Page 10] Affirmative action. There was universal objection from the participants to the dismantling of affirmative action programs in various US jurisdictions, through propositions, referenda, court rulings and lack of political will. Participants roundly criticized the common misrepresentation that affirmative action constitutes "reverse discrimination", noting that affirmative action is crucial to redressing centuries of sanctioned racial discrimination and color-based inequalities.

[Page 10] Reparations. Reparations for slavery and unpaid slave labor, as well as for dispossession of Indian lands placed high on the participants list of priority issues for the US government to address—although there was no agreed-upon form that they should take. For example, official acknowledgment and apology, and the funding of community-building and reconciliation programs, were recognized as appropriate steps. In the international context, debt relief for "Third World" countries, in particular those in Africa, was fully supported as a form of reparation for slavery and colonialism.[28]

Fifth Theme: Strategies

THE APPROACH WAS FOCUSED: subjugate the United States to "international standards," with NGOs in commanding positions.

- [Page 12] The U.S. must ratify a laundry list of five United Nations treaties and six International Labor Organization Conventions (which remained unratified for constitutional reasons). The U.S. must also accept UN jurisdiction to hear complaints, with NGOs monitoring U.S. compliance;
- [Page 13] All U.S. governments [federal and state], inter-governmental organizations, and international financial institutions are to perform a race-impact analysis before decisions are taken.
- [Page 13] All affected NGOs must be at the negotiating table when congressional approval of economic and trade policies is being sought.

The *Report* summarized the Leadership's discussions in thirty-three recommendations for U.S. positions to be taken at the World Conference Against Racism, with pointers on how to select and run the U.S. delegation.

That's what the NGOs sent to the U.S. Inter-Agency Task Force on the World Conference some time in mid-2001.

Adopting the *Report* would obviously transfer power and overcome opponents. It would also detonate the Gimme-Gimme State.

It wasn't just planning to smash the law, but to transform everything American, its economy, its society, its founding principles, into something post-American.

Why?

And numerous large foundations were paying NGOs millions to do it. Why?

IN 1987, DAVID ROMEYN HUNTER addressed the annual meeting of the leading U.S. progressive funding alliance, the National Network of Grantmakers (NNG), in a semi-retirement speech titled, "If I Had It to Do over Again."

Hunter was the widely respected godfather and guru of a whole generation of progressive social change funders. Hunter had gotten his start in 1959 as a philanthropoid at the Ford Foundation, where his inner city anti-poverty programs became the prototype for President Lyndon Johnson's War on Poverty.

He then served as executive director of the radical Stern Fund for more than a quarter of a century, putting activists and donors together "on issues of social and economic justice."

He preached that philanthropy's job was "extending democracy in the world." His democracy was democratic socialism.

Many philanthropoids—but only a few members of their boards— listened to him.

Hunter's Stern Fund could afford to be radical because its leftist donor, Sears heir Philip Stern, had ordered his foundation to spend itself out of existence in one generation. No successors, no contrary grants.

David Hunter had harsh words for those he disagreed with:

> The defenders of privilege can fight hard, too.... Anti-democratic people are sitting in the seats of power [the Reagan administration], and they are not just sitting there. They are changing things. Social change, if you will, but not the kind of social change we had in mind when we started to use that term.[29]

He urged "some ideals beyond materialistic individualism and jingoism, some explicitly stated values that would help us move toward a more democratic and egalitarian society."

He asked the donors "to think and act systematically, to take *systems transformation* as our target rather than amelioration of the symptoms of system malfunctioning."

> Obviously, a serious effort of this kind will challenge some sacred cows and gore some oxen. How much of our destiny can we leave to market forces? How much gap between haves and have nots can a society that pretends to be a democracy tolerate? Should there be limits to the wealth any person should have or control? How much can and should national sovereignty be limited? Questions like these stir the blood. But why shouldn't foundations help to raise and explore them.[30]

WHY

THE FORM OF GOVERNMENT is the "house" or structure in which a people lives, shaping their quality of life and chances to prosper.

At stake in the progressive revolution is what form of government shall prevail in the United States, indeed, in the world.

Progressives see their revolution, not always clearly, through two not always clear ideologies: multiculturalism and transnationalism.

Like all ideologies, these are political and intellectual doctrines that "construct" the world so that its leaders:

- appear as liberators of the oppressed;
- give new norms to live by;
- and seem destined for the role.

And, like all ideologies, they attract intellectuals and true believers while leaving the average person indifferent.[31]

Analyzing these ideologies—multiculturalism and transnationalism—could tell us something of what form of government these progressive revolutionaries seek, which might help us estimate their probability of success.

W HILE THE PROGRESSIVE PHOENIX tried to rise from its ashes in the face of Republican gains in 2004, a young Achilles from Illinois won election to the U.S. Senate. All these progressives had been the tutor of Barak Obama.

C H A P T E R   1 7   N O T E S

1. Joel Garreau, "300 Million and Counting," *Smithsonian*, October, 2006, p. 99.
2. International Human Rights Law Group, *A Call to Action to the United Nations* (Washington, D.C., August 4, 2000) www.globalrights.org/site/DocServer/ Call-to-Action_-_Final.pdf?docID=210 accessed January18, 2007. The three presenters were Wade Henderson (Leadership Council for Civil Rights), Julian Bond (NAACP), and Mary Frances Berry (Chair, U.S. Civil Rights Commission). *See* the group's own paid news release: PR Newswire, "U.S. Civil Rights Leaders Call on UN to Examine the U.S. Criminal Justice System," Washington, D.C., July 21, 2000, www.highbeam.com/doc/1G1-63606506.html (fee service), accessed January 18, 2007. *See also* Inter Press Service Staff, "Rights-U.S.: UN Hears Complaints of Racist Justice System," *Inter Press Service English News Service*, August 15, 2000, www.highbeam.com /doc/ 1P1-36509422.html (fee service) accessed January 18, 2007.
3. Mithre J. Sandrasagra, "Leaders Urge Call to Action: Activists Insist UN Should Investigate Racial Discrimination Against Blacks by Administrations," *Sacramento* [California] *Observer*, November 29, 2000, www.highbeam.com/ doc/1P1-79644880.html (fee service) accessed January 18, 2007.
4. Full racial disclosure: My legal name is Ronald Henri Arnold. I am a white male of English, French (Acadian), Irish, Scottish, and Native American (Cherokee) descent, blood type A negative, born in Houston, Texas to third-generation Texans, maternal line Henri from Nova Scotia through Louisiana. My wife, born Janet Ann Parkhurst, is a white female of Scottish and English descent, born in Boston to naturalized Canadian immigrants (matrilineal fifth-generation Cape Breton Island, Nova Scotia, 1840s from Lochmaddy, North Uist, Outer Hebrides, Scotland, Clan MacDonald of Sleat). We have three daughters, six grandchildren (two boys, four girls) with white fathers of English and German descent, three granddaughters with a Korean father, and one adoptive grandson with a Black father.
5. Cornel West, *Race Matters, With a New Preface* (Boston: Beacon Press, revised edition 2001, first published 1993), p. 18. West appears in *The Matrix Reloaded* and *The Matrix Revolutions,* and provides philosophical commentary on all three *Matrix* films in *The Ultimate Matrix Collection* along with Ken Wilber, theorist of consciousness and founder of the Integral Institute. I have heard West many times on NPR's *Tabas Smiley Show*.
6. Frantz Fanon (1925-1961), Martinique-born French psychiatrist, later Algerian revolutionary, *Black Skin, White Masks* (London: Pluto Press, new edition 1986), p. 114. First published in 1952 in French under the title *Peau Noir, Masques Blancs* by Editions Du Seuil, Paris. I have visited his birthplace in Fort-de-France, on Martinique (now a full *department* of France with a McDonald's, no less). A school is named for Fanon in La Trinité, creoles resent metropolitan French tourists, the economy is tourism and bananas, unemployment is high but the welfare system works. Fanon wouldn't like it.
7. *Ibid*, p. 197.
8. Black dramatist Tanya Barfield wrote her 2006 masterpiece *Blue Door* to make these points. The New York-based playwright did for Yoruba incantation what John Steinbeck did for the Hebrew word *timshel* ("thou mayest") in *East of Eden*—found timeless meaning in ancient words. She provided her lead char-

acter, a Black mathematics professor who has lost his wife, his job, and his identity, with courage from an ancestral ghost whose African songs, family stories, and jokes restore his soul—with help from a magic blue door that keeps good spirits in and bad spirits out. Barfield said, "humor and songs have both been major coping mechanisms for oppression." Like Steinbeck, she ended her drama of legacy, coping, and redemption with foreign words hanging in the American air.

9. Johnnetta Betsch Cole, "What Hip-Hop Has Done To Black Women," *Ebony*, March 2007. *See also*, Johnnetta Betsch Cole and Beverly Guy-Sheftall, *Gender Talk: The Struggle for Women's Equality in African American Communities* (New York: One World/Ballantine, 2003). For a sympathetic treatment of hip-hop, *see* James McBride, "Hip-Hop Planet," *National Geographic*, April, 2007.

10. Inter Press Service Staff, "Rights: Civil Rights Leaders Highlight U.S. Racial Biases," Inter Press Service English News Service, October 25, 2000, www.highbeam.com/doc/1P1-36510142.html (fee service) accessed January 18, 2007. Inter Press Service is a non-profit cooperative news agency established in 1964 "to serve civil society" and based in Rome, Italy.

11. *Ibid.*

12. John Fonte, "Liberal Democracy vs. Transnational Progressivism: The Future of the Ideological Civil War Within the West," *Orbis*, Foreign Policy Research Institute, Washington, D.C., Vol. 46, Issue 3, Summer, 2002.

137. United Nations Treaty Series, *International Convention on the Elimination of All Forms of Racial Discrimination*, opened for signature Dec. 21, 1965, 660 UNT.S. 195, entered into force Jan. 4, 1969, Article 4(a).

14. *Ibid*, Article 4(b).

15. *Ibid*, Article 7.

16. U.S. Senate ratification: Congressional Record, Senate, International Convention on the Elimination of All Forms of Racial Discrimination, p. S7634, June 24, 1994.

17. *Ibid.* Silently edited solely to remove numerical section references.

18. No author, "Balancing the Budget," *Christian Century*, December 6, 2000. National Council of Churches General Secretary Robert Edgar is quoted as saying, "Last year the business office managed $77 million." www.findarticles. com/p/articles/mi_m1058/is_34_117/ai_68147076, accessed January 15, 2007.

19. Bio of Mary Robinson at http://en.wikipedia.org/wiki/Mary_Robinson.

20. Mary Robinson, "Bigotry and Bias are Alive and Well," *International Herald Tribune*, March 23, 2000. www.highbeam.com/doc/1P1-25552515.html (fee service), accessed January 19, 2007.

21. Jane Fritsch, "The Diallo Verdict: The Overview; 4 Officers in Diallo Shooting are Acquitted of All Charges," *New York Times*, February 26, 2000, p. A1.

22. Lani Russell Lewter, "UN criticizes U.S. human rights violations," *New York Amsterdam News*, December 6, 2000. Amsterdam News, based in New York City, is part of the BlackPressUSA Network.

23. A report synthesized the three meetings into a 28-page document, but it was submitted only to the U.S. Inter-Agency Task Force on the World Conference (federal executives from the State Department, Attorney General's Office, Interior Department, Small Business Administration, and others). The

report was never made public. The Hudson Institute's John Fonte obtained a copy and made it available to me, which is posted at www.freezinginthedark. com/LeadershipMeetings.pdf.

24. Allison N. Stewart (Rapporteur), *Report of the US Leadership Meetings on the World Conference Against Racism: Submission to the Inter-Agency Task Force on the World Conference* (Washington: International Human Rights Law Group, no date, probably mid-2001). Online at www.freezinginthedark.com/ LeadershipMeetings.pdf.

25. It wasn't clear whether the participants meant "access to capital" or simply "access to money"—capital being "accumulated goods, possessions, and assets, used for the production of profits and wealth"—since they expressed dislike of accumulating possessions and disapproval of profits and wealth, and said nothing about production. **Definition of "capital"**: Joseph R. Nolan and Jacqueline M. Nolan-Healy, *Black's Law Dictionary, Sixth Edition* (St. Paul, Minnesota: West Publishing Company, 1990), p. 208.

26. Song, "Oh the World Owes Me a Living (Deedle Dardle Doodle Deedle Dum)," originally appeared in Walt Disney's February 1934 Silly Symphony, "The Grasshopper and the Ants," sung by Goofy (voiced by Pinto Colvig). The Disney movie release version was written by Leigh Harline and Larry Morey; the sheet music version was written by Frank Churchill ("Who's Afraid of the Big Bad Wolf?"). The tune became Goofy's signature for more than 15 years of Disney cartoons.

27. William Walker, "Yale's History Tied to Slavery: Study – Paper heats up debate over U.S. reparations," *Toronto Star*, August 30, 2001.

28. On February 24, 2007, Virginia became the first state to "acknowledge with profound regret the involuntary servitude of Africans and the exploitation of Native Americans." The General Assembly's resolution called for "reconciliation among all Virginians," but did not authorize reparations claims. Bob Gibson, "Lawmakers pass road, slavery bills," *Charlottesville* (Virginia) *Daily Progress*, February 25, 2007.

29. David Hunter's speech was published in the Winter 1987 issue of *The Network*, the newsletter of The National Network of Grantmakers, as quoted in Alan Rabinowitz, *Social Change Philanthropy in America* (New York: Quorum Books, 1990), p. 114.

30. *Ibid.*

31. Lewis S. Feuer, *Ideology and the Ideologists* (New York: Harper & Row, 1975), pp. 1-13; 181-186.

CHAPTER 18

THE BINARY TRAP

WHEN WE READ the *Call to Action* or the *Report of the Leadership Meetings*, we don't see much we'd ordinarily call "multiculturalism"— Wade Henderson isn't just saying that tolerance and cultural diversity are good, Julian Bond isn't just saying that discrimination and insensitivity are bad, and all the other signers aren't just saying let's go eat ethnic tonight and get to know each other with kindness and respect.

And Susan B. Berresford certainly didn't hand out more than 44 million Ford Foundation dollars to convince Americans with different origins that they should try to get along under one government like crabby French and English-speaking rivals manage to do in Canada, where multiculturalism was invented in 1971 as official policy to head off a violent separatist movement in French-speaking Quebec.[1]

The authors of *A Call to Action* and the *Report* wanted something else. Trying to understand them is not easy.

They're living a political philosophy—elaborated in the second half of the 20th Century—that says the injustices minorities suffer aren't just America failing to live up to the democratic principles upon which it was founded, but that the principles themselves—Enlightenment rationalism, individual rights, freedom and equality under law, majority rule with democratic representation, national unity—are defective and must be rejected.

301

Multiculturalist progressives reject the very idea of Enlightenment rationalism. Former president of Senegal, the late Léopold Senghor, wrote in 1961 of the early Black radicals in France, Aimé Césaire, Léon Damas, and himself:

> [W]e threw ourselves like an unleashed sword into an assault on European values that we summed up by the trilogy: discursive reason, technology, the market economy, i.e. Capitalism.[2]

Multiculturalist progressives also attack the very idea of electoral democracy. Kumi Naidoo (Ph.D. Oxford, 1989), leader of CIVICUS: World Alliance for Citizen Participation, asserts:

> [T]he formal institution of electoral systems does nothing to guarantee genuine democracy. We have the form of democracy without the substance. In fact, electoral democracy runs the risk of becoming in many societies a preordained elite-legitimization process.[3]

Not a critique the American electorate has eagerly embraced.

James Ceaser, professor of government at the University of Virginia, nailed the invisible principle behind the strident multicultural discourse we see in *A Call* and the *Report*: it is neither multi nor cultural.[4]

It is on the contrary binary: everybody is laid out on a two-dimensional grid as the Oppressor or the Oppressed—the privileged or the marginalized, the victimizer or the victim. You're either one or the other.

Also, the oppressors—white males, heterosexuals, Anglos—and the oppressed—African Americans, Asian Americans, Latinos/Latinas, Native Americans, Semitic people, gays, women—aren't all cultures: Being male or female is biology, not "culture" (usually thought of as a society's way of life), but politics required them to be cultures even if it made the theory fuzzy.

Neither multi nor cultural.

Only oppressors and victims.

All defined by race, ethnicity and gender.

Which has a number of interesting consequences: First, if you can only be either an oppressor or a victim, and that depends only on race, ethnicity and gender, then you're stuck with whatever you're born into.

You're a permanent member of a group first and a free individual last.

Second, to multiculturalists, the key political unit is *the group*, not the individual citizen. Rights and entitlements go to the group first—race, ethnicity, gender. Solidarity is compulsory.

Your individual capacity for choice is subordinate.

Third, such group consciousness spawns preferences for victim groups: For example, campus speech codes have asserted that racial epithets directed against minorities are racist, but racial epithets directed against Caucasian males (honkey, redneck, whitey, cracker) are not a form of racism—"on the theory that racism is defined as hostility plus power rather than as mere hostility," according to Duke University law professor Stanley Fish.[5]

Who defines the terms controls the universe of discourse.

You could design a hierarchy of oppressions along several dimensions:
Top: White straight male = oppressor = racist.
Bottom: Black lesbian = oppressed = victim.
Buy into that matrix and you buy your own shackles, whips, and noose.
You've given your soul to the grid:
The oppressed forever hate the oppressors.
The oppressors forever despise the oppressed.
Your life script has been written for you by an ideology.[6]

You're trapped in your group.
Oppressor or victim.
Your identity.

BINARY STARS

Progressive icons laid the foundations for Ceaser's binary breakdown, particularly feminist philosopher and cultural historian Riane Eisler (degrees in sociology and law, University of California), whose popular book, The Chalice and The Blade: Our History, Our Future (New York: Harper & Row, 1987) portrayed prehistoric European inhabitants as divided into "partnership cultures" (indigenous, peaceful, egalitarian, and matriarchal) and "dominance cultures" (invading, warlike, hierarchical, patriarchal), which Eisler built into a theory of how modern oppressor-victim binary relations began.

Supporter Ashley Montagu called it "the most important book since Darwin's Origin of Species"; critics condemned Eisler's work as being derivative, contrived, and an agenda-laden public relations screed for her Center for Partnership Studies, funded by New Visions Foundation.

Eisler's work relied heavily on the original research of archeologist Marija Gimbutas (1921-1994) and her goddess-worship theory of Neolithic society, which posited the central and venerated position of women in the unconscious of early European people; this order of things changed with the incursions by Kurgan groups (4300-2800 B.C.) and the European world moved "from matrilineal to patrilineal."

Gimbutas clearly identified her analysis as interpretive and speculative "archaeomythology," but it was adopted as more concrete reality by eager enthusiasts among feminists such as Eisler and neopagans such as Starhawk (pseudonym of Miriam Simos, San Francisco-based ecofeminist, anarchist and witch), whose 2004 film Signs Out of Time traced the life and work of Gimbutas.

The task of multiculturalism, like all ideologies, is to liberate: to change the dominant culture, to strengthen victim groups and weaken oppressor groups.

The liberators themselves are never victims, always superior beings.

But there are problems.

Philosophy Professor Brian Berry warned that multiculturalism actually harms the groups it seeks to help, for example, by weakening "capitalist oppressors" to the point that they flee or die and redistribution systems have no payments to transfer.[7]

Plus, the success of the ideology is largely dependent upon the spirit of compassion, generosity and willingness that characterizes most Western democracies; any real oppressor would simply show them what to do with their ideology.[8]

More to the point, victim groups each have their own intolerances that other victim groups won't tolerate—deep cultural beliefs and cherished histories that define who they are and distinguish "us" from "them." But no group will give those up. Think of Latino prejudice against gays, which gays insist Latinos relinquish. The harder you push, the harder they push back. Think of Jesse Jackson and "Hymietown" and the response of Jews Against Jackson. Think of Tevye the milkman in *Fiddler on the Roof*: on the one hand... on the other hand... on the other hand... there *is* no other hand.[9]

Then, too, empowered victims have a nasty habit of becoming The Vengeful New Oppressors. Nietzsche was right.[10]

Enforced tolerance degenerates into the implosive mind-binder, "How much intolerance of intolerance won't you tolerate?"

BLENDER WITHOUT A TOP

THE THEORY THAT JUSTIFIES ALL THIS was developed by a few academics as activists lived it.

The late Iris Marion Young (professor of Political Science, University of Chicago) gave multiculturalism its first academic alias in her 1990 book, *Justice and the Politics of Difference*.

The politics of difference, Young tells us, is not the politics of equal justice; it's a way to get *social* justice:

> I argue that where social group differences exist and some groups are privileged while others are oppressed, social justice requires explicitly acknowledging and attending to these group differences in order to undermine oppression.[11]

What her "explicitly acknowledging and attending to" means in practical terms is that equality under law must sometimes be overridden by favoring an oppressed group with "special measures" such as hiring quotas, driver testing in one's native language, compensation for ancestral slavery, gay marriage laws, and so on. [12]

It means bolstering group self-esteem by official acknowledgements that could range from subsidizing racial, ethnic and gender festivals, to declaring public holidays, to creating victim group bureaucracies with police power, to surrendering national sovereignty in favor of international social norms unfettered by constitutional constraints.

Harvard law Professor Frank Schnidman once made a relevant point to me: the police power is not given to American government by the Constitution; rather it is an inherent power of all governments to legislate on behalf of the public health, safety, welfare, or morals of their citizens. In the United States, the Constitution is a *limitation* on the use of that power. The United Nations is not like the United States.[13]

Like all ideologies, Young's comes with a load of extra baggage.

Young's politics of difference is an elaborate, spun-out theory. She begins with a sustained theoretical analysis of oppression—it is made of five elements: exploitation, marginalization, powerlessness, cultural imperialism and violence. Then she:

- excoriates welfare capitalism,
- laments the impossibility of impartiality,
- deplores white insults to black bodies,
- calls merit a myth, and
- drubs America for failing to provide perfect community.

When she gets through, there's not much left.

Young blisters the politics of rationalism and universalism, particularly as embodied in the American Declaration of Independence, which valued individuals for their personal contribution, not their aristocratic pedigree— or their pain:

> We hold these truths to be self-evident, that all men are created equal, that they are endowed by their Creator with certain inalienable Rights, that among these are Life, Liberty and the pursuit of Happiness. That to secure these rights, Governments are instituted among Men, deriving their just power from the consent of the governed.[14]

That's hypocrisy: the universalist "all men" is merely a mask for oppression. It wasn't universal at all, since "the United States had its own oligarchic horrors in the form of slavery and the exclusion of women from public life."[15]

Even the bloody civil war that defeated American slavery and the later suffrage and civil rights victories that created today's pluralist America couldn't wash away the sins of Enlightenment rationalism: the Founders "explicitly justified the restriction of citizenship to white men on the grounds that the unity of the nation depended on homogeneity and dispassionate reason."[16]

> ## ALASDAIR CHALMERS MacINTYRE
>
> Moral philosopher Alasdair MacIntyre dealt more straightforwardly than Young with the serious issues of justice and rationalism in two works, *After Virtue* (1981) and *Whose Justice? Which Rationality?* (1988).
>
> Where Young focused on specific ethical debates such as racism and feminism, MacIntyre does not attempt to resolve the conflicts of rival justices or competing rationalities, nor does he sink into moral relativism, but presents "the best theory so far" of how things are and of how we ought to act, defending "internal goods" such as good character and good judgment against "external goods" such as money, power and status, making him a stern critic of capitalism but not a raging opponent.
>
> MacIntyre focuses on what makes a good person, rather than what makes a good action or good rules, an individualistic focus that eluded collectivist Young. MacIntyre studied competing moral traditions and their history to identify the "best theory so far," making his philosophy intellectually adventurous, more like a vehicle than a destination.
>
> Young's multiculturalism, conversely, has already arrived at its stultifying binary end point.[17]

Dispassionate reason then gets hammered: Young tells us the rationalism, science, and technology that built America into an industrial power are a form of "white, bourgeois, male, European bias:"

> In thinly veiled metaphors of rape, the founders of modern science construct nature as the female mastered and controlled by the (masculine) investigator. The virtues of the scientist became also the virtues of masculinity—disembodied detachment, careful measurement and the manipulation of instruments, comprehensive generalizing and reasoning, authoritative speech backed by evidence.[18]

In short, Young's take on multiculturalism is a twisty maze leading us from a passionate condemnation of racial and gender bias to a comprehensively generalized and reasoned attack on comprehensive generalization and reason, and to authoritative speech backed by evidence against authoritative speech backed by evidence, thence to advocacy against the entire foundation of America's form of government. Okay, that wasn't short.

CATHARSIS CENTRAL

CANADIAN ACADEMIC CHARLES TAYLOR (professor of philosophy and political science, McGill University, Montreal) gave multiculturalism its other alias in a 1994 essay titled, "Multiculturalism: Examining the Politics of Recognition."[19]

Taylor defines the politics of recognition as simplicity itself: "Due recognition is not just a courtesy we owe people. It is a vital human need."

Then things get complicated.

What happens when you ask *government* to provide the vital human need for recognition?

Questions arise.

Can a democratic society treat all its members as equals and also recognize their specific cultural identities?

Should government try to ensure the survival of specific cultural groups?

Is political recognition of ethnicity or gender essential to a person's dignity?

Taylor considers two kinds of recognition in today's political scene, which he calls the *Politics of Universalism,* whose emphasis is on equal dignity of all citizens, and the *Politics of Difference,* whose emphasis is on the uniqueness of their identities:

> With the politics of equal dignity, what is established is meant to be universally the same, an identical basket of rights and immunities; with the politics of difference, what we are asked to recognize is the unique identity of this individual or group, their distinctness from everything else. The idea is that it is precisely this distinctness that has been ignored, glossed over, assimilated to a dominant or majority identity. And this assimilation is the cardinal sin against the ideal of authenticity.[20]

What's so sinful about everybody being assimilated into having an identical basket of rights and immunities?

It doesn't guarantee outcomes.

The problem is the right to life, liberty and the pursuit of happiness.

Just the pursuit. Not the happiness.

In the politics of equal dignity, you have to make your own way in the world. If a group, a cultural tradition, a religious dogma—whatever—survives and thrives, then, that's great. If it falters and disappears, well, that's sad. The right to pursue it is what matters, what makes liberty liberty.

It has no binary trap.

The politics of recognition wants to guarantee outcomes: the right to a vital human need, recognition. Guarantee the happiness.

How would we do that in America? Should Congress become "the national cry room and catharsis center for all sorts of hurts and grievances that would, at first glance anyway, seem to be private issues"?[21]

Taylor, an Anglophone from Quebec, had seen the power of recognition denied. He lived through the 1960s and '70s when many car bombs and letter bombs showed how desperate some Francophones were to preserve their French language and to keep their French-Canadian culture from being assimilated into the English majority and possibly annihilated.[22]

Despite the not-very-soothing effect of official bi-lingualism and bi-culturism in Canada, Taylor knew the underlying problem would fester on—the separatist Parti Québécois reminds binary Canadians every day.

Taylor has his own load of extra baggage: gentle wisdom.

These two modes of politics, then, both based on the notion of equal respect, come into conflict. For one, the principle of equal respect requires that we treat people in a difference-blind fashion. The fundamental intuition that humans command this respect focuses on what is the same in all. For the other, we have to recognize and even foster particularity. The reproach the first makes to the second is just that it violates the principle of nondiscrimination. The reproach the second makes to the first is that it negates identity by forcing people into a homogeneous mold that is untrue to them.[23]

What's a decent form of government to do?

Theology Professor Edward T. Oakes answered: "Society is being asked to provide two mutually contradictory supports to each individual: one based on his abstract humanity and the other on his unique particularity, and the two simply cannot be made to parse in the same political syntax."[24]

The authors of *A Call to Action* and the *Report of the US Leadership Meetings* are asking for just that: keep equal rights, but make mine special.

That, the Constitution cannot do.

B UT THE EUROPEAN UNION CAN AND DOES.
Member states, for example, have hate speech laws that would not pass constitutional muster in the United States. And gun control laws, and genetically modified food bans, and impossible industrial emission limits, and dozens of other attacks against free markets, private property, individual liberty, and limited government.

The European Union's form of government does not resemble that of the United States. It is post-democratic. Its power resides principally in the European Commission (EC), the EU's executive body. With the European Parliament and the Council of the European Union, it is one of the three main institutions governing the Union.

The Commission consists of a President, chosen by the European Council, and 27 Commissioners, one appointed from each member state of the EU. They are supported by a large bureaucracy of about 23,000 civil servants based in Brussels, Belgium.

The European Parliament has the power to force the entire commission to resign through a vote of no confidence, but has never done so. The threat alone, however, prompted President Jacques Santer (Luxembourg) and the whole commission to resign of its own accord when mismanagement scandals emerged in 1999.

The Commission is unelected and unaccountable to any member state. An internal white paper in 2000 asserted that the lack of accountability was the only reason for its success:

> The original and essential source of the success of European Integration is that the EU's executive body, the Commission, is supranational and independent from national, sectoral or other influences. This is at the heart of its ability to advance the interests of the European Union. For Commissioners and individual officials, it means that they shall neither seek nor take instructions from any government or from any other body. Similarly, Member States should not seek to influence Members and staff of the Commission in the performance of their tasks.[25]

Imagine a similar note about runnung America coming from the White House to Congress, the governors of the states, and the voters.

Some see that as the shape of a possible world government.

The EC white paper was part of a reform package, prompted by the Santer debacle, to "constrain the Commission's penchant for policy entrepreneurship in all areas under the sun."[26]

NGOs, unelected and totally unaccountable, have routine access and influence in the European Commission, yet its own member states do not, since commissioners are not permitted to take instructions from the government of the country that appointed them, but are supposed to represent the interests of the citizens of the EU as a whole.

This "democracy deficit" appalled two American experts, who warned of "The Alarmingly Undemocratic Drift of the European Union":

> The fact that, despite all of the constitutional constraints, the power of the [U.S.] federal government has grown steadily over the past 225 years underscores the problem. The existence of a written constitution, of a political and popular culture that features a healthy dose of mistrust toward the government, and of an independent judiciary does, though, provide a mitigating factor in the United States. These "checks and balances" are absent in the EU case.[27]

But undemocratic, unelected, unaccountability is the essence of the next progressive ideology.

THE YOUNG ACHILLES FROM ILLINOIS had learned well from his tutors. He was ready to take on that great leveler, war. He had mastered debate where men can make their mark.

Now a man of words and actions too, Barak Obama, in February 2007, declared his candidacy for President of the United States.

Democratic frontrunner Hillary Clinton had company.

CHAPTER 18 NOTES

1. The story is told even-handedly in Neil Bissoondath, *Selling Illusions: The Cult of Multiculturalism in Canada* (New York: Penguin Books, 1994).
2. Léopold Sédar Senghor, "Discours Prononcé à l'Université d'Oxford," October 26, 1961, reprinted in Irving Leonard Markovitz, *Léopold Sédar Senghor and the Politics of Negritude* (New York: Atheneum, 1969), p. 53. To give him his due, Senghor was not arguing against *all* reason, adding in 1963, "that discursive reason by itself could not comprehend the world in order to transform it; that it was necessary to add intuitive reason, which penetrated facts and things beyond the surfaces." *Ibid.*, p. 52. What he was getting at is best summarized in his famous, "L'èmotion est nègre, la raision est héllène" (emotion is Black, reason is Greek), strengthening African identity—over against Europe's, particularly against English Romantic poet Shelley's "We are all Greeks" (Preface to *Hellas*)—as having its own knowledge, for which emotion, intuition and spirit were basic. Senghor's colleague Aimé Césaire said it another way: "no race has a monopoly on beauty, on intelligence, on strength."
    Césaire's rebuttal to Europe was cutting and cryptic:

> Eia for those who never invented anything
> for those who never explored anything
> for those who never conquered anything
>
> Eia for joy
> Eia for love
> Eia for grief and its udders of reincarnated tears.

Aimé Césaire, *Notebook of a Return to the Native Land*, translated and edited by Clayton Eshleman and Annette Smith (Middletown, Connecticut: Wesleyan University Press, 2001). Originally published in French, *Cahier d'un retour au pays natal* (1939) in *Volontés* magazine, Paris.
3. Kumi Naidoo, "The New Civic Globalism," *The Nation*, May 8, 2000.
4. James Ceaser, "Multiculturalism and American Liberal Democracy," in Arthur M. Meltzer, Jerry Weinberger, and M./ Richard Zinman, *Multiculturalism and American Democracy* (Lawrence, Kansas: University Press of Kansas, 1998), *pp.* 141-42.
5. Stanley Fish, "Boutique Multiculturalism," in Meltzer, Weinberger, and Zinman, *Multiculturalism and American Democracy, op. cit.*, p. 72.
6. Such hierarchies of oppression, as the *Report* noted, create "competitive victimhood," in which the most victimized wins. Gay activists such as Warren J. Blumenfeld argue against such attitudes for thwarting coalitions between minorities and creating incentives for being victimized.
7. Brian Berry, *Culture and Equality: An Egalitarian Critique of Multiculturalism* (Cambridge, Massachusetts: Harvard University Press, 2002).
8. Roger Hewitt, *White Backlash and the Politics of Multiculturalism* (Cambridge, England, UK: Cambridge University Press, 2005).
9. **Latinos/gays**: Rona Marech, "Rights groups want Latino media to end gay pranks, on-air ridicule," *San Francisco Chronicle*, April 16, 2006, p. A1.

Fiddler on the Roof: Book, Joseph Stein; Music, Jerry Bock; Lyrics, Sheldon Harnick; based on stories by Sholom Aleichem.

10. Eric Hoffer, *The True Believer: Thoughts on the Nature of Mass Movements* (New York: Harper & Row, 1951).

11. Iris Marion Young, *Justice and the Politics of Difference* (Princeton, New Jersey: Princeton University Press, 1990), p. 3.

12. The Virginia General Assembly on February 24, 2007 became the first to approve a resolution to "acknowledge with profound regret the involuntary servitude of Africans and the exploitation of Native Americans." The resolution called for "reconciliation among all Virginians," but did not authorize reparation claims. Bob Gibson, "Lawmakers pass road, slavery bills," *Charlottesville* (Virginia) *Daily Progress*, February 25, 2007.

13. The gist of the conversation is summarized in Frank Schnidman, Stanley D. Abrams, and John J. Delaney, *Handling the Land Use Case* (Boston: Little, Brown and Company, 1984) pp. 423-24.

14. *Declaration of Independence* (1776).

15. Young, *Justice and the Politics of Difference, op. cit.* p. 155.

16. *Ibid.*, p. 111.

17. Alasdair MacIntyre, *After Virtue* (Notre Dame, Indiana: University of Notre Dame Press, 1981) and *Whose Justice? Which Rationality?* (Notre Dame, Indiana: University of Notre Dame Press, 1988). *See* Wikipedia article, http://en.wikipedia.org/wiki/Alasdair_Macintyre, accessed March 15, 2007, for sources and more extensive discussion.

18. Young, *Justice and the Politics of Difference, op. cit.* p. 126.

19. Charles Taylor, *Multiculturalism: Examining the Politics of Recognition* (Princeton, New Jersey: Princeton University Press, 1994).

20. Charles Taylor and Amy Gutman (editor), *Multiculturalism and the Politics of Recognition: An Essay* (Princeton, New Jersey: Princeton University Press, 1992).

21. Edward T. Oakes, "Attention Must Be Paid," *First Things*, 32 April 1993, 48-51.

22. Jane Jacobs, *The Question of Separatism* (New York: Vintage, 1981).

23. Taylor and Gutman, *Multiculturalism, op. cit.*

24. Oakes, "Attention Must Be Paid," *op. cit.*

25. European Commission, *Reforming the Commission: A White Paper, Part I* (Brussels: Commission of the European Communities, May 4, 2000), p. 7. http://europa.eu.int/comm/reform/index_en.htm, accessed January 22, 2007.

26. Liesbet Hooghe and Neill Nugent, "The Commission's Services," in John Peterson and Michael Shackleton, eds. *The Institutions of the European Union* (New York: Oxford University Press USA, 2006).

27. Lee A. Casey and David B. Rivkin Jr, "Europe in the Balance: The Alarmingly Undemocratic Drift of the European Union," *Policy Review* (Stanford, California: The Hoover Institution, June/July 2001).

PART VI

TRANSNATIONAL TRIUMPH

POWER MIGRATES
TO RULE THE WORLD

CHAPTER 19

POWER MIGRATES

THE AUTHORS OF *A CALL TO ACTION* and the *Report of the US Leadership Meetings* went to the Conference Against Racism in South Africa because it was a gathering of power.

Not the United Nations.

The 6,000 activists from 2,000 transnational NGOs they would meet in Durban at their own parallel conference, the NGO Forum.[1]

That's about five percent of the world's 40,000 internationally operating NGOs on all topics.[2]

They had netwar friends with an axe to grind all over the world.

Pressure without borders.
To do what?

Sometimes, short titles tell a long story. Take, for example, the book *Restructuring World Politics*. In three words it unmakes every form of government on Earth.

The long story is transnationalism.
The second ideology.

The book is about breaking down borders, fighting multinational corporations, weakening the nation-state, blocking development, eliminating capitalism, elevating the power of NGOs, bolstering indigenous peoples, and glorifying global governance—in short, what world politics is beginning to look like.[3]

315

Restructuring World Politics: Transnational Social Movements, Networks, and Norms was written by the MacArthur Consortium on Peace and International Cooperation—a group of experts "emphasizing change in global society"—and paid for by the John D. and Catherine T. MacArthur Foundation (2003 assets, $4.5 billion).[4]

Such gatherings are called "epistemic communities"—transnational networks of knowledge-based experts who define for decision-makers what problems they face and what they should do about them, i.e., consultants with a fancy name and clout to match.[5]

Our problem is that this nifty epistemic book with its short title—for all its broad expertise—doesn't begin to tell us what transnationalism is really all about, and it's particularly short on the "global governance" part of that "change in global society."

History tells us that the term "transnational" was coined in 1916 by the American writer Randolph Bourne in his *Atlantic Monthly* article, "Trans-National America."[6]

Bourne's essay—more an ancestor of multiculturalism than transnationalism—argued that the "melting pot" wasn't working, that Americans shouldn't be shocked by the immigrant refusing to be melted, and that the U.S. should accept immigrant cultures into a "cosmopolitan America" instead of forcibly assimilating them into "hyphenated English-Americans."[7]

Not much help when we're talking about restructuring world politics.

So we're going to simplify things and accept an academic definition:

Transnationalism is the movement of tangible or intangible items across state boundaries when at least one actor is not an agent of a government or an intergovernmental organization.[8]

That's the crux: it's merely *inter*national if it's only between governments, as in the United Nations.

Those pesky non-state actors are what makes it *trans*national.[9]

But what do non-state actors have to do with global governance?

TRANSNATIONALISM IS A REACTION against globalization.[10] Globalization is Harvard economist Theodore Levitt's term for the increasing convergence of markets, economies, and ways of life across the world.[11]

Increased travel, communications, trade, and investment have brought increased living standards, education, literacy, clean water, and health care to Third World nations—and further wealth to the First World.

Not everybody's happy with that.

It's not just that a middle class American couple can take a Princess cruise to West Java, sail by a gorgeous panorama of mountains, paddy fields and tea plantations, then go shoreside to try some *gado-gado* (vegetables in sauce) and *ayam goreng* (fried chicken) with the ubiquitous chili sauce *sambal* (way hot!) at a charming little 8-seat restaurant on Jalan Kepatihan, a side street a couple of blocks south of the main post office in Bandung, the capital.

It's that next door there's a Kentucky Fried Chicken outlet crammed with dozens of hungry locals talking on their cell phones (called "hand phones" in Indonesia) while waiting in line for a two-piece Kombo KFC—certified *halal* for Muslims. In actual fact, Bandung has four KFCs, four McDonald's, seven Dunkin Donuts, and hundreds of thousands of cell phones, some better than yours.

IMPORTED CULTURE can easily hybridize with local cultures, homogenizing, Westernizing, McDonaldizing, and enriching American free market capitalists (and Nokia executives in Finland).

The average citizen likes it.

Globalization means consumption—from McDonald's Happy Meals for Bandung kids to the Mercedes Benz SLR McLaren for Paris Hilton.

It means personal freedoms, technology, and cultural excitement, things like DVDs from Hollywood and Bollywood, MP3 players, Hello Kitty, pizza, MySpace, and viral videos (*Star Wars kid,* by a Quebec high school student swinging a golf-ball retriever around like a Darth Maul light saber, was leaked to the Internet, patched up by others with music and effects, and viewed over *900 million times* on the Web between 2003 and 2006).

Jerry Mander's not happy with that. His name sounds like a pun on "gerrymander," but it's real. He's the author of *Four Arguments for the Elimination of Television* (1977), and director of the International Forum on Globalization (IFOG). His view:

> Economic globalization is the greatest single contributor to the massive ecological crises of our time, yet this is an aspect that is often ignored—by the media, NGOs, policymakers, and citizens. Its inherent emphasis on increased trade requires corresponding expansion of transportation infrastructures—airports, seaports, roads, rail-lines, pipelines, dams, electric grids—many of these are constructed in pristine landscapes, often on Indigenous people's lands. Increased transport also uses drastically increased fossil fuels, adding to the problems of climate change, ozone depletion, and ocean, air, and soil pollution. Further, under trade liberalization rules, corporations have easier access to already depleted natural resources and environmental standards are harmonized to the lowest common denominator.[12]

Andrew Wheeler was right (page 171). You could argue against each of Mander's points, but it wouldn't change a thing. He's left something unsaid.

Transnationalists hate globalization with a fury. It's corporate imperialism, spreading artificial wants, exploiting sweatshop labor, ripping up the local ecology, and drowning authentic cultures in the free market capitalistic values of corporate cohesiveness, competitiveness, accumulation, wealth, individualism and personal achievement, rewarding (or punishing) risk takers, with resulting inequalities in income and power.

At root, it's really *free market capitalism* that globalization is about.

Transnationalism is a reaction against *globalizing free market capitalism*.

Transnationalists call it a corporate "race to the bottom"—moving operations overseas and from country to country seeking the lowest cost labor and resources to improve profits.

Only an all-powerful world government, or new global norms—or a fundamental shift in human nature—can stop it.

All the rest flows from that.

Including the *Report of the US Leadership Meetings on the World Conference Against Racism* (see Theme One).

Restructuring Global Norms

NEW REGULATORS ARE EMERGING to govern world trade.

They're non-governmental accreditation organizations that set standards and certify labor and environmental practices for compliant corporations. Factories, forests, farms, fisheries, and more can now be certified as socially or environmentally sound.[13]

This is the convergence of transnationalism and what leftists call Corporate Social Responsibility (usually capitalized) or CSR. CSR is a left-wing project to force corporations to provide free services beyond the interests of their companies, shareholders, and the law by making them pay for the social and environmental preferences of pressure groups or their designated beneficiaries. Certification is one of the most effective tactics of Corporate Social Responsibility advocates.

The idea of private certification has been around a long time (Underwriters Laboratories was founded in 1894). Environmental certification goes back at least to 1990, when the Rainforest Alliance's Smart Wood program approved the first certified forest, a teak plantation in Indonesia (on Java, but not close to Bandung).

In 1992, the United Nations Conference on Environment and Development (UNCED, the "Rio Earth Summit") released its mammoth 900-page meddling document, *Agenda 21*, which recommended:

Governments, in cooperation with industry and other relevant groups, should encourage expansion of environmental labelling and other environmentally related product information programmes designed to assist consumers to make informed choices.[14]

Those "other relevant groups" included social and labor certification groups: Social Accountability International and the Apparel Industry Partnership were organized in 1997, United Students Against Sweatshops and the Fair Labor Association in 1998; the Worker Rights Consortium came a little later, in 2001.

As we shall see, certification is an NGO tactic to gain control over corporations, telling them what to do, where to do it, how much to pay, and what losses to sustain—with corporate acquiescence.

The three best known certifiers, the Forest Stewardship Council, the Fair Labor Association, and Social Accountability International, operate by setting standards, offering certification programs, and good publicity to firms that agree to meet the standards. A relatively new approach.

United Students Against Sweatshops and its spinoff, the Worker Rights Consortium, offer no certification or good publicity. They investigate and publicize abuses, then pressure university administrators to cancel licensing contracts with manufacturers in the $2.5 billion college apparel industry that use "sweatshop" labor. A very old approach.

Tree, Spare That Woodsman

MANY TIMBER FIRMS that agreed to forest certification standards ultimately did so because they'd been battered for years by anti-timber activist group attacks—shareholder petitions, smear campaigns, lawsuits, legislative lobbying, pressure on government agencies, threatening letters to executives, protest demonstrations, blockades, site occupations, and customer intimidation, all set against a simultaneous backdrop of criminal acts including vandalism, arson, and bombing by fringe networks that were not interested in certification.[15]

The Forest Stewardship Council (FSC) got its first logging company member, Pennsylvania-based Collins Pine, because, as Vice President of Marketing Wade Mosby described it:

I was in Denmark with a client when someone came into a meeting saying, "We're being picketed. I just left the distribution yard and we've got Greenpeace out there." These guys were really scared. They thought they were going to lose their market in Europe because of the public outcry led by Greenpeace and the World Wildlife Fund.[16]

At the other end of the supply chain, Home Depot—targeted because it is the world's largest buyer of lumber—came on board under similar circumstances.

The question often asked about the genesis of The Home Depot's wood purchasing policy is "Did RAN's [Rainforest Action Network's] aggressive campaigning force the company's hand, or was this a process borne out of true social responsibility initiatives deeply rooted within the organization?"

The answer, if you ask The Home Depot, is that the company was wrestling with these issues long before the campaign banners flew. But these headline-grabbing protests did have a significant impact.

"I would say that they gave the [company's corporate] Environmental Council a sense of urgency," remembered [Home Depot Vice President Suzanne] Apple. "Purchasing wood in an environmentally responsible way was definitely on our radar screen, but what groups like the Rainforest Action Network did was help us move it to the front burner."[1]

If you read the actual headlines, Home Depot wasn't so polite when it was happening: They called the cops when RAN scared customers away in more than 600 of their parking lots, mobbed stores with activists screaming through bullhorns, stole wood products ("ethical shoplifting"), dumped wood all over the store, and invited the TV cameras to watch the fun.[18]

The facts didn't matter—Home Depot was doing a good environmental job to begin with, but RAN needed to justify its foundation grants and keep "upping the ante" with increasingly extreme tactics, as the group's President Randy Hayes told reporters. Executive Director Michael Brune said the ramping up of protests was "a way of stating your moral principles." So RAN used its own synthetic moral system, not real forest conditions, as a club.[19]

After a few years of having protesters arrested to no avail, Home Depot just caved in and joined the Forest Stewardship Council's certification program, which gradually eliminated the protests. It was less fuss, and although commodities like 2-by-4s go to price, not ideology (there is no price premium for certified lumber), they could afford to eat the additional costs.

The Forest Stewardship Council is based in Bonn, Germany, with affiliates in more than forty countries, including the Washington, D.C.-based U.S. Working Group, Inc.

FSC does not do the actual certification, it only establishes standards. FSC-accredited professional third party certifiers verify compliance by using "chain of custody" documents proving that end products have not been contaminated with non-certified impostors at any step between forest and customer.

FSC approves products with its logo, granted to those that follow all the rules.

FSC is 85% supported by foundations, 1999-2004 totals:

- Pew Charitable Trusts, $2.2 million;
- Rockefeller Brothers Fund, $450,000;
- Ford Foundation, $400,000;
- Doris Duke Charitable Foundation (American Tobacco Company money), $265,000;
- Surdna Foundation (Arlington Chemical Company money) $175,000; and
- Mary Ann Stein's Moriah Fund (RealSilk money), $170,000.

About 5% of FSC revenue comes from government grants (Austria, European Commission, Netherlands, Sweden), and the rest from user fees.[20]

The World Wildlife Fund (WWF) has been called the "incubator and the surrogate mother" of the FSC (with helpful "thought leaders" in the MacArthur Foundation and the Rockefeller Brothers Fund, long-time collaborators), but it was mainly after WWF, Friends of the Earth, and other environmental groups failed to get a binding international forest convention passed at the Rio Earth Summit that they turned to forest certification.[21]

Governments also played an important role in creating FSC:

> The governments of Austria, the Netherlands, Switzerland, and several other countries provided funding for the FSC, with Austria in particular donating roughly US$1.2 million at a critical early moment. In 1992, the Austrian parliament passed a law restricting the import of tropical timber unless it met certain conditions of forest management. The law was soon challenged as a barrier to trade under GATT [General Agreement on Tariffs and Trade]. The Austrian government rescinded the law and then donated money from that program to the nascent FSC – a fascinating case of a government offloading regulation in response to rules about "free trade."[22]

The same foundations that fund FSC also fund groups that lobby for anti-timber laws—and blockade logging operations (Rockefeller Brothers Fund and Ford Foundation support RAN, the World Wildlife Fund, and Friends of the Earth as well as FSC—Ford also supports Greenpeace).

Free enterprisers think it has the appearance of a shakedown racket by ideologically driven progressive foundations—"You join our FSC buddies (and pay the costs) or we might have to fund some blockades."

Stop-Buttons And Poverty

THE ANTI-SWEATSHOP FACTION has accused many companies with wholesome images, such as Walt Disney, Coca-Cola, The Gap, and Nike, of using sweatshops—crowded, coercive, low-paying workplaces, some with child labor, all with abusive treatment, long hours, and no job security. They assert that the outsourcing and subcontracting of manufacturing has increased worker abuses, especially in the two countries with the largest number of sweatshop workers, India and China.

Celebrated Columbia University economics Professor Jeffrey Sachs argues that sweatshops in developing nations can be a good thing: they don't replace high-paying jobs (as they would in America), and offer people an improvement over bare subsistence farming, endless physical drudgery, prostitution, trash-picking, or no work at all—and workers wouldn't take the jobs if they didn't think so.

It's a realistic cure for extreme poverty, it gave women a new independence in Bangladesh, and it gives the most desperate a foot on the ladder. It isn't the complete answer, but every poor economy has to start somewhere.[23]

Middle class sweatshop activists in wealthy countries are very all-or-nothing thinkers and tend to have only Stop-Buttons, no Go-Buttons. They don't agree with Sachs, particularly on allegations of forced or child labor.
And they have friends in high places.

The Fair Labor Association actually began as a Clinton administration "reinventing government" program: Labor Secretary Robert Reich created his "No Sweat" Initiative in 1993, partly in response to the National Labor Committee and its "fiery, charismatic director," Charlie Kernaghan in the fight to stop sweatshops, but it went nowhere until President Clinton pressured leaders of the apparel and footwear industry, labor unions, consumer groups and human rights activists at a White House meeting in 1996.[24]

They informally (and reluctantly) organized the Apparel Industry Partnership (AIP) and adopted a voluntary code of conduct, and later formally organized as the non-profit Fair Labor Association (1998, IRS exemption 1999) to run a third-party monitoring system and publicity campaign.

The idea was to inspect worker conditions, fix problems, and praise improvements.

It lost most of its NGO and union members when Clinton left office—taking heat from other progressives for consorting with the enemy and disgusted with the voluntary approach that allowed companies to inspect themselves—but continues to operate with four NGO members on a substantial budget of about $2 million a year, $75,000 from a Rockefeller Foundation grant.[25]

Social Accountability International, the other well-known anti-sweatshop certifier, evolved from Alice Tepper Marlin's Council on Economic Priorities with the help of a $1 million government grant from the Clinton administration and $600,000 from the Ford Foundation, along with smaller grants from the General Service Foundation (Weyerhaeuser heirs); the New York Mercantile Exchange Foundation, Chiquita Brands International Foundation, and several minor family foundations.[26]

Clinton also gave taxpayer money to the International Labor Organization, the American Center for International Labor Solidarity, and the International Labor Rights Fund.[27]

The new global norms being set by Corporate Social Responsibility advocates reflect the efforts of one faction of transnationalists, a faction which tries to combat economic globalization with social globalization.

Another faction sees the only way to end the reign of free market capitalism as an all-powerful world government.

But not the way you might think.

CHAPTER 19 NOTES

1. *Durban 2001, United Against Racism*, Newsletter of the World Conference Against Racism Secretariat, Issue 6, October, 2001. www.unhchr.ch/pdf/wcrnewsletter6_en.pdf, accessed April 14, 2007. *See also* Orrin C. Judd, *Redefining Sovereignty: Will liberal democracies continue to determine their own laws and public policies or yield these rights to transnational entities in search on universal order and justice?* (Hanover, New Hampshire: Smith and Kraus, Inc., 2005).

2. Helmut K. Anheier, Mary H. Kaldor, and Marlies Glasius (editors), *Global Civil Society 2005/6* (London: Sage Publications, Ltd., 2005). *See also*, Helmut K. Anheier, *Civil Society: Measurement, Evaluation, Policy* (London: Earthscan, 2004).

3. **General**: Sidney Tarrow, *The new transnational activism* (New York: Cambridge University Press, 2005); **Breaking down borders**: Arjun Appadurai, *Modernity at Large: Cultural Dimensions of Globalization*, (Minneapolis: University of Minnesota Press, 1996); **Decline of the nation-state**: Susan Strange, *The Retreat of the State: The Diffusion of Power in the World Economy* (Cambridge, England: Cambridge University Press, 1996); **World governance**: Christian Joerges, Inger-Johanne Sand & Gunther Teubner, editors, *Transnational governance and constitutionalism* (Oxford, England: Hart Publishing, 2004).

4. Sanjeev Khagram, James V. Riker, and Kathryn Sikkink, editors, *Restructuring World Politics: Transnational Social Movements, Networks and Norms* (Minneapolis: University of Minnesota Press, 2002). The MacArthur Consortium on Peace and International Cooperation links Stanford University with the Universities of Wisconsin and Minnesota.

5. The Greek word επιστήμη or *episteme* is usually translated as knowledge or science. It has most notably been used by French philosopher Michel Foucault in *The Order of Things: An Archaeology of the Human Sciences* (London: Routlege, 2001) originally published 1966 as *Les Mots et les choses: Une archéologie des sciences humaines,* arguing that what constitutes acceptable knowledge changes from period to period. Foucault's concept is reflected in transnationalism in the idea of change from the period of nation-states to the period of global civil society and its new acceptable norms.

6. Randolph Silliman Bourne (1886–1918), "Trans-National America," *Atlantic Monthly*, #118 (July 1916), pp. 86-97.

7. Edward Abrahams, *The Lyrical Left: Randolph Bourne, Alfred Stieglitz, and the Origins of Cultural Radicalism in America.* (Charlottesville: University Press of Virginia, 1986).

8. Robert O. Keohane and Joseph S. Nye Jr, "Introduction," in Robert O. Keohane and Joseph S. Nye, Jr. (editors), *Transnational Relations and World Politics* (Cambridge, Massachusetts: Harvard University Press, 1971), pp. xii-xvi.

9. Srilatha Batliwala and L. David Brown (editors), *Transnational Civil Society: An Introduction* (Bloomfield, Connecticut: Kumarian Press, 2006). Ann M Fiorini (editor), *The Third Force: The Rise of Transnational Civil Society* (Washington, D.C.: Carnegie Endowment for International Peace, 2000). Lester M. Salamon (editor), Wojciech Sokolowski (Editor), *Global Civil Society: Dimensions of the Nonprofit Sector* (Bloomfield, Connecticut: Kumarian Press, 2004).

10. Joseph Stiglitz, *Globalization and Its Discontents* (New York: W.W. Norton & Company, 2003). Jagdish Baghwati, *In Defense of Globalization* (New York: Oxford University Press USA, 2005).

11. Theodore Levitt, "Globalization of Markets," *Harvard Business Review*, May-June, 1983. The term existed before that, but Levitt's article brought it into common use.

12. Quoted in Randy Hayes, "Restructuring the Global Economy: Eradicating Breton Woods and Creating New Institutions," The 2002 Johns Hopkins Symposium on Foreign Affairs series, *Paragon or Paradox? Capitalism in the Contemporary World*, March 14, 2002.

13. Tim Bartley, "Certified Globalization: private organizations are emerging to monitor and certify global trade flow," *YaleGlobal*, August 26, 2004, http://yaleglobal.yale.edu/display.article?id=4426, accessed Jan 14, 2007. Ronnie Lipschutz and Cathleen Fogel, "Regulation for the rest of us? Global civil society and the privatization of transnational regulation" in Rodney Hall and Thomas Biersteker, *The Emergence of Private Authority in Global Governance* (New York City: Cambridge University Press, 2003).

14. Chapter 4, "Changing Consumption Patterns," Section 4.21, in *Agenda 21: Earth Summit - The United Nations Programme of Action from Rio* (New York: United Nations, 1992).

15. See my *EcoTerror: The Violent Agenda to Save Nature – The World of the Unabomber* (Bellevue, Washington: Free Enterprise Press, 1997).

16. www.collinswood.com/M3_HistoryPhilosophy/M3H5_History24.html, accessed March 4, 2007.

17. Mark Evertz, "Leading by Example: The Home Depot, Inc.: A Metafore Case Study on the convergence of business and the environment," (Portland, Oregon: Metafore, 2004), www.metafore.org/downloads/home_depot_case_study_final_081004.pdf, accessed March 13, 2007.

18. Natalie Phillips, "Activists Demonstrate at Home Depot to Protest Old-Growth Timber Products," *Knight-Ridder/Tribune Business News*, October 15, 1998. United Press International, "Five arrested in tree protest," October 29, 1998. Jen Krill, "Felling the Lumbering Giants," Multinational Monitor, Jan./Feb. 2001 - Volume 22 – Number 1 & 2, http://multinationalmonitor.org/mm2001/01jan-feb/corp5.html, accessed March 13, 2007.

19. Jim Doyle, "S.F. nonprofit a lean, green fighting machine – Rainforest Action Network hits corporations where it hurts for the good of the environment," *San Francisco Chronicle*, December 17, 2004.

20. Meridian Institute staff, "Comparative Analysis of the Forest Stewardship Council and Sustainable Forestry Initiative Certification Programs" (Washington, D.C.: Meridian Institute, 2001).

21. Timothy Synnott, "Some notes on the early years of FSC," unpublished manuscript, November 19, 2005, www.fsc.org/keepout/en/content_areas/45/2/files/FSC_FoundingNotes.doc, accessed March 5, 2007.

22. Tim Bartley, "Certified Globalization," *op. cit.*

23. Jeffrey Sachs, *The End of Poverty: Economic Possibilities for Our Time* (New York: Penguin, reprint edition 2006).

24. Andrew Ross, *No Sweat: Fashion, Free Trade, and the Rights of Garment Workers* (New York: Verso, 1997). Liza Featherstone, *Students Against Sweatshops: The Making of a Movement* (New York: Verso, 2002), *pp.* 7-8. David

Bobrowsky, "Creating a Global Public Policy Network in the Apparel Industry: The Apparel Industry Partnership," Case Study for the UN Vision Project on Global Public Policy Networks, 1999, http://www.globalpublicpolicy.net/fileadmin/gppi/Bobrowsky_Apparel_Industry.pdf, accessed March 16, 2007.

25. Wikipedia entry: Fair Labor Association, http://en.wikipedia.org/wiki/Fair_Labor_Association, accessed March 16, 2007. For negative leftist views on Social Accountability International, see Letters, "Liza Featherstone and Doug Henwood Reply" to Alice Tepper Marlin, *The Nation*, March 5, 2001, http://www.thenation.com/doc/20010305/letter, accessed March 16, 2007.

26. Department of State Washington File: Transcript: "Albright Announces Anti-Child Labor Grants," http://canberra.usembassy.gov/hyper/2001/0116/epf204.htm, accessed March 16, 2007.

27. *Ibid.*

FREEZING IN THE DARK - 326

CHAPTER 20

TO RULE THE WORLD

WORLD GOVERNMENT IS NOT GLOBAL GOVERNANCE.
World government would be a nation-state writ large, a single authority with worldwide jurisdiction over all the planet's nations and their citizens—a global federation—and power to enforce compliance.

Global governance is the opposite, what you have to do to solve problems that affect more than one country when there is no worldwide power to enforce compliance.[1]

Too bad nobody agrees on those tidy definitions.
Transnationalists indiscriminately blur the meanings to suit themselves.
But we'll try to stay tidy. Main fact:
No nation has officially put forward plans for a world government.
The United Nations wants to be a world government but has no military or taxing power of its own, and isn't even much good at global governance.
The reason is simple: it has no direct access to a constituency able to sway nation states and their governments.
Except.
Except for NGOs, a circumstance most deeply to consider.
So, throngs of NGOs promote world government.
World government advocates include the World Federalist Movement and its U.S. member, Citizens for Global Solutions; Parliamentarians for Global Action; the Centre for International Governance Innovation; One World Trust; the Institute for Global Policy; Center for the Study of Global Governance; the Committee for a Democratic UN; and quite a few others.[2]
World government has enjoyed many celebrity boosters, most notably Albert Einstein, who said after the atomic bombs dropped on Hiroshima and Nagasaki, "As long as sovereign states continue to have armaments and armament secrets, new world wars will be inevitable."
Einstein thought world federalism was therefore imminently practical, not naïve. To woo the Soviets, he declared, "Membership in a supranational security system should not be based on any arbitrary democratic standards."[3]
He was better at physics.

I realize that this subject could unintentionally evoke all sorts of other subjects. Let me dispel the most likely misunderstandings. I know that major faiths have beliefs about world government. There is no religious framework, express or implied, in what I have to say.

327

I am well aware that:

- Some Christian denominations see world government as prelude or part of the end of the world according to certain apocalyptic or millenarian doctrines;
- Islamists hold that Islam is not solely a religion, but also a social, political and legal system based upon Islamic law, so any world government could be ruled only by Islamic leaders.
- The Bahá'í Faith sees an international government as essential to fulfilling its principles of the oneness of mankind, celebration of diversity, and world peace, although another basic Bahá'í principle is non-involvement in partisan politics.

I do not wish to offend the faithful, but that's not what I'm talking about. Furthermore, I do not intend to evoke grand conspiracy theories or to gratify such theorists. I am well aware of:

- Right wing hand-wringing about the New World Order, the Rockefellers, Rothschilds, Bilderbergers, Trilateral Commission, Bohemian Grove, Illuminati, Club of Rome, Pugwash, Council on Foreign Relations, World Economic Forum, and any other mysterious rich guys who might secretly be out for world domination.
- Left wing hand-wringing about the same rich guys, and the American Empire, multinational corporations, economic globalization, world capitalism, and any other fussing about the horrible preponderance of unilateral, unipolar, hegemonic American power.

That's not what I'm talking about.

Slouching Toward World Government

THE COMMISSION ON GLOBAL GOVERNANCE (September 1992-January 1995) stands as the most credible (and controversial) public effort to date to create something resembling world government.[4]

The Commission was a private organization of twenty-eight high ranking members (*opposite*) who wouldn't mind ruling the world, given the chance. They didn't get it, but their thoughts are illuminating.

Most of their goals were trashed, or preempted by others, or ignored.

But one of them, barely on the agenda to begin with, was a politician's slogan—"political, economic and social rights for all people"—and ended by opening the way to substantial new powers for NGOs, a step in giving the United Nations direct access to a constituency for world government.

The Commission's recommendations, published in 1995 as the 400-page book, *Our Global Neighborhood*, didn't go all the way and propose a "nation-state writ large, a single authority with worldwide jurisdiction over all the planet's citizens and power to enforce compliance."[5]

GLOBAL GOVERNANCE COMMISSIONERS

Ingvar Carlsson, Sweden (co-Chairman) Prime Minister of Sweden 1986-91.
Shridath Ramphal, Guyana (co-Chairman) Secretary-General of the Commonwealth, 1975-1990.
Ali Alatas, Indonesia Permanent representative to the United Nations.
Abdulatif Y. Al-Hamad, Kuwait Director-General and Chairman of the Arab Fund for Economic and Social Development (Kuwait).
Oscar Arias, Costa Rica President of Costa Rica (1986-1990).
Anna Balletbo i Puig, Spain Member, Spanish Parliament (1979-).
Kurt Biedenkopf, Germany Minister-President of Saxony (1990-2002).
Allan Boesak, South Africa Chairman, Western Cape Region, African National Congress.
Manuel Camacho Solis, Mexico Former Minister of Foreign Affairs.
Bernard Chidzero, Zimbabwe Former Minister of Finance.
Barber Conable, United States President, World Bank (1986-1991).
Jacques Delors, France President of the European Commision (1985-1995).
Jiri Dienstbier, Czech Republic Former Deputy Prime Minister of Foreign Affairs.
Enrique Iglesias, Uruguay Former president of the Inter-American Development Bank.
Frank Judd, United Kingdom Life Peer (Baron Judd), House of Lords (1991-).
Hongkoo Lee, Republic of Korea Former Deputy Prime Minister.
Wangari Maathai, Kenya Nobel Peace Prize (2004).
Sadako Ogata, Japan United Nations High Commissioner for Refugees (1991-2001).
Olara Otunnu, Uganda President of the International Peace Academy in New York.
I.G. Patel, India Governor of the Reserve Bank of India (1977-1982).
Celina Vargas do Amaral Peixoto, Brazil Director Getulio Vargas Foundation.
Jan Pronk, Netherlands Deputy Secretary-General of UNCTAD (1980-1985).
Qian Jiadong, China Ambassador and Permanent Representative in Geneva to the United Nations.
Marie-Angelique Savane, Senegal Director of the Africa Division of the UN Population Fund.
Adele Simmons, United States President, John D. and Catherine T. MacArthur Foundation (1989-1999).
Maurice Strong, Canada Secretary-General of Earth Summits 1972 and 1992.
Brian Urquhart, United Kingdom Involved in creation of the United Nations (1945).
Yuli Mikhailovich Vorontsov, Russia Ambassador to the United States (1994-1999); Ambassador to the United Nations (1990-1994).

In fact, the Commission seemed alarmed that anyone might even suggest they were interested in such a thing. Its report stressed that global governance "does not imply world government or world federalism."[6]

Instead it proposed remaking the United Nations into a much more powerful (and grasping) institution, still a long way from a happy federation of world nation states and considerably more insidious.

The Commission's eight key reforms (including a UN standing army and global taxing authority) would eliminate the veto power of the permanent members of the Security Council (China, France, Russia, the United Kingdom, and the United States), elevating the Third World into a voting majority with sufficient clout to incrementally plunder the industrialized nations in the name of equality, with NGOs whispering in the ears of all parties on the way down.

That wouldn't likely promote happy world federalism.

But it would recast the United Nations as just a bigger nation state, one with legions of NGO meddlers, that the rest of the world—particularly nations with industry to plunder—must guard against. Or opt out.

Kissing A Lot Of Frogs

THE COMMISSION ON GLOBAL GOVERNANCE didn't ooze out of some secret backroom of the global rich. For a decade it gestated uneasily in the mind of German politician Willy Brandt (1913-1992), the Cold War Chancellor of West Germany, and leader of its Social Democratic Party.[7]

He was an unlikely parent for world government. His most muscular legacy was his can't-we-just-be-friends policy of improving relations with communist neighbors, East Germany, Poland, and the Soviet Union. Angry countrymen called it "high treason" and "weak." Brandt was forced to resign after his close aide, Günter Guillaume, was found to be an East German spy. He departed with the reputation of a weak, treasonous dupe.[8]

The Socialist International didn't mind, and kept him as president from 1976 to his death from colon cancer in 1992 at age 78.

After disgrace in government, commissions became Brandt's signature career accomplishment, thanks to World Bank President Robert McNamara.

In January, 1977 McNamara announced an international commission of respected influentials, hoping to break out of the political impasse between the developed North and the developing South (all of Latin America, Africa and most of Asia below the Soviet Union, including the Middle East).[9]

The Group of 77—a loose coalition of developing nations demanding lower trade barriers and higher trade preferences—was deadlocked with the developed nations, which had their own sagging economies to worry about and resisted any radical new costs in trade and development aid.

By September, McNamara had convinced a reluctant Brandt to chair the "Independent Commission on International Development Issues"—a North-South binary trap commission. It was to be a frustrating trial by fire that led Brandt to the Commission on Global Governance a decade later

Brandt went to work recruiting 20 others, not so much experts as highly experienced politicians like himself. Members included a former President, three former Prime Ministers, several ambassadors and other senior officials as well as *Newsweek* and *Washington Post* publisher Katherine Graham, and former London-based Secretary-General of the British Commonwealth, Sir Shridath Ramphal of Guyana, a popular South American known as "Sonny."[10]

Oddly, the Brandt Commission had nobody to report to. The World Bank was neither host nor sponsor. All the money and facilities came from elsewhere, mostly from private foundations and European governments.[11]

Brandt carefully balanced members half-and-half between the developed and developing countries, but made sure that four of the five northern politicians were socialists with a pronounced pro-South bias—Brandt, Olof Palme (Sweden), Edgar Pisani (France), and Jan Pronk (Netherlands).

Edward Heath, former conservative prime minister of the United Kingdom, and Peter G. Peterson, chairman of the Federal.Reserve Bank in New York (and Nixon's secretary of commerce), were exasperated.

An anti-North slant pervaded the Commission's findings, based on Keynesian welfare economics and the trendy "mutual interest" thesis.

The North was to pay for a *compulsory* 20-year Marshall Plan to take the produced wealth of developed states and parcel it out to the undeveloped.

Brandt: "We are looking for a world based less on power and status, more on justice and contracts; less discretionary, more governed by rules."[12]

His "mutual interest" vision of "political, economic and social rights for all people"—the slogan was Brandt's—wasn't very mutual:

"The interconnected nature of the global economy means that the self interest of the North needs to be sacrificed in the short term if they are to ensure their own survival as well as that of those in the South."[13]

The Commission went far afield. It hired 16 experts to do background papers on food and hunger, interdependence, industrialization, economic cooperation, energy, disarmament, world trade and the world monetary order. They asked hundreds of research institutes for reports on recent work.

It took ten meetings in different parts of the world and two stormy years of arguments to complete their task, which ended in deadlock.

Members disagreed so intensely that unanimous approval of their report became possible only when Ted Heath for the North and Sonny Ramphal for the South agreed to write the final compromise document as a team.[14]

When it was done in 1980, the Brandt Commission published its direful report, *North-South: A Program for Survival*. Brandt said in his Foreword: "This report raises not only classical questions of war and peace, but also the questions of how can one defeat hunger in the world, overcome mass misery, and meet the challenge of the inequality in living conditions between rich and poor. To express it in a few words: This report is about peace."[15]

Who paid for it? The German Marshall Fund of the United States, the Ford Foundation, the Friedrich Ebert Foundation and the Friedrich Naumann Foundation (Germany), and the International Development Research Center of Canada.

The governments of Denmark, the Netherlands, Norway, Sweden, United Kingdom, and the OPEC Fund also contributed.

The whole thing cost about $750,000.[16]

The report was lionized in the press, translated into 21 languages, and had almost no effect. The timing couldn't have been worse.

Margaret Thatcher was elected in the United Kingdom and Ronald Reagan in the United States. Keynesian economics was out. Free market capitalism was in.

Although thousands of people worldwide marched in support of Brandt's proposals—early versions of today's anti-globalization rallies—nothing went right for Brandt. When 22 heads of government (including Thatcher and Reagan) accepted his invitation to a North-South Summit (in Cancun in 1981), their attempt at dialogue failed, the developed countries rejected the Brandt Report, and the Group of 77 was seriously weakened.[17]

It institutionalized the debate between the capitalist and socialist models of global development, but the Brandt Commission was a flop.

Willy Brandt seems to have taken it personally. He wanted a Phase II.

The Commission released an even more horrendous report in 1983, *Common Crisis, North-South: Cooperation for World Recovery.*[18]

Phase II, same result: all talk, no action.

That cost another $350,000, paid by the German Marshall Fund of the United States and the governments of Canada, West Germany, Kuwait, the Netherlands, and the Commission of the European Communities.[19]

GETTING STRONG

Brandt was fed up with uncooperative nations. In 1985 he told a New York award ceremony honoring him for devotion to the Third World that "national attempts at crisis management are no longer an adequate response to the global dimension of the problems."[20]

It was time to press for "the subordination of national sovereignty to democratic transnationalism," as the Socialist International later reported.[21]

But how? Another commission wasn't likely. Maybe a foundation. Hoping, Willy Brandt established his Development and Peace Foundation in Bonn in 1986 as a tool to "globalize politics"—if nations won't give you political, economic, and social rights for all people, transnationalize them by boosting NGOs—with colleague Kurt Biedenkopf (page 327) as co-founder.[22]

Foundation conferences with NGOs weren't splashy like his grand commission, but they had experts and credibility. He barely had time to get used to them when his big break came: the Berlin Wall fell on November 9, 1989. It soon became clear that the entire Soviet empire was crumbling.

No Cold War. Everything's changed. New threats, new opportunties. Great pretext for a new commission to throttle those uncooperative nations, to create that world without borders, to make it One World, as his foundation's flagship publication was named.

Think globally, act locally? René Dubos (United Nations Conference on the Human Environment, 1972) coined that famous motto all wrong.

Think globally, *act globally.*

D ifficult but not impossible. If anyone could pull *that* off, it was Maurice (pronounced "Morris") Strong, wealthy industrialist, World Bank official, UN factotum—secretary-general of the 1972 UN Conference on the Human Environment in Stockholm; director, UN Development Program; and Under Secretary General of the United Nations since 1985—and most-hated mysterious rich guy (after David Rockefeller) of conspiracy theorists.[23]

Strong was thinking about the end of the Cold War the same as Brandt. A lot of socialists were. In fact, a special session of the North-South Roundtable on "The Economics of Peace" had been called for mid-January, only two months away. The main presenter was to be Dr. Mahbub ul Haq, a brilliant Pakistani economist who had been the Roundtable's chairman (1979-1984).[24]

Brandt knew him well: he had been an Eminent Adviser to his own Brandt Commission (it was he who equated aid with peace). Dr. Haq would discuss "the post-Cold War world and its need for a new concept of global security."

When Dr. Haq spoke, socialists listened. It looked like his session—new ideas from a man long respected in elite policy circles—would provide some excellent fodder for a new commission, and yes, Strong would be interested.

The Roundtable would be held in San Jose, Costa Rica, hosted by President Oscar Arias, who would no doubt also be interested.

Several other prominent people were coming who might be interested as well, including old friend Robert McNamara, Brian Urquhart (former UN Under Secretary General for Special Political Affairs), Sweden's Minister of Disarmament, Inga Thorsson, and perhaps Saburo Okita, Japan's foremost economist, member of the United Nations World Commission on Environment and Development, and the Roundtable's vice-chairman.[25]

Willy Brandt wasted no time. He scheduled a meeting for January to take advantage of whatever Maurice Strong got out of the Roundtable session, perhaps even Dr. Mahbub ul Haq in person.[26]

The guest list for Brandt's meeting was never published. All the sources merely repeat some version of the official explanation of how Brandt started the Commission on Global Governance:

> In January 1990, he invited to Königswinter, Germany, the members of the [Brandt] Commission and individuals who had served on the Independent Commission on Disarmament and Security Issues (the Palme Commission), the World Commission on Environment and Development (the Brundtland Commission), and the South Commission (chaired by Julius Nyerere).[27]

It didn't say who. The place gave no clue: Königswinter is a resort town ten miles up the Rhine from Bonn. Everybody seems to hold such gatherings there (it's also headquarters of the generous Friedrich Naumann Foundation).

Who was there at the beginning? Best guess: based on the outcome, Maurice Strong and Dr. Mahbub ul Haq both joined Willy Brandt in Königswinter, along with Sonny Ramphal and Jan Pronk, among others. But not any of the commission leaders whose work they built upon.[28]

1980-82: Independent Commission on Disarmament and Security Issues
   Olof Palme, Prime Minister of Sweden (assassinated, 1986)
   • *Blueprint for Survival:* disarmament in the Cold War era
1983-87: World Commission on Environment and Development
   Gro Harlem Bruntland, former Prime Minister of Norway
   United Nations World Commission on Environment and Development
   • "Sustainable development" report, *Our Common Future*
1987-90: Independent International South Commission
   Julius Kambarage Nyerere, retired President of Tanzania and noted
   theorist connecting socialism with African communal living
   • *The Challenge to the South:* self-sufficiency and global relations

---

Palme was dead, but his deputy, Ingvar Carlsson, who took over as Swedish Prime Minister, very likely *was* at Königswinter. Brundtland, on the other hand, had a big environmental conference in Moscow in mid-January and likely didn't get back in time. Julius Nyerere was preparing for the Cyprus plenary of his South Commission in May (and three more after that), and then hoped to retire to his childhood home village of Butiama in western Tanzania.

What could Mahbub ul Haq have said at Königswinter that might rule the world? Follow his reasoning. Ask what could make it happen:

This meeting takes place at an extraordinary moment of human history. The dramatic reduction of East-West tensions and the surge of democracy in many parts of the world provides us a unique opportunity for a new way of ordering world relationships. A new vision of the world after the cold war needs to be developed in which territorial security shall be achieved through negotiations and not through military interventions; in which persistence of global poverty, economic inequities and social injustices are regarded as major threats to peace; in which protection of global commons is viewed as protection of humankind's common future; and in which collective security lies in adherence to the rule of law.[29]

It was a precis of his "human development theory" (*opposite*), which would debut in a United Nations report in May. It closely matches the final text of *Our Global Neighborhood* five years later. So does his six-point agenda:

• The redefinition of the concept of security and the development of a vision of a post-cold war world;
• big reductions in military spending, conventional armed forces and armed transfers, the elimination of chemical weapons, and rapid progress towards the elimination of nuclear weapons;

- using the "peace dividend" from reduced military expenditure to ensure greater human development in both developing and developed countries;
- easing the economic and environmental imbalances underlying many existing international and national tensions;
- strengthening the UN and other international and regional machineries for conflict resolution; and
- reaffirming and extending the code of conduct contained in the UN Charter covering the renunciation of the use of military force, unilateral intervention in the affairs of other nations and the shipment of arms.[30]

M A H B U B UL H A Q

Mahbub ul Haq (1934-1998) was a world renowned Pakistani economist who created The Human Development Index, a comparative measure of life expectancy, literacy, education, and standard of living—a shopping list for poor nations—and used since 1990 by the UN Development Program for its annual Human Development Report.

He was the World Bank's director of policy planning (1970-1982) and Pakistan's Minister of Finance and Planning (1982-1984).

Dr. Haq was one of the founders of *human development theory*, which merges ecological economics, sustainable development, welfare economics, and feminist economics into a system for measuring well-being ("things beyond money"), denouncing material growth unless for social welfare, and insisting that rich nations pay for everybody.

He created the backbone agenda for what would become the Commission on Global Governance. At a special session of the North-South Roundtable in Costa Rica in January 1990, he proposed "a new concept of global security, with the orientation of defense and foreign policy objectives changed from an almost exclusive concern with military security to a broader concern for overall security of individuals from social violence, economic distress and environmental degradation, which would require attention to causes of individual insecurity and obstacles to realization of the full potential of individuals." He redefined security.

Who defines the terms controls the universe of discourse.

Dr. Haq's six-point agenda was adopted by the participants at Willy Brandt's Königswinter meeting, combined with recommendations from members of the Palme, Brundtland and Nyerere commissions, and given to a Working Group comprised of Ingvar Carlsson, Shridath Ramphal and Jan Pronk as the basis of their memorandum to the *Stockholm Initiative* conference a year later, which Dr. Haq attended.

That would reform the United Nations toward Brandt's unspoken goal of subordinating national sovereignty to democratic transnationalism.

Dr. Haq's theory didn't emphasize some cogs and wheels essential to making his juggernaut roll: the NGOs. That omission had to be rectified before the Königswinter meeting could get to its real purpose, rigging a convincing call for another (expensive) international commission.

The problem was with the United Nations: the committee that controls NGO access has always done its best to limit NGO rights and power, despite a provision in the UN Charter providing them "consultative status" with the Economic and Social Council (ECOSOC). The rationale was that NGOs must have fewer rights than observer delegations from specialized agencies or governments that were not ECOSOC members. What to do?[31]

Maurice Strong was a wily politician, unlike Dr. Haq. When he ran the UN Conference on the Human Environment in Stockholm back in 1972, he sidestepped the NGO Committee and allowed unofficial NGO conferences alongside the official diplomatic sessions. They were called "the forum," and attracted journalists and even the diplomats.[32]

Forums were chaotic affairs infested with microphone grabbers, debates, street theatre, films, NGO newspapers (they first appeared at the 1972 forum, produced by Teddy Goldsmith's *Ecologist* magazine and Friends of the Earth) and a stew of ideas far beyond the official UN program.[33]

Strong's Stockholm forum was the first to have a direct impact on an official conference agenda: NGO demonstrations against whaling forced the decision of the diplomats to vote for a moratorium on commercial whaling.[34]

Strong had invited a number of unaccredited green groups, just to be fair, of course. Making the demonstrations more impressive was "coincidence."

Being a wily politician, Strong knew the limits to trickery. Forums had grown in size and public impact, but hadn't given NGOs the internal access and control over the official agenda they needed now that reforming the United Nations itself was the agenda.

This Commission on Global Governance, if it were to be worth the effort, had to give NGOs real power to thwart nation states.

Strong and Ramphal had seen what NGOs could do as members of the Brundtland Commission, which organized public hearings in over 15 capitals on five continents, consulting with hundreds of NGO representatives.

NGO networks made the commission's report, *Our Common Future*, a bestseller with global influence on public opinion and legislation.[35]

Strong wanted NGOs to get security passes, not just to committee meetings and planning sessions, but also to all the buildings, including the lounges, bars, and restaurants used by the diplomats, so they could chat with them informally and thus influence meetings and councils they couldn't get into.

But how could you get NGOs into the General Assembly so they could put their items on the United Nations agenda, speak up on issues, maybe even vote? Tough question. They'd think of something when the time came.

So, the Königswinter gathering had its two-pronged agenda, reforming the UN to match Dr. Haq's vision, and somehow giving power to NGOs.

Finally, they turned to the practical problem of convening a new commission. It must be properly invoked by a large and distinguished assembly of persuasive world leaders—all socialists, of course.

The task, then, was to call for a conference to call for a commission.

Ingvar Carlsson told the 1993 Pugwash Council what happened next:

> In April 1990, at the request of Willy Brandt, I had the honor to invite about 30 leaders from all around the world to what became known as the "Stockholm Initiative on Global Security and Governance." In the light of the end of the Cold War and faced with all new risks and challenges, we examined what urgent actions had to be taken in order to promote peace, democracy, and sustainable development.[36]

Brandt had asked Carlsson to join with Jan Pronk and Sonny Ramphal (who had been a member of the Brandt Commission, the Palme Commission, the Brundtland Commission, and the South Commission) to form a Working Group and write the memorandum that would become the agenda for the Stockholm Initiative which would become the agenda for the Commission on Global Governance.[37]

This time, it went like clockwork.

On April 22, 1991, these world leaders met in conference in Sweden:

1. **Ali Alatas**, Indonesia	19. Michael Manley, Jamaica*
2. **Abdulatif Al-Hamad**, Kuwait	20. Vladlen Martynov, Soviet Union
3. Patricio Aylwin Azocar, Chile*	21. Thabo Mbeki, South Africa
4. Benazir Bhutto, Pakistan	22. Robert McNamara, United States*
5. Boutros Boutros-Ghali, Egypt	23. Bradford Morse, UnitedStates
6. *Willy Brandt*, Federal Republic of Germany	24. Babacar Ndiaye, Senegal
7. Gro Harlem Brundtland, Norway	25. Julius Nyerere, Tanzania
8. Fernando Henrique Cardoso, Brazil	26. Saburo Okita, Japan*
9. **Ingvar Carlsson**, Sweden	27. Reinaldo Figueredo Planchart, Venezuela
10. Jimmy Carter, United States*	28. *Jan Pronk*, Netherlands
11. **Bernard Chidzero**, Zimbabwe	29. *Shridath Ramphal*, Guyana
12. Bronislaw Geremek, Poland	30. Nafis Sadik, Pakistan
13. Mahbub ul Haq, Pakistan	31. Salim Salim, Tanzania
14. Vaclav Havel, Czech and Slovak Federal Republic*	32. Arjun Sengupta, India
15. *Edward Heath*, United Kingdom	33. Eduard Shevardnadze, Soviet Union*
16. **Enrique Iglesias**, Uruguay	34. **Manuel Camacho Solis**, Mexico
17. **Hongkoo Lee**, Republic of Korea	35. Kalevi Sorsa, Finland
18. Stephen Lewis, Canada	36. **Maurice Strong**, Canada
	37. **Brian Urquhart**, United Kingdom*

STOCKHOLM CONFERENCE MEMBERS

Bold = Later, Member of Commission on Global Governance
Italic = Previously, Member of Brandt Commission
* Did not attend but agreed to support the Initiative

There they elaborated the Working Group's memorandum into 28 proposals and gave it the title, "Common Responsibility in the 1990s: The Stockholm Initiative on Global Security and Governance."[38]

Proposal 28 recommended "as a matter of priority, the establishment of an Independent International Commission on Global Governance."

A COMMISSION AT LAST

The MacArthur Foundation wrote a half-million-dollar check "For analysis of forces of global change and examination of major issues facing the world community, with recommendations for how international institutions can be reformed or strengthened."[39]

It was addressed to a house in Geneva, Switzerland—on the Avenue Joli-Mont not far from the airport—a house donated by the Canton of Geneva that served as the secretariat of the Commission on Global Governance.

More money would be coming from the Ford Foundation and the Carnegie Corporation of New York. And the governments of Canada, Denmark, India, Indonesia, the Netherlands, Norway, Sweden and Switzerland. And Kuwait's Arab Fund for Economic and Social Development and the World Humanity Action Trust in the United Kingdom.[40]

It was finally happening.

At the Stockholm meeting, Willy Brandt had spoken to Gro Harlem Brundtland and Julius Nyerere about leadership for the Commission on Global Governance.

He had never planned to chair it himself. He was 77 and not well. He wanted it split between North and South, as he had done with members before, and picked Ingvar Carlsson and Sonny Ramphal as co-chairs.

They liked the idea. Brandt soon issued two invitations.[41]

It took the rest of 1991 and a quarter of 1992 for Carlsson and Ramphal to recruit 26 members, arrange funding and facilities and finish preparations.

Maurice Strong had his hands more than full as Secretary General of the Earth Summit in Rio and wouldn't be available until well after the garbagemen had cleaned up the mess from the gigantic conference in June, the one where Teresa Heinz and John Kerry spoke French—and where 2,400 representatives from 650 NGOs were accredited and 17,000 people showed up for the forum.[42]

Once committed and provided with documents, the 26 members studied the thick agenda separately and eventually divided themselves into four Working Groups: 1) global values, 2) global security, 3) global development, and 4) global governance.[43]

Everything was based on Dr. Haq's expanded definition of "security."

By April of 1992, the two co-chairs had things sufficiently organized to visit United Nations Secretary General Boutros Boutros-Ghali and explain the Commission, which had no connection to the UN. Carlsson and Ramphal needed his blessing for credibility, and got it, but not on the scale they had hoped, considering he had joined them at the Stockholm conference.

In fact, Boutros-Ghali merely said some nice words, but did nothing beyond authorizing token UN funding and faint recognition. The UN money was actually obtained by their Roundtable friend Saburo Okita (who was reportedly at the Königswinter meeting) from two UN trust funds supported by the government of Japan, where he was once Minister of Foreign Affairs.[44]

An apocryphal story circulated hinting that Boutros-Ghali had noted that their agenda seemed to make much of giving a voice to NGOs, citizen movements, and transnational organizations, but none of their 28 members came from a civil society background.

It was indeed an embarrassing omission and pointed up the simple fact that nation-based politicians still pulled all the strings, regardless of their devotion to transnationalizing national sovereignty.

Nevertheless, they were setting in motion a process that would increase the power of NGOs to absorb the sovereignty of nation states.

Carlsson and Ramphal had already arranged for a vast consultation round with civil society organizations. They planned contacts with more than 50 leading global NGO networks to ask them to disseminate information about the commission to their member organizations and solicit direct feedback. Three regional consultations were set, in Latin America, Africa, and Asia.[45]

In May, a few weeks after the meeting with Boutros, the commission settled its secretariat's small staff at the house on Geneva's Avenue Joli-Mont. They were equipped and instructed to receive direct NGO feedback and make sure it actually helped discussion within the commission.

Looking ahead, the staff pre-scheduled commissioners to meet with NGO leaders in Geneva on at least two occasions. Discussions with NGOs were also set during the commission's planned meetings in New York, Mexico City, Delhi, and Tokyo.

Three seminars were to be held at Harvard and Cambridge, a conference at the London School of Economics, a symposium at Norway's Foreign Affairs Ministry in Oslo, and another symposium at the United Nations University in Tokyo.

It was overkill with a vengeance.

In September, the commission gathered in Geneva for the first of its eleven official meetings. They were off and running.

Willy Brandt never saw any of it.

Less than a month after the inaugural meeting, he died at his home in Unkel, a small town on the right bank of the Rhine, October 8, 1992.[46]

Five Aces to the UN

You can't understand what the Commission on Global Governance did in its report without understanding Willy Brandt and Mahbub ul Haq. We do.

The final report, *Our Global Neighborhood, was* launched at the World Economic Forum in Davos, Switzerland, on January 26, 1995.[47]

The blurbs for it are slathered with gooey lawyer-speak that hides intent and counts on worn-out value words—"a global ethic," "shared norms," "a new vision"—to mask the plunder of industrial nations that's really in the text.

The commission posted a Website that summarized the report's many recommendations into an "easy-to-read" Top 8 Proposals. Verbatim:

The report includes proposals to:

1 Reform the Security Council, so that it becomes more representative and maintains its legitimacy and credibility
2 Set up an Economic Security Council to have more effective - and more democratic - oversight of the world economy
3 Establish a United Nations Volunteer Force so that the Security Council can act more quickly in emergencies
4 Vest the custody of the global commons in the Trusteeship Council, which has completed its original work
5 Treat the security of people and of the planet as being as important as the security of states
6 Strengthen the rule of law worldwide
7 Give civil society a greater voice in governance.
8 Explore ways to raise new funds for global purposes, e.g. a tax on foreign currency movements, and charges for using flight lanes, sea-lanes and other common global resources.[48]

Let's try that again in plain English, so it accurately reflects the text.

The report's proposals would really:

1 Reform the Security Council, so that poor nations can first outvote rich nations, then eliminate their veto power, then loot the North's treasuries by majority rule
2 Set up an Economic Security Council to control global capital flows and global means of production by taxation, then transfer the wealth of rich nations to poor nations
3 Make the UN a military power with a standing army loyal to the Security Council
4 Give the UN territory: assert title and jurisdiction over nonterritorial oceans, the atmosphere, outer space, and Antarctica, administered by the Trusteeship Council
5 Reduce the power of nation states by giving the UN direct access to a global constituency through granting more authority to friendly NGOs (see 7),
6 Eliminate the individual right to be protected from government interference; hold citizens of all nations subject to prosecution
7 Create two new UN bodies, the Forum of Civil Society to give NGOs direct access to the General Assembly, and the Council for Petitions, to give NGOs power to file complaints of any threat to "security," using Dr. Haq's expanded definition.
8 Give the UN taxing power: an Economic Security Council tax on foreign currency movements, and Trusteeship Council charges for using flight lanes, sea-lanes, and other "common global resources."[49]

The Commission on Global Governance had clear but limited impacts.

Report card on the report:

1 Reform the Security Council: Failed. Permanent members still have veto power. There are still ten rotating non-permanent members elected for two year terms.

2 Set up an Economic Security Council: Failed. The existing Economic and Social Council (ECOSOC) is unchanged, powers still limited.

3 Establish a United Nations Volunteer Force: Failed. UN Peacekeeping Forces still may only be employed when both parties to a conflict accept their presence.

4 Vest the custody of the global commons in the Trusteeship Council: Failed. The Council was set up in 1945 to decolonize all trust territories, the last of which (Palau) became independent in 1994. The Council now exists only on paper. UN Reforms proposed by Kofi Annan in 2005 would completely eliminate it.[50]

5 Treat the security of people and of the planet as being as important as the security of states: Partial success. Dr. Haq's broad "security" concept is widely accepted by NGOs and even business: over 3,300 companies pledged to "adopt sustainable and socially responsible policies" in the UN Global Compact of 2000.[51]

6 Strengthen the rule of law worldwide. Partial success. The International Criminal Court was established in 2002 by the Rome Statute (a treaty) to prosecute individuals for genocide, crimes against humanity, war crimes, and the crime of aggression. The United States signed the treaty, but later "unsigned" it to avoid Law of Treaties obligations to refrain from "acts which would defeat the object and purpose" of treaties signed but not yet ratified.[52]

7 Give civil society a greater voice in governance. Largely successful. The Forum of Civil Society and Council for Petitions got no support, but Boutros Boutros-Ghali told a 1994 conference of NGOs at UN headquarters, "I want you to consider this your home." NGOs now have security passes to all the buildings, lounges, bars, and restaurants used by the diplomats. Their influence pervades governments from town councils to national agencies. "The new reality is that non-governmental organisations are now considered full participants in international life," says Peter Willetts, Professor of Global Politics at City University, London.[53]

8 Explore ways to raise new funds for global purposes: The taxing power failed, and the proposed 1998 World Conference on Global Governance did not happen, but the 2000 Millennium Summit resulted in the UN's Millennium Declaration, which continued the call for redistributing the wealth of the North to poor countries of the South. In 2002, the Monterey Consensus that resulted from the International Conference on Financing for Development held in Monterey, Mexico obtained commitments from the U.S. for more development aid, which is now very large, but socialist countries, especially those in Scandinavia, complain that the amount is still a small percentage of the U.S. gross domestic product and should be larger.[54]

Reducing the power of nation states by giving the UN direct access to a global constituency was a brilliant idea, most clearly seen by Maurice Strong and Mahbub ul Haq. Non-profits in the 22 leading nations employed 19 million people, making it a $1.1 trillion industry. Taken as a separate economy, it would be the 8th largest in the world, ahead of Brazil, Russia and Canada.

A wily politician, Strong calculated that the United Nations could gain global control by using civil society organizations as a tool to influence and reshape the governments of nations, making them more amenable to genuine world federation.

But he forgot one thing.
Civil society might want to rule the world itself.

THE SECOND SUPERPOWER

I N 1999, THE "BATTLE OF SEATTLE" against the World Trade Organization startled the world by showing that the synergy of Ralph Nader's Citizens Trade Campaign, labor unions, environmental groups, thousands of local students, and a determined anarchist black bloc swarm could shut down key negotiations between major nation states—a very loud echo of 1980's marches for the Brandt Commission.[55]

Restructuring World Politics correctly noted that the Battle of Seattle "was not an isolated, spontaneous event but rather a carefully planned tactic of an increasingly coordinated and powerful movement against globalization that often targets international organizations such as the WTO, the World Bank (WB) and the International Monetary Fund (IMF)."[56]

Not coincidentally, more than 40 wealthy foundations—some of them foreign—gathered in Seattle on the eve of the riots to create the Funders Network on Trade and Globalization (a working group of the Environmental Grantmakers Association, which is a project of the Rockefeller Family Fund).[57]

In early 2003, a news analysis on the front page of the *New York Times* talked about the huge global antiwar demonstrations against President George W. Bush's planned invasion of Iraq, concluding "that there may still be two superpowers on the planet: the United States and world public opinion."[58]

"Second superpower" became the instant motto of the global anti-war movement. Greenpeace picked up the phrase in its news releases. Within a month, UN Secretary General Kofi Annan used it in two speeches. Activists grappled it to their souls with hoops of steel. It became the global progressives' all-purpose nostrum, just take Second Superpower and feel better right away.

Dr. James F. Moore of Harvard Law School's Berkman Center for Internet and Society invited furious attacks with his Weblog, *The Second Superpower Rears Its Beautiful Head*, for dumbing it down, removing the politics, dulling the edge, and suffusing it with a sappy Pollyanna-Meets-The-Tooth-Fairy sweetness, which battle-scarred campaigners found offensive:

It is a new form of international player, constituted by the "will of the people" in a global social movement. The beautiful but deeply agitated face of this second superpower is the worldwide peace campaign, but the body of the movement is made up of millions of people concerned with a broad agenda that includes social development, environmentalism, health, and human rights. This movement has a surprisingly agile and muscular body of citizen activists who identify their interests with world society as a whole—and who recognize that at a fundamental level we are all one.[59]

Wikipedia offered a more modest, less ripe description: "The Second Superpower is a term used to conceptualize a global civil society as a world force comparable to or counterbalancing the United States of America."[60]

ALTHOUGH DOZENS OF GLOBAL IDEOLOGUES vie for leadership of that world force, American anti-globalization guru David C. Korten has a slight edge: he's written more books on civil society ruling the world and helped form more civil society groups to do it than most of the rest—and he's bagged big bucks from foundations to do it with.

Korten (MBA and Ph.D., Stanford) is a one-man epistemic community, the personal embodiment of *Restructuring World Politics,* breaking down borders, fighting multinational corporations, weakening the nation-state, blocking development, eliminating capitalism, elevating the power of NGOs, bolstering indigenous peoples, and glorifying global governance. He's Mr. *Transnational Social Movements, Networks, and Norms,* all in one tidy package.[61]

Korten's not just brainy, he's a cunning student of human frailty (his Stanford undergraduate degree was in psychology). His appeal lies in a simple, accessible, three-pronged approach, telling us what's wrong, then telling us what's right, then telling us what to do.

He tells us what's wrong in his 1995 book, *When Corporations Rule the World.* The trade journal *Publishers Weekly* said of it, "This well-documented, apocalyptic tome describes the global spread of corporate power as a malignant cancer exercising a market tyranny that is gradually destroying lives, democratic institutions and the ecosystem for the benefit of greedy companies and investors."[62]

He tells us what's right in his 1999 book (launched at United Nations headquarters), *The Post-Corporate World: Life After Capitalism.* This time, *Publishers Weekly* waxed considerably less rhapsodic: "In four sections of three or four chapters each, Korten lays out how it happened and what we can do about it, using model communities that have already begun to 'treat money as a facilitator, not the purpose, of our economic lives.'"[63]

He tells us what to do in his 2006 book, *The Great Turning: From Empire to Earth Community.* It reads like a Riane Eisler script for some improbable motivational film with a title like *Revenge of the Norms* or *Marx in Love. Publishers Weekly* somehow missed it.[64]

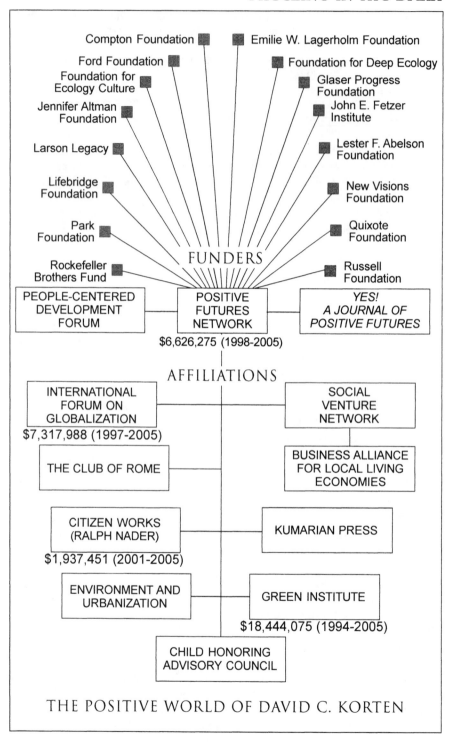

Compton Foundation • • Emilie W. Lagerholm Foundation

Ford Foundation • • Foundation for Deep Ecology

Foundation for Ecology Culture • • Glaser Progress Foundation

Jennifer Altman Foundation • • John E. Fetzer Institute

Larson Legacy • • Lester F. Abelson Foundation

Lifebridge Foundation • • New Visions Foundation

Park Foundation • • Quixote Foundation

Rockefeller Brothers Fund • FUNDERS • Russell Foundation

| PEOPLE-CENTERED DEVELOPMENT FORUM | POSITIVE FUTURES NETWORK | YES! A JOURNAL OF POSITIVE FUTURES |

$6,626,275 (1998-2005)

AFFILIATIONS

| INTERNATIONAL FORUM ON GLOBALIZATION | SOCIAL VENTURE NETWORK |

$7,317,988 (1997-2005)

| THE CLUB OF ROME | BUSINESS ALLIANCE FOR LOCAL LIVING ECONOMIES |

| CITIZEN WORKS (RALPH NADER) | KUMARIAN PRESS |

$1,937,451 (2001-2005)

| ENVIRONMENT AND URBANIZATION | GREEN INSTITUTE |

$18,444,075 (1994-2005)

| CHILD HONORING ADVISORY COUNCIL |

THE POSITIVE WORLD OF DAVID C. KORTEN

If Eisler was derivative of Gimbutas, Korten is twice derivative.

Like Eisler, Korten's bottom line is a return to Eden, a restoration of "partnership cultures" (he even uses Eisler's phrase), by getting rid of 5,000 years of "Empire," his generic term for organizing human relationships by "dominator hierarchy," again using Eisler-cum-Gimbutas jargon.

He also says that things are getting so bad so fast that we must reform now before we destroy ourselves and everything else on Earth.

The difference is that Korten has a huge personal following, a vast network of like-minded colleagues, and very rich mentors intent on building a civil society that just might be able to usurp the power to rule the world (*see diagram opposite*).

- He's co-founder and board chair of his flagship group, the Positive Futures Network. It publishes *Yes! A Journal of Positive Futures*.[65]
- He's founder and president of the People-Centered Development Forum, a low-budget repository for his writings and ideology.[66]
- He was a co-founder of the International Forum on Globalization, a global coalition of social justice, environmental and anti-corporate activists, some more stellar than Korten, including John Cavanagh of the way-left Institute for Policy Studies, Randy Hayes of Rainforest Action Network , Vandana Shiva, physicist and winner of all kinds of leftish awards including the 1993 Right Livlihood Award, Teddy Goldsmith of *The Ecologist* magazine (the late billionaire Sir Jimmy Goldsmith was his brother), and Jerry Mander (page 317), program director of Doug Tompkins' Foundation for Deep Ecology.[67]
- He's a member or advisor of the remaining groups in the diagram.

Korten's roadmap to global rule by civil society may sound twee enough to make you wonder who would build the airplanes, arrest the bad guys, and run the sewage plants in his Eden—or even whether his Paradise has planes and crooks and indoor plumbing—but he is adamant that "a different world is possible" (an iconic slogan of social globalists) and has drawn the positive peace-and-love future in enough detail to look like he's right, give or take a few untended potholes.

The only question is, would you want to live in such a darling world?

Korten says that, "to secure its future, the human species must turn away from the dominator way of Empire to the partnership way of Earth Community, as defined by the principles of the Earth Charter."[68]

The charter's preamble:

We stand at a critical moment in Earth's history, a time when humanity must choose its future. As the world becomes increasingly interdependent and fragile, the future at once holds great peril and great promise. To move forward we must recognize that in the midst of a magnificent diversity of cultures and life forms we are one human family and one Earth community with a common destiny. We must join together to bring forth a sustainable global society founded on respect for nature, universal human rights, economic justice, and a culture of peace. Towards this end, it is imperative that we, the peoples of Earth, declare our responsibility to one another, to the greater community of life, and to future generations.[69]

WELL, WELL, WELL.
The Earth Charter.

We just *knew* that Maurice Strong had to turn up again somewhere.

The Earth Charter was his idea.

It was a way to snag that direct constituency of millions clamoring to form a true world government. Korten was one of the snagged.

It first showed up in 1987, when the United Nations World Commission on Environment and Development—the Brundtland Commission (Strong was one of its commissioners)—called for a new charter to guide the transition to sustainable development. At Strong's insistence.[70]

Nobody paid the slightest attention. Strong was about to go through a Brandt-like disillusionment with nation states.

In 1992, while preparing for the Rio de Janeiro Earth Summit, Strong established his Earth Council in Geneva, Switzerland to promote his Earth Charter. He hoped to use his position as Secretary General of the Summit—formally the UN Conference on Environment and Development—to convince delegates to adopt his Charter, but all he got out of it was the anemic Rio Declaration, a blah statement of the achievable consensus at the time.

That did it. The wily politician gave up on national governments and decided to go directly to the source: he'd engineer a civil society initiative with millions of supporters to legitimize his Earth Charter idea and let *them* cram it down government throats. If all went well, they'd end up *de facto* governments themselves. A real Second Superpower, *making* global policy, not just ineffectually taking to the streets against American global policy.

It took two years for the right opportunity to come along, but in 1994 Mikhail Gorbachev was just forming his Green Cross International, and Strong got together with him. They would co-chair a new grand commission: the Independent Earth Charter Commission.

With the help of Dutch colleague Jan Pronk, who was now Minister for Development Co-operation, they got the government of the Netherlands to throw in some money, then called on Sonny Ramphal to work his magic as commissioner and recruiting agent for the final slate of 19 commissioners.

It took a while, but the Earth Charter Commission launched in 1997 with a North-South cross section of civil society, including Kenya's Green Belt activist Wangari Maathi, Argentinian singer Mercedes Sosa, John Hoyt of the Humane Society of the United States (which gave Michael Ansara's fund-raisers such a huge cut of the take—page 225), and Stephen C. Rockefeller, a former dean of Joshua Mailman's alma mater, Middlebury College, now chair of Rockefeller Brothers Fund, which supported Korten.

The Earth Charter is a 2,400-word document released in 2000 by the Earth Charter Commission. It contains uncredited concepts of Dr. Mahbub ul Haq as well as of Maurice Strong, and is organized around 16 principles:

1. Respect Earth and life in all its diversity.

2. Care for the community of life with understanding, compassion and love.

3. Build democratic societies that are just, participatory, sustainable and peaceful.

4. Secure Earth's bounty and beauty for present and future generations.

5. Protect and restore the integrity of Earth's ecological systems, with special concern for biological diversity and the natural processes that sustain life.

6. Prevent harm as the best method of environmental protection and, when knowledge is limited, apply a precautionary approach.

7. Adopt patterns of production, consumption and reproduction that safeguard Earth's regenerative capacities, human rights and community well being.

8. Advance the study of ecological sustainability and promote the open exchange and wide application of the knowledge acquired.

9. Eradicate poverty as an ethical, social and environmental imperative.

10. Ensure that economic activities and institutions at all levels promote human development in an equitable and sustainable manner.

11. Affirm gender equality and equity as prerequisites to sustainable development and ensure universal access to education, health care and economic opportunity.

12. Uphold the right of all, without discrimination, to a natural and social environment supportive of human dignity, bodily health and spiritual well-being, with special attention to the rights of indigenous peoples and minorities.

13. Strengthen democratic institutions at all levels, and provide transparency and accountability in governance, inclusive participation in decision-making, and access to justice.

14. Integrate into formal education and lifelong learning the knowledge, values and skills needed for a sustainable way of life.

15. Treat all living beings with respect and consideration.

16. Promote a culture of tolerance, nonviolence and peace.

The Charter provoked criticism as well as praise. Its quasi-religious tone offended numerous Christian groups, its socialist economic principles were condemned by libertarians, and its disregard for the sovereignty of nation states insulted conservatives.

THE 16 PRINCIPLES OF THE EARTH CHARTER

The Commission pretty much did what Strong hoped. Touted as the product of "the largest global consultation process ever associated with an international declaration," the Earth Charter was endorsed by thousands of organizations representing millions of individuals.

It got a splashy send-off in June, 2000, at a special ceremony at The Peace Palace in The Hague, Netherlands, Queen Beatrix attending.

The Charter has since been fostered by Strong's original Earth Council, plus six key Earth Council affiliates around the world, and the Earth Council Alliance, a network of 28 powerful global organizations, including former President Bill Clinton's private foundation, as well as an NGO in China.[71]

The Earth Council's news releases tend to mention national agencies and heads of state almost as an afterthought.

Maurice Strong had his direct global constituency.

So what if Korten and his ilk had a mind of their own?

They were all singing Haq and Strong's Earth Community song:

The Earth Charter's inclusive ethical vision proposes that environmental protection, human rights, equitable human development, and peace are interdependent and indivisible. It provides a new framework for thinking about and addressing these issues.

A framework of names and addresses to mobilize big protests in 2003? You watch out, now. All that eyewash might make your brain blurry.

HOW WE REALLY GOT THE UN

DOROTHY B. ROBINS IS NOT A FAMOUS NAME.
Perhaps it should be, because she witnessed and documented the real backstory of the United Nations.

She was an official of the League of Nations Association during its tumultuous transformation into the United Nations Association. She saw people and documents few others saw.

Perhaps we don't know about her because she wrote a book about it with the hackneyed title, *Experiment in Democracy*, which currently brings up 1,279 entries on Amazon.com, one of them hers, if you can find it.[72]

It's the subtitle that grabs you: *The Story of U.S. Citizen Organizations in Forging the Charter of the United Nations*.

Robins unfolds a tale that we should have known but didn't, one that reads like a novel of political intrigue and slapstick comedy, not real history.

All historians know that serious planning for the United Nations began a few days after the Nazi invasion of Poland on September 1, 1939—not by that name and not with any preconceived shape, but something to replace the League of Nations (which the United States never joined, and which had obviously failed to stop aggression) with a new postwar international organization capable of preventing war and averting economic disasters such as the Great Depression.[73]

Upon the outbreak of World War II in Europe, President Franklin D. Roosevelt and Secretary of State Cordell Hull immediately went into action. Assuming an Allied victory, they began intensive and secret research and planning not only for the long-term problems of the war, but also to plan for the subsequent peace.

Some historians are aware that only 12 days after Hitler's blitzkrieg hit Poland, a prominent NGO came to the State Department proposing a confidential War and Peace Studies Project, including postwar plans.[74]

The NGO was the Council on Foreign Relations. The visitors were Executive Director Walter H. Mallory and Hamilton Fish Armstrong, editor of the group's prestigious journal, *Foreign Affairs*. Their contact was assistant secretary of state George S. Messersmith—also a CFR member.

Messersmith immediately took them to meet Secretary of State Cordell Hull and Undersecretary Sumner Welles—also a CFR member. The two officials approved the secret project and Hull appointed Dr. Leo Pasvolsky, director of the Division of Special Research, to work with CFR on "long-range problems bearing on the postwar future."[75]

COUNCIL ON FOREIGN RELATIONS

Influential foreign policy organization established in 1921 in New York City with 108 distinguished founding members, stemming from a group of scholars known as "The Inquiry," President Woodrow Wilson's foreign policy advisory group (1917-1919) on strategy for the post-World War I peace, including formation of the League of Nations. CFR included many luminaries such as John Foster Dulles, Averell Harriman, and members of the Rockefeller family, who were regular benefactors. The Rockefellers funded the entire World War II War and Peace Studies Project, which was so secret the Council's own members not directly involved were completely unaware of the study group's existence. Some Council members were later put in uniform to conduct studies as military officers. The Council's institutional memory of all the failures of the League of Nations made its members key in early planning for the United Nations to avoid repeating mistakes. The Council's roster of State Department officials, corporate executives, and its great influence on foreign policy has made it a perennial focus of conspiracy theories.

In November of 1939, Columbia University history professor James T. Shotwell, also president of the League of Nations Association (and CFR member) created the Commission to Study the Organization of Peace, a who's who of international relations scholarship in the fields of education, government, business, and labor (Shotwell was a founder of the International Labor Organization in 1919). CSOP's eminent scholars worked closely with the State Department, and a year later published two major reports: "The Problems Before Us" and "The Organization of Peace."[76]

Also in 1939, the National Peace Conference (founded 1907), unaware of the CFR or Commission's work, began planning a World Government Day for November 11, 1940, and on April 9, 1941, sent an open letter to President Roosevelt signed by 150 civic leaders asking that "a responsible government agency be set up," to "reassure the people that our Government is taking adequate steps" to protect "freedom of expression, freedom of belief, freedom from want and freedom from fear in the postwar world."[77]

Thus, more than two years before the United States entered World War II, the government had a secret NGO partner, a semi-open NGO collaborator, and a membership NGO petitioner planning for a United Nations that would not materialize for six more years.

December 7, 1941: Japan simultaneously attacked Pearl Harbor, the U.S.-controlled Philippines, Thailand, Malaya and Hong Kong. During his December 9 announcement of the declaration of war with Japan, Germany and Italy (the Axis, or "Tripartite Pact" nations), President Roosevelt said, "We are going to win the war and we are going to win the peace that follows," first public hint that a post-war peace-keeping plan was in progress.[78]

Government and NGO researchers immediately addressed the problem of isolationist factions in Congress—they had thwarted the League of Nations and might thwart plans for a new postwar international organization.

On December 22, Secretary Hull created a public relations front to head off isolationists: the Advisory Committee on Post-War Foreign Policy, which was to include "prominent persons from outside the Government."[79]

In August 1943, Hull and his staff had secretly drafted a model Charter of the United Nations, designed primarily to forward American interests.[80]

It was not until 1944 that Allied victory became certain. Then it was time to put the State Department's long-hatching publicity plan into action.

A new Division of Public Liaison began to enlist large numbers of influential, mostly elite, non-governmental organizations to promote "United States membership in the Postwar International Organization."[81]

The United Nations took center stage in August 1944 as the Big Four (the United States, Soviet Union, United Kingdom and China) met at an estate called Dumbarton Oaks in the Georgetown area of Washington, D.C.[82]

Forty-five Allied nations had already created the postwar economic order at the United Nations Monetary and Financial Conference in Bretton Woods, New Hampshire, and now all eyes turned to postwar security.[83]

The Dumbarton Oaks Conference—the "Washington Conversations on International Peace and Security Organization"—negotiated the makeup of the United Nations, including which states would be invited as members, the General Assembly, the formation of the Security Council, and the right of veto for permanent members, which was highly controversial.

The details were made public in the Dumbarton Oaks Declaration on October 7, 1944—which followed Hull's model United Nations Charter closely—ending with "several questions are still under consideration," to be answered at the United Nations Conference, still unscheduled.[84]

Opposition appeared instantly. The America First Party, Americans United, and 33 other organizations refused to put national sovereignty and economic prosperity in the hands of any international body, and organized fierce campaigns to block Senate ratification of the United Nations.[85]

But the State Department had already gone into high gear to drown out the opposition and generate as much fanfare as possible. Its liberal colleagues in the Commission to Study the Organization of Peace had held a big meeting in New York City with representatives of over 50 national and community-service organizations to "take the Dumbarton Oaks Educational Campaign to millions of people"—if the government needed the public's help, the groups would get the public to help.[86]

The attendees elected a Planning Committee, which included leaders from the National Peace Conference, Writers' War Board, League for Fair Play, General Federation of Women's Clubs, Church Peace Union, Synagogue Council of America and League of Nations Association—including Dorothy B. Robins, whose name is not famous.[87]

The Planning Committee was the beginning of the problem.

But it didn't show yet. Their coordination of the Dumbarton Oaks Educational Campaign went perfectly. They grew to more than 200 "in" groups.

The State Department's helper network sponsored "Victory Caravans," speaker tours, radio broadcasts, comic strips, newsletters, movie newsreel features, newspaper advertising, questionnaires to get more recruits—the gamut of PR tools available at the time, including newfangled opinion polls.[88]

The Woodrow Wilson Foundation distributed 318,000 copies of the Dumbarton Oaks Proposals to supporters: their tabulation of churches alone showed "23,909 copies to Protestant churches, 12,000 to Catholic churches, 1,206 to Jewish congregations and 1,000 to Negro churches."

The Congress of Parents and Teachers distributed charts, booklets, and discussion outlines to its state presidents.

The International Ladies Garment Workers Union sent its directors film-strips on Bretton Woods.

The State Department cultivated the American Federation of Labor, the American Bar Association, National Council of Churches, the Federation of Women's Clubs, Consumers League, the National Farm Bureau Federation, American Friends Service Committee, Business and Professional Women's Clubs, as well as the National Association for the Advancement of Colored People and the National Education Association.

More than 1,000 other groups volunteered without special invitation.

In February, 1945 the Yalta Conference ended by setting the place and date for the final step: San Francisco, April 25, 1945.

By then the job was done. Opinion polls showed that the in-groups had won public support for the State Department's mission. But Cordell Hull, the "Father of the United Nations," wasn't there. He had resigned in ill health, and Undersecretary of State Edward Stettinius was now Secretary.[89]

Then things got out of hand, as they will in democracies.

The in-groups wanted a voice in creating the United Nations.

(Conspiracy theorist note: Maurice Strong was 16, still in grade eleven in Manitoba. He didn't do it. Not that he wouldn't have.)

They had devoted nine months of their lives to winning support for it.

The State Department owed them a place at the table.

Group leaders told the Planning Committee to poll all the groups and select a "Core Committee" to go to San Francisco.[90]

Secretary Stettinius, not the brightest bulb in the marquee, didn't know what to do. The San Francisco Conference, officially the United Nations Conference on International Organization (UNCIO), was set to open soon. The United States was sending only diplomats. Over 1,200 groups were coming and over 200 of them were *his*. Even if he authorized his groups, a mob of interested, unruly, and demanding American civilians at such a high level, historic, crucial conference would—who knows what?

Stettinius was in no position to say no. He still needed loyal NGOs to lobby the Senate for ratification after the United Nations was created.

But more than two hundred groups asked for tickets to San Francisco.

The State Department then did what bureaucracies rarely do: something totally new. They agreed to send a limited number of groups, but only 42 (*opposite*), as "Consultants" to the American delegation—whatever that meant. "Consultant" was left undefined because Stettinius wasn't sure.

It was Pandora's Box.

The Core Committee was not pleased, because nearly two hundred of their people in those 42 groups wanted to go to San Francisco.

So the State Department said each "Consultant" could bring along two "Associate Consultants"—whatever *that* meant.

The Core Committee still wasn't pleased. Nearly 200 of their in-groups were not selected as Consultants (too bad about the 1,000 uninvited groups).

So the State Department allowed 160 in-groups to send "Observers," and begged the Consultants to keep them happy with their lesser role—give them speeches, call special meetings for them, sponsor dinners for everybody who showed up, get Hollywood celebrities to rub shoulders with them, anything to keep them happy. It was an explosive situation, since they each felt their group deserved the same recognition as the 42 official Consultant groups.

Then, two weeks before the San Francisco Conference was to open, President Roosevelt died of a cerebral hemorrhage. America was devastated.

Harry Truman was President, and not known for enthusiasm toward the United Nations. Would he postpone the meeting? The NGOs held their breath.

No problem. The new President told Stettinius to go ahead as planned.

What could have easily turned into a chaotic zoo turned into a stunning demonstration of what popular scientist Kevin Kelly fifty years later would call "the hive mind" in his book *Out of Control*. The 42 disparate, grasping, and sometimes mutually hostile groups reshaped the United Nations in their own image, one group doing this, another that, groping toward an end they could not see, blind to their cohesiveness and grace, yet emerging with the seeds of power to one day rule the world. But not without a few scary lurches.[91]

1. American Association for the United Nations	22. Foreign Policy Association
2. American Association of University Women	23. General Federation of Women's Clubs
3. American Bar Association	24. Kiwanis International
4. American Council on Education	25. Lions International
5. American Farm Bureau Federation	26. National Association for the Advancement of Colored People
6. American Federation of Labor	27. National Association of Manufacturers
7. American Jewish Committee	28. National Catholic Welfare Conference
8. American Jewish Conference	
9. American Legion	29. National Congress of Parents and Teachers
10. American Section-International Chamber of Commerce	30. National Council of Farmer Cooperatives
11. American Veterans Committee	31. National Education Association
12. Americans United for World Organization	32. National Exchange Club
13. Carnegie Endowment for International Peace	33. National Federation of Business
	34. National Foreign Trade Council
14. Catholic Association for International Peace	35. National Grange
15. Chamber of Commerce of the United States	36. National Lawyers Guild
	37. National League of Women Voters
16. Church Peace Union	38. National Peace Conference
17. Congress of Industrial Organizations	39. Railway Labor Executives Association
18. Council on Foreign Relations	40. Rotary International
19. Disabled American Veterans of the World War	41. Veterans of Foreign Wars of the United States
20. Farmers Union	42. Women's Action Committee for Victory and Lasting Peace
21. Federal Council of Churches of Christ in America	

NGO CONSULTANT ORGANIZATIONS

UNITED NATIONS CONFERENCE ON INTERNATIONAL ORGANIZATION

DEPARTMENT OF STATE BULLETIN XII, SAN FRANCISCO, APRIL 22, 1945

One of the American delegates, Virginia Gildersleeve, Dean of Barnard College, told the Core Committee that, to keep the Charter short, there would be no specific mention of the Commission on Human Rights, or a number of their other burning needs.

Brevity was official policy, and the Charter was still regarded as fundamentally a security document.

A flurry of Consultant activity made short work of that.

Separate bunches took separate actions.

The religious and civil rights bunches wanted a new purpose listed, "To promote respect for human rights and fundamental freedoms."

Read Chapter I, Purpose 3 in the Charter:

To achieve international co-operation in solving international problems of an economic, social, cultural, or humanitarian character, and in promoting and encouraging respect for human rights and for fundamental freedoms for all without distinction as to race, sex, language, or religion

The 42 groups did that. Then socialist sociologist W.E.B. Du Bois of NAACP (and raging anti-colonialist) demanded that the Charter's trusteeship system, already set up to decolonize the world, must also provide human rights protection. The National Peace Conference helped.

Read Chapter XII, Article 76:

The basic objectives of the trusteeship system shall be:
a. to further international peace and security
b. to promote the political, economic, social, and educational advancement of the inhabitants of the trust territories, and their progressive development towards self-government or independence as may be appropriate to the particular circumstances of each territory and its peoples and the freely expressed wishes of the peoples concerned, and as may be provided by the terms of each trusteeship agreement;
c. to encourage respect for human rights and for fundamental freedoms for all without distinction as to race, sex, language, or religion, and to encourage recognition of the interdependence of the peoples of the world.

The 42 groups did that. Then the education bunch wanted to expand the role of the Economic and Social Council with a general provision for social and educational functions, and most bunches called for the creation of a Human Rights Commission.

Read Chapter X, Article 62, Section 2:

The Economic and Social Council shall set up commissions in economic and social fields and for the promotion of human rights, and such other commissions as may be required for the performance of its functions.

The 42 groups did that. Then the industry, labor, and agricultural bunches (and Rotary clubs) found it useful to formalize ongoing "economic discussions" with the United Nations, and the education bunch later joined to recommend making themselves permanent fixtures.

Read Article 71:

> The Economic and Social Council may make suitable arrangements for consultation with non-governmental organizations which are concerned with matters within its competence. Such arrangements may be made with international organizations and, where appropriate, with national organizations after consultation with the Member of the United Nations concerned.

The 42 groups did that. They created today's exclusive and jealously guarded "consultative status" with no idea what they had done.

The National Association of Manufacturers. The Chamber of Commerce. The American Federation of Labor. The National Education Association. The NAACP. Rotary clubs. *Rotary clubs.* Rotarians even helped change the opening words of the Charter from "We the States" to "We the Peoples."

After the fact, the results look so simple and planned and orderly.

While it was happening, it was like Kevin Kelly's story of flying an airplane by committee. The Flock Mind catches on after a few scary lurches.

Certainly, nobody expected such influence and power to flow from what started as a State Department publicity stunt.

Archibald MacLeish, Assistant Secretary of State for cultural affairs (previously Librarian of Congress), who had been given the task of herding the Consultants said of it before the outcome was known:

> Frankly, this was an experiment—but I don't know of a better experiment in the democratic process. And if we do succeed in getting a democratic charter and a democratic peace, the Consultants and the millions of Americans they speak for and speak to will be entitled to a good share of the credit and the glory.[92]

The world didn't turn out as quite as MacLeish hoped, but, for good or bad, an interested, unruly, demanding mob of American civilians shaped the United Nations Charter to suit their own disparate, grasping, and sometimes mutually hostile purposes.

And that's how we really got the UN.

And how NGOs really got Consultative Status.

It's like the lyrics from the old John Lennon song *Beautiful Boy*, "Life is just what happens to you while you're busy making other plans."[93]

NGO Consultative Status is just what happened to the State Department while it was busy making plans for a security organization.

That may not make us feel better about it, but at least we know.

Thank you, Dorothy B. Robins, whose name is not famous.

CHAPTER 20 NOTES

1. Gernot Erler (Minister of State), "Defining Global Governance," Berlin, German Federal Foreign Office, 2006. www.auswaertiges-amt.de/diplo/en/Infoservice/Presse/Rede/2006/061004-Erler-GlobalGovernance.html, accessed March 5, 2007.

2. For a general discussion see the Wikipedia entry under World Government at http://en.wikipedia.org/wiki/World_government.

3. Walter Isaacson, *Einstein: His Life and Universe* (New York: Simon & Schuster, 2007), p. 490.

4. The Website of the Commission on Global Governance, now defunct, is archived at http://web.archive.org/web/20020124121152/www.cgg.ch/, accessed April 19, 2007..

5. The Commission on Global Governance, *Our Global Neighborhood: The Report of the Commission on Global Governance* (New York: Oxford University Press USA, 1995).

6. *Ibid*, "Chapter One: A New World."

7. Willy Brandt was born Herbert Ernst Karl Frahm to Martha Frahm, an unwed mother. He never met his father, John Möller, an accountant from Hamburg. He took the name Willy Brandt in 1933 to avoid detection by Nazi agents as he fled to Norway to avoid persecution as a member of the Social Democratic Party.

8. Viola Herms Drath, *Willy Brandt: Prisoner of His Past* (Radnor, Pennsylvania: Chilton Book Company, 1975).

9. Online at www.brandt21forum.info/About_BrandtCommission.htm, accessed April 2, 2007.

10. The full roster is in Frédéric Lapeyre, *The outcome and impact of the main international commissions on development issues - Working Paper No. 30* (Geneva: International Labor Office, May 2004), p. 57.

11. Ibid., p. 13.

12. The Brandt Commission, *North-South: A Program for Survival* (Cambridge, Massachusetts: The MIT Press, 1980), p. 65.

13. *Ibid*.

14. Leonard Downie Jr., "New Ideas on Global Cooperation Unveiled," *Washington Post*, December 19, 1979, p. A23.

15. *North-South*, Foreword, *op. cit.*.

16. Online, www.brandt21forum.info/About_BrandtCommission.htm, accessed April 2, 2007.

17. The Summit was the "International Meeting on Cooperation and Development," assessment of failure is in Lapeyre, p. 14.

18. Independent Commission on International Development Issues, *Common Crisis - North-South Co-operation for World Recovery* (New York: Macmillan, 1983).

19. Online, www.brandt21forum.info/About_BrandtCommission.htm, accessed April 2, 2007.

20. Online, www.sef-bonn.org/en/about/history/index.php?f=inhalt, accessed April 3, 2007.

21. No author, "Socialist Internationalist Stockholm Initiative Aims for Stronger World Government," *EcoSocialist Review, publication of the Democratic Socialists of America*, Summer 1991. Online, www. reformwatch.net/fitxers/83.pdf, accessed April 2, 2007.

22. Brandt's foundation was known in German as Stiftung Entwicklung und Frieden. Online, www.sef-bonn.org/en/about/history/index.php?f=inhalt, accessed April 3, 2007.

23. **Maurice Strong**: Highly sanitized official Canadian government biography is at www.dfait-maeci.gc.ca/department/skelton/Strong_bio-en.asp, accessed April 23, 2007. A Wikipedia entry is more detailed: http://en.wikipedia.org/wiki/Maurice_Strong, accessed March 22, 2007.

24. **Meeting**: Richard Jolly and Deepayan Basu Ray, *National Human Development Reports and the Human Security Framework: A review of Analysis and Experience* (Sussex, UK: Institute of Development Studies, 2006). Online at http: //hdr.undp.org/docs/network/hdr_net/NHDRs_and_the_Human_Security_Framework_Final_Draft.doc, accessed March 26, 2007. **The North-South Roundtable:** a project of the Society for International Development, created in 1957 by British economist Barbara Ward (1914-1981), guru of transfer payments as a proportion of GNP from North to South and the concept of a long "shopping list" of social subsidies owed to each individual. She was known as a "distributist" (of other people's money). There was more to being a human being, Ward argued, than producing wealth.

25. Jolly and Ray, *Reports, op. cit.,* footnote 15.

26. Lapeyre, *Outcome, op. cit.,* p. 33.

27. "How the Commission was Formed," on the Website of the Commission on Global Governance, now defunct, archived at http://web.archive.org/web/20020124121152/www.cgg.ch/, accessed April 19, 2007.

28. This conjecture is based on intensive comparison of documented locations in January, 1990 for each of the participants.

29. "Roundtable on Economics of Peace," North South Roundtable, Online at www.ns-rt.org/html/activities_nsrt_1.htm#11, accessed March 26, 2007.

30. *Ibid.* Dr. Haq's agenda was adopted by the Roundtable as a whole. **Mahbub ul Haq profile**: Wikipedia at http://en.wikipedia.org/wiki/Mahbub_ul_Haq, accessed March 26, 2007. *See* Craig N. Murphy, *The United Nations Development Programme: A Better Way?* (Cambridge, UK: Cambridge University Press, 2006), p. 243. *See also,* Nitin Desal, "Heartbeat - tribute to development economist Mahbub ul Haq - Obituary," *UN Chronicle,* Volume 35, Fall 1998, which mentions "being Mahbubed" in an affectionate context. **The Working Group**: "Preface," *The Stockholm Initiative on Global Security and Governance, "Common Responsibility in the 1990's,"* Stockholm, Office of the Prime Minister of Sweden, 1991. Published by Stiftung Entwicklung und Frieden, Bonn, 2nd edition 1991.

31. An extensive discussion of the problem is in Peter Willetts, *"The Conscience of the World" - The Influence of Non-Governmental Organisations in the UN System* (Washington, D.C.: Brookings Institution Press, 1996), Chapter 2. NGO consultative status covers all the work of the Economic and Social Council, along with the operational programs in developing countries, the specialized agencies, and UN conferences.

32. *Ibid.* See online version of Chapter 2 at www.staff.city.ac.uk/p.willetts/NGOS/CONSSTAT.htm, accessed March 28, 2007.

33. *Ibid.*

34. *Ibid.*

35. World Commission on Environment and Development, *Our Common Future,* (New York: Oxford University Press USA, paperback edition, 1987).

36. Ingvar Carlsson, "Global Governance," in Joseph Rotblat and Sven Hellman (editors), *A World at the Crossroads: New Conflicts, New Solutions : Annals of Pugwash 1993* (Hackensack, New Jersey: World Scientific Publishing Company, 1994), p. 85.

37. "Preface," *The Stockholm Initiative, op. cit.*

38. *The Stockholm Initiative, op. cit.*

39. Grant description, John D. and Catherine T. MacArthur Foundation, Foundation Center database, record number 3519657, retrieved through Dialog database No. 27 (fee service).

40. Lapeyre, *Outcome, op. cit.*, p. 64.

41. As told in Commission on Global Governance, *Our Global Neighborhood, op. cit.*, Preface by Ingvar Carlsson and Sridath Ramphal.

42. UN Website for UNCED at www.un.org/geninfo/bp/enviro.html, accessed April 12, 2007. See also, Willets, *Conscience, op. cit.*

43. Lapeyre, *Outcome, op. cit.*, p. 63.

44. **UN trust funds:** *Ibid.*, p. 64. **Okita at Königswinter:** James E. Goodby, Vladimir I. Ivanov, and Nobuo Shimotomai, editors, *"Northern Territories" and Beyond: Russian, Japanese and American Perspectives* (Westport, Connecticut: Praeger Publishers, 1995), p. 5.

45. All facts about the work process of the commission in this section are in Lapeyre, *Outcome, op. cit., pp.* 63-64.

46. For a summary of Brandt's life, *see* "Nobel Peace Prize Curriculum Vitae for Willy Brandt, Nobel Peace Prize, 1971," at http://nobelprize.org/nobel_prizes/peace/laureates/1971/brandt-cv.html, accessed April 12, 2007.

47. Commission on Global Governance, *Our Global Neighborhood, op. cit.* **Davos release:** Lapeyre, *Outcome, op. cit.*, p. 63.

48. http://web.archive.org/web/20020221182811/www.cgg.ch/index.html.

49. Text of *Our Global Neighborhood* contains proposals that either explicitly state or directly imply my assertions.

50. The Wikipedia entry adequately covers this point at http://en.wikipedia.org/wiki/United_Nations_Trusteeship_Council, accessed March 14, 2007.

51. http://en.wikipedia.org/wiki/United_Nations_Global_Compact, accessed April 14, 2007.

52. http://en.wikipedia.org/wiki/International_criminal_court, accessed April 14, 2007.

53. Chadwick Alger, "Evolving roles of NGOs in member state decision-making in the UN system," *Journal of Human Rights*, Volume 2, Issue 3 September 2003, pages 407 - 424. *Also,* telephone conversation with Henry Lamb of the Ecological Conservation Organization describing his personal experience as an NGO leader in United Nations meetings. *See also,* Willetts, *"The Conscience of the World," op. cit.*

54. http://en.wikipedia.org/wiki/Monterrey_Consensus, accessed April 14, 2007. **Non-profit economy:** "Johns Hopkins-led Study Finds Nonprofit Sector is a Burgeoning, Economic Force," Nov. 8, 1998, www.jhu.edu/news_info/news/home98/nov98/nonprof.html.

55. Steven Perlstein, "Protest's Architect 'Gratified'; D.C.-Based Activist Brought Diverse Groups Together," *Washington Post*, December 2, 1999. **Black bloc:** "A black bloc is an affinity group that comes together during some sort of protest, demonstration, or other event involving class struggle, anti-capitalism, or anti-globalization. Black clothing and masks are used to make the

bloc appear to be one large mass, promote solidarity, create a clear revolutionary presence, and also to avoid being identified by authorities." http://en.wikipedia.org/wiki/Black_bloc, accessed March 5, 2007..

56. Sanjeev Khagram, James V. Riker, and Kathryn Sikkink, editors, *Restructuring World Politics: Transnational Social Movements, Networks and Norms* (Minneapolis: University of Minnesota Press, 2002). p. 3.

57. Funders Network on Trade and Globalization, www.fntg.org/about/index.html, accessed January 12, 2007. Two of the foreign foundations were the JMG Foundation (part of the fortune of the late dual British/French billionaire, Sir Jimmy Goldsmith), based in the United Kingdom but not registered there; the French-American Charitable Trust, a Bermuda trust; *See also*, www.mott.org/sitecore/content/Globals/Grants/2006/200100285_04_ Environmental%20Grantmakers%20Association%20and%20 Funders%20 Network%20on%20Trade%20 and%20 Globalization.aspx, accessed February 27, 2007.

58. Patrick E. Tyler, "A New Power In the Streets," *New York Times*, February 17, 2003.

59. James F. Moore,*The Second Superpower Rears Its Beautiful Head*, Berkman Center for Internet and Society, Harvard Law School, Cambridge, Massachusetts. Online at http://cyber.law.harvard.edu/people/jmoore/second superpower.html, accessed April 4, 2007.

60. http://en.wikipedia.org/wiki/Second_superpower, accessed April 15, 2007.

61. http://en.wikipedia.org/wiki/David_Korten, accessed July 31, 2007.

62. David C. Korten, *When Corporations Rule the World* (San Francisco, Berrett-Koehler Publishers, 1995). *Publishers Weekly* review is in the Amazon.com page for the book.

63. David C. Korten, *The Post-Corporate World: Life After Capitalism* (San Francisco, Berrett-Koehler Publishers, 2000). *Publishers Weekly* review is in the Amazon.com page for the book.

64. David C. Korten, *The Great Turning: From Empire to Earth Community* (San Francisco, Berrett-Koehler Publishers, 2000).

65. www.yesmagazine.org, accessed August 1, 2007.

66. www.pcdf.org, accessed August 1, 2007.

67. www.ifg.org, accessed August 1, 2007.

68. http://en.wikipedia.org/wiki/David_Korten, accessed June 30, 2007.

69. Charter history is at http://en.wikipedia.org/wiki/Earth_Charter, accessed June 3, 2007..

70. A robust narrative is Elaine Dewar, *Cloak of Green* (Toronto: James Lorimer & Company, Publishers, 1995), p. 249*ff*.

71. The story is told in part at www.earthcharter.org, accessed June3, 2007. Dewar has the backstory, p. 395*ff*.

72. Dorothy B. Robins, *Experiment in Democracy: The Story of U.S. Citizen Organizations in Forging the Charter of the United Nations*, (New York: The Parkside Press, 1971). Expanded from Robins' doctoral dissertation at New York University at Washington Square, "U.S. Non-Governmental Organizations and the Educational Campaign from Dumbarton Oaks 1944 through the San Francisco Conference 1945."

73. *Ibid.* p. 4.

74. Laurence H. Shoup and William Miner, *Imperial Brain Trust: The Council on Foreign Relations and United States Foreign Policy* (New York: Authors Choice Press, 1977), p. 119. Thoroughgoing Marxian analysis, with a Foreword by G. William Domhoff.

75. *Ibid*, p. 119, and Robins, *Experiment, op. cit.*, p. 6.

Council on Foreign Relations Profile: Official history, Peter Grose, *Continuing the Inquiry: The Council on Foreign Relations from 1921 to 1996* (New York: Council on Foreign Relations: 1996). Quintessential conspiracy theory, Caroll Quigley, *Tragedy and Hope: A History of the World in Our Time* (San Pedro, California: G.S.G. & Associates, Inc., new edition, 1975, originally Macmillan, New York, 1966). Measured assessment: James Perloff, *The Shadows of Power: The Council on Foreign Relations and the American Decline* (Appleton, Wisconsin: Western Islands Publishers, 1988).

76. Commission to Study the Organization of Peace, *Building Peace: Reports of the Commission to Study the Organization of Peace, 1939, 1972* (Lanham, Maryland: Scarecrow Press, 1973).

77. Robins, *Experiment, op. cit.*, p. 29.

78. Franklin D. Roosevelt, "Declarations of a State of War with Japan, Germany, and Italy" (Radio address by the President of the United States broadcast from the White House, on Tuesday, December 9, 1941.) The Avalon Project at the Yale Law School. www.yale.edu/lawweb/avalon/wwii/dec/dec06.htm, accessed April 10, 2007.

79. Cordell Hull, "Secretary Hull's letter to President Roosevelt suggesting the establishment of the Advisory Committee on Post-War Foreign Policy, December 22, 1944," in Robins, *Experiment, op. cit.*, Appendix I, p. 163.

80. The Cordell Hull Birthplace & Museum State Park, "The Legacy of Cordell Hull," www.cordellhullmuseum.com/history.html, accessed April 10, 2007.

81. Robins, *Experiment, op. cit.*, (citing a mimeographed statement in the "Doris Cochrane files" of the Department of State, location not specified), p. 35 and note 3, p. 265. Scholarly comment in Kenneth Colegrove, "The Role of Congress and Public Opinion in Formulating Foreign Policy," *The American Political Science Review,* Vol. 38, No. 5 (October, 1944), *pp.* 956-969.

82. Ernest R. May and Angelike E. Laiou (editors), The Dumbarton Oaks Conversations and the United Nations, 1944-1994 (Cambridge, Massachusetts: Harvard University Press, 1998).

83. For a contemporary account, *see* Mabel Newcomer, *Monetary plans for the United Nations,: A layman's guide to proposals of the Bretton Woods conference* (Washington, D.C.: American Association of University Women, 1944).

84. A contemporary assement is in "Dumbarton Oaks and San Francisco," *Time,* April 30, 1945, http://www.time.com/time/magazine/article/0,9171,797395, 00.html , accessed April 25, 2007.

85. Robins, *Experiment, op. cit., pp.* 55-56, pp. 73-74.

86. *Ibid., pp.* 40-41.

87. *Ibid.*, p. 43.

88. Details in these paragraphs are found in Robins, *Experiment, op. cit.*, Chapter IV, "Developing the Campaign," *pp.* 57-80.

89. "Biography," *Cordell Hull, The Nobel Peace Prize 1945*, http://nobelprize.org/ nobel_prizes/peace/laureates/1945/hull-bio.html, accessed April 20, 2007.

90. This story is contained only in Robins, *Experiment, op. cit.*, Chapter VI, "San Francisco Conference April-June 1945," pp. 100-139. The Du Bois episode is in Carol Anderson, *Eyes off the Prize: The United Nations and the African American Struggle for Human Rights, 1944–1955* (Cambridge, UK: Cambridge University Press, 2003).

91 Kevin Kelly, *Out of Control: The New Biology of Machines, Social Systems, and the Economic World* (New York: Basic Books, 1994)., *pp.* 8-11.

NGO consultant list: in Robins, *Experiment, op. cit.*, Appendix XXII, "Official list of consultants from national organizations to the United Nations Conference on International Organization in San Francisco, as carried in Department of State Bulletin, XII (April 22, 1945), 724-725," *pp.* 207-210.

United Nations Charter: online at www.un.org/aboutun/charter/, accessed April 2, 2007.

92. Robins, *Experiment, op. cit.*, p. 105.

93. www.john-lennon.com/songlyrics/songs/Beautiful_Boy_Darling_Boy.htm.

PART VII

FREEZING IN THE DARK

THE ENERGY GAP

FREEZING IN THE DARK - 364

CHAPTER 21

THE ENERGY GAP

G LOBAL WARMING CAN BE READ SEVERAL WAYS.
It can be read as a scientific discovery and subject of research.
It can be read as a political campaign with policy objectives.
It can be read as an anti-corporate movement of social change.
It can be read as a personal moral and ethical belief system.
It can be read as an apocalyptic religious cult.
It can be read as catastrophile propaganda.
It can be read as a virus.

The more you merge these readings, the more you forget your manners.

Science historically thrives on disagreement. Skeptical criticism, open-ended arguments, overturned theories, shifted paradigms, disputed facts, vituperative personal attacks, and conflicting opinion about what science is and who's doing it right are its meat and potatoes (or tofu and tahini). The hate-fest between Noam Chomsky and George Lakoff over who's right about linguistics (page 125) is science as usual. The last thing you'd expect of such an enterprise is *consensus*. Even laymen know that reality doesn't care who votes for it. And, count on it, some scientists will disagree with *that*.

Now merge global warming science with global warming politics.

Global warming science becomes political science. Most global warming scientists are government-funded. In order to protect their funding, they produce government science, which is the same sort of oxymoron as military intelligence. The scientists have become politicians, forming factions, negotiating truth, counting votes, rigging outcomes, proclaiming consensus, and declaring themselves winners. As winners, they demand political power to plan all human activities worldwide. Your consent is not required. Your belief and obedience are.

365

Now merge global warming political scientists with an anti-corporate movement of social change.

The political scientists begin to look like Maurice Strong replicas, sound like recordings of the Earth Charter, sprout a lot of Ph.D.s that act like David Korten, cultivate colleagues in the Union of Concerned Scientists, the Sierra Club, Campaign for America's Future, Steelworkers Union, Human Rights Watch, and the Ford Foundation, then work on viral messages that will lead a mass global public to belief and obedience.

Now merge movement ideology with personal belief systems.

True believers get that way through several stages: first, discontent with their lives, then contact with a movement participant, who introduces them to a group of believers, who guide them to redefine their personal needs in terms of global warming ideology—sincere belief that "environmental protection, human rights, equitable human development, and peace are interdependent and indivisible"—and the commitment decision to surrender to the ideology, then testifying publicly to the experience, and, finally, group support for their new belief and obedience. Or opprobrium for doubt.

Now merge true believers into an apocalyptic religion.

Well, think about it. Global warming has a myth of the Fall: the loss of harmony between man and nature caused by our materialistic society using fossil fuels. It has an End of the World dogma. It has Al Gore as Pope and his film *An Inconvenient Truth* as Bible. It has apostles who voted Pope Al an Oscar, an Emmy, and a Nobel. It has skeptics as heretics, SUV drivers as sinners, Hybrid drivers as saints, Compact Fluorescent Lamp buyers as novices, and offsets as indulgences to bless yourself as "carbon neutral" even if you keep your five homes and private jet. It has bicycling to work as a ritual of observance. It has the No Impact Movement as a demonstration of commitment. It has evil fossil fuel sellers to tempt you into heat, light, and transport. It has zealous missionaries. It threatens hell for infidels. It promises redemption if only you believe, but don't do anything else. Smile. It's a joke. Sort of. Anyway, don't try this in court; it's not a real religion under the law.

Now merge apocalyptic religion into catastrophile propaganda.

Catastrophiles see the Heat Death of Earth with both fear and yearning. They dread it, but they really want it to happen just to prove you were wrong.

Now consider this whole mélange as a virus. It's a self-replicating message that moves from person to person, like AOL's Instant Messenger without the Internet, overwhelming your mental DNA with fear and guilt, wrapping around your brainstem, and driving you to belief and obedience.

You have the choice to not believe, to not obey. Exercising that choice is a crap shoot with the usual perils of resisting social norms or civil authority.

But something happened in 2004 that looked very much like an outbreak of global warming virality from contagions five and ten years earlier. Two smart guys said the environment, social justice and security are solidly linked, just like the 1994 Commission on Global Governance and the Earth Charter of 2000. But they thought it was something new. It was like viral amnesia.

OBTUSE OBITUARY

THERE'S A DEAD BODY IN THE ROOM, and it's starting to stink.
It's the corpse of the environmental movement, or ought to be, said veteran issue entrepreneur Michael Shellenberger and widely-experienced polling sidekick Ted Nordhaus.[1]

They weren't talking about the movement's dismal showing in Election 2004's exit polls. This was several weeks *before* the election, and they were debuting their own provocative essay, *The Death of Environmentalism,* at the annual retreat of the Environmental Grantmakers Association.

The two critics had a knack for snappy openings:

> Over the last 15 years environmental foundations and organizations have invested hundreds of millions of dollars into combating global warming.
> We have strikingly little to show for it.[2]

From two hard-left ideologues, that was *heresy.*
What followed was worse, heresy and *treason*:

> We have become convinced that modern environmentalism, with all of its unexamined assumptions, outdated concepts and exhausted strategies, must die so that something new can live.

That nasty knifing won Shellenberger and Nordhaus the epithet, "The Reapers," among environmentalists. Yet they took care to stress that this was not just a tirade, but a well researched and tightly focused analysis:

> We started by getting clear about our vision and values and then created a coalition of environmentalists, unions, and civil rights groups before reaching out to Reagan Democrats and other blue-collar constituents who have been financially wrecked by the last 20 years of economic and trade policies....These working families were a key part of the New Deal coalition that governed America through the middle of the last century.

Yes, we've heard all that before—rejuvenation, Lakoff, framing, rising from the ashes, blah, blah, blah. Invoking the big-government past won The Reapers another soubriquet, "The Throwbacks," among conservatives and libertarians, the few that paid any attention at all.

Okay, then, what did The Throwback Reapers have in mind?

> Today we have in our hands the power to reverse global warming, create millions of new jobs in the clean-energy economy, create a "race to the top" in social and environmental performance by corporations and governments, create poison-free products made from materials that can be continuously recycled, reduce crime, and increase the quality of life for people living in cities.

Whoa! I had followed their earlier attacks against Maxxam Corporation in California's venomous "Redwood Wars" and thought that these two diatribal Lords of Invective must be reading from somebody else's script.[3]

That was just too positive.

They spoke of rejuvenating our nation's economy.

They spoke of creating the next generation of American industrial jobs.

They spoke of treating clean energy as an economic and security mandate to rebuild America.

They said that America needs to hope again, to dream again, to think big, and to be called to the best of our potential by tapping the optimism and can-do spirit that is embedded in our nation's history.

Wow!

That's so joyous it sticks to your shoes.

Grand slam.

It was called the Apollo Alliance, evoking the Kennedy era moon shot.

But there was something odd about *The Death of Environmentalism*: the fact that The Reapers debuted it at an Environmental Grantmakers Association annual gathering of deep-pocketed foundation executives who underwrite the environmental establishment (held on Kauai that year).

It broke the First Commandment of the Philanthropoid, as Mark Schmitt noted:

> Thou Shalt Not Air a Movement's Dirty Laundry In Front of the *Funders.* Never mind that funders already know the dirty laundry, and probably are responsible for two-thirds of it, and that it's in no one's interest to keep them ignorant, it Just Isn't Done.[4]

Then why did they do it?

Simple: one of the deep-pocketed foundation executives paid them to.

Who? Nathan Cummings Foundation's environment program director, Peter Teague, who commissioned *The Death of Environmentalism*.[5]

The real question was why he did that.

THE IDEA

DAN CAROL WAS IN LOS ANGELES when the planes hit the twin towers.[6] Unlike most Americans that September morning, he didn't watch the terrorist attacks on television, even though he was a tuned-in, successful, busy, media-savvy political strategist visiting clients about new generation media campaigns.

He was 43. He had a wife and two kids and a mortgage. He had plenty to think about and plenty to think with. Smart, talented, eclectic, cutting edge, hip, futuristic, committed partisan, the quintessential progressive.

But different. He exuded hope.

And a tough realism.

The night of September 10, he had stayed at the new home of a colleague's parents who had no TV yet. He went to bed thinking about the project he was just finishing up for Ben Cohen of Ben & Jerry's Homemade Ice Cream—the Internet component of Business Leaders for Sensible Priorities, a campaign to cut defense spending and give more money to social programs and kids.

It was set to launch in four days, on September 14, 2001.

Dan Carol heard about the American disaster from his wife Joyce Berman, who called him in the morning from their home in Eugene, Oregon.

Time stopped. Disbelief. Anger. Grief. Realization.

There would be no meetings today. Or any day soon. His plane ticket was useless. But his rental car stood in the driveway.

He rolled north thirteen hours straight. On the way up Interstate 5, he listened to the world change.

Leaving the Los Angeles basin and over Tejon Pass. *People were losing their lives and loved ones.*

Through the San Joaquin Valley toward Sacramento. *Shock.*

Beyond Redding and Mount Shasta. *Rage.*

Nightfall past Medford and Roseburg. *Loss.*

"I heard September 11, I didn't really see it," he told me. "But the sense of disassociation allowed me to think about what's next."

The September 14 project launch he had been building toward since early summer?

That dog is not going to hunt.

Then where to? What next?

Calls to patriotism. Calls to war.

That much was obvious.

The anger and frustration are going to drive thinking and policy.

What else should we do? How should we harness that energy?

His mind roiled, chunks of experience riding like tectonic plates on the mantle of his adaptive unconscious, driven to an unseen convergence boundary.

All his life had he looked away, to the future, to the horizon. As a young undergraduate he majored in philosophy—and public interest research groups. He got a Master's in regional planning. He went to the Congressional Budget Office as an energy and environment policy analyst. Ron Brown hired him to upgrade Democratic National Committee research. He directed research for the 1992 Clinton-Gore campaign, served as new technology consultant to the Congressional Institute for the Future, formed his own firm to pioneer new iDemocrat network politics, like he was doing for his Los Angeles clients.

And now this.

"When I got back late that night, my wife greeted me, half asleep—one in the morning, whatever it was—and I spent several hours watching. I had this palpable sense that I had missed an incredible cultural moment."

What little good can we get out of this situation?

"My brain went to memories of my grandfather talking about Victory Gardens and scrap metal drives during World War II. And Richard Nixon's 1974 call to make America energy independent after the OPEC oil crisis. Conservation and more domestic energy production."

In a Malcolm Gladwell *blink* moment The Idea appeared.[7]

The tectonic plates in his mind converged and formed a new continent.

Dan Carol began writing a long proposal. Top quotes:

The Opportunity:
Channeling Anger and Frustration into Something Positive

With the September 11 tragedy comes opportunities. Opportunities to highlight the precarious position the United States continues to find itself in through its dependence on foreign oil. And opportunities to finally mobilize the grassroots energy and political willpower do something about it.

The Campaign:
What We'd Hope to Achieve

We believe that a carefully crafted, 6-month campaign has the potential to achieve the following goals:

• Convince the Federal Government to launch a grand-scale "moon shot" effort on energy independence. A multi-billion dollar crash in-dependence program would change our need to "engage" in the Middle East from taking oil to bringing democracy. And it would appeal not just to the environmental faithful and cultural creatives, but to Joe Six Pack types and patriots who tend to favor isolationist rhetoric. In essence, we'd seek to create a "patriotic pivot" on message and leverage this opportunity to direct federal dollars to a place that makes sense.

• Build a grassroots community of several hundred thousand sup-porters who are committed to the effort, and willing to pressure their elected officials to back it as well.

• Fundamentally change the dynamics of this debate by redefining energy independence as something associated with excitement and achievement, rather than pain and sacrifice.

When John F. Kennedy talked about going to the moon, he talked about going to the moon. He did not make endless speeches about "raising taxes to pay for this," "tightening our belts to support Apollo," etc. We need to focus on the end goal – energy independence, freedom from dependency, and the restoration of our national sovereignty. That is what will engage our target audiences.[8]

Dan Carol had conceived the Apollo Alliance in a blink.

Conception was one thing. Delivery was another.

It wasn't as though he could shop it around the progressive community every day, but he tried. Between cancelling the launch of Ben Cohen's project, then helping Jim Hightower get his Rolling Thunder Down Home Democracy Tour going, he evangelized everyone who would listen.

Dan Weiss, former Sierra Club political director, had gone to Art Malkin and Don Ross's M+R Strategic Services and nobody there wanted to tackle it, not Malkin, not Ross, not Weiss, not any of their colleagues. And the AFL-CIO's Gerry Shea, special assistant for government affairs, didn't either.

"People weren't yet connecting the dots between national security, new jobs and renewable energy, and the connection to foreign oil," said Carol.

Mahbub ul Haq had redefined security in much the same way. But Carol's redefinition wasn't clicking, wasn't controlling the universe of discourse.

Then one day in the fall of 2001 he was talking to Bob Borosage (Chapter 15)—they had known each other since 1989 when Carol was with the Democratic National Committee—and the Moon Shot Memo came up.

Borosage liked Carol, thought he was smart. Borosage's Campaign for America's Future was a good place to incubate ideas. Some incubated better than others, so Borosage said he'd look at the Memo and think about it.

He did. And he connected the dots.

About the same time, Carol was talking to Joel Rogers—they had known each other since 1995, after Carol had moved his consulting company from Washington, D.C. to Oregon—and the Moon Shot Memo came up.

Rogers is a University of Wisconsin professor of law, political science, and sociology, director of the Center on Wisconsin Strategy (COWS)—and a certified influential, selected by *Newsweek* as one of the 100 Americans most likely to affect U.S. politics and culture in the 21st century.[9]

Rogers said he'd look at the Memo. He connected the dots, too.

One paragraph stood out for its strategic potential:

We should not slam on oil companies, or talk about fighting pollution, greenhouse gasses, or saving the rain forest. This campaign is about energy independence. If we focus on that, we will succeed, and the other goals will follow. In the long run, there will undoubtedly be different visions and thorny politics regarding clean coal, drilling on US public lands, and so on, but these challenges should not get in the way of our earliest message and coalition opportunities to define the FY 2003 energy debate our way and to emphasize the need for jobs now.

Be positive. *"The other goals will follow."* Delphic.

By early 2002 they were holding weekly three-way conference calls, trying to make something of The Idea.

They faced serious internal problems. The Blue-Green Working Group (pages 50-51) had blown apart, leaving a wide breach between environment and labor. Was there something in energy independence that could heal it?

Borosage focused on economic revitalization. Positive.
Rogers focused on progressive capacity. Positive.
Carol focused on energy independence. Positive.

Before summer, 2002, they sorted things out well enough to make a proposal to the Hewlett Foundation's Hal Harvey. It got them a $75,000 grant, "For the initial phase of the Green Growth Initiative."[10]

"Apollo Alliance" was too grandiose for a grant application coming from a fledgling that was still just an egg, but "Green Growth" sounded positive enough and a lot more realistic. And it melded the three focuses.

The grant was made "to analyze the potential of energy efficiency, renewable energy, and smart growth to create high-skill high-wage jobs for American workers."[11]

Translated out of foundationese, that meant polls and focus groups to test the public appeal of a huge program of government funding for energy-efficient urban and regional redevelopment, federal subsidies for wind, solar, and biofuel corporations, scientific analyses proving its job-making power—and silently penalizing fossil fuels into oblivion.

The importance of government power to these men cannot be overstated.
Borosage and government we know from Chapter 15.

Rogers says his political goal is "finding a successor to the institutions and mass politics of social democracy and the Keynesian welfare state."[12]

Carol told me flatly, "Government should invest in infrastructure. If you put me up against a wall, that's the last thing I want to give away."

All very well, but translated into workaday chores, that meant hiring someone to knock on doors, get labor unions and green groups together, and get community groups, faith groups, businesses, everybody, signed on to the broad coalition necessary to turn their lofty ideas into federal law.

D AN CAROL FOUND HIM BY ACCIDENT. It was at a Washington dinner held by his firm, Carol/Trevelyan Strategy Group.

Alice Hendricks, an employee, brought along her husband, Bracken.

He got to talking with Dan about community economics and regionalism. Bracken, it seems, held a Master's in Public Policy and Urban Planning from Harvard and spoke the language. Carol said, "We bonded."

It turned out that Hendricks had also been deep in Democratic politics: Special Assistant to the Office of Vice President Al Gore, a wonk in the Department of Commerce's Interagency Climate Change Working Group, the President's Council on Sustainable Development, and the White House Livable Communities Task Force. He was an expert on environmental policy. He knew all the power players. More important, they knew him.[13]

Then, too, his wife was the daughter of the AFL-CIO's Chief of Staff Bob Welch, a fact not lost on Borosage or Rogers. He could heal the breach.

Bracken Hendricks became the Apollo Alliance's first executive director.

GUERILLAS IN THE MIST

O N JULY 30, 2002, A MAN NAMED JAMES D. RANGE, Washington lawyer and former congressional staffer, filed registration papers for a new Delaware corporation, the Theodore Roosevelt Conservation Partnership, Inc.[14]

• He got a $250,000 grant from Ted Turner's foundation just to help out.[15]

• He got a $50,000 grant from the Surdna Foundation, "For general support for motivating hunters and fishermen to participate more actively in national forest management decision-making."[16]

The SHOT Show (Shooting, Hunting, & Outdoor Trade) is a legendary gun-lover's extravaganza held each year in Orlando, Florida. At the 2003 SHOT Show, James D. Range was presented with *Outdoor Life* magazine's prestigious 2002 Conservation Award for his work to establish the Theodore Roosevelt Conservation Partnership (TRCP).[17]

TRCP's slogan: "Guaranteeing you a place to hunt and fish."

Simultaneously, plaudits came in from eight members of Congress, five Republicans and three Democrats, giving it the look of a right-leaning group.

U.S. Sen. Pete Domenici (R-NM), then-chairman of the Senate Energy and Natural Resources Committee, set the tone for the other seven:

"Jim Range has been one of those rare individuals who has dedicated his life to bringing opposing parties together to unite for a common good. He did it as a senior staff in the United States Senate working on clean air, clean water, and wildlife issues. He is still doing it in the conservation field now with the Theodore Roosevelt Conservation Partnership. I truly believe that if extremists on both sides of the environmental spectrum could learn from Jim's wisdom and work, the whole country would be better off."

All eight congressional panegyrics were like that.[18]

You couldn't put your finger on it, but there was something off about Jim Range and his Theodore Roosevelt Conservation Partnership.

SLOGGING

B RACKEN HENDRICKS HAD DONE A LOT BY THE FALL OF 2002. He and Joel Rogers had spent many Sunday mornings on the phone hammering out an all-important breach-healing document: the Apollo Ten Point Plan.

1. Promote Advanced Technology & Hybrid Cars
2. Invest In More Efficient Factories
3. Encourage High Performance Building
4. Increase Use of Energy Efficient Appliances
5. Modernize Electrical Infrastructure
6. Expand Renewable Energy Development
7. Improve Transportation Options
8. Reinvest In Smart Urban Growth
9. Plan For A Hydrogen Future
10. Preserve Regulatory Protections.[19]

It was not some airy vision they just whipped out and passed around. Getting official endorsements from the International bodies of labor unions was tough work. Very tough work.

Each point in that plan was individually crafted and recrafted to meet the hopes and needs and demands of skeptical unions and green groups in the early Apollo coalition.

They needed hard data and specific deliverables.

What's the overall budget for this program? *Financial studies.*

What's going to happen to our environmental agenda? *Negotiations.*

What's our piece of the action? *More negotiations.*

What's going to happen to our jobs? *Negotiations and a little finesse.*

How do we pitch this to the public? *Focus groups and poll testing.*

The Machinists wanted to know.

The Sierra Club wanted to know.

The Paper and Chemical Workers wanted to know.

The Natural Resources Defense Council wanted to know.

And the Textile and Garment Workers, Transit Employees, the Service Employees, Electrical Workers, and Sheet Metal Workers wanted to know.

And the League of Conservation Voters, Union of Concerned Scientists, Greenpeace, and National Wildlife Federation wanted to know.

The Green Growth Initiative—its name already changed to the Apollo Project—quickly ran out of money.

JOEL ROGERS HAD AN IDEA where he could find some more. He and Bob Borosage had separately received small grants from a big New York foundation for studies on economic revitalization and progressive capacity building.[20]

Lance Lindblom was an old friend of Rogers. He was as blond as his tree-bloom namesake, had been a philanthropoid with the Ford Foundation, and before that with the Soros Open Society operation.[21]

He had been president and CEO of Nathan Cummings Foundation for two years now. Cummings had been obsessed with boosting the blue-green labor-environment concept, even before Lindblom got there, and even after an extensive remake in 2001 with new quarters and new officers.

A proposal for a large grant to continue the effort with the parallel Apollo project might be well received.

Cummings had sunk $75,000 in 2000 into the Blue-Green Working Group (*see* Chapter 4) and $300,000 in 2002 into the Labor Institute for a pilot program to turn rank-and-file union members green. The Institute worked with five groups to put thousands of union members through its educational program:[22]

- The Sierra Club;
- The Natural Resources Defense Council (NRDC);
- The Service Employees International Union (SEIU);
- The United Steelworkers of America;
- The Union of Industrial and Needle Trades Employees (UNITE).

Cummings also gave $200,000 to an unlikely grantee, the Public Health Institute, "to create a prototype 'Green Union'" with United Steelworkers District 11 "to educate the rank and file about environmental issues, with an emphasis on global warming."[23]

When Rogers contacted Lindblom, his proposal was well received.

NATHAN CUMMINGS FOUNDATION
2005 assets, $481,024,999 Grants paid, $16.8 million
Established in 1949 in New York, endowed by the fortune of Nathan Cummings, founder of Sara Lee Corporation.

Cummings originally funded programs to "enhance understanding between Jews and non-Jews," bring health care delivery to the poor, and support the arts.

It developed into a major contributor to far-left causes during the 1990s, then went through a total overhaul in 2001 with new headquarters, a new president (Lindblom, salary $260,000, benefits $60,144), and new prescriptive grantmaking strategies to foster far-left groups with the political power to change public policy.

Programs included social justice, the environment and a ferocious anti-corporate thrust that saw the foundation itself filing shareholder resolutions.

All this is paid for by Cummings investments in ExxonMobil, ConocoPhillips, Chevron, Occidental Petroleum. Anadarko Petroleum, Duke Energy (coal, nuclear), El Paso Corp (natural gas), and many more—plus 25,999 shares of database firm Acxiom (*page 262*).

COMMONISTS

PETER BARNES AND DAVID BOLLIER had established their reputations as advocates of the commons, conceived as all things "that Americans own as a people—forests, minerals, government R&D, the broadcast airwaves, public schools, cultural spaces"—and deplored them "being taken over by private business interests, often with the full complicity of our government."[24]

Barnes caught the public's eye with his 2001 book, *Who Owns the Sky: Our Common Assets and the Future of Capitalism*, with its Sky Trust concept of imposing a nationwide CO_2 emissions cap-and-trade permit scheme on all industry and giving an equal share of the revenues to each citizen.[25]

A year later, Bollier raised eyebrows with his *Silent Theft: The Private Plunder of Our Common Wealth*. Ralph Nader said of it, "*Silent Theft* defines, with sure handed authority, a grand new mission for the beleaguered

American commonwealth—that it should be governed by civic values not commercial, unaccountable supremacies."[26]

On September 16, 2002, Common Assets Defense Fund was registered in California with Barnes and Bollier as board members. Its address was listed as the Blue Mountain Center in New York, a pet project of AMAX mining heir, Adam Hochschild; Harriet Barlow, the Center's director, was a board member of the new group.[27] Its purpose statement:

> Common Assets Defense Fund was formed to preserve the public assets of the United States. Common Assets include the air, the water, the airwaves used by TV and radio, and the Internet. Collectively such assets are worth more than our entire privately owned property put together, worth more in dollars, and worth more in terms of health, happiness, and quality of life.[28]

For all its lofty lefty ambition—assigning government property rights to non-profit use with an unaudited financial statement—it lacked the socialistic sweep and grandeur of 1994's Global Governance Commission report and 2000's Earth Charter. It was more parochial, but that made it more possible.

The executive director selected was a charming young Bay Area man who had previously been the youngest Sierra Club president (1996-1998), credited with rejuvenating a moribund, aging group: Adam Michael Werbach.

Now he was 29 and president of his own media consulting and film business, Act Now Productions—named after his 1997 go-get-'em book, *Act Now, Apologize Later* (which was badly panned by *Library Journal* as "shallow, disappointing...MTV sound bites and Generation X platitudes").[29]

Two weeks after the Common Assets group was registered, with a job paying $45,832 waiting, he married Emilyn Dene Merrill at the Ahwahnee Hotel in Yosemite National Park, California, Rabbi Helen Cohn officiating.[30]

PHILANTHROPESTS

NOT LONG BEFORE JOEL ROGERS contacted Lance Lindblom concerning an Apollo Project grant, Cummings got a new environment program director—another Bay Area man—named Peter Teague.

Teague landed with Cummings after a stint as executive director of San Francisco's Horizons Foundation (1999-2001), and previous work as senior program officer at Drummond Pike's Tides Foundation, where his grab-bag portfolio included the environment; economic, social and environmental justice; community organizing; gay, lesbian, bisexual and transgender rights; harm reduction; AIDS; and democratic renewal.[31]

He had worked as environmental policy advisor to California Democrats including Rep. Leon Panetta, Sen. Diane Feinstein and Sen. Barbara Boxer.

Teague also got to know a Bay Area professor who was doing a little consulting work for some activist groups.

He immediately grasped the strategic power of the professor's work with cognitive framing.

George Lakoff, of course.

One of Teague's first official acts at Cummings was to ask Lakoff to advise some grantees on basic framing and how to broaden their appeal. He didn't have to sell Lindblom on a grant for Lakoff, because Lindblom had already given Lakoff a $20,000 Cummings grant two years earlier.[32]

Teague said, "I wanted to make him available to all grantees, so they could turn to him whenever necessary."[33]

Right away, Lakoff got $100,000 for his Rockridge Institute through a Cummings Presidential Authority Grant—one with Lindblom's signature.[34]

Lakoff began traveling the country on Cummings money, giving talks to thousands of activists and leaders and making them think differently about communications and language.[35]

Early in 2003, he got a call from an aide of Senator Byron Dorgan, head of the Senate Democratic Policy Committee, who had been reading *Moral Politics*, and we know the rest of that story from Chapter 11.

Teague made sure Lakoff got another $375,000 from Cummings, so he could teach "vision and values" to progressives all over the country.[36]

In 2004, George Soros gave him $250,000, too.[37]

Now we can see why Lakoff's talks were free: they weren't.

THE APOLLO PROJECT PROPOSAL FOR A BIG CUMMINGS GRANT came across Teague's desk with the Barnes, Bollier, Barlow and Werbach proposal for a big Cummings grant

That meant three non-profits were doing The Ask: Borosage's Institute for America's Future, Rogers' COWS, and Barnes's Common Assets group.

Teague wanted a fourth party.

Michael Shellenberger was a Bay Area denizen like Teague had been—he lived in El Cerrito, a few miles up Interstate 80 from Lakoff's Rockridge Institute in Berkeley. (See the caveat about Shellenberger at endnote 37/38.)

Teague had put him in touch with Lakoff and Michael became a convert.

Shellenberger's background was hard-left, working for anti-corporate, anti-globalization Global Exchange in San Francisco before starting a spinoff public relations firm in 1996, Communication Works.[38]

His little PR firm grew into a big PR firm. In 2001, Shellenberger and co-founder Tony Newman merged it with the ultra-left Washington-based Fenton Communications—Ira Arlook of Citizen Action fame (and a co-founder of the Campaign for America's Future), was a Fenton executive.

When Teague came to Cummings, Shellenberger was going through a big split with the Fenton group. He told one reporter that he quit "to question our most basic assumptions about what it will take for progressives to start winning again." Whatever happened, it meant he was available.[39]

Rumors said he approached Teague with an anti-SUV campaign.

True or not, Teague told him about Apollo.

Shellenberger then ginned up Americans for Energy Freedom, a really great-sounding name to add to the Apollo lineup, but not incorporated, not exempt, just one guy, Mike Shellenberger, doing business as.

Cummings did what any prescriptive foundation would: it told them to join forces and split the money. Borosage's IAF would get a special $75,000 right away, and Common Assets and IAF would each get $225,000 in 2003. The next year IAF and CADF would each get $275,000 and COWS would get $150,000, then a $275,000 pass-through from IAF in 2005. Shellenberger's cut would be passed-through in 2004, $68,502 from IAF and $112,500 from CADF for a total of $181,002. Not quite what the originals had in mind.[40]

NOW THE ORIGINAL APOLLO PROJECT TEAM HAD A DECISION TO MAKE. Do they tell Cummings "no, thanks," or do they take the money and get some new partners who might not see things quite the same as they did?

Cummings knew some great researchers at the University of Illinois who could complete their economic studies—the researchers had already done some very good regional work for another Cummings grantee, the Center for Law and the Environment.

Common Assets? They held Barnes and Bollier in high regard. Werbach might get a little overtorqued on intergenerational issues now and then, but he sounded really excited about the Apollo approach and seemed like a nice guy.

Shellenberger was an unknown quantity.

Although other funding prospects lay just over the horizon, some of their service union allies were getting antsy about moving too slowly (even though industrial unions worried about going too fast).

They took the money.

Except for Dan Carol. Ironically, the guy who thought the whole thing up worked pro bono.

So, in early 2003, the University of Illinois group completed the stalled economic research and analysis, and Apollo finished polling and focus group testing. The studies showed that "large-scale public investment in efficiency measures and currently available clean energy alternatives could produce as many as four million good jobs nationally."

Over 70% of respondents to the public opinion survey approved of the idea of a "ten-year, $300 billion investment in America's future."

That was what they needed. They used the data to talk their allied unions and green groups into formal endorsements.[41]

The Apollo Alliance launched in June, 2003 at the Take Back America Conference in Washington's Marriott Wardman Park Hotel. It was the first time all the co-founders—Borosage of the Institute for America's Future, Rogers of COWS, Werbach of the Common Assets Defense Fund, Shellenberger of Americans for Energy Freedom, and Carol of Carol/Trevelyan Strategy Group—were in the same room.[42]

Apollo's problems started immediately.

Werbach and Shellenberger lost faith in Bracken Hendricks' coalition building. They wanted Shellenberger as executive director. But the originals fought them off and Hendricks remained. Teague was not pleased.

The Common Assets group then got on Adam Werbach for spending too much time on Apollo tasks and not enough on their other projects—the Peter Barnes Sky Trust, the Spectrum Project (challenging for-profit use of the airwaves), and the Water Project (to block coal-bed methane development)—so Dan Carol, who came on as a board member in late 2003, had to stand up for Werbach and Apollo. Barnes and Bollier withdrew to the advisory board.

That Water Project was a hidden thorn. It was an overt attack on oil companies. It contravened Dan Carol's original strategic principle for Apollo:

> We should not slam on oil companies, or talk about fighting pollution, greenhouse gasses, or saving the rain forest. This campaign is about energy independence.

Common Assets was not about energy independence

It was particularly pernicious because the United States is effectively energy independent in natural gas, cleanest of the fossil fuels. The United States produces nearly three-quarters of its natural gas consumption on our own soil, not the Middle East, and all but 2 percent of the rest comes by pipeline from Canada, not the Middle East—a comfortable self-sufficiency.[43]

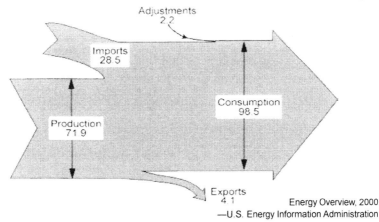

Energy Overview, 2000
—U.S. Energy Information Administration

The catch: natural gas self-sufficiency required more than 18,000 new wells *each year* to keep up with demand—unlike oil, gas does not accumulate in vast underground oceans, but in smaller pockets with short production lives.[44]

Next catch: Environmentalists blocked drilling in the richest areas and were blocking more. Slow down new wells and fall behind demand. Stop and kill energy independence in natural gas. Most natural gas goes to industry and its union jobs. Common Assets Defense Fund was drifting away from the Apollo Alliance—becoming an energy killer, not an energy seeker.

But that wasn't what caused the rupture.

NoDOG

I N APRIL OF 2004, while those troubles were brewing in the Apollo Alliance, the Washington-based anti-mining Mineral Policy Center (MPC) changed its name to Earthworks, began a merger with a Colorado group, the Oil and Gas Accountability Project, and arranged for partnerships with groups such as the Montana-based Center for Science in Public Participation.

They did that because software millionaire Paul Brainerd's foundation told them to. Brainerd did it politely but firmly in a "challenge grant."[45]

The money wanted Mineral Policy Center to lose that geeky name (is it a think tank?) for something cool and turn their highly successful anti-mining corporate campaign strategy against oil and gas.

Earthworks President Stephen D'Esposito said, "The grant changed the way we look at the organization and opened up new possibilities for us."

Understatement. The foundation had redirected their exempt purpose.

I N SEPTEMBER OF 2004, the Oil and Gas Accountability Project, now based in Earthworks' K Street office in Washington, D.C., held a workshop out West in Denver titled, *Corporate Energy Campaigning: Using Financial Pressure for Conservation*. It was co-hosted by a Canadian group, Dogwood Initiative. Dogwood's newsletter told the story:

> Participants came from the Yukon, Alberta, BC, Ontario, Alaska, Montana, Colorado, Wyoming, New Mexico, Louisiana, and Maine. They have been fighting the impacts of the oil industry on their communities and environment. Traditional approaches like community organizing, government relations, legal challenges, and public education have served them well. All agree, however, that new tools are needed.
>
> As scandals create demand for stricter corporate governance, our ability to influence industry increases. Financiers—whether they are shareholders, banks, insurance companies or other entities—are risk averse, and we have strategies to enhance risk to create leverage.
>
> We gathered experts who have successfully used these strategies— experts on financing and corporate research, shareholder activism, credit ratings, and corporate dialogue. Our experts were drawn from a "who's-who" of successful corporate campaigners. *Friends of the Earth* and *Rainforest Action Network* sent trainers, and people from *AmazonWatch* and the *Burma Project* were involved in the preparation.
>
> The workshop's biggest success was the support generated for a new continental fossil fuel campaign. The activists created a Steering Committee, and approved organizing principles, criteria for target selection, and a short-list of target companies.
>
> The coming months should be very interesting, as the foundation is put in place to hit one target corporation's operations across North America—creating political risks, threatening their social licence and right to operate, launching lawsuits; and educating investors, bankers, credit raters, and insurers on undisclosed liabilities.[46]

It was a replay of Ray Rogers' original 1974 corporate campaign idea and Midwest Academy's 1998 brochure dictum:

> Being right is not enough.
> An organization must also have the power to compel the person who makes the decision to give the group what it wants. In every case there are strong forces on the other side that are trying to make that decision go in the wrong way. Strategy is about getting that power. The key lies in figuring out the cost to the Decision Maker of various actions that your organization can take in the public arena, so that you can get concessions for not taking them. This is why thinking strategically matters.

The principle is still somewhere between a protection racket and blackmail. And it's still not illegal. Perhaps that will change.

The new campaign's target was independent oil and gas companies, not Big Oil.

The independents are Little Oil.

They don't own refineries or filling stations.

The average independent drilling company has 12 employees.

Average time in business, 23 years.

Independents drill 90 percent of our new oil and gas wells, produce 82 percent of our natural gas and 68 percent of U.S. oil.

About half their operations are on federal government land.[47]

They are the oil and gas sector most vulnerable to corporate campaign attacks by well-funded energy-killing non-profits.

The *Corporate Energy Campaigning* workshop was the precursor to a multi-year strategy designed to:

- attack small independent oil companies in the Rocky Mountain West;
- make people cringe at horror stories from select "victim groups;"
- publish drilling site photos framed to upset nature lovers;
- commission "scientific" reports on toxic terror from drilling;
- threaten small companies with corporate campaigns if they didn't sign "do it right" codes of conduct that killed profits;
- lobby for laws to "slow down" the number of wells drilled.[48]

ON NOVEMBER 15, 2006, Earthworks registered web addresses for a project called No Dirty Oil and Gas, www.nodirtyoilandgas.com and org.[49] NoDOG for short.

Energy independence was not their plan.

It was a deliberate, cold-blooded, old-style, supersize-me, energy-killer corporate campaign with lots of groups and lots of money.

No dirty oil and gas? No oil and gas drilled in America. Period.

BACK TO PHILANTHROPESTS

FOR WHATEVER REASON—policy, ideology, personal pique, slighting Lakoff (Dan Carol didn't even meet Lakoff until late 2003, when the professor was just an enthusiastic fan of Apollo's framing and not one of its creators), or some other reason—in early 2004 Peter Teague decided to commission Michael Shellenberger to write *The Death of Environmentalism.*

Shellenberger brought in old chum Ted Nordhaus.

It was nearly the death of the Apollo Alliance.

THE CUBAN ROLODEX

MICHAEL SHELLENBERGER REGISTERED AS A FOREIGN AGENT with the U.S. Department of Justice on May 20, 2004.[50]

In the middle of the Apollo project, he got a new client: Hugo Chávez, pal of Cuban dictator Fidel Castro and darling of the American Left for diverting oil money to the poor as president of Venezuela, fifth-largest oil producer in the world and fourth-largest oil supplier to the United States.

Shellenberger's private consulting firm, Lumina Strategies LLC, got a six-month, $60,000 subcontract from the Venezuela Information Office (VIO) to help Chávez out of a tough spot: 3.6 million of his fellow citizens had signed a petition to boot him out of office and he faced a recall referendum to do just that. The *San Francisco Chronicle*'s headline said Shellenberger would be working to "help build Chávez's image, provide polling data."[51]

There was more to it than that.

Chávez was adored by the slum dwellers but almost nobody else. He had survived a brief coup in early 2002, resumed office understandably furious, and demanded more money for his huge and contentious social programs. He seized control of the national oil company, Petróleos de Venezuela (PDVSA), prompting oil workers to strike, trying to force him out of office.

Venezuela's oil exports crashed and imports were soon required. Chávez fired PDVSA's top management and dismissed 18,000 skilled employees.[52]

A court ruled the firings illegal, but Chávez ignored it.

The outraged opposition group *Súmate* presented the National Electoral Council (CNE) with about 3.2 million recall signatures in August 2003, but they were rejected on the grounds they had been collected before the mid-point of Chávez's presidential term, a legal disqualification.[53]

In November 2003, the opposition collected a new set of signatures, with 3.6 million names produced in four days. The CNE rejected the petition again, saying only 1.9 million signatures were valid, provoking riots that left 9 dead, 339 arrested and over 1,200 injured. Momentum for the recall grew.

Hugo Chávez was not the sort of person to lose a recall vote. He would have to do some things that might not go down well with his enthusiastic leftist supporters in the United States, who were perhaps more important to his power agenda than those in his own country—things like publishing the names of petition signers and firing those in government jobs.

He would need some diversionary tactics as well as image polishing. Shellenberger, who was fluent in Spanish, asked to help.

The day before his foreign agent registration was filed, Shellenberger addressed a proposal to Deborah James, executive director of the Venezuela Information Office.[54]

James had come to the VIO from Global Exchange (*profile next page*), like Shellenberger, who had worked for them as a staff researcher while in graduate school in 1995 and signed them a year later as his first big client when he started his PR firm, Communication Works.

Shellenberger wrote to James, "I am proposing to work intensively with the VIO on strategy and media relations for six months starting on June 1."

His letter evidently formalized prior discussions. He already knew quite a bit about the Chávez problem as well as what Deborah James needed to provide her Venezuelan superiors:

The services I am proposing can be divided into two categories: strategic and media relations.

1. On the strategic counsel side, I recommend you use me for regular strategy calls, coordination with lobbying, trips to Caracas, overseeing advertising, polling, specific exchanges, Internet activism and other projects.

2. On the media relations side, I recommend you use me to pitch stories proactively, gently correct wrong stories, work with Andres and the Ambassador on the U.S. tour and editorial board approach, and coordinate announcements coming out of Caracas.

II. ACTIVITIES and DELIVERABLES
   1. Oversee media relations
      a. Respond to breaking news.
      b. Develop and oversee media strategy relating to *reparo* and referendum process.
      c. Travel to Venezuela for *reparo*.
      d. Work with Caracas staff and others to get stories out.
   2. Participate on regular strategy calls.
   3. Travel to Venezuela up to once a month.
   4. Write and work to place op-eds.
   5. Work with Embassy and VIO to organize U.S. tour
      • Speeches, editorial board visits, and think-tank visits to New York, Chicago, Miami, Dallas, Houston, Ft. Worth, San Diego, L.A., and San Francisco in late May, before *reparo*.
      • Help arrange and attend meetings.
      • Help prepare Ambassador.
   6. Internet Activism

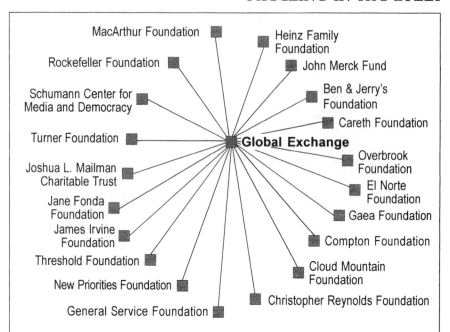

MacArthur Foundation

Rockefeller Foundation

Schumann Center for
Media and Democracy

Turner Foundation

Joshua L. Mailman
Charitable Trust

Jane Fonda
Foundation

James Irvine
Foundation

Threshold Foundation

New Priorities Foundation

General Service Foundation

Heinz Family
Foundation

John Merck Fund

Ben & Jerry's
Foundation

Careth Foundation

Global Exchange

Overbrook
Foundation

El Norte
Foundation

Gaea Foundation

Compton Foundation

Cloud Mountain
Foundation

Christopher Reynolds Foundation

FOUNDATION FUNDERS - GLOBAL EXCHANGE

Global Exchange, a combination human rights NGO, travel agency, and coffee store, was incorporated December 28, 1987, in San Francisco, California, Kirsten Moller, executive director.

Co-founders were Kevin Danaher and his wife Medea Benjamin.

Danaher (Ph.D. Sociology, University of California at Santa Cruz) is a noted anti-globalization activist and author of *Globalize This! The Battle Against the World Trade Organization and Corporate Rule* (2000) and *Insurrection: The Citizen Challenge to Corporate Power* (2003).

Medea Benjamin, born Susie Benjamin, renamed herself in college after the Greek mythological character Medea, sorceress who murdered her three sons to spite her husband Jason for taking a new wife (Masters, Public Health., Columbia University; Masters, Economics, New School for Social Research) and is a high profile anti-war, anti-corporate, pro-Cuba activist.

Global Exchange began by providing "reality tours" to human rights problem areas such as Cuba, Palestine, and Zapatista-held Mexico, hoping to recruit travelers as activists against the Cuban Embargo and for other anti-American issues. They have built a substantial cadre of activists.

Global Exchange spent $1.2 million of its $4.1 million 2005 revenue on reality tours and sold $1.8 million in coffee and other goods at a profit of over $950,000. Socialist ideology, capitalist methodology.

The group is highly networked, with ties to Joshua Mailman's Social Venture Network, the Energy Action anti-oil coalition, and the government of Hugo Chávez in Venezuela, where "reality tours" boomed.

"Andres" is Venezuela's Minister of Communication and Information, Andres Izarra.

"The Ambassador," of course, is Venezuela's Ambassador to the United States, Bernardo Alvarez Herrera.

Reparo, well, that's a little complicated.

"Reparo" translates as "repair," meaning "signature repair" in this case, which referred to a five-day period given by the National Electoral Council so the owners of disputed petition signatures could confirm that they did in fact want Chávez gone and did in fact support the recall referendum.

Reparo was so important to Chávez because he could stop the vote if his opposition couldn't validate at least 2.4 million signatures.

Reparo turned up 2,436.830 valid signatures.

Chávez had to stand for recall.

So he granted citizenship to half a million illegal aliens in a crude vote-buying scheme and "migrated" existing voters away from their local election office—to fix the results in his favor.[55]

At referendum time, the American firm of Penn, Schoen & Berland did exit polls that showed Chávez losing by a 60-40 margin, but the official results put Chávez winning by 58 to 41 percent, as we saw in Chapter 16. Doug Schoen, who saw Milosevic do it, said, "I think it was a massive fraud."[56]

Former U.S. President Jimmy Carter said, "the results were accurate."[57]

Aftermath: *Súmate* had received a $53,400 grant from the National Endowment for Democracy to use for "election education."[58]

Like NED's grant to Serbia's opposition, as we saw in Chapter 7, their grant was used "to promote voter education," meaning to teach observers how to stop Chávez from stealing the election. Clearly, that didn't work.

Chávez prosecuted four *Súmate* officials, including founder Maria Corina Machado (mother of 3), for high treason and conspiracy for accepting funds from the U.S. Congress.[59]

Nobody prosecuted Shellenberger for accepting more than that from the Venezuelan government.

S HELLENBERGER HAD LOTS OF FRIENDS to "build Chávez's image." Before he arrived, British Trotskyist Alan Woods, editor of the website In Defense of Marxism, founded "Hands Off Venezuela."[60]

After he departed, U.S. Congressman José Serrano (D-NY) invited Chávez to give a speech to Bronx community groups focused on the "socialism of the 21st century." Chávez told them that this new socialism must be based in Christianity: "A new Christian Socialism; the first great socialist was Christ."[61]

The Arca Foundation (Chapter 14), with its long history of funding Castro supporters, just pumped some more money into pro-Chávez causes.[62]

The familiar names that popped up led a State Department official to smile and say, "The Venezuelans just got the Rolodex from Cuba."[63]

BLIP ON THE RADAR

AURICE STRONG'S EARTH COUNCIL ALLIANCE sponsored the 2004 Annual William J. Clinton Foundation Energy Forum in New York City.[64]

The topic was the relationship between energy policy and security, development and climate change.

The dots were connecting.

Who defines the terms controls the universe of discourse.

COGNITIVE DISSONANCE

HELLENBERGER AND NORDHAUS presented *The Death of Environmentalism* in October 2004. Nobody quite knew what to make of it.

Foundation directors and philanthropoids were baffled why Peter Teague, one of their own, paid these two guys to dump on the environmental movement in front of its funders.

Mark Schmitt noted that Peter Teague was his friend, and wrote, "There's a lot in this essay...some of it right on, some of it a bit crazy, some of it vacuous and new-agey (particularly the epigraphs about death opening each section, and of course that insufferable management-consultant aphorism that the Chinese ideogram for "crisis" is a combination of danger and opportunity), some of it beyond my capacity to evaluate, but all very much worth reading. It's written to provoke, and provoke it did."[65]

Carl Pope, head of the Sierra Club, was *really* provoked. He had signed on to co-chair the Apollo Alliance, and shot back a fierce 6,000-word reply charging that "the not so hidden agenda is 'fund us instead.'"[66]

The Reapers didn't foster trust between Pope and the Apollo Alliance.

Then Adam Werbach gave a speech titled, "Is Environmentalism Dead?" beginning with the words, "I am here to perform an autopsy."[67]

In his speech, he claimed that in late 2002 he sat across the table from Peter Teague in a New York eatery, having a get-to-know-the-funder chat.

"Peter," I said, "Environmentalism is dead. There won't be environmental programs at foundations in five years."

He looked down, feeling guilty for airing dirty laundry to a funder.

I looked back up at Peter, and he was smiling. "I agree," he said. "I've been thinking the same thing."

If that's true, why didn't Teague come clean at the time?

Why fund Apollo in 2003 and sabotage it in 2004?

Shellenberger then co-authored an essay titled "Getting Tough on Oil" with Ross Gelbspan, militant author of *Boiling Point: How Politicians, Big*

Oil and Coal, Journalists and Activists Are Fueling the Climate Crisis.[68]

The mine workers were not pleased.

This wasn't about energy independence anymore.

Borosage, Rogers and Carol found themselves doing damage control instead of coalition building. Carol sent a rebuttal to Grist.com emphatically stating that the *Death* message was not Apollo's position.[69]

So they faced another decision: say goodbye to Teague's man and therefore Teague's grants? Or grin and bear it?

They told Shellenberger to leave Apollo.

They told Adam that he and Common Assets could stay, but he decided to leave with Shellenberger. They became tighter than anyone knew.

A year or so later, Werbach, by then appointed a San Francisco public utilities commissioner, officiated at the wedding of Nordhaus and Sara Mann, a San Francisco lawyer, with Shellenberger as best man.[70]

Two months after that, Shellenberger and Nordhaus registered a non-profit called the Breakthrough Institute in Oakland, California.[71]

They rode the crest of their celebrity into a book deal with Houghton Mifflin. Title: *Break Through: From the Death of Environmentalism to the Politics of Possibility.*

In 2005, after Shellenberger and Werbach departed, Nathan Cummings Foundation zeroed out all four of the Apollo Alliance groups.

APOLLO'S WEBSITE SAID *The Apollo Alliance is a joint project of the Institute for America's Future and the Center on Wisconsin Strategy.* Only the two.

It is one of the few examples of a non-profit taking its program back from a prescriptive foundation and taking the consequences with it.

Whatever else you could say of Borosage and Rogers, they got balls.

Apollo found other funding. It acquired a powerful 12-person national steering committee, 23 distinguished members for its national advisory board, 35 labor union endorsements, 23 environmental group endorsements, nods of approval from a number of state governors—a veritable Democratic Party love fest—and dozens of partner groups, both non-profits and businesses.

The Apollo Alliance also got a new executive director, Jerome Ringo, who had been elected chairman of the board of the National Wildlife Federation in 2005, the first African American to lead a major environmental group.

By 2007, Apollo had incubated long enough. It became a stand-alone. And its origins came home to roost:

> This campaign is about energy independence. If we focus on that, we will succeed, and the other goals will follow. In the long run, there will undoubtedly be different visions and thorny politics regarding clean coal, drilling on US public lands, and so on...

It was time for the other goals, different visions, and thorny politics.

GUERILLAS WITHOUT MIST

ON JANUARY 13, 2007 at the SHOT Show in Orlando, Florida, Jim Range's Theodore Roosevelt Conservation Partnership introduced its new branch, the Union Sportsmen's Alliance (USA), comprised of 20 strongly Democrat labor unions.

It came with a $1.2 million check to TRCP from the unions.[72]

Not so right-leaning after all.

And now the Democrats controlled Congress, lusting after a No-Energy Energy Policy to kill off fossil fuels, and searching for the keys to it.

On March 27, 2007, the House Natural Resources Committee held a hearing titled, "Access Denied: The Growing Conflict Between Fishing, Hunting, and Energy Development on Federal Lands."[73]

It was chaired by Rep. Nick Rahall, Democrat of West Virginia, who had introduced H.R. 6, a comprehensive No-Energy Energy Bill, in January.

The hall outside the Morris K. Udall Hearing Room was so jammed with people wearing union jackets that an oil and gas delegation couldn't get in.

Rollin D. Sparrowe, Ph.D., gave testimony for the Theodore Roosevelt Conservation Partnership, saying he brought 40 years of wildlife experience to the hearing. Of the oil and gas industry, he testified:

> Realistically, their job is to develop gas and oil and produce as much as possible. Their associations and company lobbyists have pursued "the wildlife question" as an impediment and our government has listened to them and largely ignored the conservation community's many appeals to slow down and "do this right."[74]

The NoDOG strategy.

"Slow down," make sure those new wells needed each year never get drilled. "Do this right," kill off independent oil and gas producers with rules nobody can follow. Shove the drill rigs offshore. End our self-sufficiency in natural gas, pinch industry, and let the Union Sportsmen's Alliance wonder how they got so much time to hunt and fish. And no money to fill the gas tank.

Dr. Sparrowe did not say that his Partnership had received $300,000 from the Doris Duke Foundation "For campaign to educate public about state wildlife planning process and to generate support for those plans."[75]

Or that the campaign helped send 75,000 formal comments against energy leasing to Colorado's natural resources director, who responded by backing a 15-20-year ban on oil and gas operations in the state's Little Snake Resource Area. Energy killer.[76]

Dr. Sparrowe did not say that his Partnership had received $600,000 from Gordon Moore's private foundation. Moore is the co-founder of giant computer chipmaker Intel. His foundation's assets exceed $5.3 billion.

The Moore Foundation's stated purpose for the grant: "to change the course of energy development on public lands." Energy killer.[77]

TRCP was part of a huge foundation-funded network (*pages 390-391*).

The message is clear. The half of independent oil and gas operations on federal lands will be banned from operating there.

America's self-sufficiency in natural gas will be banned with it.

"STOP DRILLING!" is not an energy policy.

Issue entrepreneurs like Jim Range and Earthworks' Stephen D'Esposito have the ear of congressmen like Nick Rahall because they have very rich progressive funders who give them the money to "educate the public."

Do lawmakers understand that "protecting wildlife" will kill our energy independence in natural gas? And drive prices at the pump higher?

I MET KATHLEEN SGAMMA at a barbecue at 4 Eagle Ranch in the Colorado Rockies near Wolcott. She's manager of government affairs (in plain English, that's lobbying) for IPAMS, the Independent Petroleum Association of Mountain States, based in Denver.

We talked about the impact of the Roosevelters.

She was still smarting from serious losses to Earthworks (and others) in the 2007 state legislative sessions of New Mexico, Colorado, and Wyoming—a slew of new habitat and surface rights laws to "slow down" drilling.[78]

But she still had the presence of mind to catch the Roosevelters in a good one: TRCP had put out a press release two weeks after Rep. Nick Rahall introduced his anti-oil and gas energy reform bill, H.R. 2337.

It was headlined, *Sportsmen Support Congressional Reform of Energy Development on Federal Public Lands.* It didn't mention Rahall's bill.[79]

The release began, "Survey results show that the vast majority of respondents believe the most important uses of our public lands are for providing fish and wildlife habitat and outdoor recreation opportunities. Only 29% rated energy development as a top priority and 79% oppose unlimited energy development on federal public lands." Sounds bad for energy.

TRCP President and CEO George Cooper even used the predictable NoDOG motto, "Why not slow down and do it right?"

The poll was called "Sportsmen's Attitudes Toward Energy Development in the Rocky Mountain West," done for TRCP by Virginia survey firm Responsive Management, which interviewed 1,617 hunters and anglers.

Does that sound like a payoff to Rep. Rahall for his wonderful hearing?

Then TRCP followed the rules of transparency. They posted the survey itself on their website. So Sgamma took a look. She found that:

- 54% of Rocky Mountain state respondents support increasing the amount of energy development on public lands.
- A majority (52%) of sportsmen agree that America needs increased energy development in the Rocky Mountain West.
- A mere 16% of sportsmen are dissatisfied with the current pace of energy development in the West.
- 71% do not think that energy development on public lands has negatively affected their personal hunting and fishing experiences in the past 5 years.

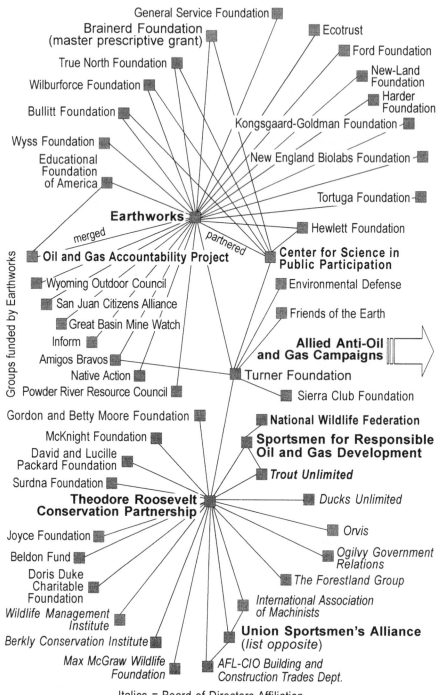

General Service Foundation

Brainerd Foundation
(master prescriptive grant)

Ecotrust

Ford Foundation

True North Foundation

New-Land
Foundation

Wilburforce Foundation

Harder
Foundation

Bullitt Foundation

Kongsgaard-Goldman Foundation

Wyss Foundation

Educational
Foundation
of America

New England Biolabs Foundation

Tortuga Foundation

Earthworks

Hewlett Foundation

merged

partnered

Groups funded by Earthworks

Oil and Gas Accountability Project

**Center for Science in
Public Participation**

Wyoming Outdoor Council

Environmental Defense

San Juan Citizens Alliance

Friends of the Earth

Great Basin Mine Watch

Inform

**Allied Anti-Oil
and Gas Campaigns**

Amigos Bravos

Native Action

Turner Foundation

Powder River Resource Council

Sierra Club Foundation

Gordon and Betty Moore Foundation

National Wildlife Federation

McKnight Foundation

**Sportsmen for Responsible
Oil and Gas Development**

David and Lucille
Packard Foundation

Surdna Foundation

Trout Unlimited

**Theodore Roosevelt
Conservation Partnership**

Ducks Unlimited

Joyce Foundation

Orvis

Beldon Fund

*Ogilvy Government
Relations*

Doris Duke
Charitable
Foundation

The Forestland Group

*Wildlife Management
Institute*

*International Association
of Machinists*

Berkly Conservation Institute

Union Sportsmen's Alliance
(*list opposite*)

*Max McGraw Wildlife
Foundation*

*AFL-CIO Building and
Construction Trades Dept.*

Italics = Board of Directors Affiliation

NODOG: CONNECT THE ANTI-OIL AND GAS DOTS

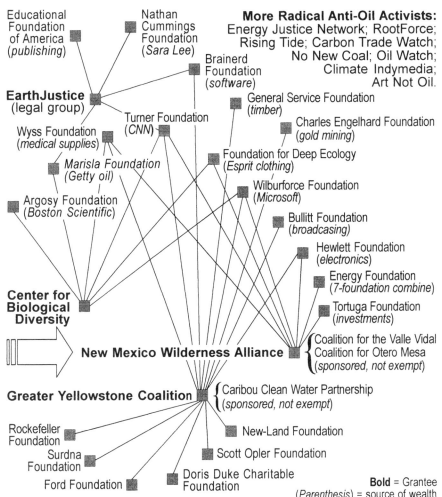

Educational Foundation of America (*publishing*)

Nathan Cummings Foundation (*Sara Lee*)

More Radical Anti-Oil Activists:
Energy Justice Network; RootForce; Rising Tide; Carbon Trade Watch; No New Coal; Oil Watch; Climate Indymedia; Art Not Oil.

Brainerd Foundation (*software*)

EarthJustice (legal group)

Turner Foundation (*CNN*)

Wyss Foundation (*medical supplies*)

Marisla Foundation (*Getty oil*)

Argosy Foundation (*Boston Scientific*)

General Service Foundation (*timber*)

Charles Engelhard Foundation (*gold mining*)

Foundation for Deep Ecology (*Esprit clothing*)

Wilburforce Foundation (*Microsoft*)

Bullitt Foundation (*broadcasing*)

Hewlett Foundation (*electronics*)

Energy Foundation (*7-foundation combine*)

Tortuga Foundation (*investments*)

Center for Biological Diversity

New Mexico Wilderness Alliance

Coalition for the Valle Vidal
Coalition for Otero Mesa
(*sponsored, not exempt*)

Greater Yellowstone Coalition

Caribou Clean Water Partnership
(*sponsored, not exempt*)

Rockefeller Foundation

Surdna Foundation

Ford Foundation

New-Land Foundation

Scott Opler Foundation

Doris Duke Charitable Foundation

Bold = Grantee
(*Parenthesis*) = source of wealth

International Union of Bricklayers & Allied Craft Workers	United Steel Workers of America
	International Brotherhood of Electrical Workers
International Brotherhood of Boilermakers, Iron Ship Builders, Blacksmiths, Forgers & Helpers	International Association of Machinists and Aerospace Workers
	American Postal Workers Union
Utility Workers Union of America	United Association of Plumbers & Pipe Fitters
Operative Plasterers & Cement Masons International Association	International Association of Fire Fighters
	Sheet Metal Workers International Association
International Union of Elevator Constructors	International Association of Bridge, Structural, Ornamental, & Reinforcing Iron Workers
United Mine Workers of America	
United Union of Roofers, Waterproofers, & Allied Workers	Bakery, Confectionery, Tobacco Workers and Grain Millers International Union
International Association of Heat, Frost Insulators, & Asbestos Workers	International Union of Painters & Allied Trades
Brotherhood of Railroad Signalmen	Transportation Communications International Union

Sgamma wrote a full set of talking points about the survey, then got together with IPAMS' communications manager Joe Bargas to write a news release. They talked Executive Director Marc Smith into releasing it.

Headline: "Results of Theodore Roosevelt Conservation Partnership survey 'encouraging'—*In spite of rhetoric, survey shows sportsmen support energy development in the Intermountain West.*"[80]

Sgamma blistered TRCP: "The obstructionist environmental group's constant assertions that sportsmen are opposed to energy development are not supported by their own data."

Marc Smith, whose IPAMS delegation was the one that encountered all the union jackets outside Rahall's hearing, said, "It's just a tactic to drive a wedge between sportsmen and energy companies. We have good operating partnerships with a number of wildlife groups. We work seriously with them on responsible development." He shook his head at TRCP's survey.

TRCP then removed the survey and news release from their website. Not so transparent.

But that was okay, IPAMS had already posted them on its own website.

Unfortunately, comeuppances do not congressional policy make.

Rahall's H.R. 2337, "The Energy Policy Reform and Revitalization Act of 2007," was characterized by the Congressional Budget Office as "a framework of national strategies to protect natural resources affected by the production, distribution, and use of energy." (Energy's not a natural resource?)

It mostly slowed issuance of drilling permits on federal lands by a factor of three, extending approvals from 30 days to 90 days.[81]

"Slow down." "Do it right." Suffer the consequences. No oil and gas.

Energy independence was not Rahall's plan. *Energy* was not his plan.

Perhaps some bright young lawmaker will introduce a bill to require the Congressional Budget Office to do a "Net Gain or Loss of BTUs" assessment of all bills that come through its doors. Just to keep Congress honest.

CHASING BTUs

A BTU IS AN ENERGY MEASUREMENT. It stands for British Thermal Unit. It's defined as the amount of heat required to raise the temperature of one pound of water by one degree Fahrenheit. It's used to describe the heat value (energy content) of fuels and the power of heating and cooling systems, such as furnaces, stoves, barbecue grills, and air conditioners.[82]

So the BTUs in your car's gas tank are the same as in your home heating or a factory or a moon rocket. Doesn't matter if it came from a hydroelectric dam or a nuclear power plant or the fireplace in the den. It's energy. BTUs measure energy.

Now let's talk about energy independence.

Great idea, to convert to clean energy made in the USA.

Here's the problem:

The United States Energy Information Administration says that in 2006, the U.S. consumed 99.53 quadrillion BTUs of energy.
Of this,
— 40% came from oil
— 23% from coal
— 22% from natural gas
— 8% from nuclear
— 2.9% from biomass, including ethanol, biodiesel and wastewood
— 2.8% from conventional hydroelectric power dams
— *less than 1% came from geothermal, wind, and solar combined.*[83]

If you count from biomass to the bottom, "clean energy" is missing 93 quadrillion BTUs that we needed to run the country. 96 without hydro.
The Energy Gap.

All the energy-killer non-profits and their fatal foundations and the progressive activists and gurus and lawmakers and civil society world rulers we've seen in this book are creating an energy gap that will get out of hand and we'll be lucky to live through it.
If you're a serious progressive busy eliminating fossil fuels, and you're not fond of nuclear power plants or those river-blocking hydroelectric dams either, you'd better slow down your energy-killing spree and do it right with those much-touted "sustainable clean energy alternatives" or you'll get your clean energy economy before there is one.
The Energy Crunch.

The trouble is, the rest of us have to be there with you.
The title of this book might mean something to everybody then.

Progressives, your Phoenix is risen: you now have the power to destroy.
Can you create?
Can you show us 93 quadrillion BTUs? 80 quadrillion? 50? 25? 10?
Or is that the real question?

REAL QUESTIONS

I PERSONALLY TAKE THE APOLLO ALLIANCE TO BE A GOOD-FAITH EFFORT to do what its rhetoric says: clean energy, good jobs, energy independence.
I also take it to have strayed from its original "this campaign is about energy independence" to embrace "other goals, different visions and thorny politics," things many of us consider to be questionable or foolish.
That's a problem. But for now, what about energy independence?
First, they don't intend to do it by creating 93 quadrillion more BTUs.

They intend to do it by rebuilding America to be energy efficient, which means we could run on much less, perhaps as little as 50 quadrillion BTUs.

While they're reworking the homes and factories and cars, trains and roads and pipelines and all the other infrastructure, they'll promote vast increases in clean energy production—biomass, geothermal, wind, solar.

They'll do all this, says Dan Carol, through policy-driven programs.

What does it mean, "policy-driven?"

Generally, it's rules and laws that make everyone do what a policymaker wants them to do, approximately the opposite of "market-driven."

Specifically, what does Apollo want everyone to do?

In eight words, Fill all your needs with clean American energy.

Sounds good. I'd do that. But I'd read the fine print first.

Policy: "The general principles by which a government is guided in its management of public affairs."[84]

That's *Black's Law Dictionary*. It can be annoyingly vague.

So, policy is about public affairs. What's that got to do with you and me?

Public policy: "The principles under which the freedom of contract or private dealings is restricted by law for the good of the community."[85]

That's also *Black's Law*. Word for word. Read it again. It's the nub of "policy-driven" and it's the nub of the Apollo Alliance.

Apollo's price for filling all your needs with clean American energy is laws that restrict your freedom of contract and restrict your private dealings.

That's severely choice-limiting. It could change our form of government. If we let it.

Apollo has some great ideas, but don't forget that it's part of The Vast Left Wing Conspiracy, the progressive social change revolution.

So let's go into this with our eyes open.

But let's go into it.

P HIL ANGELIDES BECAME APOLLO'S CHAIR when it went stand-alone in September 2007. He's a Harvard grad (government, 1974). He was the Democratic nominee for Governor of California who got Terminatored by incumbent Arnold Schwarzenegger in the 2006 elections.[86]

And, most importantly, he was California State Treasurer, 1998-2006.

As Treasurer, Angelides was a trustee of:

• the California Public Employees' Retirement System ($250 billion)
• the California State Teachers' Retirement System ($157 billion)
• both affiliated with the Council of Institutional Investors.($3 trillion).

As Chair of Apollo, he still knew where all the money was.

And it knew where he was

A lot of it was invested in businesses that could profit from the Apollo agenda, a consideration not to be dimissed.

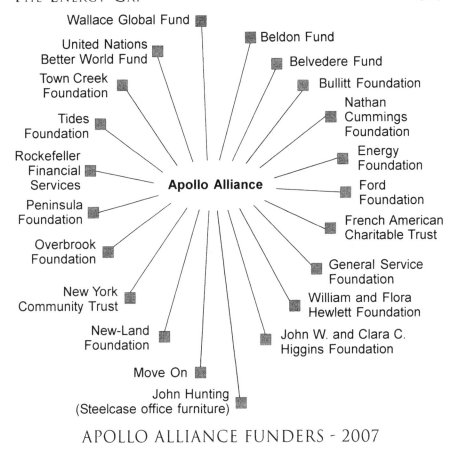

Wallace Global Fund

United Nations
Better World Fund

Town Creek
Foundation

Tides
Foundation

Rockefeller
Financial
Services

Peninsula
Foundation

Overbrook
Foundation

New York
Community Trust

New-Land
Foundation

Move On

John Hunting
(Steelcase office furniture)

Beldon Fund

Belvedere Fund

Bullitt Foundation

Nathan
Cummings
Foundation

Energy
Foundation

Ford
Foundation

French American
Charitable Trust

General Service
Foundation

William and Flora
Hewlett Foundation

John W. and Clara C.
Higgins Foundation

Apollo Alliance

APOLLO ALLIANCE FUNDERS - 2007

Angelides took over an organization on the cusp of functional strategic power. Apollo had not only garnered many vital endorsements, it was also testing its scalability with state and local chapters, it had convinced Rep. Jay Inslee (D-WA) to introduce the New Apollo Energy Act of 2005 (and again in 2007), it had held an Apollo Summit with 160 leaders including Sen. Hillary Clinton, and secured funding from more than 20 donors (*diagram above*).

Jerome Ringo shifted to president. Apollo was back on the launch pad.

APOLLO'S AGENDA HAD MATURED. It was still based on the Ten Point Plan, but it had advanced to the critical questions of how to design and deploy workable ways to create clean energy jobs and achieve energy independence, equipped with model financing strategies, specific carbon-cutting targets, and energy-saving policies. It had emerged in sufficient detail to raise some nuts-and-bolts questions and support a thoughtful critique.

A cursory scan of the Apollo agenda shows that it consists of only two major features: subsidies for the good, restrictions for the bad.

Apollo itself provides neither, but is a power and pressure group to drive policymakers to enact the subsidies and restrictions

A deeper scan shows that Apollo's agenda for the most part recommends existing government programs and promotes existing clean energy non-profit groups and for-profit businesses. Not so radical as it might seem.

What's original is the scope. Putting all the existing ideas together gives you a breathtaking look at what Apollo's energy independence really takes (*graphic opposite*), replete with different visions and thorny politics.

A thorough examination of the Apollo agenda separates the content (what it's about) from the context (who's doing it and why).

Who's doing the Apollo Alliance is nearly 100 percent Democrats—officers, advisors, congressional supporters, consultants, the works.

Why Apollo's doing it is energy independence, national security, CO_2 control for global warming, and organized labor employment.

What Apollo is about is policies that are leftist, but point to results that non-leftists could support—energy independence, for instance.

To non-leftists, energy independence can stand on its own feet without the different visions and thorny politics. So can energy efficiency.

But the Apollo Alliance offers no way to avoid the visions and politics.

If we support Apollo, what are we doing to ourselves? Is it worthwhile, or even possible, to get beyond the ideological conflicts between leftists and non-leftists to find an energy future we might both agree on?

Dan Carol, the *blink*-father of Apollo, had a suggestion.

TRANSPARTISANSHIP IS ONE OF THOSE NEW MEMES among the cognoscenti. It acknowledges the validity of ideas across the familiar left-right political spectrum, but tries to see them pragmatically and find effective solutions to social and political problems without the left-right split—a way to agree without surrendering and to disagree without being disagreeable.

It might be helpful for non-leftists and the Apollo Alliance.

An outfit called Reuniting America specializes in small gatherings of people from widely divergent ideologies who try to be transpartisan about various issues. I was fortunate enough to have a couple of old friends who had been to some of their events.[87]

I talked to Grover Norquist, president of Americans for Tax Reform. He's the "Investment Banking Matrix" guru in Rob Stein's *Conservative Message Machine's Money Matrix* PowerPoint (and was surprised to find out how much money he controlled when I told him about it). Grover had participated in one of Reuniting America's events, the Second Conference on Democracy in America, in 2005.

Smart electrical grid
- integrate all sources
- computer control
- regional/local generation
- local power storage
- efficient transmission
- improved distribution
- terrorism-proof
- stable failproof grid
- continual innovation

Air travel
- efficient engines
- biofuel research
- ultralight composite airframes
- offsets in ticket price

Agriculture
- integrated output
- wind and solar
- food, feed, fiber, fuel
- land lease for big wind
- solar to get off the grid
- corn and cellulosic ethanol
- animal waste for biogas methane
- tree growing for carbon sequestering
- steep farmland and food price increases

Housing
- energy saving construction
- efficient appliances
- jobs-housing linkage fees
- employer assisted housing
- transit-linked mortgages
- zoning exclusions
- urban infill

Retrofit buildings
- commercial, industrial, residential
- energy efficient system upgrades
- heating, lighting, refrigeration, ventilation, elevators, air conditioning replacement

Market development
- geothermal electricity
- solar/photovoltaic
- wind power

Emissions cap and trade authorities
- regulator sets emissions limit (cap)
- regulator divides limit into permits
- regulator sells permits up to set limit
- businesses buy permits and then sell them to each other as necessary and possible (trade)
- revenues returned to program

Private investment
- Social Venture Network
- subsidy-seeking funds
- social responsibility funds

Research & Development
- hydrogen fuel cell development
- carbon capture technology
- sequestered coal

Policy-driven finance
- Public bonds for retrofitting
- Public bonds for renewable energy
- State development authorities
- State revolving loan programs
- State pension funds directed to energy projects

Public transportation
- new transit starts
- maintain passenger trains
- regional high-speed rail
- improved roads and bridges

Private transportation
- regulations and mandates
- fuel mileage minimum
- emissions control
- junker buyback and scrap
- hybrid and flexfuel mandates
- alternative fuel vehicle market support

Entertainment and amusement
- energy efficient hotels and parking
- efficient rides and attractions

Workforce
- displacement and retraining
- "Just Transition" payoffs
- green jobs for the disadvantaged
- job quality standards
- apprenticeships

Subsidies:
Manufacturing:
existing federal programs
Manufacturing Extension Partnership
Industrial Technologies Program
Industry of the Future

Self-contained health care
- energy self-sufficient hospitals, emergency rooms, medical offices, hospices, and birthing centers

Federal mandates
- renewable fuel standards
- renewable portfolio standards
- renewable energy tax credits

Open space and wildlands
- forbidding clean energy development on lands Apollo's environmental constituency excludes

TIP OF A VERY BIG ICEBERG
APOLLO ALLIANCE AGENDA EXEMPLARS

I mostly wanted to know if he was able to work with any of the leftists at the conference on subsequent issues. Yes, he said, on Internet freedom. He felt the left-right coalition worked well together.

Then I called Fred Smith, president of Competitive Enterprise Institute, who had been to a different Reuniting America gathering, a leadership retreat on Transpartisan Search for National Energy Security in mid-2006.

Al Gore was there, too. Fred said it wasn't possible to team up with anyone later. He remarked that Gore was more reasonable in a small group than before the cameras, but one attendee was a zealous global warming believer who called others global warming deniers—evoking Holocaust deniers. This charming fellow recommended treason charges. A loyal climate cultist, but not so transpartisan. I'll do a big rant about that later.

So, there's a fifty-fifty track record. Not a wild win, but not hopeless.

I like a lot of Apollo's goals, so I'll give them my transpartisan best and ask that they do the same for me. I'll watch to be sure I'm not a cheap date doing all the trans- while they're doing all the partisan.

To repeat my baselines from page 18, in a word, I believe in choice. I believe in private property, free enterprise, small government, fiscal prudence, avoiding foreign entanglements, the maximum personal liberty consistent with public safety, and a rule of law designed to enhance that liberty. I believe that protected private property rights are the basis of any free economy.

Specifically, I'm for absolute Internet freedom. I'm for gun rights and religious freedom. You can't run a complex society without bureaucracy, but citizens need a check against abuses. I think government funding for health, safety, welfare, and education is proper. I think that subsidies for agriculture, business and industry are a proper counterbalance to regulation. I tolerate mandates if funded and appealable. I support review of corporate charters of both for-profit and non-profit organizations, and truth in advertising for both.

As in all things of our "too too solid flesh," my preferences get bashed and trashed same as Shakespeare's Hamlet. I just don't get morose about it.

Okay, Apollo, here are my transpartisan mid-course corrections for you:

REBUILDING AMERICA'S INFRASTRUCTURE IS A NO-BRAINER. Start with the Interstate Highway System. It's 50 years old. A bridge collapsed in Minneapolis. Congestion is massive in cities. Time to rebuild the whole thing.

With so many industrial renewal, small business, and rural aid programs already on the books it would be hypocritical to say, "Hey, that's Big Government" to Apollo's proposals for government aid for renewable energy projects. Of course it is. But it's aid to private enterprise. That messy mixed economy.

Some of the other specifics aren't so clearcut, like "Smart Growth" that won't let people live where they want to, but tries to push them into urban infill spaces. I have problems with that, but I've also had a lot of experience helping people with zoning rules. I know that the zoning power is as close to absolute as any power that government has, so I'll only ask that Apollo give the locals a vote on Smart Growth to keep it from being Dumb No Growth.

A UTOMOTIVE FUEL EFFICIENCY STANDARDS are so controversial that Rep. John
Dingell (D-MI), chairman of the U.S. House Energy and Commerce
Committee, proposed a 50-cent tax on a gallon of gasoline and suspension of
mortgage deductions for homes over 3,000 square feet—to drive the point
home that if we believe global warming is so serious that it's worth hurting
the automobile industry, isn't it worth hurting everyone? Speak, Apollo.[88]

G LOBAL WARMING DOESN'T TERRIFY ME as much as its adherents do, and in
particular the Believe Or Die set, like those who sent five death threats
to Timothy Ball, a former climatology professor at the University of Winnipeg
in Canada for questioning how much man was affecting climate change.
    Is the Apollo Alliance honor bound to speak out on this issue and to
loudly condemn and anathemize the Atmospheric Al qaeda?[89]
    Speak, Apollo.

D O THE MATH: TRACK AND PUBLISH ANNUAL STATUS REPORTS on our progress
toward energy independence and clean energy's projected contribution to the mix. The Apollo Alliance website and literature are so smogged
with pep-talk that realistic projections are needed as a catalytic converter.
    An Apollo-friendly renewable energy policy group called "25x25"
predicts renewables will provide 25 percent of our energy by 2025.[90]
    Apollo wants $300 billion over ten years.
    Will that buy us less than one-fourth of energy independence?
    Will we have to buy three or more additional ten-year installments?

    Apollo could be more credible to non-leftists who aren't impressed with
pep-talks by prominently posting a chart like the one on page 395 (free, from
the U.S. Energy Information Administration) next to a projection like this:

    In 2025, the U.S. will consume 50 Quadrillion BTUs of energy.
    Of this,
    — 25% will come from oil
    — 25% will come from natural gas
    — 25% will come from sequestered clean coal
    — 25% will come from geothermal, biomass, wind, and solar.

    Of course, I just made that up. But correctly done annual charting is a
radically simple way to answer the key energy independence question:
    Are We There Yet?
    Just Show Us The BTUs. Show us where we are. Show us where we're
going. That's absolutely essential. It would give America some idea of how
much clean energy contributed to the mix each year as well as confidence that
we're not flying blind into The Energy Gap.
    And wouldn't it be a powerful thwart to NoDOG.?
    Speak, Apollo.

G REAT EXPECTATIONS AREN'T SO GREAT. Ethanol has a terrible carbon and economic footprint. With ethanol's 51-cent-per-gallon subsidy, soaring production pushed corn prices up, caused tortilla riots in Mexico, diverted farms from food, and pushed *all* U.S. food prices up 6.7 percent in 2007. Sky-high farmland prices mean young farmers can't afford farms. Ethanol production also uses natural gas. Apollo acknowledges that, saying we can make up for it planting trees to sequester the carbon (which only works until the tree dies, when the carbon comes back during decay—and if we can bless ethanol production with offsets, why not oil and gas?). But to the point: ethanol production has three outputs: one-third ethanol, one-third spent feedstock, and one-third CO_2. Clean energy or the corn lobby?[91]

Speak, Apollo.

A POLLO IS NOW ON RECORD WITH "the long-term goal of weaning America off fossil fuel." I respectfully submit that that's a wrong-headed goal. For one thing, weaning means feeding baby enough other food to survive and thrive, and it's nowhere in sight. Daddy would be smarter over such a long haul to invest in cleanup technologies to produce more oil and natural gas on our own soil, just as research into sequestered coal is already on Apollo's list.

Doesn't obstinately writing off oil and gas smell like you're sinking back into hatred of corporations and not emerging with innovative transpartisan ideas for energy independence?[92]

Speak, Apollo.

C ONSEQUENCES: Since Apollo isn't likely to come off the goal of ending oil and gas, what do you do with the oil and gas people who no longer have a place to work, particularly the small independents with 12 employees?

Apollo people have recommended "Just Transition," a sort of safety net that provides retraining, job finding aid, and temporary wage replacement money from the federal treasury.

There are two problems with this concept. The first is there's nothing "just" about killing somebody's job for the sake of somebody else's policy. The least they could do is honestly call it forced displacement reparations.

Second is the lack of displacement reparations for two very important classes of the displaced: shareholders and business owners, the people who have their own money invested.

If Apollo is to be fair, shareholders must receive dollar-for-dollar new-for-old stock trades in comparably profitable clean companies.

Business owners must receive a new clean business with as much profit potential as the old one taken from them by somebody else's policy.

If we're going to play Welfare State, shouldn't we attend to the welfare of all, the defeated social outcasts of the former fossil fuel capitalist class included?

Speak, Apollo.

M Y TRANSPARTISAN FINALE: I'll go along with Apollo's less intrusive parts to obtain the benefits. I keep coming back to an insistence on knowing that there will be benefits, that we won't fall into The Energy Gap. The Apollo Alliance must do America this non-negotiable, transpartisan favor:

Show Us The BTUs. Show us where we are. Show us where we're going.

Bridge The Energy Gap First; I'll bet most of us will come aboard.

Keep flying blind into the dark? Houston, we have a problem.

Will you do the math? Will you Show Us The BTUs?

Speak, Apollo.

O H, YES. ONE LAST THING: I'd like a seat on the Apollo Alliance's board of advisors. Wouldn't you? Wouldn't all of us?

Speak, Apollo.

CONSIDERED OPINION

T HE JUNE 1951 ISSUE OF *ASTOUNDING SCIENCE FICTION* ran a story by British writer Eric Frank Russell titled, "...And Then There Were None."[93]

It was set in a world based on the premise that in a truly free society no person may coerce another in any manner, that at any juncture, a person may simply say, "FIW"—meaning Freedom - I Won't!—and that answer must be accepted as valid.

The watchword of Russell's society was, "MYOB"—meaning Mind Your Own Business.

We don't live in that world.

It's just another social system that doesn't work in real life.

Like progressivism

I think progressives need to learn a little MYOB.

I think progressives need to respect a little FIW.

They probably won't, so I'm saying this just to make sure my voluntary good will toward Apollo doesn't come across as surrender to its ideology.

They have some good ideas. They have some not so good.

Energy independence? Include me in.

Energy efficiency? Include me in.

Global peace and global warming? Include me out.

I don't believe those claims.

Why would I work with them, then?

The usual: I get some of what I want, they get some of what they want. We may even get some good ideas from each other.

I also have the quirky habit of admiring some of my opponents as much as I admire some of my friends.

If progressives remember their manners, fine.

If they get drunk with power, well, you know.

MYOB.

And by the way, FIW.

CODA

We're done.
    We've been through a lot together.
    Gina Glantz to Dan Carol. America Coming Together to NoDOG.
    George Soros and the Open Society Network to Lance Lindblom and the Nathan Cummings Foundation
    We've seen what those "all other reforms" are, from everybody using nicer lightbulbs to civil society ruling the world.
    There is no big ending that ties all the loose ends together because this isn't a novel.
    Real life is mostly loose ends.
    In politics, it's never over.

    If you were waiting for that big rant about global warming believers, here it is:

        If global warming is natural, and we all commit suicide, we won't stop the warming.
        If global warming is man-made, and it's reached the tipping point, and we all commit suicide, we won't stop the warming.
        If global warming is anything else, it's all politics, and in this too too solid world, we'll do something we'll have to amend later when it doesn't work.

    If you think you can make the climate do what you want, go ahead.
    Just try not to kill us all in the process.

    "STOP DRILLING!" is not an energy policy.
    We need some Energy Keepers to counterbalance the Energy Killers.
    Get it? Don't kill the energy we've got before we get the energy we want.
    Bridge the Energy Gap First.
    And keep accounts to make sure.
    Show Us The BTUs.

    So, to progressives of good faith, do that, just Show Us The BTUs and I bet we'll trade you transpartisan support.
    To the rest, It's The Energy Gap, Stupid.

    What difference does it make?
    Warm and bright. Freezing in the dark.
    Life or Death.

    Now, let's get on with it and see what you can do about The Vast Left Wing Conspiracy.

1. Mark Hertsgaard, "A Challenge to Enviros," *The Nation*, January 3, 2005.
2. Blockquotes this page: Michael Shellenberger and Ted Nordhaus, "The Death of Environmentalism: Global Warming Politics in a Post-Environmental Age," www.thebreakthrough.org/images/Death_of_Environmentalism.pdf, accessed December 12, 2004. The website is registered through proxies, which hides actual registrants.
3. http://watchpaul-articles.blogspot.com/2007/01/aeb-shellenbergernational-pr.html.
4 Mark Schmitt, "The Death of _____ism," *The Decembrist* (blog), February 10, 2005, http://markschmitt.typepad.com/decembrist/2005/02/the_death_of_.html, accessed August 5, 2006.
5. Shellenberger and Nordhaus, "The Death of Environmentalism," *op. cit., pp.* 4-5. Teague's motives in commissioning this divisive piece have never been made clear. He did not respond to my repeated requests for an interview and did not respond to repeated requests for replies to written questions submitted by email. I have no reason to believe any of my statements about him are false.
6. Interview with Dan Carol, Portland, Oregon, June 13-14, 2007.
7. Malcolm Gladwell is the author of *Blink: The Power of Thinking Without Thinking* (Boston: Little Brown, 2005), which explores the power of the trained mind to make snap decisions that are better than carefully planned and considered ones.
8. Dan Carol, Memo, "Energy Independence - The Political Opportunity," September 12-18, 2001, 7 pages. Provided by Dan Carol on May 11, 2007 by email.
9. http://law.wisc.edu/faculty/biog.php?ID=396, accessed June 10, 2007.
10. The William and Flora Hewlett Foundation, Form 990, 2002, Schedule 5, page 45 of 110.
11. http://home.ourfuture.org/aboutus/about_caf_iaf.html, accessed June 10, 2007.
12. http://law.wisc.edu/faculty/biog.php?ID=396, accessed June 10, 2007.
13. Hendricks has since moved to John Podesta's Center for American Progress. Bio at www.americanprogress.org/experts/HendricksBracken.html, accessed July 22, 2007.
14. District of Columbia Department of Consumer and Regulatory Affairs, Registered Organization File Number 251571 dated 5/18/2005. http://mblr.dc.gov/corp/lookup/status.asp?id=42133, accessed June 23, 2007.
15. Turner Foundation, Form 990, 2002, Statement 16, page 30 of 35.
16. Surdna Foundation, Annual Report, 2002.
17. www.trcp.org/pr_range.aspx, accessed June 10, 2007.
18. *ibid.*
19. www.apolloalliance.org/strategy_center/a_bold_energy_and_jobs_policy/ten_point_plan.cfm, accessed June 10, 2007.
20. Nathan Cummings Foundation Form 990-PF, 2002, Statement 16, pages 11 and 25 of 27.
21. www.nathancummings.org/bios/000062.html, accessed June 10, 2007.
22. Nathan Cummings Foundation Form 990-PF, 2001, Statement 17, page 41 of 53. Nathan Cummings Foundation Form 990-PF, 2002, Statement 16, page 14 of 27.
23. Nathan Cummings Foundation Form 990-PF, 2003, Statement 19, page 12 of 17. Nathan Cummings Foundation Annual Report 2003, page 15.
Nathan Cummings Foundation Profile: Form 990-PF, 2001 through 2005. and website.

24. David Bollier, "Reclaiming the Commons," http://www.bollier.org/reclaim.htm, accessed June 21, 2007

25. Peter Barnes, *Who Owns the Sky: Our Common Assets and the Future of Capitalism* (Washington, D.C.: Island Press, 2001).

26. David Bollier, *Silent Theft: The Private Plunder of Our Common Wealth* (London and New York: Routledge, 2002). Nader remark, review at www.amazon.com/ Silent-Theft-Private-Plunder-Common/dp/product-description/0415932645, accessed July 7, 2007.

27. California business registration: C2467777, 9/16/2002, address Blue Mountain Center, Blue Mountain Lake, NY12812-0109. **Barlow:** Blue Mountain Center, Form 990-PF, 2002, Statement 14.

28. Common Assets Defense Fund, Form 990, 2002, Statement 1.

29. Adam Werbach, *Act Now, Apologize Later* (New York: HarperCollins, 1997). Bad review: Wilda Williams, "Prepub Alert," *Library Journal*, 6/15/97.

30. Werbach wedding: Weddings/Celebrations, "Lyn Merrill, Adam Werbach," *New York Times*, September 29, 2002.

31. Teague bio, http://www.nathancummings.org/bios/000338.html, accessed June 22. 2007.

32. Nathan Cummings Foundation Form 900-PF, 2000, Contact List, page 99.

33. Amanda Griscom Little, "Don't Think of the Environment - Enviros recruit Lakoff for reframing project, but concerns mount that he might leave them in the lurch," *Muckraker*, March 29, 2005.

34. Nathan Cummings Foundation Form 900-PF, 2002, Statement 16, page 24 of 27.

35. Noam Scheiber, "Wooden Frame – Is George Lakoff misleading Democrats?" *The New Republic*, May 23, 2005.

36. Nathan Cummings Foundation Form 900-PF, 2003, Statement 19, page 15 of 17.

37. Open Society Institute, Form 990-PF, Grants to U.S. Charities, page 61.

Shellenberger caveat: Mr. Shellenberger replied to my request for review with this message: "I received and reviewed the pages you sent me from your forthcoming book. If you print them in their current form, you will be publishing assertions that are inaccurate and misleading. You are obviously not interested in doing fair or objective reporting, and thus I am not interested in cooperating with you." Mr. Shellenberger's refusal to correct the record is regrettable, but I have no reason to believe that any statement about him in these pages is false, having relied on the public record shown in my footnotes, and information from credible sources close to the events. I have no intention to mislead readers, so I inform you that Mr. Shellenberger denies my assertions. However, I stand by my story unless and until any factual inaccuracy is identified, when I will be pleased to correct it.

38. David Armstrong, "Communication Works joins the ranks of politically correct spin doctors," *San Francisco Examiner*, August 5, 1997. *See also*, http://web.archive.org/web/20030715191645/www.luminastrategies.com/whoweare.html, accessed July 8, 2007.

39. Marc Polonsky, "Michael Shellenberger On Why Liberals Need To Abandon Complaint-Based Activism," *The Sun Magazine*, http://www.thesunmagazine. org'350 _Shellenberger.pdf, accessed August 2, 2006.

40. Amounts are found in the Form 990 reports of the organizations for years noted.

41. Nathan Cummings Foundation, Annual Report, 2003.

42. www.commondreams.org/news2003/0602-02.htm, accessed June 11, 2007.

43. The chart is at www.eia.doe.gov/emeu/aer/eh/total.html, accessed June 12, 2007.

44. Douglas Jehl, "Boom in Natural Gas Drilling Can't Match Soaring Demand," *New York Times*, July 22, 2001.
45. The complete story is in the Brainerd Foundation's website, Earthworks Profile, at http://brainerd.org/grantees/profiles/ew.php, accessed June 12, 2007.
46. Will Horter, "How Can We Respond? United Financial Pressure," *Lands and People* (newsletter of Dogwood Initiative, Vancouver, British Columbia, Canada), October 2004, page 9 (follow-on of breakover article from page 1, Will Horter, "Can Fossils Fuel Our Future?"). www.dogwoodinitiative.org/documents/LandsPeople/LP_0410.pdf, accessed August 10, 2007.
47. Independent Petroleum Association of Mountain States, "Building a Sustainable Energy Future," page 2, www.ipams.org/media/docs/2007/Callup07broch.pdf, accessed June 12, 2007.
48. *American Oil & Gas Reporter*, "Group Sets Plan to Stop Oil and Gas," July 2007, page 49.
49. NoDOG is a carbon copy of Earthworks' No Dirty Gold campaign, www.nodirtygold.org/home.cfm. No Dirty Oil and Gas wesbite registration, www.networksolutions.com/whois/results.jsp?domain=nodirtyoilandgas.org, registrant name, Alan Septoff, registrant organization Earthworks. URLs accessed May 20, 2007.
50. Foreign Agents Registration Act filings, U.S. Department of Justice, File #5567. See also, Aleksander Boyd, "Venezuela's Information Office Hires Michael Shellenberger," June 22, 2004, London, www.vcrisis.com/index.php?content=letters/200406221843, accessed August 3, 2006.
51. Robert Collier, "Venezuelan politics suit Bay Area activists' talents - Locals help build Chavez's image, provide polling data," *San Francisco Chronicle*, August 21, 2004.
52. Juan Forero, "Venezuela Tries to Lure Oil Investors," *New York Times*, December 19, 2003
53. Wikipedia, "Venezuelan Recall Referendum, 2004," http://en.wikipedia.org/wiki/Venezuelan_recall_referendum,_2004, accessed June 14, 2007.
54. The Shellenberger-James letter is posted at www.vcrisis.com/schellenberger.pdf, accessed August 3, 2006.
Global Exchange Profile: Global Exchange Form 990, 1998-2005, and Wikipedia entries under Global Exchange, Kevin Danaher and Medea Benjamin.
55. J. Michael Waller, *What to Do About Venezuela*, Occasional Papers Series No. 6, (Washington, D.C.: Center for Security Policy, May 2005), page 6.
56. Michael Barone, "Exit polls in Venezuela," *U.S. News and World Report*, August 20, 2004.
57. Mary Beth Sheridan, "Chavez Defeats Recall Attempt - Monitors Endorse Venezuelan Vote; Margin Is Wide," *Washington Post*, August 17, 2004; Page A1.
58. National Endowment for Democracy, "NED Venezuela grants approved FY 2003," www.ned.org/grants/venezuelaFacts.html, accessed August 21, 2007.
59. Associated Press, "Chavez Calls Watchdog Group a Top Enemy," *CBS News*, December 3, 2005. www.cbsnews.com/stories/2005/12/03/ap/world/main D8E8MNGO6.shtml?CMP=ILC-SearchStories, accessed June 14, 2007.
60. www.handsoffvenezuela.org/about_us_3.htm, accessed June 14, 2007.
61. Bernardo Delgado, "Supporters Celebrate President Chavez's Return to Venezuela from New York," September 21, 2005, www.venezuelanalysis. com/news.php?newsno=1760, accessed December 15, 2005.
62. Arca Foundation Form 990-PF 2004, 2005.

63. Pablo Bachelet, "Venezuelan oil sales to American poor: Chavez builds base with grass-roots circles in U.S.," *Miami Herald,* November 21, 2005.
64. www.earthcouncilalliance.org/en/alliances/index.html, accessed July 14, 2007.
65. http://markschmitt.typepad.com/decembrist/2005/02/the_death_of___.html, accessed August 5, 2006.
66. http://deathofenvironmentalism.com/documents/shellenberger_final_response.doc, accessed, August 10, 2006.
67. www.grist.org/news/maindish/2005/01/13/werbach-reprint/, accessed June 16, 2007.
68. www.globalexchange.org/war_peace_democracy/oil/1155.html, accessed August 4, 2007. Ross Gelbspan, *Boiling Point: How Politicians, Big Oil and Coal, Journalists and Activists Are Fueling the Climate Crisis—And What We Can Do to Avert Disaster* (New York: Basic Books, 2004).
69. Amanda Griscom Little, "Over Our Dead Bodies - Green leaders say rumors of environmentalism's death are eatly exaggerated - Responses: Dan Carol, board member of the Apollo Alliance." www.grist.org/news/maindish/2005/01/13/little-responses/#carol, accessed August 15, 2007.
70. www.tedandsarawedding.com/our%20wedding.html, accessed August 4, 2007.
71. California Secretary of State, Corporation Registration Number C2934002.
72. www.trcp.org/unionsportsmensalliance.aspx, accessed May 25, 2007.
73. http://resourcescommittee.house.gov/index.php?option=com_ jcalpro&Itemid=32 extmode=view&extid=25, accessed May 25, 2007.
74. http://resourcescommittee.house.gov/images/Documents/20070327/testimony_ sparrowe.pdf, accessed May 20, 2007.
75. Doris Duke Charitable Foundation, Form 990-PF, 2005, Part XV, Statement 19B, page 36 of 51.
76. http://dnr.state.co.us/news/press.asp?PressId=4488, accessed July 20, 2007.
77. The Gordon E. and Betty I. Moore Foundation, Form 990-PF, 2005, Statement 16A.
78. News release: "National Precedent Set by New Landowner Protection Law," Oil and Gas Accountability Project, May 29, 2007.
79. News release: "Sportsmen Support Congressional Reform of Energy Development on Federal Public Lands," Theodore Roosevelt Conservation Partnership, May 31, 2007.
80. News release: "IPAMS: Results of Theodore Roosevelt Conservation Partnership survey 'encouraging'," Independent Petroleum Association of Mountain States, June 28, 2007.
81. Congressional Budget Office, Cost Estimate, H.R. 2337, Energy Policy Reform and Revitalization Act of 2007, July 13, 2007. www.cbo.gov/ftpdocs/83xx/doc8320/hr2337.pdf, accessed August 14, 2007.
82. http://en.wikipedia.org/wiki/British_thermal_unit, accessed July 20, 2007.
83. Monthly Energy Review, August 2007, Table 1.3: Energy Consumption by Source (Quadrillion Btu), United States Energy Information Administration, www.eia.doe.gov/emeu/mer/pdf/pages/sec1_7.pdf, accessed August 23, 2007.
84. Entry, "Policy," *Black's Law Dictionary, Sixth Edition* (St. Paul, Minnesota: West Publishing Company, 1990), p. 1,157.
85. Entry, "Public Policy," *Black's Law Dictionary, Sixth Edition* (St. Paul, Minnesota: West Publishing Company, 1990), p. 1,157.
86. http://en.wikipedia.org/wiki/Phil_Angelides, accessed, September 15, 2007.
87. www.reunitingamerica.org/, accessed August 10, 2007.

88. "Put up or shut up on global warming: Dingell puts a fair price tag on the high cost of saving energy, *Detroit News*, www.detnews.com/apps/pbcs.dll/article?AID=/20070809/OPINION01/708090308/1008, accessed August 9, 2007.

89. Tom Harper, "Scientists threatened for 'climate denial,'" *Sunday Telegraph* (UK), March 11, 2007, www.telegraph.co.uk/news/main.jhtml?xml=/news/2007/03/11/ngreen211.xml, accessed June 20, 2007.

90. www.25x25.org/, accessed August 4, 2007.

91. "Mexicans stage tortilla protests," *BBC News*, February 1, 2007. http://news.bbc.co.uk /2/hi/americas/6319093.stm, accessed August 23, 2007. Mark Yancey, "Biofuels: Everything you wanted to know, but were afraid to ask," www.ipams.org/resources/presentations/07AnnualMeeting/Mark_Yancy.pdf, accessed August 23, 2007. Lester R. Brown, "INSIGHTS: Supermarkets and Service Stations Now Competing for Grain," www.ens-newswire.com/ens/jul2006/2006-07-15-insbro.asp, accessed August 23, 2007. Alana Herro, "Food Prices Surging, Raising Hunger Concerns," Worldwatch Institute, June 6, 2007.

92. www.apolloalliance.org/strategy_center/model_financing_strategies/revbonds.cfm, accessed August 23, 2007.

93. Full description and plot at http://en.wikipedia.org/wiki/The_Great_Explosion, accessed September 14, 2007.

FREEZING IN THE DARK - 408

EPILOGUE

THE CALL

RING RING.

Hello?

Yes, just a minute.

Here, it's for you.

BIBLIOGRAPHY

This selection includes numerous works not mentioned in the text, which, together with citations in the chapter endnotes, comprises a comprehensive survey of the literature that shaped *Freezing In The Dark*.

Edward Abrahams, *The Lyrical Left: Randolph Bourne, Alfred Stieglitz, and the Origins of Cultural Radicalism in America*. (Charlottesville: University Press of Virginia, 1986).

Nelson W. Aldrich, Jr., *Old Money: The Mythology of America's Upper Class* (New York: Alfred A. Knopf, 1988).

Saul D. Alinsky, *Rules for Radicals: A Pragmatic Primer for Realistic Radicals* (New York, Random House, 1971; Vintage Books Edition, 1972, 1989).

Gar Alperovitz, *America Beyond Capitalism: Reclaiming Our Wealth, Our Liberty, and Our Democracy* (Hoboken, New Jersey: John Wiley & Sons, 2004).

Carol Anderson, *Eyes off the Prize: The United Nations and the African American Struggle for Human Rights, 1944–1955* (Cambridge, UK: Cambridge University Press, 2003).

Helmut K. Anheier, *Civil Society: Measurement, Evaluation, Policy* (London: Earthscan, 2004).

Arjun Appadurai, *Modernity at Large: Cultural Dimensions of Globalization*, (Minneapolis: University of Minnesota Press, 1996).

Ron Arnold, *EcoTerror: The Violent Agenda to Save Nature – The World of the Unabomber* (Bellevue, Washington: Free Enterprise Press, 1997).

Ron Arnold, *Undue Influence: Wealthy Foundations, Grant-Driven Environmental Groups, and Zealous Bureaucrats That Control Your Future* (Bellevue, Washington: Free Enterprise Press, 1999).

John Arquilla and David Ronfeldt, *The Advent of Netwar* (Santa Monica, California, RAND Corporation, January 25, 1996).

John Arquilla and David Ronfeldt, *Networks and Netwars: The Future of Terror, Crime, and Militancy* (Santa Monica, California, RAND Corporation, January, 1996).

Dennis T. Avery and S. Fred Singer, *Unstoppable Global Warming: Every 1,500 Years* (Lanham, Maryland: Rowman and Littlefield Publishers, 2007).

Jagdish Baghwati, *In Defense of Globalization* (New York: Oxford University Press USA, 2005).

Wayne E. Baker, *America's Crisis of Values: Reality and Perception*, (Princeton, New Jersey: Princeton University Press, 2005).

Peter Barnes, *Who Owns the Sky: Our Common Assets and the Future of Capitalism* (Washington, D.C.: Island Press, 2001).

Michael Barone, *Hard America, Soft America: Competition vs. Coddling and the Battle for the Nation's Future*, (New York: Crown Forum, 2004).

411

Srilatha Batliwala and L. David Brown (editors), *Transnational Civil Society: An Introduction* (Bloomfield, Connecticut: Kumarian Press, 2006).

Jean Baudrillard, *Simulacra and Simulation* (translated by Sheila Faria Glaser) (Ann Arbor: University of Michigan Press, 1994) Originally published in French as *Simulacres et simulation*, by *Éditions Galilée,* Paris, 1981.

Brian Berry, *Culture and Equality: An Egalitarian Critique of Multiculturalism* (Cambridge, Massachusetts: Harvard University Press, 2002).

Neil Bissoondath, *Selling Illusions: The Cult of Multiculturalism in Canada* (New York: Penguin Books, 1994).

Sidney Blumenthal, *Rise of the Counter Establishment: From Conservative Ideology to Political Power*, (New York: Crown, 1986).

David Bollier, *Silent Theft: The Private Plunder of Our Common Wealth* (London and New York: Routledge, 2002).

Heather Booth, Steve Max and Harry Boyte, *Citizen Action and the New American Populism* (Philadelphia, Temple University Press, 1986).

Harry C. Boyte, *The Backyard Revolution: Understanding the New Citizen Movement* (Philadelphia, Temple University, 1980).

Robert L. Bradley, Jr. and Richard W. Fulmer, *Energy: The Master Resource - An Introduction to the History, Technology, Economics and Public Policy of Energy* (Dubuque, Iowa: Kendall/Hunt Publishing Company, 2004).

Brandt Commission, *North-South: A Program for Survival* (Cambridge, Massachusetts: The MIT Press, 1980).

David Brock, *Blinded by the Right: Conscience of an Ex-Conservative* (New York: Crown, 2002).

Aimé Césaire, *Notebook of a Return to the Native Land*, translated and edited by Clayton Eshleman and Annette Smith (Middletown, Connecticut: Wesleyan University Press, 2001).

Johnnetta Betsch Cole and Beverly Guy-Sheftall, *Gender Talk: The Struggle for Women's Equality in African American Communities* (New York: One World/Ballantine, 2003).

Commission on Global Governance, *Our Global Neighborhood: The Report of the Commission on Global Governance* (New York: Oxford University Press USA, 1995).

Commission to Study the Organization of Peace, *Building Peace: Reports of the Commission to Study the Organization of Peace, 1939, 1972* (Lanham, Maryland: Scarecrow Press, 1973).

Gary Delgado, *Organizing the Movement: The Roots and Growth of ACORN*, (Philadelphia: Temple University Press, 1986).

Elaine Dewar, *Cloak of Green* (Toronto: James Lorimer & Company, Publishers, 1995).

G. William Domhoff, *Who Rules America? Power, Politics, & Social Change*, (New York: McGraw-Hill, 1998, 5th Edition 2005)

Viola Herms Drath, *Willy Brandt: Prisoner of His Past* (Radnor, Pennsylvania: Chilton Book Company, 1975).

Paul Driessen, *Eco-Imperialism: Green Power Black Death* (Bellevue, Washington: Free Enterprise Press, 2003)

Thomas R. Dye, *Top Down Policymaking*, (New York: Chatham House, 2001).

Thomas R. Dye, *Who's Running America: The Bush Restoration*, (Upper Saddle River, New Jersey: Prentice Hall, 1996, 7th Edition 2002).

Frantz Fanon, *Black Skin, White Masks* (London: Pluto Press, new edition 1986).

Liza Featherstone, *Students Against Sweatshops: The Making of a Movement* (New York: Verso, 2002)

Lewis S. Feuer, *Ideology and the Ideologists* (New York: Harper & Row, 1975).

Paul Feyerabend, *Science in a Free Society* (London: Verso, 1978).

Eamon Fingleton, *In Praise of Hard Industries: Why Manufacturing, not the information economy, is the key to future prosperity* (Boston: Houghton Mifflin, 1999.

Ann M Fiorini (editor), *The Third Force: The Rise of Transnational Civil Society* (Washington, D.C.: Carnegie Endowment for International Peace, 2000).

Joan Flanagan, *The Grass Roots Fundraising Book: How to Raie Money in Your Comunity* (Chicago: Contemporary Books, 1992)

Michel Foucault, *The Order of Things: An Archaeology of the Human Sciences* (London: Routlege, 2001).

John Kenneth Galbraith, *American Capitalism: The Concept of Countervailing Power*, (Cambridge, Mass., The Riverside Press, 1952).

Ross Gelbspan, *Boiling Point: How Politicians, Big Oil and Coal, Journalists and Activists Are Fueling the Climate Crisis—And What We Can Do to Avert Disaster* (New York: Basic Books, 2004).

Leo W. Gerard, Archon Fung, Teresa Hebb, and Joel Rogers, *Working Capital: The Power of Labor's Pensions* (Ithaca, New York: Cornell University Press, 2001).

Georgie Anne Geyer, *Americans No More: The Death of Citizenship*, (New York: The Atlantic Monthly Press, 1996).

Malcolm Gladwell, *Blink: The Power of Thinking Without Thinking* (Boston: Little Brown, 2005).

Peter Grose, *Continuing the Inquiry: The Council on Foreign Relations from 1921 to 1996* (New York: Council on Foreign Relations: 1996).

Richard N. Haass, *The Opportunity: America's Moment to Alter History's Course* (New York: PublicAffairs, 2005).

Rodney Hall and Thomas Biersteker, *The Emergence of Private Authority in Global Governance* (New York City: Cambridge University Press, 2003).

Morton H. Halperin, Jerry Berman, Robert Borosage and Christine Marwick, *The Lawless State: The Crimes of the U.S. Intelligence Agencies* (Washington: Center for National Security Studies, 1976).

Stuart L. Hart, *Capitalism at the Crossroads: The Unlimited Business Opportunities in Solving the World's Most Difficult Problems* (Upper Saddle River, New Jersey: Wharton School Publishing, 2005).

Howard C. Hayden, *The Solar Fraud: Why Solar Energy Won't Run the World* (Pueblo West, Colorado: Vales Lake Publishing, 2005).

Roger Hewitt, *White Backlash and the Politics of Multiculturalism* (Cambridge, England, UK: Cambridge University Press, 2005).

Robert Higgs and Carl P. Close (editors), *Re-Thinking Green: Alternatives to Environmental Bureaucracy* (Oakland, California: The Independent Institute, 2005).

Adam Hochschild, *Half the Way Home: A Memoir of Father and Son* (Boston: Houghton Mifflin Company, 2005).

Eric Hoffer, *The True Believer: Thoughts on the Nature of Mass Movements* (New York: Harper & Row, 1951).

Jeffrey Hollender and Stephen Fenichell, *What Matters Most: How a Small Group of Pioneers Is Teaching Social Responsibility to Big Business, and Why Big Business Is Listening* (New York: Basic Books, 2004).

Elwood M. Hopkins, *Collaborative Philanthropies: What Groups of Foundations Can Do That Individual Funders Cannot* (New York: Lexington Books, 2005).

Christopher C. Horner, *The Politically Incorrect Guide to Global Warming (and Environmentalism)* (Washington, D.C.: Regnery Publishing, Inc., 2007).

James Davison Hunter, *Culture Wars: The Struggle to Define America*, (New York, Basic Books, 1992).

Independent Commission on International Development Issues, *Common Crisis - North-South Co-operation for World Recovery* (New York: Macmillan, 1983).

Walter Isaacson, *Einstein: His Life and Universe* (New York: Simon & Schuster, 2007).

Christian Joerges, Inger-Johanne Sand & Gunther Teubner, editors, *Transnational governance and constitutionalism* (Oxford, England: Hart Publishing, 2004).

Robert Matthews Johnson, *The First Charity: How Philanthropy Can Contribute to Democracy in America*, Cabin John, Maryland: Seven Locks Press, 1988).

Richard Jolly and Deepayan Basu Ray, *National Human Development Reports and the Human Security Framework: A review of Analysis and Experience* (Sussex, UK: Institute of Development Studies, 2006).

Orrin C. Judd, *Redefining Sovereignty: Will liberal democracies continue to determine their own laws and public policies or yield these rights to transnational entities in search of universal order and justice?* (Hanover, New Hampshire: Smith and Kraus, Inc., 2005).

Arnold S. Kaufman, *The Radical Liberal, new man in American politics* (Palo Alto, California: Atherton Press, 1968).

Michael T. Kaufman, *Soros: The Life and Times of a Messianic Billionaire*, (New York: Alfred A. Knopf, 2000).

Kevin Kelly, *Out of Control: The New Biology of Machines, Social Systems, and the Economic World* (New York: Basic Books, 1994).

Robert O. Keohane and Joseph S. Nye, Jr. (editors), *Transnational Relations and World Politics* (Cambridge, Massachusetts: Harvard University Press, 1971).

Sanjeev Khagram, James V. Riker, and Kathryn Sikkink (editors) *Restructuring World Politics: Transnational Social Movements, Networks, and Norms*, (Minneapolis: University of Minnesota Press, 2002).

David C. Korten, *The Great Turning: From Empire to Earth Community* (San Francisco, Berrett-Koehler Publishers, 2000).

David C. Korten, *The Post-Corporate World: Life After Capitalism* (San Francisco, Berrett-Koehler Publishers, 2000).

David C. Korten, *When Corporations Rule the World* (San Francisco, Berrett-Koehler Publishers, 1995).

Philip Kotler and Nancy Lee, *Corporate Social Responsibility: Doing the Most Good for Your Company and Your Cause* (Hoboken, New Jersey: John Wiley & Sons, Inc., 2005).

George P. Lakoff, *Moral Politics: How Liberals and Conservatives Think*, (Chicago: University of Chicago Press, 1996, 2nd edition, May 1, 2002).

George P. Lakoff and Mark Johnson, *Metaphors We Live By*, (Chicago: University of Chicago Press, 1980, 2nd edition, April 15, 2003).

George P. Lakoff, *Don't Think of an Elephant! Know Your Values and Frame the Debate—The Essential Guide for Progressives*, (White River Junction, Vermont: Chelsea Green Publishing Company, 2004).

Marcel Leroux, *Global Warming - Myth or Reality? The Erring Ways of Climatology* (New York: Springer, 2005).

Michael Lind, *Up From Conservatism: Why the Right is Wrong for America* (New York: Free Press, 1996).

Bjørn Lomborg, *Cool It: The Skeptical Environmentalist's Guide to Global Warming* (New York: Knopf, 2007).

Amory B. Lovins, E. Kyle Datta, Odd-Even Bustnes, Jonathan G. Koomey, and Nathan J. Glasgow, *Winning the Oil Endgame: Innovation for Profits, Jobs, and Security* (Snowmass, Colorado: Rocky Mountain Institute, 2005).

Alasdair MacIntyre, *After Virtue* (Notre Dame, Indiana: University of Notre Dame Press, 1981).

Alasdair MacIntyre, *Whose Justice? Which Rationality?* (Notre Dame, Indiana: University of Notre Dame Press, 1988)

Michael J. Malbin, editor, *The Election after Reform: Money, Politics and the Bipartisan Campaign Reform Act.* (Lanham, Maryland: Rowman and Littlefield, 2005).

Jarol B. Manheim, *Biz-War and the Out-of-Power Elite: The Progressive-Left Attack on the Corporation,* (Mahwah, New Jersey, Lawrence Erlbaum Associates, 2004)

Jarol B. Manheim, *The Death of a Thousand Cuts: Corporate Campaigns and the Attack on the Corporation* (Mahwah, N.J.: Lawrence Erlbaum Associates, 2001).

Irving Leonard Markovitz, *Léopold Sédar Senghor and the Politics of Negritude* (New York: Atheneum, 1969).

Arthur M. Meltzer, Jerry Weinberger, and M. Richard Zinman, *Multiculturalism and American Democracy* (Lawrence, Kansas: University Press of Kansas, 1998).

Patrick J. Michaels, *Meltdown: The Predictable Distortion of Global Warming by Scientists, Politicians, and the Media* (Washington, D.C.: Cato Institute, 2004).

Patrick J. Michaels, *Shattered Consensus: The True State of Global Warming* (Lanham, Maryland: Rowman and Littlefield Publishers, Inc., 2005).

James Miller, *Democracy is in the Streets: From Port Huron to the Siege of Chicago* (Cambridge, Massachusetts: Harvard University Press, 1987, 1994)

Charles Wright Mills, *The Power Elite,* (Oxford: The Oxford University Press, 1956)

Craig N. Murphy, *The United Nations Development Programme: A Better Way?* (Cambridge, UK: Cambridge University Press, 2006).

Waldemar Nielsen, *The Golden Donors: A New Anatomy of the Great Foundations* (New York: Truman Talley Books / E. P. Dutton, 1985)

James Perloff, *The Shadows of Power: The Council on Foreign Relations and the American Decline* (Appleton, Wisconsin: Western Islands Publishers, 1988).

C. K. Prahalad, *The Fortune at the Bottom of the Pyramid* (Upper Saddle River, New Jersey: Wharton School Publishing, 2005).

Alan Rabinowitz, *Social Change Philanthropy in America* (New York: Quorum Books, 1990).

Dorothy B. Robins, *Experiment in Democracy: The Story of U.S. Citizen Organizations in Forging the Charter of the United Nations,* (New York: Parkside Press, 1971).

Steven J. Rosenstone and John Mark Hansen, *Mobilization, Participation, and Democracy in America* (New York: Macmillan, 1993).

Andrew Ross, *No Sweat: Fashion, Free Trade, and the Rights of Garment Workers* (New York: Verso, 1997).

Dimitrios Roussopoulos and C. George Benello (editors), *The Case for Participatory Democracy: Prospects for a New Society,* (Tonawanda, New York: Black Rose Books, 2003).

Jeffrey Sachs, *The End of Poverty: Economic Possibilities for Our Time* (New York: Penguin, reprint edition 2006).

Lester M. Salamon (editor), Wojciech Sokolowski (Editor), *Global Civil Society: Dimensions of the Nonprofit Sector* (Bloomfield, Connecticut: Kumarian Press, 2004).

Gene Sharp, *The Politics of Nonviolent Action – Part 1: Power and Struggle; Part 2: Methods of Nonviolent Action; Part 3, Dynamics of Nonviolent Action,* (Boston: Porter Sargent Publishers, 1973).

Gene Sharp, *From Dictatorship to Democracy: A Conceptual Framework for Liberation,* (Cambridge: Albert Einstein Institution, 1993).

Laurence H. Shoup and William Miner, *Imperial Brain Trust: The Council on Foreign Relations and United States Foreign Policy* (New York: Authors Choice Press, 1977).

George Soros, *The Bubble of American Supremacy: Correcting the Misuse of American Power* (New York: PublicAffairs, 2004).

Leon Stein, *Out of the Sweatshop: The Struggle for Industrial Democracy,* (New York City: Quadrangle/New York Times Book Company, 1977).

Neal Stephenson, *Snow Crash* (New York: Bantam, 1992).

Joseph Stiglitz, *Globalization and Its Discontents* (New York: W.W. Norton & Company, 2003).

Susan Strange, *The Retreat of the State: The Diffusion of Power in the World Economy* (Cambridge, England: Cambridge University Press, 1996).

Sidney Tarrow, *The new transnational activism* (New York: Cambridge University Press, 2005).

Charles Taylor, *Multiculturalism: Examining the Politics of Recognition* (Princeton, New Jersey: Princeton University Press, 1994).

David Vogel, *Lobbying the Corporation: Citizen Challenges to Business Authority,* (New York, Basic Books, Inc., 1978).

David Vogel, *The Market for Virtue: The Potential and Limits of Corporate Social Responsibility* (Washington, D.C.: Brookings Institution Press, 2005).

Adam Werbach, *Act Now, Apologize Later* (New York: HarperCollins, 1997).

Cornel West, *The American Evasion of Philosophy: A Genealogy of Pragmatism* (Madison: The University of Wisconsin Press, 1989).

Cornel West, *Race Matters, With a New Preface* (Boston: Beacon Press, revised edition 2001, first published 1993).

Juan Williams, *My Soul Looks Back in Wonder: Voices of the Civil Rights Experience,* (New York, N.Y., Sterling Publishing Company, Inc., 2004).

Peter Willetts, *"The Conscience of the World" - The Influence of Non-Governmental Organizations in the UN System* (Washington, D.C.: Brookings Institution Press, 1996).

World Commission on Environment and Development, *Our Common Future,* (New York: Oxford University Press USA, paperback edition, 1987).

Walter B. Wriston, *The Twilight of Sovereignty : How the Information Revolution Is Transforming Our World* (New York: Scribner Book Company, 1992).

Byron York, *The Vast Left Wing Conspiracy* (New York: Crown Forum, 2005).

Iris Marion Young, *Justice and the Politics of Difference* (Princeton, New Jersey: Princeton University Press, 1990).

INDEX